LYCURGAN ATHENS AND THE MAKING OF CLASSICAL TRAGEDY

Through a series of interdisciplinary studies this book argues that the Athenians themselves invented the notion of 'classical' tragedy just a few generations after the city's defeat in the Peloponnesian War. In the third quarter of the fourth century BC, and specifically during the 'Lycurgan Era' (338–322 BC), a number of measures were taken in Athens to affirm to the Greek world that the achievement of tragedy was owed to the unique character of the city. By means of rhetoric, architecture, inscriptions, statues, archives and even legislation, the 'classical' tragedians (Aeschylus, Sophocles and Euripides) and their plays came to be presented as both the products and vital embodiments of an idealised Athenian past. This study marks the first account of Athens' invention of its own theatrical heritage and sheds new light upon the interaction between the city's literary and political history.

JOHANNA HANINK is Assistant Professor of Classics and Robert Gale Noyes Assistant Professor of Humanities at Brown University, where she is also a member of the Graduate Field Faculty in the Department of Theatre Arts and Performance Studies. She works primarily on the intellectual and performance cultures of classical Athens and has published widely on Athenian tragedy and its reception in antiquity.

LYCURGAN ATHENS AND THE MAKING OF CLASSICAL TRAGEDY

JOHANNA HANINK

CAMBRIDGE
UNIVERSITY PRESS

University Printing House, Cambridge CB2 8BS, United Kingdom

One Liberty Plaza, 20th Floor, New York, NY 10006, USA

477 Williamstown Road, Port Melbourne, VIC 3207, Australia

4843/24, 2nd Floor, Ansari Road, Daryaganj, Delhi - 110002, India

79 Anson Road, #06-04/06, Singapore 079906

Cambridge University Press is part of the University of Cambridge.

It furthers the University's mission by disseminating knowledge in the pursuit of education, learning and research at the highest international levels of excellence.

www.cambridge.org
Information on this title: www.cambridge.org/9781107697508

First published 2014
First paperback edition 2017

A catalogue record for this publication is available from the British Library

Library of Congress Cataloging in Publication data
Hanink, Johanna, 1982–
Lycurgan Athens and the making of classical tragedy / Johanna Hanink.
pages cm. – (Cambridge classical studies)
Includes bibliographical references and index.
ISBN 978-1-107-06202-3 (hardback)
1. Athens (Greece) – History. 2. Lycurgus, approximately 390 B.C.-approximately 324 B.C. 3. Greek drama (Tragedy) – History and criticism. 4. Tragedy. 5. Greece – Civilization – To 146 B.C. 6. Literature and society – Greece – Athens. I. Title.
DF285.H36 2014
882′.0109162 – dc23 2014010189

ISBN 978-1-107-06202-3 Hardback
ISBN 978-1-107-69750-8 Paperback

CONTENTS

ILLUSTRATIONS

ACKNOWLEDGEMENTS

I am grateful to a number of people who have helped this book along, from its beginnings as a Ph.D. thesis to its publication. First among these is my Ph.D. supervisor, Richard Hunter, whose knowledge and patience were essential ingredients both to my studies and to this work. I was also fortunate enough to benefit from the encouragement and erudition of James Diggle, who generously read and commented upon early drafts and made my time at Cambridge possible. As ever, Simon Goldhill asked the right questions and pushed for the big ideas, and kept me from forgetting the forest for the sake of the trees. Patricia Easterling and Peter Wilson were generous and challenging examiners of the Ph.D., and I thank them for their insight and suggestions. I am also indebted to Robin Osborne for his helpful comments at many stages of the process. Other teachers, too, have left their mark on me and on this book: Benjamin Acosta-Hughes, H. D. Cameron, Marco Fantuzzi, Mark Griffith, Erich Gruen, Leslie Kurke, Emily Mackil, Donald Mastronarde and Andy Stewart have each indirectly shaped the thoughts that I have set down here.

A number of funding bodies made the completion of this book possible. On this count I owe debts of gratitude to the Cambridge Classics Faculty, the Cambridge Overseas Trusts, Queens' College (for a Walker Studentship) and the Gates Cambridge Foundation. A bursary from the Hellenic Society enabled me to spend three idyllic weeks (in the spring of 2010) at the Fondation Hardt in Vandœuvres, Switzerland. In 2011 a Tytus Fellowship from the Department of Classics at the University of Cincinnati provided a humid summer of access to a remarkable library and some very collegial classicists. In recent years Brown University and my colleagues in the Department of Classics have proven enormously giving – of time, resources and other intangible means of support.

While in Cambridge I had the good fortune of being surrounded by an extraordinary cohort. David Butterfield, Lyndsay Coo, Ian Goh, Foivos Karachalios, Emily Kneebone, Marden Nichols, Jeanne Pansard-Besson, Shaul Tor and Lacey Wallace were all great friends and colleagues during my time in graduate school. During those years Daniel Cook was always a patient inspiration. My new colleagues and friends at Brown University have also been enormously encouraging, and I am particularly grateful for the *paréa* of Elsa Amanatidou, Nancy Khalek, Kostis Kornetis, Eng-Beng Lim, Stratis Papaioannou, Felipe Rojas and Adele Scafuro. I also benefitted enormously from discussing the ideas in this book with Jonas Grethlein during my first year at Brown. Lacey Wallace offered invaluable support and encouragement during the book's revisions. Athena Kirk has inspired me for a decade with her knowledge of various Hellenisms. Anna Uhlig has been a vital source of friendship and an intellectual better half; this book would be much the worse had she not cast her penetrating eye over the entire typescript. Several students at Brown have also offered helpful feedback and enjoyable conversation: I am most grateful of all to Trigg Settle, Eric LaPointe, Charles Pletcher and Zach Rothstein-Dowden.

Peter Bing, Paola Ceccarelli, Eric Csapo, Richard Hunter, Stephen Lambert, Benjamin Millis, Christina Papastamati-von Moock, Antonis Petrides and Peter Wilson each allowed me access to forthcoming work of theirs. This book would not have been possible without their generosity.

I wish also to thank my family for their love and support: my parents Dean and Maureen; Mary, Emily, Bear and Molly Hanink and Sarah, Matt, Hannah and Madelyn Westergard.

This book is dedicated to James Diggle, a remarkable teacher to whom I owe far more than can be accounted for here.

SHORT TITLES AND ABBREVIATIONS

Standard abbreviations for ancient authors and texts as well as for reference works have been used, but the following should be noted:

Agora 16	Woodhead, A. G. (1997) *Inscriptions: The Decrees. The Athenian Agora Vol. 16.* Princeton.
CEG	Hansen, P. A. (1983–1989) *Carmina epigraphica graeca* (2 vols.). Berlin.
CGFPR	Austin, C. (1973) *Comicorum graecorum fragmenta in papyris reperta*. Berlin and New York.
Csapo–Slater	Csapo, E. and Slater, W. J. (1995) *The Context of Ancient Drama*. Ann Arbor.
*DFA*²	Pickard-Cambridge, A. (1988) *The Dramatic Festivals of Athens*. Second edition (1968) revised with a new supplement (1988) by J. Gould and D. M. Lewis. Oxford.
DNP	Cancuk, H. and Schneider, H., eds. (1996–2003) *Der neue Pauly: Encyclopädie der Antike*. Stuttgart.
FdD III	*Fouilles de Delphes, III: Épigraphie.* (1929–) Paris.
FGE	Page, D. (1981) *Further Greek Epigrams*. Cambridge.
FGrH	Jacoby, F. (1923–1958) *Die Fragmente der griechischen Historiker*. Berlin and Leiden.
GP	Gow, A. S. F. and Page, D. L. (1968) *The Garland of Philip*. Cambridge.

GV	Peek, W. (1955) *Greichische Vers-Inschriften*. Berlin.
IE	Clinton, K. (2008) *Eleusis: The Inscriptions on Stone. Documents of the Sanctuary of the Two Goddesses and Public Documents of the Deme* (3 vols.). Athens.
IG	*Inscriptiones Graecae*. (1913–) Berlin.
Lambert	Lambert, S. D. (2008) 'Polis and theatre in Lykourgan Athens: the honorific decrees', in *Μικρός Ιερομνήμων: Μελέτες εις Μνήμνη Michael H. Jameson*, ed. A. P. Matthaiou and I. Polinskaya. Athens: 53–85.
Le Guen	Le Guen, B. (2001) *Les associations de technites dionysiaques à l'époque hellénistique*. Vol. I: *Corpus documentaire*. Paris.
LSJ	Liddell, H. G. and Scott, R. (1940) *A Greek–English Lexicon, 9th edn revised and augmented by H. S. Jones*. Oxford and New York.
Meiggs–Lewis	Meiggs, R. and Lewis, D. M. (1971) *A Selection of Greek Historical Inscriptions to the End of the Fifth-Century BC*. Oxford.
Millis–Olson	Millis, B. W. and Olson, S. D. (2012) *Inscriptional Records for the Dramatic Festivals in Athens*. Leiden.
Rhodes–Osborne	Rhodes, P. J. and Osborne, R. (2003) *Greek Historical Inscriptions, 404–323 BC*. Oxford and New York.
Schwenk	Schwenk, C. J. (1985) *Athens in the Age of Alexander: The Dated Laws and Decrees of 'The Lykourgan Era'*. Chicago.
SH	Lloyd-Jones, H. and Parsons, P. (1983) *Supplementum Hellenisticum*. Berlin.
SOD	Stork, P., Ophuijsen, J. M. and Dorandi, T. (2000) 'Demetrius of Phalerum: the sources, text and translation', in *Demetrius*

	of Phalerum: Text, Translation and Discussion, ed. W. W. Fortenbaugh and E. Schütrumpf. New Brunswick, NJ: 1–310.
Stephanis	Stephanis, I. (1988). *Διονυσιακοὶ τεχνῖται*. Heraklion.

Unless otherwise noted, fragments of tragic drama follow the texts and use the numbering of:

TrGF	(1971–2004) *Tragicorum Graecorum fragmenta* (5 vols.). Göttingen.
Vol. I	Snell, B. ed. (1986) *Didascaliae tragicae, catalogi tragicorum et tragoediarum testimonia et fragmenta tragicorum minorum.* Corrected and augmented by R. Kannicht. Göttingen.
Vol. II	Kannicht, R. and Snell, B. eds. (1981) *Fragmenta adespota, testimonia, volumini I addenda, indices ad volumina I et II.* Göttingen.
Vol. III	Radt, S. ed. (1985) *Aeschylus*. Göttingen.
Vol. IV	Radt, S. ed. (1977) *Sophocles*. Göttingen.
Vol. V	Kannicht, R. ed. (2004) *Euripides* (2 fascicles). Göttingen.

Unless otherwise noted, fragments of comic drama follow the texts and use the numbering of:

PCG	Kassel, R., and Austin, C. (1983–2001) *Poeti comici graeci* (8 vols.). Berlin.

All translations into English are by the author except where otherwise noted.

REFERENCE CHRONOLOGY

Year(s)	Archon	Event(s)
c. 355–337		Eubulus administrator of *theorikon* treasury (the theoric fund)
c. 350		Construction renewed on the 'Lycurgan' Theatre of Dionysus (first planned/begun under Pericles)
347/6	*Themistocles*	Peace of Philocrates (spring; just after the Great Dionysia)
346/5	*Archias*	Aeschines, *Against Timarchus*
347/6–343/2		The *Fasti* (*IG* ii^{2} 2318) first inscribed at some point
343/2	*Pythodotus*	Aeschines and Demosthenes, *On the False Embassy*
341/40	*Nicomachus*	Astydamas victorious at the Great Dionysia; awarded honours
338/7	*Chaerondes*	Battle of Chaeronea (summer)
338–322		The 'Lycurgan Era'; Lycurgus son of Lycophron, of Butadae overseer of the Athenian treasury
336/5	*Pythodelos*	King Philip II of Macedon assassinated at the theatre in Aegae; Alexander the Great ascends to the throne (autumn)
332/1	*Nicetes*	Alexander the Great founds the city of Alexandria (7 April); Alexander's theatre festival in Phoenicia (spring); First attested 'Assembly in [the Theatre of] Dionysus'
331/30	*Aristophanes*	Lycurgus, *Against Leocrates*

Reference chronology

Year(s)	Archon	Event(s)
330/29	*Aristophon*	Aeschines, *Against Ctesiphon*; Demosthenes, *On the Crown*
c. 330		Lycurgan law on scripts and statues of the three tragedians; Aristotle, *Poetics*
325/4	*Anticles*	Death of Lycurgus
324/3	*Hegesias*	Death of Alexander the Great (10 June)
324/3–323/2		Lamian War; Athens falls to Macedon
323/2	*Cephisodorus*	Death of Aristotle
322/1	*Philocles*	Demosthenes commits suicide
320/19	*Neaechmus*	'Lycurgan' Theatre of Dionysus completed

INTRODUCTION: THROUGH THE LYCURGAN LOOKING GLASS

The Peloponnesian War concluded in the spring of 404 BC when an Athens overcome by siege and hunger at last surrendered to Sparta. Not long afterwards, the Spartan general Lysander undertook to replace the Athenian democracy with the oligarchic regime that would come to be known as the Thirty Tyrants. The Athenians initially resisted this devastating reversal of their constitution, but Lysander responded with the grave warning that the city had already been caught in violation of the terms of peace by failing to tear down its walls. He promised to take the case to the Peloponnesian League and, according to Plutarch, the ensuing assembly of those allies saw proposals to sell the Athenians into slavery, raze the city to the ground and give over the Attic countryside to the grazing of sheep.[1] Xenophon, in his narrative of the end of the war, reports that no Athenians had slept the night after the news of the previous summer's defeat at Aegospotami: instead they passed its dark hours mourning the dead, but also lamenting 'much more for themselves, thinking that they would suffer the same things as they had wrought upon the Melians, colonists of the Lacedaemonians, when they conquered them by siege, and upon the Histiaeans and the Scionaeans and the Tornaeans and Aeginetans and so many other Greeks'.[2] When the war did conclude the next spring it seemed that this was precisely the fate that Lysander and the rest of his League had planned. What could have changed their minds?

According to Plutarch's account, the allies had their second thoughts at the banquet after the assembly. There a

[1] Plut. *Lys.* 15.2; compare the account at Xen. *Hell.* 2.19–20. On how the proposed destruction of the city in 404 was remembered in fourth-century Athens see Steinbock (2013) 280–341.

[2] Xen. *Hell.* 2.2.3.

certain Phocian man entertained the gathered leaders by singing the choral *parodos* of Euripides' *Electra*.[3] At the performance 'all were bent to pity, and it came to seem a merciless deed to destroy and make an end of a city so illustrious and which had produced such men'; that is, such men as the poet Euripides.[4] Elsewhere, in his *Life of Nicias*, Plutarch also writes of how after the previous decade's disaster of the Sicilian Expedition some of the Athenians enslaved in Sicily had been 'saved by Euripides' because they were able to teach Sicilians portions of his plays.[5] Now with the entire Peloponnesian War at a final and bitter end, all of Athens apparently owed its salvation to one tragic poet.

We should certainly suspect the historicity of Plutarch's anecdote. Yet the notion that Athenian tragedians had the power to save their city and its citizens was potent enough to be repeated many times in the ancient tradition about classical drama.[6] In Aristophanes' *Frogs*, which premiered at the Lenaea of 405, just over a year before the war ended, the character of Dionysus posed the question to 'Aeschylus' and to 'Euripides' of how Athens might assure its own salvation (σωτηρία).[7] At the end of the play Dionysus, hoping that the vehicle of that salvation would be one of the city's great (dead) playwrights, chooses to resurrect Aeschylus: 'I came down here for a poet,' Dionysus explains to Pluto in the final scene of the play, 'so that the rescued (σωθεῖσα) city might lead its choruses'.[8] When the curtain falls, Dionysus is poised to return to Athens with Aeschylus in tow, optimistic that the great tragedian of the past will secure the city's future. Plutarch, writing nearly half a millennium later, also saw a tragic poet as the

[3] Plutarch quotes Eur. *El.* 167–8, the first two lines of the play's *parodos*. See Steinbock (2013) 319–23 on the (more likely) reasons that Athens was spared and 331–6 and on the role that the Phocians did actually play in reversing the city's fate.

[4] Plut. *Lys.* 15.3.

[5] Plut. *Nic.* 29.2–4.

[6] On this conceit see also pages 188–90. Another late anecdote, recorded by Pausanias (born about a half century after Plutarch), links an act of mercy on the part of Lysander with the power of the Athenian tragedians: when the Lacedaemonians invaded Attica, their general (i.e. Lysander) had a dream that he saw Dionysus bidding him to pay the 'new siren' the honours that are due to the dead. The general interpreted the 'new siren' to mean the recently deceased Sophocles: Paus. 1.21.1–2.

[7] Ar. *Ran.* 1435–6.

[8] Ar. *Ran.* 1419–20.

man to whom the city of Athens owed its collective life: Aristophanes' Dionysus had erred only in his choice of tragedian for the job.

None of the three great classical tragedians whose works have survived to this day – Aeschylus, Sophocles and Euripides – lived to see their city's defeat by Sparta in the Peloponnesian War, let alone to hear the story that a play by one of their number preserved Athens from obliteration. Euripides died sometime in the year 406 BC and Sophocles followed shortly after in 405. For the Dionysus of the *Frogs*, the death of Sophocles was itself a nail in the coffin of Athens' great tragic tradition: at the outset of the play the god announces to Heracles that he is about to journey to Hades in search of a 'clever' or 'good' (δεξιός) poet, 'because [such poets] no longer exist and the ones who are left are bad'.[9] The *Frogs* marks an early dramatisation of a deep nostalgia for the three great tragedians, but one which continued to regard the deceased poets as at odds and in competition with each other, even within the Underworld.

In the latter decades of the fourth century, however, only a few short generations after the *Frogs*, the contribution of the fifth-century tragedians would come to be viewed as a unified one, embodied atop a single statue base. Their singular achievement would be cast as a crowning glory of Athens, one of the greatest gifts that the city had bestowed upon Hellas as a whole. The new vision of 'classical' tragedy that developed during the second half of the fourth century is nearly impossible to disentangle from what we now perceive as the fifth-century dramatic triumph. In the light of the last few decades of scholarship, one could hardly dispute that for many years after the passing of Attic tragedy's 'historical moment' (to borrow Vernant's famous formulation), the city's tragic theatre industry remained very much alive and well.[10] It is, of course, only

[9] Ar. *Ran.* 72: οἱ μὲν γὰρ οὐκέτ' εἰσίν, οἱ δ' ὄντες κακοί.

[10] Vernant (1972) 13–17, on 'Le moment historique de la tragédie en Grèce'. For defences of the continued liveliness of the tragic theatre in the fourth century see esp. Easterling (1993) and Le Guen (1995), who both write against what Easterling

with a retrospective gaze that we follow Aristophanes in seeing a rupture in the tragic tradition after the death of Sophocles, a rupture that seems even more violent because of its close coincidence with the end of the Peloponnesian War. Yet already in late classical Athens, a deep and gaping fissure – however imaginary – divided the theatrical landscape between an era that died with Euripides and Sophocles and one which was born with all subsequent production.

The first signs of these contours are evident in the *Frogs*, in which Aeschylus, Euripides and to a lesser extent Sophocles (whose death shortly before the play's premiere may have limited his comedic 'participation'), are positioned as the only serious contenders for the Underworld's Chair in Tragedy. Outside of Old Comedy, however, Greek literature of the fifth century is surprisingly silent on the subjects of tragedy and tragedians. One searches with little success in the works of Herodotus and Thucydides for mentions of tragic drama or playwrights. Herodotus' most extensive discussion comes in the form of his story about the playwright Phrynichus, who was fined thousands of drachmas for reminding the Athenians of a painful event in Ionian history with his play *The Sack of Miletus*.[11] Thucydides, on the other hand, never directly discusses tragic drama.[12] And excepting those mentions of tragic *choregiai* undertaken as liturgies by wealthy Athenians, the tragic theatre rarely appears in the oratory of the fifth and early fourth centuries; the most notable exception is Isocrates' criticism of the old practice of parading the surplus allied tribute – along with the year's war orphans – before the allies

(1993) 59 calls the 'stereotype of sudden and total collapse' of drama after the fifth century.

[11] Her. 6.121, the only passage of his which contains forms of the word δρᾶμα. At 5.67 he mentions that the Sicyonians honoured Adrastus with 'tragic choruses'. He also tells of Aeschylus' innovation in making Artemis the daughter of Demeter in one of his plays (2.156.6), yet given the theme of the *Histories* it is noteworthy, as Ford (2009) 817 remarks, that Herodotus makes no mention of Aeschylus' *Persians*.

[12] He does identify the Peace of Nicias that ended the Archidamian War in 421 as having been sworn 'just after the Great Dionysia': Thuc. 5.20.1. The terms of the peace were to be renewed annually by the Athenians at the celebration of the Hyacinthia in Sparta and by the Lacedaemonians in Athens at the Great Dionysia (5.20.3).

gathered at the Great Dionysia.[13] Plato, evoking the life of the late fifth-century city, does have his Socrates refer on a number of occasions to the great tragedians, and the *Symposium* paints a particularly vivid picture of everyday 'dramatic' life in its setting at the celebration of Agathon's first tragic victory. But rich though the Platonic dialogues may be in abstract discussions of tragedy and in theatrical *obiter dicta*, they offer reconstructed pictures of the city's fifth-century cultural life rather than direct reflections upon the space that tragedy occupied in Plato's own Athens. Not until the second half of the fourth century, in the wake of another Athenian military and political disaster, do we find another torrent of discourse centred upon the 'politics' of tragic drama. At the heart of this new discourse, robust in prose and poetry alike, are questions about the relationships between imperial Athens and tragedy's perceived fifth-century zenith, as well as between the present-day city and its theatrical heritage.

The relative explosion of 'tragic' material occurs in the third quarter of the fourth century, the period that this book will examine in detail. Now, once again, it would seem that the city was calling upon its tragedians to come to its aid in a time of crisis. The Macedonian victory over the Greeks at the Battle of Chaeronea in 338 heralded more loudly than ever Macedon's imperial ambitions in Greece. With the future of Athenian independence in question, the city was forced to re-evaluate which institutions, legacies and virtues defined its uniqueness both in the Greek world and beyond. At this point in the city's history, an impulse to what Hans-Joachim Gehrke has called 'intentional history' (*intentionale Geschichte*) was accordingly strong: the Athenians sought to mould the shape of the past in an attempt to define their identity and direct the course of their future.[14] It is no coincidence, then, that the decades of the Macedonian ascendancy mark one of the liveliest and most

[13] Isoc. 8.82 (*de Pace*). He also occasionally refers briefly to tragic drama, but does not reflect upon it as an Athenian institution (for a brief exception see Isoc. 12.168). On Isocrates' references to poetry see Papillon (1998) 43–8.

[14] Gehrke (2001) and (2010); perhaps the clearest definition of the term is offered by Luraghi and Foxhall (2010): intentional history 'is the projection in time of the elements of subjective, self-conscious self- categorization which construct the identity of a group as a group'; they emphasise that 'A key issue is that of social agency in

important chapters in the history of Athenian drama and in the evolution of what, in time, would become the tragic corpus that we possess today. On the one hand, this was the period in which the entire body of classical tragedy began to boil down to a common performance repertory and a selection of plays that would serve as standard texts among the educated elite for centuries to come. Even more significantly, however, it was also the era in which the seeds were first planted of the notion that Greek tragedy had been a uniquely and quintessentially Athenian triumph. Attic tragedy has long been regarded as a fundamental aspect of the broader phenomenon of the 'Athenian miracle', but if we wish to confront that 'miracle' honestly we must also acknowledge that it was the Athenians themselves who, especially in the latter part of the fourth century, began constructing the pedestal upon which their drama still stands in the modern imagination.[15]

This book will present a detailed case as to how, in the third quarter of the fourth century BC, a number of measures were taken in Athens to affirm to the Greek world that the cultural achievement of tragedy was owed to the special qualities of the city that had first fostered it. By means of rhetoric, architecture, inscriptions, statues, archives and even legislation, these years saw the 'classical' tragedians and their plays packaged and advertised as the products and vital embodiments of the city's idealised past. The evidence of these efforts comes to us primarily from the years between the Peace of Philocrates, ratified by Athens and Philip II of Macedon just days after the Great Dionysia was celebrated in 346, and the Lamian War, which ended with Athenian defeat in 322. At the conclusion of that war, fought in the aftermath of Alexander the Great's death, Athens ceded its independence to Macedon and saw Antipater installed as the city's regent. These years largely coincide with the lifetime of Alexander, who was born in Pella in

the formulation of ideas, notions and stories about the past, and how these become, or aspire to become, possessions of a whole community' (9).

15 Mitchel (1970) poses this rhetorical question with respect to the Lycurgan Era more generally: 'For Athens [Lykourgos] was the founder of the classical tradition, and if the tradition had not begun to crystallize under Lykourgos in the 330s and 320s, one may well ask when and under whom it would have had its start?' (52).

356, succeeded his father Philip II of Macedon to the throne in 335 and died in Babylon in 323. The second half of the period, my primary object of study, closely corresponds to what is now commonly known as the 'Lycurgan Era'; that is, the era traditionally bounded by the Athenian defeats at Chaeronea in 338 and in the Lamian War, and dominated by the political career of Lycurgus son of Lycophron, of the deme of Butadae. The principal administrator of the city's public treasury during that era, Lycurgus is regarded today as these years' pre-eminent Athenian statesman.[16]

Lycurgus stood at the forefront of many of his city's efforts to shape its memory of classical tragedy and to capitalise upon the economic and diplomatic potential of the still-vibrant Athenian theatre industry. As Graham Oliver has recently reminded us, however, we should be wary of seeing a total break between the middle decades of the century and the beginning of Lycurgus' tenure at the head of state finances in 338.[17] Lycurgus' (and Lycurgan-Era) policies show strands of continuity from previous decades, particularly from the 350s and 340s, when as head of the city's theoric fund Eubulus occupied a position in the city comparable to the one that Lycurgus later held.[18] Already during Eubulus' administration we find evidence of Athens' growing interest in the strength and promotion of its theatre industry. Recently scholars have also begun to question whether Lycurgus has lent his name deservingly to the years of his own administration.[19] Nevertheless, here I shall be referring to the era as 'Lycurgan' both for the sake of convenience

[16] Lycurgus' tenure extended from 336/5–325/4. For a recent review of the chronology of Lycurgus' political career and the problem of which office he held (ὁ ἐπὶ τῆς διοικήσεως) between 336/5 and 325/4 (in a succession of four-year terms, the last cut short by his death) see Friend (2009) 61–3. For the dates of the public offices held by Lycurgus see Develin (1989); for overviews of his political career see esp. Humphreys (1985) and Mitchel (1970) ch. 2 'The Program'.

[17] Oliver (2011).

[18] For an overview of Eubulus' administration see Cawkwell (1963).

[19] See in particular Brun (2005) and Rhodes (2010), who both qualify the period's traditional identification as 'Lycurgan'. Rhodes nevertheless points out that it is 'reasonable to think of the Lycurgan period as of the Periclean period, as long as we are clear about what we are claiming and what we are not': Lycurgus was certainly 'one of the most prominent men in Athens', though he was by no means singlehandedly responsible for his city's policies or finances (88).

and because there is good evidence that a number of the initiatives that I discuss either were associated with him or seem to cohere with his broader vision for the city. Oftentimes and as has become convention, my references to 'Lycurgan' initiatives serve as a shorthand for policies enacted not just by Lycurgus, but by his circle of like-minded citizens.

The process of tragedy's classicisation in the Lycurgan Era would prove to be of substantial consequence for the shape of the tragic corpus that managed to outlast antiquity. It is generally accepted, for example, that Lycurgus' reaffirmation of Athens' own tragic *tre corone*, a kind of canon already dramatised by the *Frogs* of 405, helped to pave the way for the survival of works by the same three tragedians – and those tragedians alone – to the present day. What has received less than due attention, however, is the striking overlap between the tragedies for which there is an indirect fourth-century tradition and those plays which have been preserved:[20] testimonia for Aeschylus' *Choephori*, Sophocles' *Ajax*, *Antigone*, *Electra*, *Oedipus Tyrannus* and *Philoctetes* and Euripides' *Hecuba*, *Hippolytus*, *Iphigenia in Aulis*, *Iphigenia in Tauris*, *Medea*, *Orestes* and *Trojan Women* all appear among our fourth-century prose sources and comic fragments. It is also an oft-invoked (though still sobering) statistic that, of the 300 or so plays supposedly written by Aeschylus, Sophocles and Euripides, only thirty-three, or about one tenth, survive.[21] In the light of those numbers, we should regard it as exceptionally noteworthy that roughly half of the tragedies that Aristotle mentions by name in the *Poetics* can be found on that list of thirty-three.[22] While the *Poetics* itself was surely influential in shaping the body of tragic texts that we have

[20] See however Easterling (1997b) 212–20 and (1993) 564 for the earliest processes of 'canon' formation (and the importance of reperformance to those processes) in the fourth century.

[21] The *Suda* (s.v. each of the tragedians' names) reports that Aeschylus wrote 90 plays, Sophocles 90 or 'as some say many more' (ὡς δέ τινες καὶ πολλῷ πλείω) and Euripides either 75 or 92.

[22] Surviving plays identifiably mentioned in the *Poetics*: Aesch. *Cho.*; Soph. *Ant.*, *El.*, *OT*; Eur. *IA*, *IT*, *Or.*, *Med.*; Aristotle is also likely referring to *Prometheus Bound* at 1456a2–3. Lost plays mentioned include Aesch. *Niobe*, *Philoctetes*, *Daughters of Phorcys*; Soph. *Tereus*, *Tyro* and *Wounded Odysseus*; Eur. *Cresphontes*, *Melanippe the Wise* and *Philoctetes*.

today, the other witnesses to many of the plays which Aristotle mentions suggest that, by the 330s, the wheels of canonisation were already in motion for the tragic poets and their individual corpora. Though typically overlooked by historians of the theatre, the mass of other surviving texts and documents from this part of the fourth century constitutes significant evidence for that process, a process whose end results would shape a great portion of Western literary and dramatic history.

Together the sources also attest to contemporary Athenian attempts to reconceptualise the very idea of tragic drama by presenting it as an historical institution that was exclusively the product and possession of the Athenian demos. Scholars have long been interested in the relationship between tragedy and the fifth-century Athenian Empire as well as in identifying expressions and critiques of Athenian imperialism latent within the tragic texts.[23] Debates continue today about the extent to which the tragic plays engaged with a uniquely Athenian civic ideology when they first premiered, and these debates are far from being resolved. But despite the many open and lingering questions about the relationship between tragedy, democracy and the fifth-century empire, texts from the latter half of the fourth century – an era in which the Athenian polis no longer reigned politically supreme – attest to highly conscious attempts in Athens to forge ideological links between the city's character and its theatrical history.

During this period, in 339 BC, 'old' (*palaion*) comedy also joined the programme of the Great Dionysia, alongside the productions of 'old tragedy' that had been in place since 386.[24] This addition speaks further to Athens' heightened attention to its theatrical past during this period, and a study of Athens' delicate relationship with its comic past (and the era of liberal free speech that it represented) is also to be desired. Yet

[23] This topic is vast, but for tragedy as an expression of Athenian imperialism see esp. Kowalzig (2006) on tragedy's appropriation of the Athenian allies' mythical histories, and Kurke (1997) on its absorption of 'foreign' lyric forms. Scodel (2001) offers an important account of the attention that Athens paid to its theatrical industry while the city grew as an imperial power. The bibliography of Carter (2011) marks a useful compilation of modern scholarship on the politics of fifth-century tragedies.

[24] *IG* ii^2 2318.1565–6 Millis and Olson.

the generation of comic playwriting that would come to be regarded as Greece's Golden Age of Comedy – that is, New Comedy – was still on the horizon in the third quarter of the fourth century. Tragedy already occupied a central place in the city's *imaginaire* largely thanks to its early success outside of Athens, as well as to the attention that it had received from 'Old' comic playwrights such as Aristophanes. A spectacular era of tragic production had coincided with the political *floruit* of Athens, and this chronology was not lost on later generations of Athenians.[25] In particular, the evidence for the cultural programme advanced in the 330s points to a developing civic narrative designed to connect the city's illustrious history with its signature art form. This narrative actively bound the achievements of fifth-century drama and the figures of the great tragedians to idealised visions of both the Athenian past and the city's 'national' character.

The third quarter of the fourth century, and more specifically the Lycurgan Era, may mark relatively untravelled territory for many students of fifth-century tragedy. Yet as readers confronting the tragic plays that survive, we should bear in mind that these decades created a filter which cannot be removed from any critical lens that we apply to the fifth-century material today. Both the qualitative and quantitative dimensions of the present-day tragic corpus show the clearest signs of first having come into focus during these years, when the first recorded attempt to stabilise, protect and preserve the works of Aeschylus, Sophocles and Euripides was supposedly made by Lycurgus himself. Only a decade or so earlier (between 347/6 and 343/2), during Eubulus' tenure as overseer of the theoric fund, the records of victors at the Great Dionysia upon which we rely

[25] Aeschylus' first victory came in 484 (so the *Parian Chronicle*), just six years before the formation of the Delian League in 478 (cf. Thuc. 1.96); his *Oresteia* was produced in 458, four years before the treasury of the Delian League is usually thought to have been moved to Athens (i.e. in 454/3, though the treasury may have been moved earlier). Athens was defeated by Sparta in the Peloponnesian War in 404, about two years after the death of Euripides and one year after that of Sophocles. Pausanias synchronises Sophocles' death with Athens' surrender to Sparta in 404: Paus. 1.21.1–2 (n. 6 above).

so heavily (as did our Alexandrian predecessors) for information about dramatic chronology were first inscribed.[26] At about the same time, in 346 BC, the first known instance of tragic quotation in an Athenian courtroom appears, in Aeschines' speech *Against Timarchus*. Aeschines also constitutes one of our most important sources for the 'preplay ceremony' at the Great Dionysia that saw the parade of war orphans in the theatre, even though by his day the tradition was no longer upheld.[27] Indeed, much of what we know, or think that we know, about the cultural, festal and civic contexts of fifth-century tragedy derives from the fourth-century sources that I shall be discussing here.

A truly remarkable body of evidence for both the reception of classical tragedy and the vitality of the contemporary theatre clusters in the Lycurgan Era. The year 330 alone saw the delivery of three orations in Athens (Lycurgus' *Against Leocrates*, Aeschines' *Against Ctesiphon* and Demosthenes' *On the Crown*) which collectively bear witness to a variety of ideas about the role of classical tragedy in the education of the demos, the importance of the Theatre of Dionysus as an historical monument to festivals past and the significance of the Great Dionysia as an occasion for Athenian self-presentation to both citizens and foreign visitors. This same year is the traditional date for the Lycurgan law which called for the first ever official copies of the tragic texts and commissioned public statues of their authors. And though archaeological and epigraphic records now offer evidence to the contrary, it is telling of ancient perceptions that our literary sources attribute the completion of a reconstructed Theatre of Dionysus to Lycurgus himself.[28] In the late 330s Aristotle, who had returned to Athens from Macedon in 335, is likely to have delivered the lectures whose substance is partially preserved in the *Poetics*, and not to be overlooked are his efforts to amass the historical records of

[26] *IG* ii^2 2318.
[27] See esp. Goldhill (1987) on the 'preplay ceremonies' at the Great Dionysia.
[28] See Papastamati-von Moock (forthcoming) and the discussion on pages 95–103.

victors at the Great Dionysia. Stephen Lambert's recently compiled corpus of Lycurgan-era theatre inscriptions vividly (if fragmentarily) attests to a variety of innovations with respect to the management of the Athenian theatre and to the city's capitalisation upon its cultural heritage.[29] Prominent among these initiatives was an urgent use of civic honours both to retain famous actors and to encourage private investment in the ongoing construction of the new theatre. In the same period stelai recording honorific decrees were also first displayed within the sanctuary of Dionysus, and thus became yet another object of the theatregoer's gaze.

But the importance of the Lycurgan Era to the history of theatre is not confined to what it tells us about Athens' dramatic past and present. In the third quarter of the fourth century we also find foreshadowed a number of the developments that, in full flower during the third and second centuries BC, would reshape the Greek world's theatrical landscape. These later years marked the critical decades in which Greece's theatrical heritage was most actively being transmitted to and, starting no later than the momentous first tragic production of Livius Andronicus in 240 BC, adapted by Rome. In hindsight, the years of Lycurgus' own lifetime marked a significant crossroads in terms of Athens' own history (as the city came to inhabit what we know as its 'Hellenistic' identity) as well as for the historical development of the theatre: it is here that we can locate not only a re-evaluation of the fifth-century heritage in Athens, but also the early consolidation of the highly developed Hellenistic, Panhellenic industry.

At its heart this is a literary study in cultural history that is concerned most of all with the discourses that steered and shaped the transmission of classical tragedy in fourth-century Athens. The significance of the Lycurgan theatre programme has long been recognised by epigraphists and archaeologists of the theatre, who have already laid critical groundwork for further research into the period's theatre-related economy,

[29] Lambert (2008).

inscriptions and architecture.[30] Yet the programme's significance for literary and dramatic history remains to be fully appreciated. Here it is my aim to redress this lacuna by keeping the fifth-century plays as much in the foreground as possible, but also by attending carefully and even primarily to the many literary texts that bear witness to the cultural currents that I describe. Literary texts are invaluable witnesses to the discourses and conflicts whose end results are recorded on and in the ancient stones, and the evidence that they provide is integral if we hope to understand the many textured complexities of Athens' relationship with its theatrical and 'tragic' past in this period.

The first part of this book brings together a variety of evidence for the Lycurgan theatre programme, and engages in a series of close and contextualising readings of the texts that bear witness to it. Here the epigraphic and material records provide critical tools for the analysis of the literary texts. In the second part, I slightly extend my chronological scope. These chapters each consist in a genre-based case study that traces shifting views of classical tragedy in the later fourth century: through oratory, comic fragments and Aristotle. In discussing the pre-Lycurgan oratorical conflicts of Aeschines and Demosthenes, I look more carefully to the Eubulan roots of Lycurgus' theatrical vision; my study of comedy is the most expansive in its reach across much of the century. Though I do not return specifically to the Lycurgan Era until the final chapter, primarily a reading of Aristotle's *Poetics* as a work of theatre history, each of the discussions in the second part of the book relies in its conclusions upon the outline of the Lycurgan theatre programme that I construct in the first.

My guiding interest throughout is thus in the poetics of theatrical heritage during the Lycurgan Era (and to some extent

[30] For epigraphy see especially Millis and Olson (2012) and Lambert (2008); on the economy and finances of the Athenian theatre industry from Eubulus to Lycurgus see Csapo and Wilson (forthcoming). Csapo, Goette, Green and Wilson's forthcoming edited volume on Greek theatre in the fourth century contains a number of important and relevant pieces, some of which do extend the horizon of work in this area to the literary. For studies in the history of the period see n. 35 below.

beyond), but essential to my overarching argument is the question of how changing political circumstances came to affect the Athenians' conceptualisation of their city and the role of tragic drama therein. On many points it is therefore difficult to distinguish literary from historical questions. Lycurgan Athens developed and presented its theatre industry largely in reaction to the expansion of the Macedonian empire and the challenge that Macedon posed to Athens' standing within the Greek world. A handful of recent studies have begun to investigate the Macedonians' appreciation for Athenian tragedy and their role in tragedy's diffusion abroad, but the side of the story that remains to be considered – and which I shall begin to tell here – is that of Athens' own defensive reaction to the foreign appropriation of its most celebrated poetry and poets.[31] As theatre on an 'Athenian model' became ever more popular throughout Greece, the illustrious past of Attic tragedy also became an increasingly central emblem of Athenian civic identity and cultural heritage. Confronted with the reality of a considerably weakened political position on the international stage, Athens made ever more explicit attempts to capitalise upon its record of cultural achievement.[32] As part of those attempts, the city embarked upon a determined programme of reclaiming the fifth-century tragedians and their plays for the city that had birthed and raised them.

In recent years new historical reassessments of this period have been made possible, thanks largely to Lambert's work in preparing a fascicle for the new edition of *IG* ii (fascicle 2 of *IG* ii[3]) which comprises all of the Athenian laws and decrees (about 280 texts) from the period 352/1–322/1 BC. In the course of this work Lambert produced dozens of preparatory articles on themes in the inscriptions of the period, and together these articles offer a far more developed picture of Athens in the third quarter of the fourth century than had previously existed or indeed was possible without such an up-to-date documentary

[31] On tragedy and Macedon see esp. Moloney (2003) and Revermann (1999–2000). The rare treatments of the Athenian side of the story include Wilson and Csapo (2009) and Lambert (2008).

[32] On the epigraphic evidence for these sorts of attempts see Lambert (2008).

corpus.[33] More generally, the last decades have also seen an intensified interest in the figure of Lycurgus and the Lycurgan *Kulturpolitik*,[34] as well as in the role that a collective, idealised memory of the 'Age of Pericles' played in shaping the policies and projects of the Athenian 'silver age'.[35] Brigitte Hintzen-Bohlen in particular has made a detailed and compelling case that the 'retrospective tendencies' (*retrospektive Tendenzen*) of the Lycurgan period were not founded upon mere nostalgia, but rather that Lycurgus' programme for Athens managed to turn the city's 'golden age' into a usable past which provided new opportunities for political, fiscal and cultural innovation.[36] With the exception of the Lycurgan building programme in its entirety, such a combination of retrospection and forward-thinking ingenuity (a spectacular example of 'intentional history') was on display nowhere so much as in the state-sponsored promotion of the city's theatrical heritage.

But again, and despite the significance of the Lycurgan efforts and initiatives, this era remains remarkably under-investigated by literary scholars as a critical moment in tragedy's early reception. Even the studies of recent decades which have sought to defend the vitality of the post-fifth-century Athenian theatre focus primarily upon the first decades of the fourth century.[37] Neglect of the period may also be partially explained by a tendency for scholars interested in the theatre beyond its 'formative "golden" context' to turn their attention away from tragedy's Athenian centre in favour of investigating the ways in which non-democratic polities outside of mainland Greece appropriated and experienced the

[33] Many of these are now collected in Lambert (2012).
[34] The term of Hintzen-Bohlen (1997).
[35] For the phrase see Mitchel (1970) 28. Recent studies of Lycurgan Athens include Csapo and Wilson (forthcoming) (with an emphasis on the theatre industry), Lambert's (2012) collected papers, Azoulay and Ismard (2011), Steinbock (2011), Burke (2010), Rhodes (2010), Azoulay (2009), Wirth (1997), Hintzen-Bohlen (1995) and (1997), Engels (1992), Faraguna (1992) 195–210 and 245–85 and Vielberg (1991).
[36] Hintzen-Bohlen (1997), who calls this strategy 'Vergangenheit als Stimulation für die Gegenwart' (106).
[37] E.g. Easterling (1993); Hall (2007).

Athenian plays.[38] But the lack of a substantial study on the Athenian theatre and the construct of classical tragedy in this part of the fourth century may also be owed to the nature of our sources. Plentiful though they may be, we have no single witness to tragic production or reception in the mid-fourth century that supplies nearly so much information as Aristophanes' *Frogs* (or even *Acharnians* or *Thesmophoriazusae*) does for the age of Sophocles and Euripides; even more frustrating for the literary historian is the scarcity of sizeable fragments of fourth-century tragedy itself.

Nevertheless, the unique combination of epigraphic, archaeological and non-dramatic literary records for these years makes it possible to reconstruct a picture of Athenian theatrical discourses in the mid-fourth century that is perhaps even clearer that what we can posit for the fifth. These records are supplied by sources which generally do not appear in the standard collections of theatrical testimonia. Peter Wilson has now repeatedly drawn cautionary attention to the tendency of scholars of Greek theatre to engage solely with the testimonia contained within Pickard-Cambridge's magisterial works *The Dramatic Festivals of Athens* and *Dithyramb, Tragedy, Comedy*.[39] Yet even in the revised edition of *Dramatic Festivals* (*DFA*²), the section 'Tragedy after the fifth century BC' in the portion of the volume that is explicitly dedicated to 'The Great or City Dionysia' runs to only a single paragraph.[40] The situation is similar with respect to the testimonia for the lives of the classical tragedians, which offer evidence for diverse and

38 The phrase of Taplin (2009b) 471. As a sampling see, on Athenian tragedy in Sicily: Bosher (2012), Kowalzig (2008), Allan (2001), Dearden (1999), Griffith (1978); on Athenian tragedy in Macedon: Moloney (2003), Revermann (1999–2000); more general discussions: Taplin (1999), Easterling (1997b) and (1994).

39 Respectively *DFA*² and Pickard-Cambridge (1927), revised by Webster (1962). On the tendency to use only those sources gathered by Pickard Cambridge see, e.g., Wilson (2008) 3: 'Hundreds of these interpretative studies [i.e. of Greek drama] blithely refer to the relevant pages of Pickard-Cambridge's *The Dramatic Festivals of Athens* and *Dithyramb, Tragedy and Comedy* and take all that is said in them on trust'; cf. Wilson (2009) 18 (on the exclusion of *IG* i³ 102 from 'the standard portfolio of evidence for the history of the classical theatre') and Wilson and Csapo (2009) 50 on the comparable fate of theatre inscriptions from the end of the fourth century.

40 Pickard-Cambridge (1968) 81–2.

evolving views of these playwrights and their art form. The extensive collections of *testimonia vitae atque artis* for the tragedians found among the pages of the five volumes of *Tragicorum Graecorum Fragmenta* are immensely useful but not exhaustive. In the case of Euripides, for example, Kannicht's 107 pages of testimonia do not include the numerous passages of post-Aristophanic comedy and fourth-century oratory which contain references to the tragedian.[41] Those passages provide some of the most important contexts and evidence for the highly politicised reinvention of the Euripidean 'biography' in the Athens of the 330s, a reinvention that was indispensable to Athenian efforts in the era both to claim and to control the patrimony of the previous century's tragedy.

At this point a disclaimer is in order. This book aims to reconstruct the discourses that imagined and constructed Athens' tragic heritage, rather than to re-evaluate the work of the later tragedians either on the basis of formal poetics or in the light of their own social, political and cultural contexts.[42] Throughout the pages that follow I take for granted that the mid-fourth century was a prolific era of new tragic production in its own right, complete with celebrity playwrights, ostentatious *choregoi* and much-anticipated premieres. In an important reappraisal of the new tragedy produced in Athens during the first part of the fourth century, Patricia Easterling identified three key factors which 'tell against the complete artistic and intellectual dominance of the old plays' after the fifth century. Those factors are (1) 'the continuing prestige of the competition for new plays', (2) 'the productivity and fame of some of the fourth-century dramatists' and (3) 'the existence of family networks and traditions' that made for 'a continuity of professional expertise' with the theatrical traditions of

[41] *TrGF* 5.1 39–145.

[42] Easterling (1993) 566–7 also opens up a number of questions as to what new political and cultural resonances the fifth-century plays acquired when performed in the fourth century; see e.g. Duncan (2006) and Ferrario (2006) for work in this direction. Studies such as Taplin (2009a), a close reading of the fragments of Astydamas' *Hector*, demonstrate that research into the fourth-century tragic fragments is far from complete.

the fifth century.[43] It is precisely the position of the 'old plays' that most concerns me, but each of these three aspects of the fourth-century theatrical landscape will necessarily feature in my discussion. Even if some spectators were initially drawn to the Great Dionysia by the fame of Athens' illustrious past, the majority of plays that they saw there will have been new compositions. And significantly, it was always before the premieres of new tragedy that Athens conferred honours upon its benefactors. The celebration of the Great Dionysia in its fourth-century form served as a space within which the city could programmatically assert and perform the continuity of its past with its present. To borrow from Nicole Loraux's characterisation of the *epitaphios logos*, that 'very Athenian invention', the festival of the Great Dionysia and its dramatic performances marked another of the institutions that came to embody 'the many traces of permanence and transformation that, for us, constitute the history of Athens'.[44]

Let us return for a moment to Plutarch, whose own view of the history of this period anticipates essential aspects of my arguments. Though separated from classical Athens by more than four centuries, Plutarch recognised the significance of the Theatre of Dionysus as an edifice that housed a political stage in addition to its theatrical one. In his biographies of certain fourth-century politicians, the Great Dionysia comes to constitute a symbolic battlefield in the struggle between Athens and Macedon, as each mention of the festival in these *Lives* serves to illustrate threats that the Macedonians and their allies were making to the festival's (and to Athens') essential character.[45] Plutarch's historical accuracy is often suspicious at best, yet his reading of the broader importance of the theatre to the Athens of this period is subtle and incisive. In the chapters that follow I shall be making frequent reference to his accounts of Athens'

[43] Easterling (1993) 565. [44] Loraux (1986) 132.

[45] One thinks of e.g. Demades' scandalous *choregia*, mentioned by Plutarch in his *Life of Phocion*, discussed on pages 123–4 below; there is also Plutarch's vivid account of Demetrius Poliorcetes' debasements of the festival during his reign in Athens: because of Demetrius and his sycophants' impieties, a destructive and unseasonable cold broke out which destroyed the Athenians' crops and even forced the cancellation of the Great Dionysia's procession: Plut. *Dem.* 12.

drama industry. I do not present these accounts as reliable historical evidence, but rather as useful and revealing interpretations of the power dynamics that were once performed in the theatre space.

Nowhere does Plutarch weave together so many of the issues at the heart of this book as in a passage of his *Life of Alexander*, where the description of a festival put on by Alexander serves as an instructive allegory for Athens' struggle to retain its theatrical pre-eminence in the face of Macedon's rise. In the *Life* Plutarch records that, when Alexander the Great had returned to Phoenicia from his campaign in Egypt (in April of 331),

> θυσίας τοῖς θεοῖς καὶ πομπὰς ἐπετέλει καὶ χορῶν κυκλίων καὶ τραγικῶν ἀγῶνας, οὐ μόνον ταῖς παρασκευαῖς, ἀλλὰ καὶ ταῖς ἁμίλλαις λαμπροὺς γενομένους. (Plut. *Alex.* 29.1)
>
> he made sacrifices to the gods and held processions as well as dithyrambic and tragic competitions, which proved brilliant not only in terms of the preparations, but also with respect to the contests themselves.

These contests were particularly brilliant, Plutarch explains, because the kings of Cyprus acted as *choregoi* on the occasion, and they competed against each other with 'remarkable ambition'.[46] Nicocreon of Cypriot Salamis and Pasicrates of Soli were the most zealous of the royal competitors, for they had been allotted the most famous actors: Pasicrates received Athenodorus, while Nicocreon drew Thessalus.[47] Athenodorus and Thessalus are also listed in a fragment of the historian Chares as among the entertainers present at the mass wedding of Macedonian generals to Persian women that Alexander would orchestrate at Susa six years later, in 324.[48]

Thanks to the epigraphic sources we know that these two actors had distinguished records of performance in Athens at the Great Dionysia, most likely the venue at which they had

46 Plut. *Alex.* 29.1: ἠγωνίζοντο θαυμαστῇ φιλοτιμίᾳ.

47 For the careers of Athenodorus and Thessalus see Stephanis nos. 75 and 1200 respectively and Heckel (2006) s.v. Athenodorus [4] and Thessalus. According to Arrian, Athenodorus had joined Alexander's retinue in Egypt in 332/1: Arr. *Ana.* 3.1.4. For Thessalus see also Millis and Olson (2012) 57, 62 and 67.

48 Chares *FrGH* 125 F4 ap. Ath. 7.538f; attributed to Book 10 of Chares' *Histories of Alexander*.

earned their international fame. Athenodorus had taken the acting prize at the festival in 342 and would do so again in 329, not long after he performed for Alexander in Phoenicia.[49] He is also known to have competed in Athens – and to have lost to Thessalus – in 340.[50] Thessalus also performed at the Dionysia in 341, but by 336 was already working for Alexander. In 334, five years before the festival in Phoenicia, Alexander even used him on a diplomatic mission to Pixodarus, the satrap of Caria.[51] Alexander favoured Thessalus at the competition in Phoenicia, where the judges are said to have been the most esteemed Macedonian generals.[52] Athenodorus, however, was victorious, and though Alexander was sorely disappointed at the outcome he paid the fine that Athenodorus owed to the Athenians for having failed to keep his commitment to perform at the year's Great Dionysia.[53] To Athenodorus' mind, Alexander's festival had evidently constituted the better offer.

This account of Alexander's celebrations in Phoenicia and of the Cypriot kings' *choregiai* dates to centuries after the fact, and in both brief sketches of the affair that appear in Plutarch's corpus there is a point on which he (or perhaps Alexander) seems to have misinterpreted the Athenian choregic system.[54] The festival was supposedly organised with the model of the Athenian *choregia* in mind, yet the *choregoi* in Athens were never selected by lot (Plutarch claims that in Athens the *choregoi* were 'appointed by lot' from among the tribes).[55] But while the *Life of Alexander* may not be a reliable source for details

[49] *IG* ii² 2318.1538 (343/2 BC) and 1705 (330/29 BC) Millis and Olson.

[50] *IG* ii² 2320.23 Millis and Olson. He also competed at the Great Dionysia in 341, when Neoptolemus took the tragic actor's prize: *IG* ii² 2320 Col. II.8 10 Millis and Olson.

[51] Plut. *Alex.* 10.3. Thessalus' failure on this mission supposedly led Philip II to demand his arrest; Philip died shortly thereafter, however, and Thessalus managed to escape prison.

[52] Plut. *de glor. Alex.* 334e.

[53] Alexander is said to have proclaimed that he would rather give up part of his kingdom than see Thessalus defeated: Plut. *Alex.* 29.2; *de glor. Alex.* 334e.

[54] Plut. *Alex.* 29 and *de glor. Alex.* 334d–e.

[55] Wilson (2000) 288, who also points out that Alexander's choice of kings marked 'an appropriate equivalent to the wealthy *khoregoi* of Athens' and thus that 'Plutarch's inaccurate commentary might betray a better knowledge of the system on Alexander's part than on his own' (288).

of theatrical practice, its narrative of the festival in Phoenicia draws together a number of thematic threads in the history of the era's theatre. That kings were chosen as *choregoi*, for example, points us to the lavish parallel expenditure of the wealthy *choregoi* in Athens.[56] Plutarch's anecdote also serves to highlight the 'star power' of actors in the fourth century. We have no indication as to what plays Alexander saw performed on the occasion; in every sense it is the actors who take centre stage in this account. And if we read the anecdote with another passage from the *Life of Alexander* in mind (§10, on Thessalus' unsuccessful diplomatic mission to Caria), Thessalus' appearance at this point in the story might serve as a further reminder of the role that actors played in international relations in the 340s and 330s, decades in which they were often included in diplomatic embassies.[57]

Most importantly, however, this passage spotlights the inter-state competition in this period to secure theatrical celebrities for festival performances, competition which is here illustrated by the allusion to fines for actors who failed to fulfil their commitments to perform.[58] Plutarch's story indirectly but importantly puts us on the trail of an anxiety that seems to run just below the surface of a number of the fourth-century sources. While Macedon's power grew, Athens' grip upon its status as capital of Greek theatre was slackening. In Phoenicia Alexander did not just appropriate the Athenian choregic system and adapt it to his own ends and circumstances; he spared no expense in pilfering one of the leading actors of Athens for his own private event.[59] Studies in recent years have helped us

[56] No dramatic choregic monuments survive from this era in Athens, yet we might still note the highly ostentatious and architecturally innovative choregic monument that Lysicrates of Kikynna commissioned to commemorate his victory in the boys' dithyramb at the Great Dionysia of 335/4. On the monument see esp. Wilson (2000) 219–26, who contextualises it within the political and social climate of the time. See also the general study of Alemdar (2000), as well as Hintzen-Bohlen (1997) 88 and Knell (2000) 149–59 on the monument in the context of the Lycurgan building programme.

[57] On the use of actors as diplomats in this period (especially by Athens to Macedon) see pages 68–70.

[58] This is substantiated by the evidence of at least Aeschin. 2.19; see pages 71–2.

[59] As a thought experiment we might imagine the uproar had Laurence Olivier been poached to perform for an American millionaire in October 1963, on the eve of the

better to understand the enormous role that the Macedonian conquering elite played in spreading classical Greek tragedy throughout the *oikoumene*, or the 'civilised world'.[60] Yet Macedon's new proprietorship of tragedy met with vocal resistance from Athens. It is surely no coincidence that at the height of Macedonian expansion, and within just a few years or so of the supposed *choregiai* of the Cypriot kings, Lycurgus is said to have successfully moved his law dictating that bronze statues of Aeschylus, Sophocles and Euripides be erected in Athens and that official copies of their works be deposited in the state archive.[61]

Even the events leading up to the dramatic date of Plutarch's story foreshadow an imminent new chapter in the history of the tragic scripts, a chapter that begins with their removal from Athens. Alexander celebrated his festival in Phoenicia after returning from Egypt, where not long earlier, on the modern date of 7 April 331 BC, he had founded the city of Alexandria. Within a half-century it would be the library in that new city, and not the archive in Athens, that could boast of being the authoritative centre for the preservation of the fifth-century plays. Ironically, in the 330s the very creation of those scripts had marked efforts on the part of men such as Lycurgus to stake Athens' claim as the official and permanent home of the fifth-century plays. Those years, the years of Lycurgus' administration and of Alexander's own lifetime, provide us with a clear picture of an Athens ardently struggling to shape and to control its theatrical heritage. The story of that struggle, as revealed in poetry, speeches, statues, inscriptions, architecture and anecdotes of the era – a struggle which would in many ways come to define our own regard for Athenian tragedy today – is the story which this book seeks to tell.

premiere of his *Hamlet* at the National Theatre in London. On the Macedonians and the 'privatisation' of the theatre in the fourth century as well as the role of tragedies at the Macedonians' 'ad hoc' festivals see Csapo (2010) 172–4.

[60] See n. 31 above. [61] *Vit. dec. or.* 841f., cf. Paus. 1.21.1–2.

PART I

CLASSICAL TRAGEDY AND THE LYCURGAN PROGRAMME

CHAPTER 1

CIVIC POETRY IN LYCURGUS' *AGAINST LEOCRATES*

From the surviving corpus of Greek oratory, 331/0 BC looks to have been a particularly momentous year in the Athenian courtroom. In the late spring or early summer, Lycurgus delivered *Against Leocrates*, his narrowly unsuccessful and only surviving oration, before the court of the Areopagus.[1] Towards the end of the summer another important trial proved the finale of the more than fifteen-year public rivalry between the city's most prominent orators, Aeschines and Demosthenes.[2] In this case Aeschines brought a *graphē paranomōn*, a suit challenging the legality of a decree, against Ctesiphon, a politician and supporter of Demosthenes. Aeschines was contesting a proposal that Ctesiphon had made six years earlier, and which had called for Demosthenes to be crowned (again) in the Theatre of Dionysus in recognition of his services to Athens. During the trial Demosthenes himself addressed the court in Ctesiphon's defence, crafting his response to the charges as an argument for his own worthiness and a counter-assassination of Aeschines' character. Lycurgus appears to have lost his prosecution of Leocrates by a single vote,[3] but the margin of Ctesiphon's acquittal proved so wide that Aeschines, the one-time stage-actor turned diplomat and orator, was

[1] In *Against Ctesiphon* Aeschines remarks that this εἰσαγγελία had been brought 'just recently', πρώην (3.252). On the Areopagus in this period see Humphreys (1985) 200–1.

[2] The suit was argued a few days before the celebration of the Pythian festival (Aeschin. 3.254), which took place in the Delphic month of Boukatios (the Attic month of Metageitnion), i.e. in late summer (Wright (1891) 151; see too Burke (1977) 333 n. 12). 330 BC may also have been the year of Hyperides' speech for Euxenippus (Hyp. 4): see Colin (1946) 164.

[3] Aeschin. 3.252 implies that the votes were evenly split in the trial, tantamount to an acquittal: as Jebb (1876) 380 pointed out, 'Leokrates benefited by the precedent of Orestes.'

compelled to leave Athens and lived out the rest of his life on Rhodes.[4]

This year of high-profile court cases turns out to be the mid-point of Athens' Lycurgan Era (338–322 BC), a period that was defined by Lycurgus' administration of the city treasury and framed by two of the most significant events leading up to Macedon's definitive conquest of the city in 322: the Athenian defeats at the Battle of Chaeronea in 338 and the Lamian War of 323–22. Following the devastation of Athenian and Theban troops at Chaeronea, Athens had been stripped of its islands and control of the sea and became one of many Greek poleis to join the alliance (or 'common peace', the κοινὴ εἰρήνη) known to modern scholars as the League of Corinth. That league was organised under the authority of the victorious King Philip of Macedon,[5] and as part of the League's oath a number of Greek cities (with the notable exception of Sparta) invested Philip with the title of hegemon and swore never to overthrow his kingdom or the kingdoms of his descendants.[6] These Greek states each pledged to Macedon a certain number of soldiers who would support Philip in a campaign against Persia. The treaty between Philip and the Greek states also stipulated that no party who swore to it would destroy the *politeia* of any other, but its terms were nevertheless designed to keep the Greek cities weak and to ensure that they acknowledge Philip's supremacy.[7] Though Philip died in 336 and had since been succeeded by his son Alexander, Athens was still operating under the terms of this treaty – during a period marked by relative peace, but also by persistent anxiety about Macedonian ambitions – when Lycurgus, Aeschines

[4] So the ancient biographical tradition: on Aeschines' exile and his establishment of a school of rhetoric in Rhodes see primarily [Plut.] *Vit. dec. or.* 840c–e. For the tradition in ancient sources see Kindstrand (1982) 75–84.

[5] Bibliography on the League of Corinth is vast; for a summary of the circumstances of its formation see Rhodes (2005) 318–20.

[6] Part of an inscription (from the Acropolis) containing the oath survives: *IG* ii^3 318 = Rhodes–Osborne 76. On the terms of the alliance, see Rhodes–Osborne ad loc. and Aeschin. 3.132, Diod. Sic. 16.89 and Just. *Epit.* 9.5.1–4.

[7] Rhodes–Osborne (2003) 318.

and Demosthenes all delivered their speeches in 330. That same eventful year, Alexander the Great burned to the ground the royal palace at Persepolis and so spectacularly proclaimed to the world his definitive conquest of the Achaemenid Empire.[8]

Even if conditions of peace prevailed for the moment within the Greek world, the speeches of 330 BC afford insight into the continued internal division in Athens over the 'Macedonian Question', a division that had only been exacerbated in the aftermath of Chaeronea.[9] Nearly a decade after the battle, in 330, the memory of Chaeronea was still sufficiently potent for Lycurgus to bring a charge of treason (an *eisangelia prodosias*) relating to the defeat. Lycurgus' indictment alleged that his fellow citizen Leocrates had abandoned Athens following news of the city's loss when, as an emergency measure, a prohibition on leaving Attica was instated for citizens and metics.[10] During his speech Lycurgus asks the Athenian jurors not to grow angry with him for reminding them of the disasters which struck the city at that time.[11] He claims that, in the midst of the crisis, Leocrates turned his back on his *patris* and deigned neither to help gather the bodies nor to attend the funeral procession of those who had died defending the freedom and safety of the demos. If Leocrates had his way, Lycurgus speculates aloud, the Athenian soldiers who fell at Chaeronea would lie unburied to this day.[12] To demonstrate by

8 On the archaeological and historiographical evidence for the burning see Hammond (1992); the most elaborate ancient account is at Diod. Sic. 17.20–2.

9 Cf. Humphreys (2004) 79–80. Lycurgus also successfully prosecuted Lysicles, one of the Athenian commanders at Chaeronea ([Plut.] *Vit. dec. or.* 843d; Diod. Sic. 16.85 and 88). Lysicles, too, was put to death.

10 Lycurg. 1.16; cf. 1.36–7 and 41 on the measures themselves and Hyper. frr. 27–39 (fragments of Hyperides' defence against Aristogeiton's charge that a measure had been illegal). At 1.8 Lycurgus characterises Leocrates as ἐκλιπόντα . . . τὴν πατρίδα. See Lambert (2003a) on a decree (*IG* ii³ 416) from shortly after the battle which may offer insight into religious responses to the panic that the defeat at Chaeronea induced.

11 Lycurg. 1.16; 1.39–42.

12 Lycurg. 1.45: ὑπὲρ τῆς ἐλευθερίας καὶ τοῦ δήμου σωτηρίας. On Lycurgus' diction see Allen (2000) 6: 'Words like *patris* appear in this speech with far greater relative frequency than in any other piece of extant oratory. Lycurgus' peers generally preferred to rally people to the defense not of the *patris* but of the *polis*.'

contrast his own strong sense of the due of the dead, Lycurgus offers a short encomium of Athens and the soldiers who gave their lives for the city, in a section of the speech that looks much like an abbreviated version of the traditional *epitaphios logos*.[13]

These three speeches from the year 330 have long been recognised as valuable historical-political documents. They also, however, contain a number of references to the theatre – to actors, tragic poetry, tragedians and the Theatre of Dionysus. And although the immediate aim of Lycurgus' speech was the prosecution of Leocrates, this text in particular is especially valuable for the detailed information that it provides about Lycurgus' vision for the cultural life of his city. Later we shall revisit the case 'On the Crown', but here I shall be reading *Against Leocrates* as a first and critical piece in the puzzle of how classical tragedy was defined and reimagined in this period. This speech stands out as an extraordinary example of fourth-century oratory not least because it includes a remarkably long section dedicated to poetic quotations. Foremost among them is a lengthy fragment of Euripides' *Erechtheus*, a passage which Lycurgus frames in ways that effectively rewrite literary history. Euripides, the Athenian poet notorious for anti-democratic leanings and who enjoyed the greatest fame abroad, becomes in Lycurgus' hands the paradigm of an Athenian citizen. A close reading of Lycurgus' remarks will help to establish an essential background for each of my subsequent discussions of the evidence for 'classical' tragedy's formulation in this era. Lycurgus' verbal strategies in the speech are subtle and require detailed unpicking, but without an understanding of them it will be impossible to construct a broader picture of his vision for the theatre.

[13] Lycurg. 1.46–51. Lycurgus introduces his remarks as εὐλογίαι, 1.46. Loraux (1986) 126 called this section a 'fictional epitaphios' whose centre is 'the image of Greek freedom being buried'; cf. Dobson (1919) 278: Lycurgus' 'tendency towards the epideictic style is also seen in his treatment of his subject-matter; thus §§ 46–51 are nothing but a condensed funeral speech on those who died at Chaeronea'.

Poetic problems in *Against Leocrates*

The only surviving oration of the fifteen which he is said to have written,[14] Lycurgus' *Against Leocrates* stands out amongst Greek oratory for both the range and quantity of its poetic quotations.[15] Particularly extraordinary is his extended discussion of poetic quotations, which occurs over sections 100–10. Three of these (the quotations of Euripides, Homer and Tyrtaeus) are unusually long, while the final two are Simonidean epigrams commemorating the Spartan dead of Thermopylae and the bravery of the Athenians at Marathon.[16] If we take into account Lycurgus' preliminary and concluding remarks upon the poetic passages, these sections of the oration come to look like a cohesive digression on the value of poetry to the citizens and so to the state as a whole. Lycurgus' introductions to the lines by the three named poets are also exceptional, for nowhere else in surviving Greek rhetoric does the speaker provide such extended commentary upon multiple poets.[17] By means of his discussion, Lycurgus aims to cast these poets as embodiments of the values which their poetry espouses, and further ascribes to each poet's historical figure a rhetorical and ideological importance equal to that of the poetry itself.[18]

[14] [Plut.] *Vit. dec. or.* 843b; Harpocration gives the names of fourteen orations in his *Lexicon of the Ten Orators*; the *Suda* s.v. Λυκοῦργος (λ 824) provides a slightly different list.

[15] In the course of the transmitted speech Lycurgus quotes over one hundred lines of epic, tragedy, elegy and epigram, much of which (with the exception of Homer) is not otherwise attested. The only comparable speech on these grounds is Aeschines' *Against Timarchus*. Lycurgus' *Against Leocrates* also contains an unusually large number of citations of documents (decrees, oaths and laws), many of which are likely to be inauthentic: Davies (1996) 31–2. On poetic quotations in Greek oratory see esp. Scodel (2007) 133–42, Ford (1999), Wilson (1996) and Ober and Strauss (1990). Spina (1980–1), devoted exclusively to poetic quotations in *Against Leocrates*, emphasises Lycurgus' use of poetry as *paradeigmata*. On poetry's power to 'enliven' a speech cf. Ar. *Ves.* 579–80. In the *Rhetoric* Aristotle claims that the 'poets and all other famous people whose judgements are well known' constitute the 'ancient witnesses' (παλαιοὶ μάρτυρες) at an orator's disposal (*Rhet.* 1.1375b).

[16] Simonides XXI and XXII *FGE*; see esp. Page's discussion of Lycurgus' citation *ad* XXI.

[17] The only other extended discussion of a poet's character appears in Aeschines' *Against Timarchus*, where the poet in question is again Euripides: Aeschin. 1.153: see the discussion at pages 134–43.

[18] Cf. Albini (1985) 354.

Even in antiquity Lycurgus was noted for his tendency to use poetry, in addition to mythical and historical exempla, in his speeches. Hermogenes of Tarsus, a Greek orator active during the reign of Marcus Aurelius, voiced disapproval of Lycurgus' frequent use of extraneous digressions (παρεκβάσεις) 'upon myth and historical events and poetry'.[19] Hermogenes complains that these digressions had only the appearance of rhetorical 'forcefulness' (δεινότης), and similar criticism of Lycurgus' oratorical style would persist in scholarship on *Against Leocrates* until the end of the twentieth century.[20] But the speech is puzzling for reasons other than the unusual amount of poetic 'digressions' that it contains.[21] Historians have been troubled, for example, by the relative insignificance of the defendant – Leocrates was only a coppersmith – as well as by Lycurgus' own concession that Leocrates had not broken any pre-existing law.[22] During the speech, Lycurgus warns the Areopagites that in issuing their verdict they must act not only as jurors (δικασταί) but also as lawmakers (νομοθέται), because the lawmakers of the past had neglected to legislate against these sorts of crimes.[23] More perplexing still is that prior to Leocrates' trial Lycurgus had already made an example of a prominent Athenian whom he also accused of violating the post-Chaeronea emergency measures. At section 53 of *Against Leocrates* he boasts of the conviction (with death sentence) that he has already secured against Autolycus, a member of the Areopagus who sent his wife and sons away at the news of the battle's outcome.[24] The ancient *hypothesis* to *Against Leocrates* even points out that 'the subject of the speech resembles that

[19] Hermog. 2.11.183–5: ἐπὶ μύθους καὶ ἱστορίας καὶ ποιήματα. See Spina (1980–81) 17–19 for ancient judgements regarding Lycurgus' rhetorical ability.

[20] E.g. Perlman (1964) 168; Burtt (1962) 10; Petrie (1922) xxxvii; Dobson (1919) 279; and Jebb (1876) 376.

[21] The speech is 'generally recognized as being one of the most idiosyncratic and non-representative texts in the classical Athenian oratorical corpus': so Allen (2000) 6.

[22] Cf. e.g. Allen (2000) 10, Burke (1977) 330–1 and Burtt (1962) 10.

[23] Lycurg. 1.19; cf. 53–4. See Humphreys (1985) 201–4 on the role and scope of the powers of the *nomothetai* during the Lycurgan Era.

[24] Autolycus is called 'τὸν Ἀρεοπαγίτην' in [Plut.] *Vit. dec. or.* 843d, where we are told that Lycurgus prosecuted Aristogeiton, Autolycus and Leocrates for cowardice (δειλία, 843e).

of the *Against Autolycus*', and with Autolycus executed it does indeed seem curious that, as Danielle Allen puts it, 'Lycurgus then turned to frying smaller fish'.[25]

Partially because of the peculiarities of both the case and the speech, a tendency has developed to see Lycurgus as having used the soapbox afforded (or intentionally created) by the trial of Leocrates as an opportunity for airing his broader ideas about the direction of the city. These ideas touched upon the way in which prosecutions should be conducted, how Athenians should view their own civic history, the nature and role of religion in Athens, and even the strategies by which the city might respond to further Macedonian aggression.[26] Lycurgus' oratory was no doubt intended to have consequences beyond the courtroom, and the portion of the speech that he devotes to poetic citations should accordingly be treated as evidence for the ideological foundations of his programme for Athens.

Euripides' *epitaphios mythos*

Lycurgus begins to quote poetry extensively at section 100, two-thirds of the way into the speech, with a lengthy passage from Euripides' lost play *Erechtheus*.[27] Like other Euripidean tragedies from the period of the Archidamian War, the *Erechtheus* 'dramatises a glorious but costly moment in the legendary history of Athens'.[28] Earlier in the speech, at section 80, Lycurgus began to appeal to the past for historical examples of patriotism and reverence for the gods (he mentions the *Plataiomachoi* and their oath, the noble death of the

[25] Allen (2000) 9.

[26] Allen (2000), Ober (2006), Vielberg (1991) and Burke (1977) respectively.

[27] Eur. F 360 = 12 Sonnino. Euripides also mentions the story at *Ion* 277–80; [Plut.] reports Euripides' version (μέμνηται Εὐριπίδης ἐν Ἐρεχθεῖ) in the *Parallela Minora* 310d; cf. the summary from [Demaratus] *Subjects of Tragedy* (Τραγῳδούμενα), *FrGH* 42 F 4. For the myth see also [Apollodorus] *Bib.* 3.15.4 and Hyginus *Fab.* 46, 238.2. See Harding (2008) 42–7 on treatments of the Erechtheus story in Atthidography.

[28] Cropp (1995) 148. Sonnino (2010) discusses Euripides' tendency during the period of the Archidamian War (431–421 BC) to treat 'in forma dramatica i miti nazionali del *logos epitaphios*' (41). Cf. Loraux (1986) 65; see also the case study of Steinbock (2013) ch. 3 on the burial of the 'Seven against Thebes' in tragedy and oratory.

Athenian king Codrus and the filial piety of a man who stayed behind to save his father during an eruption of Mount Etna), and by section 98 he has come to the story of Erechtheus, the ancient and fabled Athenian king.[29] Lycurgus prefaces his quotation of Euripides' play with a summary of the legend: when Eumolpus and the Thracians attacked Athens, Erechtheus consulted the Delphic oracle about how he might secure a victory against them.[30] The oracle's response was that he must sacrifice his daughter; Erechtheus obeyed and so was able to expel the invaders.[31] Other surviving fragments of Euripides' play reveal the high price that Erechtheus and the Athenians paid for their victory. In a show of unity with their sacrificed sister, Erechtheus' other daughters committed suicide, and despite the sacrifice of his daughter Erechtheus himself died in battle as he led the Athenians to victory over Thrace.[32]

Euripides' tragedy probably premiered in the later 420s, certainly not after 412.[33] Though lost to us today, the 'indirect tradition' (i.e. the evidence of ancient texts that refer to classical tragedy) suggests that *Erechtheus* was relatively well known in antiquity. Lysistrata quotes a line from it in

[29] Lycurgus himself belonged to the Eteoboutadai *genos*, which traced its descent from Boutes and Erechtheus: see Lambert (2010). On historical exempla in fourth-century oratory see Steinbock (2013) and Hobden (2007) 490, with bibliography.

[30] Lycurg. 1.98 φασὶ γὰρ Εὔμολπον κτλ.

[31] Connelly (1996) has (controversially) argued that the story of Erechtheus and the sacrifice of his daughter constitutes the 'mythical reference behind the images' of the central scene on the East Frieze of the Parthenon.

[32] Athena's speech *ex machina*, in which she gives orders for the burial of the girls, the hero cult of Erechtheus and Praxithea's new status as Athena's priestess, is preserved on the Sorbonne papyrus (F 370 beginning at l. 55). On the plot of the play see recently Calame (2011) 5: 'In the *Erechtheus* the *metabasis* is twofold: first comes the voluntary and united sacrifice of the two sisters following the execution of the sacrificed young girl, then the death in combat of Erechtheus himself as a result of Poseidon's anger at the loss of Eumolpos.'

[33] Cropp (1995) 155 and Sonnino (2010) 32 both suggest premieres at the Great Dionysia of 422 (accepted by Calame (2011)); for the date see Jouan and Van Looy (2002) 98–9 and Sonnino's discussion at 27–34. See also Sonnino 133–5 on an Italian *pelike* (420–410 BC) ascribed to Polychorus (Museo della Siritide inv. 35304) which may depict a scene from *Erechtheus*. Calame (2011) emphasises the play's likely performance 'at the end of the first phases of the Peloponnesian war, and probably in connection with the beginning of the reconstruction of the temple of Athena Polias, better known as the Erechtheion'.

Aristophanes' *Lysistrata*,[34] and one of its poetic phrases is parodied in *Thesmophoriazusae*.[35] Anaxandrides, a comic playwright of the mid-fourth century, wrote an *Erechtheus* that may have satirised Euripides' treatment.[36] Ennius also composed an *Erechtheus*, and its few surviving fragments do appear to rework the Euripidean play.[37] Centuries later, Plutarch would record that after the Peace of Nicias had been sworn between Athens and Sparta in 415 BC, the people 'gladly listened to choruses singing things such as "I shall leave my spear for spiders' webs to entwine,"' and Stobaeus identifies this verse as belonging to Euripides' tragedy.[38]

Lycurgus' courtroom invocation of *Erechtheus*, a play that staged an outside invasion from the north and its threat to the very survival of Athens, may have resonated with particular strength in 330 BC.[39] With their recent memory of Chaeronea, the members of Lycurgus' jury and audience must have been keenly aware of the city's continued vulnerability in the face of Macedon's mounting power and ambition. Only five years before Lycurgus delivered his *Against Leocrates*, Alexander the Great had razed the city of Thebes, supposedly killing six thousand of its inhabitants and enslaving another 30,000.[40] Demosthenes had also invoked the story of Eumolpus' invasion in the *epitaphios logos* that he was elected to deliver for those who

[34] Ar. *Lys.* 1135 = Eur. F 363: εἷς μὲν λόγος μοι δεῦρ' ἀεὶ περαίνεται (attributed by a scholion 'erroneously placed at 1131' (Cropp 1995 ad loc.)).

[35] Eur. F 369d: Ἀσιάδος κρούματα; cf. Ar. *Th.* 120: κρούματά τ' Ἀσιάδος. Both plays date to 411.

[36] According to the *Parian Chronicle* Anaxandrides' first victory was in 376 BC (*FGrH* 239 A70 = Anax. T 3).

[37] Ennius F LX–LXII Jocelyn.

[38] Plut. *Nic.* 9.5: κείσθω δόρυ μοι μίτον ἀμφιπλέκειν ἀράχναις = Eur. F 369.1 = Sonnino 10; cf. Stob. 4.14.4.

[39] Quotation from Cropp (1995) 154; Calame (2011) 8 also discusses the contemporary relevance of Lycurgus' citation.

[40] Diod. Sic. 17.11.1–14.1. Later that year, when Alexander the Great demanded that Athens give up the ten most vocal opponents of his in the city – including Demosthenes and Lycurgus – Phocion supposedly urged the men to remember the example set by the Hyacinthids, the daughters of Erechtheus, and sacrifice themselves (Diod. Sic. 17.15.2). If this was the case, Lycurgus' invocation of this chapter in Athens' mythical history may have been viewed as bold in the light of his own alleged refusal to sacrifice himself.

died at the Battle of Chaeronea in 338.[41] In that speech he lists the Athenians' expulsion of the Thracians among the achievements of the 'ancestors of the present generation', characterising Eumolpus' invasion as a threat not just to Athens but to all of Greece.[42] He explains how, after the ancestors defeated the invading Amazons, they

καὶ τὸν Εὐμόλπου καὶ τῶν πολλῶν ἄλλων στόλον οὐ μόνον ἐκ τῆς οἰκείας, ἀλλὰ καὶ ἐκ τῆς τῶν ἄλλων Ἑλλήνων χώρας ἐξήλασαν. (Dem. 60.8)

also drove away the army of Eumolpus and of many others not only from their own land, but even from the lands of the other Hellenes.

Demosthenes goes on to recount how King Erechtheus delivered his own daughters, the Hyacinthids, to their deaths in order to save the city.[43] This noble example, he claims, had inspired the bravery of the Erechtheids (i.e. the members of the Erechtheid *phylē*)[44] at the Battle of Chaeronea. Those men had recognised how shameful it would be if

τὸν μὲν ἀπ' ἀθανάτων πεφυκότα πάντα ποιεῖν ἕνεκα τοῦ τὴν πατρίδ' ἐλευθερῶσαι, αὐτοὶ δὲ φανῆναι θνητὸν σῶμα ποιούμενοι περὶ πλείονος ἢ δόξαν ἀθάνατον. (Dem. 60.27–8)

one born from the immortals [i.e. Erechtheus] should have sacrificed everything for the freedom of his fatherland, but they should appear to have regarded their mortal bodies as more important than immortal glory.

The Athenians' victory over Eumolpus was in fact a commonplace of Athenian epideictic oratory, and particularly of the *epainos*, or encomiastic, section of the traditional *epitaphios logos*.[45] The story's popularity in the Athenian rhetorical

[41] The speech is now generally accepted as genuine. For a summary of the authenticity debate surrounding the oration see Frangeskou (1999) 323 n. 10. Thomas (1989) 210 suggests that 'The absence of the usual Demosthenic spirit is explained by the genre.' On points of contact between Dem. 60 and the Lycurgan 'mini-*epitaphios*' (Lycurg. 1.46–51) see esp. Loraux (1986) 393 n. 210.

[42] Dem. 60.7.

[43] On the identification of Erechtheus' daughters with the Hyacinthids see Phanodemus *FGrH* F 3; see also n. 40 above.

[44] The Erechtheids may have been regarded as a particularly valiant tribe: a casualty list of its members who died in war (numbering 172) survives from the year 459 BC (Meiggs–Lewis 13).

[45] Thomas (1989) 218 highlights four topics from the 'legendary period' that recur in funeral orations: the expulsion of the Amazons; the expulsion of Eumolpus and

tradition is further illustrated by Socrates' praeterition of it in Plato's *Menexenus*. Socrates invokes the story as part of his quasi-parodic performance of an *epitaphios logos*, which he claims to have been taught by Pericles' mistress Aspasia:

Εὐμόλπου μὲν οὖν καὶ Ἀμαζόνων ἐπιστρατευσάντων ἐπὶ τὴν χώραν καὶ τῶν ἔτι προτέρων ὡς ἠμύναντο ... ὅ τε χρόνος βραχὺς ἀξίως διηγήσασθαι, ποιηταί τε αὐτῶν ἤδη καλῶς τὴν ἀρετὴν ἐν μουσικῇ ὑμνήσαντες εἰς πάντας μεμηνύκασιν· (Pl. *Men*. 239b)

My time is too short to narrate adequately ... how [sc. the πατέρες] drove off Eumolpus and the Amazons and others still earlier when they invaded their land: the poets, since they have beautifully praised them in song, have already commemorated their *aretē* for everyone.[46]

Isocrates, too, recalled the legends of the Amazons and Thracians in his *Panathenaicus*, as well as in the *Panegyricus*, an epideictic speech that draws on many of the same traditions and *topoi* as the funeral orations.[47]

The mythical theme of the Thracian invasion may have been standard in Athenian public oratory, but Lycurgus' *Against Leocrates* features a striking innovation in its manner of presentation. Here, for the first time in the surviving tradition, the story of Erechtheus becomes equated with the version of events that had been dramatised by Euripides.[48] And Lycurgus does far more in prefacing his quotation than simply attribute the lines to their poet. He also stresses that we must commend not just the verses, but the man who wrote them: for Lycurgus the achievement of the play lays primarily in Euripides' recognition of the story as a valuable historic *exemplum*. Lycurgus embarks upon this quotation, and upon the whole of his discussion of poetry, with the claim that 'One would justly

the Thracians; the expulsion of Eurystheus and salvation of the Heraclids; and the Athenian acceptance of the Argives' request to bury their dead after the attack of the 'Seven' on Thebes. On the commonplaces of the *epainos* see Ziolkowski (1981) 74–137 and Loraux (1986) 241–51; on the conceit of the Athenian past in the *epitaphios* see also Grethlein (2010) 118–23.

46 Cf. Demosthenes 60.9. For the 'time is not sufficient' formula in the *epainos* see Ziolkowski (1981) 132, on the trope that poets have glorified the dead see ibid. 128–9.

47 Carey (2007b) 242; see Isoc. 12.193 and 4.68 respectively.

48 On Lycurgus' assimilation of the event to the Euripidean narrative see Falappone (2006) 68–74 (esp. 69, with bibliography at n. 13).

praise Euripides' (δικαίως ἄν τις Εὐριπίδην ἐπαινέσειεν, Lycurg. 1.100) for being a good poet, and in particular for choosing to write a play about the story of Erechtheus' sacrifice. Following this preface, he goes on to recite the entire monologue which Euripides had composed (πεποίηκε) for Praxithea, the wife of Erechtheus and the mother of the sacrificed child. Here it is especially noteworthy that Lycurgus himself, and not the court clerk, will have recited Praxithea's lines. In other near-contemporary speeches that make use of multi-line poetic quotations, the orator usually bids the clerk to read out the verses, often using the same imperatives as when he commands the clerk to read out laws (νόμοι), testimony of witnesses (μαρτυρία), decrees (ψηφίσματα) or other documents: 'read', or 'say' (ἀνάγνωθι; λέγε).[49] But here in the absence of any such command, the jurors will have heard in Lycurgus' single voice a plurality of voices (Praxithea's, Euripides' and Lycurgus' own) blended together in united praise of Athens.

Praxithea – or rather Lycurgus-as-Euripides-as-Praxithea – begins the speech by explaining that she has 'many reasons' for which she will give her child over to be killed, the primary one being that 'I could have no other city better than this one.'[50] Athens is the greatest of cities, Praxithea argues, first and foremost because 'we are *autochthones*'.[51] She explains that, to her mind, the purpose of having children at all is to provide guards for the fatherland and for the altars of the gods. She reasons that the ruin of one home counts for far less than the destruction of an entire city and claims that if she had sons rather than daughters she would gladly send them forth into battle:

[49] Another notable exception occurs in *Against Timarchus*, when Aeschines refers to the Homeric verses 'which I am now about to recite' (ἃ ἐγὼ νυνὶ μέλλω λέγειν, Aeschin. 1.144).

[50] That Praxithea, the mother of the child, is here the one to justify the sacrifice effectively prevents her husband's myth from tottering too close to the paradigm of Agamemnon, who sacrificed his daughter and suffered his wife's retribution (Praxithea explicitly declares, 'I hate women who chose life for their children over the *kalos*', F 360.30–1). Calame (2011) 5 nevertheless suggests that 'Just as Agamemnon must atone for the sacrifice of Iphigenia, perhaps Erechtheus' violent death is another price to pay for the murder of a young girl sacrificed in the name of the state.'

[51] On the space that Praxithea's creates for a view of female Athenian autochthony see Calame (2011).

men who die in battle share a common tomb (τύμβος κοινός) and equal good repute (εὔκλεια), but by dying for the city her daughter shall have the honour of receiving her own garland. As Lycurgus himself so often does, Euripides' Praxithea cites a desire to honour the laws of her Athenian ancestors (the πρόγονοι);[52] she then concludes with the declaration that, if everyone who dwelled in Athens loved it as much as she, then the fatherland (πατρίς) would never suffer any harm.[53]

Later in antiquity, Plutarch would regard Praxithea's speech as a beautiful encomium of Athens. In his work *On Exile* he consoles his exiled addressee with the observation that few of the greatest and wisest men are buried in their own country. To illustrate his point he invokes the example of Euripides, who by his own choice finished his life at the court of Archelaus in Macedon. And yet, Plutarch asks, 'who ever delivered such an encomium of his fatherland as Euripides?'; he then goes on to quote lines 7–10 of Praxithea's speech.[54] The speech as a whole is encomiastic, but it also shares a number of tropes in common with one encomiastic tradition in particular, namely the Athenian *epitaphios logos*. These include, for example, the claims that Athens is the greatest of all the Greek cities; that the Athenians' autochthony is a unique and defining indicator of their greatness; that those who die in battle enjoy enduring fame and glory; and that the ancestral laws and traditions are of preeminent importance.[55] Lycurgus' very decision to quote tragic poetry also implicitly recalls yet another commonplace of the funeral oration, namely that the poets of the past have already glorified the Athenians who died defending the fatherland.[56] For Lycurgus, Euripides certainly must have stood among the front ranks of such poets: as Peter Wilson has observed, here Lycurgus' choice of quotation implies 'a very nostalgic view of

[52] Lycurgus himself mentions the πρόγονοι more than twenty times in this speech.

[53] On the lines see esp. the commentary of Sonnino (2010) 248–88.

[54] Plut. *Mor.* 604d *de Exilio*: τίς γὰρ εἴρηκε τῆς ἑαυτοῦ πατρίδος ἐγκώμιον τοιοῦτον, οἷον Εὐριπίδης; on Plutarch's quotation see Sonnino (2010) 248.

[55] On these tropes see esp. Loraux (1986) ch. 5 ('The Funeral Oration as a Political Genre') and Ziolkowski (1981) 103–28. For the relationship of Euripides' *Erechtheus* with the *epitaphios logos* see Sonnino (2010) 36–42.

[56] Cf. Ziolkowski (1981) 128–9.

tragedy that virtually assimilates it to the profoundly idealizing genre of the *epitaphios logos*'.[57]

An Attic epitaph may further confirm the more general assimilation of tragic poetry and the discourse of the *epitaphios logos* in this period. The language of Praxithea's speech and of Lycurgus' own reverberates, as Christos Tsagalis has demonstrated, in the epitaph for Diognetos, son of Euadetos of Paiondai. Diognetos was an Athenian who died in war, most likely at the Battle of Chaeronea. Tsagalis argues that the combination of rhetorical echoes in Diognetos' epitaph is the 'result of a complex set of literary influence stemming from Euripidean tragedy on the one hand, and the rhetoric of the Funeral Orations tailored to the needs of forensic framework on the other'.[58] The epitaph, inscribed on a monument discovered at Brauron, runs as follows:

> εἴ τις τῶν ἀγαθῶν μνείαν ἔχει ἐν δορὸς ἀλκεῖ, πρῶτον κρίνων
> {ων} ἂν τόνδε δίκης μετέχοι·
> ἀντὶ γὰρ ἧς ψυχῆς ἀρετῆι πόλιν ἐστεφάνωσεν, θεσμοὺς οὐ
> παραβὰς εὐδοκίμων προγόνων. (*CEG* 594)

> If one of the brave is remembered for the force of his spear, it would be right to award the first prize to this very man.
> For instead of his life, he crowned the city with his virtue without trespassing the laws of his glorious ancestors.
> (Trans. Tsagalis)

Tsagalis highlights the last two lines in particular, which distinctly recall lines 45–52 of Praxithea's monologue. At the end of her speech Praxithea declares that 'there is no account on which, for the sake of one life, I would not save my city', where

[57] Wilson (1996) 314. The view is 'nostalgic' in that it sees Euripides' tragedy as a straightforward vehicle for the glorification of Athens. Wilson surmises that Euripides' play interrogated this myth, and perhaps called into question the words and actions of the play's Athenian characters. Lycurgus' quotation may therefore have served to cast Praxithea's words in a different light than they had appeared in the play: Wilson (1996) 312–14; cf. too Albini (1985), who contends that the speech gives a representative sense neither of *Erechtheus* nor of the Euripidean *corpus*. Salamone (1976) argues that the outlook of *Against Leocrates* is however 'tragic' in its emphasis on the need for retribution: 'Il mondo della Leocratea è lo stesso mondo dei tragici con l'arcaica concezione della θεοβλάβεια' (50).

[58] Tsagalis (2007) 13.

Diognetos' 'for instead of his life' (ἀντὶ γὰρ ἧς ψυχῆς) in line 4 of the elegiac epitaph repeats nearly the same wording as Praxithea (and so presumably Lycurgus) had formulated in iambic trimeters: ἀντὶ γὰρ ψυχῆς μιᾶς (F 360.51).[59] The resonances in Diognetos' epitaph of both the *Erechtheus* passage and of other formulations that appear in *Against Leocrates* suggest that other citizens, too, recognised common ground between the ideological expressions in Praxithea's speech and those found in orators such as Lycurgus and the givers of *epitaphioi logoi*.[60]

Lycurgus also attributes the same kind of ideology to Euripides himself. When at last he has finished reciting Praxithea's lines, he returns to praising the poet who authored them: Athenians ought to take to heart the example of this family's personal sacrifice, but Euripides is to be particularly praised for the way in which he chose to tell the story, and especially for the lines 'which he made the child's mother say'. Euripides 'portrayed' (ἐποίησε) this woman as loving her country more than she loved her children,[61] and 'showed' (ἐνδεικνύμενος) that if women can be courageous enough to make such a sacrifice, men should be able to display unsurpassed goodwill (ἀνυπέρβλητον ... εὔνοιαν) for their fatherland – and not flee from or disgrace it, as Leocrates did. Lycurgus' language here consistently emphasises Euripides' agency as a poet: he 'composed' (πεποίηκε) the speech for Praxithea, 'portrayed' (ἐποίησε) her in a certain way, and in so doing 'showed' (ἐνδεικνύμενος) the moral of his story.[62] Euripides' very choice of subject material should thus, Lycurgus argues, be rated as nearly equal to the great historical deed which the tragedy commemorates. That choice only confirms the status of Euripides as a paradigmatic Athenian patriot, and as a valid and necessary witness in the case at hand.

[59] Tsagalis (2007) 11. [60] For these see Tsagalis (2007) 12–13.

[61] The verb ποιέω is commonly used of 'portraying' or 'crafting' characters; cf. e.g. Arist. *Po.* 1453b28–9: Εὐριπίδης ἐποίησεν ἀποκτείνουσαν τοὺς παῖδας τὴν Μήδειαν ('Euripides depicted Medea as killing her children').

[62] Lycurg. 1.100.

The good poet and the good citizen

Poetry is rarely quoted in our corpus of Attic oratory, and all of the speeches that do cite poetic verse date to the third quarter of the fourth century.[63] More specifically, these speeches – the three surviving orations by Aeschines, Demosthenes 18 and 19 and Lycurgus' own *Against Leocrates* – all belong to the years between the Peace of Philocrates in 346 and Demosthenes' 'crown' trial in 330. In each case, the orations are of considerable public importance and accompany high-profile cases.[64] Yet the comments that Lycurgus makes about Euripides are without parallel even within the small group of Athenian speeches that do bring poetry to bear. This section of *Against Leocrates* stands as a witness to Lycurgus' efforts to harness the name of Euripides to the glorification of Athens, but its most remarkable features have passed unnoticed in studies both of this speech and of poetic citations in oratory more generally. While Lycurgus seeks to link 'Euripidean' civic ideology with that of the Athenian *epitaphios logos*, his introduction of the poet also uniquely borrows from another sphere of Athenian civic discourse, namely the language of honorific decrees. By framing his remarks on Euripides in the city's official language of praise, Lycurgus suggests that Euripides' contributions to Athenian society were comparable to those of the political and financial benefactors who received public recognition from the demos.[65]

Let us revisit Lycurgus' first mention of Euripides, which is accompanied by an explanation as to why the poet deserves praise:

δικαίως ἄν τις Εὐριπίδην ἐπαινέσειεν, ὅτι τά τ' ἄλλ' ἦν ἀγαθὸς ποιητής, καὶ τοῦτον τὸν μῦθον προείλετο ποιῆσαι, ἡγούμενος κάλλιστον ἂν γενέσθαι τοῖς πολίταις παράδειγμα τὰς ἐκείνων πράξεις, πρὸς ἃς ἀποβλέποντας καὶ θεωροῦντας συνεθίζεσθαι ταῖς ψυχαῖς τὸ τὴν πατρίδα φιλεῖν. (Lycurg. 1.100)

63 Scodel (2007) 134.
64 Scodel (2007) 134, who notes that 'Nobody quotes poetry in a private oration.'
65 For the honorific decrees of the Lycurgan Era see Lambert (2004), (2006) and (2007), all collected in Lambert (2012).

One would justly praise Euripides since, in addition to being a good poet in all other respects he also chose to treat this story, considering their deeds [i.e. those of Erechtheus' family] the finest example by which the citizens, in gazing upon and considering them, might accustom their hearts to loving their fatherland.

In this introduction Lycurgus first takes care to establish that Euripides was a good (*agathos*) poet. Fourth-century oratory contains a handful of other instances in which the speaker characterises a poet as *agathos* immediately before citing the poet's verses. Two of these instances occur in speeches of Aeschines. In *Against Timarchus* of 346 BC, Aeschines responds to Demosthenes' citation of Homer and the 'other poets' with the claim that he, too, knows something about poetry and so shall be calling upon poets as witnesses. Like Lycurgus, he enjoins the jurors to 'look' into certain authors for their moral wisdom:

θεωρήσατε ἀποβλέψαντες, ὦ Ἀθηναῖοι, εἰς τοὺς ὁμολογουμένως ἀγαθοὺς καὶ χρηστοὺς ποιητάς, ὅσον κεχωρίσθαι ἐνόμισαν τοὺς σώφρονας καὶ τῶν ὁμοίων ἐρῶντας, καὶ τοὺς ἀκρατεῖς ὧν οὐ χρὴ καὶ τοὺς ὑβριστάς. (Aeschin. 1.141)

By looking, men of Athens, into the poets generally agreed to be good and worthy, you shall see how much they considered moderate men who loved their own kind to be differentiated from those who lack moral restraint and who are *hybristai*.

Aeschines soon quotes two of these 'good and useful poets': Homer, 'whom we rank among the oldest and the wisest of the poets',[66] and Euripides, who is 'as wise as any of the poets'.[67] By first suggesting that Homer and Euripides are commonly held to be 'good' and 'useful', Aeschines prepares the jury to accept *a priori* the truth, or rather his interpretation, of their verses.[68] In his 343 BC speech *On the False Embassy*, Aeschines also describes the poet Hesiod as *agathos*, just before citing lines from *Works and Days* about how one's reputation (φήμη)

[66] Aeschin. 1.142: ὃν ἐν τοῖς πρεσβυτάτοις καὶ σοφωτάτοις τῶν ποιητῶν εἶναι τάττομεν.

[67] Aeschin. 1.151: ὁ τοίνυν οὐδενὸς ἧττον σοφὸς τῶν ποιητῶν Εὐριπίδης; see pages 137–9.

[68] See Ford (1999) on the way in which orators would argue 'for a particular "reading" of a text that was often old and not perfectly clear in its implications' (232). The courtroom could thus in a sense be converted into a 'literary salon' where the meanings of difficult texts were debated (254).

never entirely dies.[69] There, too, he first asserts the poet's good character in order to ensure that the jurors will view the verses as bearing a credible moral authority.[70] Aeschines and Lycurgus' strategy of citation is therefore two part: first the orator claims that everyone knows that the poet whom he is about to quote is 'good'; he then assertively presents his reading of that poet's verses as the only correct interpretation, the true meaning intended by the poet. For Aeschines and Lycurgus alike a poet's status as *agathos* is also sanctioned by time. They never use the adjective to describe a living poet; in fact contemporary poets are never mentioned in the extant speeches. The poets whom the orators quote and call *agathoi* are always situated within a vaguely remote and idealised past.[71]

The notion that a poet who is 'good' must necessarily also be a good man, an *anēr agathos*, also appears (and is interrogated) in several Socratic dialogues.[72] When, for example, Socrates reports Diotima's account of the nature of intellectual creativity in the *Symposium*, he explains that everyone should wish to produce offspring (ἔκγονα) of the sort that have been engendered by the 'good' poets, such as Homer and Hesiod. In Socrates' report Diotima also argues that these sorts of 'intellectual' offspring provide their parents with undying fame, just as Lycurgus contends that Euripides should (still) be celebrated for his *Erechtheus*.[73] But in the *Republic*, Socrates elaborates a different account of the *agathos* poet, in a speech that looks much like a direct and 'point-by-point' refutation of his own account of Diotima's speech in the *Symposium*.[74] According to the Socrates of the *Republic*, the 'good poet' cannot exist, because a poet who is also *agathos* would renounce the pursuit of poetic spectres (φαντάσματα) and instead direct his efforts

69 Aeschin. 2.144.

70 On ἀγαθός as part of the 'moral vocabulary' of forensic oratory see Dover (1974) 63–4.

71 Cf. Scodel (2007) 140.

72 Cf. especially Pl. *Symp.* 196e and 209d, *Lys.* 206b, *Ion* 533e–535a, *Rep.* 598e–599e and to a lesser extent *Cra.* 398b and *Phdr.* 236d.

73 Pl. *Symp.* 209d: ἀθάνατον κλέος and μνήμη. For a discussion of this passage and the use of pregnancy/birth metaphors for poets' creative production see Hunter (2009) 110–16.

74 Asmis (1992) 344–7.

towards accomplishing the kinds of deeds that poets memorialise:

πειρῷτο ἂν πολλὰ καὶ καλὰ ἔργα ἑαυτοῦ καταλιπεῖν μνημεῖα, καὶ εἶναι προθυμοῖτ' ἂν μᾶλλον ὁ ἐγκωμιαζόμενος ἢ ὁ ἐγκωμιάζων. (Pl. *Resp*. 9.599b)

he would then endeavour to leave behind many and beautiful works as memorials of himself, and would much prefer to be the one praised than the one who praises.[75]

In the very process of attempting to define the 'good poet', then, the Socrates of the *Republic* ends in claiming that the very category is inherently paradoxical: the 'good poet' cannot exist, because anyone who is good will produce works (ἔργα), and not the mere shadows (εἴδωλα) of poetry.[76]

Despite the apparent irreconcilability of these two arguments (and the difficulty of establishing any 'true' Platonic position on poetry more generally), both take for granted that a poet must first be a 'good' man in order also to be called *agathos* with respect to his poetry.[77] This essential notion is one to which Lycurgus clearly subscribes in this passage of *Against Leocrates*, where he explicitly connects the praiseworthiness of Erechtheus' sacrifice with the nobility of Euripides' decision to dramatise it: for Lycurgus it was precisely Euripides' own principles that prompted him to choose such fine material and to portray his characters so nobly. In the framework of Lycurgus' speech, a poet's status as *agathos* is therefore more properly a character trait than a marker of his verses' purely aesthetic qualities.

[75] On the passage see esp. Murray (1996) ad loc., Asmis (1992) 351–4 and Ferrari (1989) 129–31.

[76] This is a key 'Platonic' criticism of poetry, namely that 'poets see imitation as good in itself, as a process of knowledge or understanding, regardless of what is imitated': Ferrari (1989) 120.

[77] This same premise appears to underlie Isocrates' claim in *Against the Sophists* that *paideusis* alone cannot make men into writers (λόγων ποιητάς) who are ἀγαθοί (Isoc. 13.15). The connection between the *agathos* man and the *agathos* poet is perhaps most explicitly stated centuries later by the geographer Strabo: 'We do not say that the *aretē* of poets is the same as that of carpenters or blacksmiths. Their *aretē* partakes of nothing noble or serious, but that of the poet is linked to that of the man, and no one can become a good poet without first having become a good man' (Str. 1.2.5).

With the suggestion of a conceptual link between the *agathos* poet and the *agathos* man in mind, we can begin to tease out more fully Lycurgus' remarkable rhetorical strategies. When Lycurgus first introduces Euripides he declares that someone would rightly 'praise' (ἐπαινέσειεν) him because, in addition to being 'a good poet in all other respects', he chose to dramatise the *mythos* of Erechtheus. The verb ἐπαινέω is common in fourth-century prose,[78] and Lycurgus uses it again when he prefaces his quotation of Homer:

> βούλομαι δ' ὑμῖν καὶ τὸν Ὁμήρον παρασχέσθαι ἐπαινῶν.
> (Lycurg. 1.102)
>
> I wish also to commend Homer to you, praising (him).

In the context of Homeric poetry, the verb ἐπαινέω seems to have had a special meaning, as a term used specifically for the recitation of Homeric verse. Modern discussions of 'Homeric *epainos*' tend to centre upon the passages in Plato's *Ion* in which Ion uses the verb ἐπαινέω to describe what he does in rhapsodic competition: Ion claims to 'praise Homer' (Ὅμηρον ἐπαινῶ).[79] Socrates, too, uses this formulation when he argues that 'praising Homer' is precisely the nature and purpose of Ion's profession, even if he will not allow that Ion is competent at some craft (τέχνη) or personally possesses any special knowledge (ἐπιστήμη) that enables him to do so.[80] On the basis of the passages in Plato's *Ion*, Gregory Nagy has even argued that ἐπαινέω is 'the technical word used by *rhapsōidoi* for the notion of "recite Homer"',[81] later elaborating that Ὅμηρον ἐπαινεῖν means 'to "quote" Homer…in a specific context and for a specific purpose'.[82] Other scholars place more emphasis on the aim of the Homeric 'praiser' (ἐπαινέτης) to publicise Homer's

[78] Capuccino (2005) 161 notes that variations of ἐπαινῶ/ἔπαινος occur more than 300 times in Plato.

[79] Pl. *Ion* 536d; cf. Pl. *Resp.* 10.606e–607a, where Socrates implies that Homer's 'encomiasts' claim that Homer had 'educated Greece' (τὴν Ἑλλάδα πεπαίδευκεν).

[80] Pl. *Ion* 541e. Socrates also calls Ion an ἐπαινέτης of Homer at 536d and 542b.

[81] Nagy (1979) 98 n. 4. [82] Nagy (2002) 27.

'excellence as an educator of society': 'to praise Homer' was to cite his poetry with acknowledgement of his 'paideutic value, and the model for living that he provides'.[83]

We need not insist upon an exact interpretation of 'Homeric *epainos*' to recognise that such a concept is well attested in the fourth century. The parallels are sufficient to suggest that, when Lycurgus uses the verb to introduce Homer, he is also referring to a recognisable discourse of Homeric 'praise'. The verb ἐπαινέω is especially appropriate to the context, and even crucial to Lycurgus' meaning, because it belongs to a specific and technical vocabulary of Homeric performance.[84] This exegesis of Lycurgus' introduction to Homer then serves to cast his comments upon Euripides in a new light. In Lycurgus' ἄν τις Εὐριπίδην ἐπαινέσειεν we have a phrase that recalls Ὅμηρον ἐπαινεῖν, where Lycurgus is certainly presenting an argument in favour of Euripides and 'the model for living that he provides'.[85] By introducing Euripides as the object of ἐπαινέω, Lycurgus is suggesting that Euripides' verses, too, possess great moral authority, and that his tragedies are accordingly worthy of an 'official' status in Athens, akin to that which the Homeric poems enjoyed.

Lycurgus' special use of the verb ἐπαινέω adds further texture to this passage and another programmatic layer to his presentation of Euripides. But the very first words that Lycurgus uses to introduce Euripides also reward careful rereading:

[83] Capuccino (2005) 163 (translated from the Italian).

[84] Velardi (1989) 34 (translated from the Italian). He renders the Greek: 'Voglio produrvi anche Omero facendovene l'*épainos*'. Velardi's discussion is prompted largely by Reiske's emendation of Lycurgus' words to βούλομαι δ' ὑμῖν καὶ τῶν Ὁμήρου παρασχέσθαι ἐπῶν. On Reiske's roundly rejected conjecture see Velardi (1989) 35 with n. 59.

[85] 'Euripidean *epainos*' also appears in Aristophanes' *Clouds* in a line that uses language similar to Lycurgus' formulation. When Strepsiades has finished explaining to the Chorus how and why his son beat him up, Pheidippides interjects that he beat his father justly: it was because he failed to 'praise' Euripides, the wisest [of poets] (οὔκουν δικαίως, ὅστις οὐκ Εὐριπίδην ἐπαινεῖς, | σοφώτατον, 1377–8). In a fragment of Aristophanes' *Gerytades* a use of ἐπαινέω with respect to Aeschylus also seems to be in line with Ion and Socrates' use of the verb for Homer: ἐν τοῖσι συνδείπνοις ἐπαινῶν Αἰσχύλον (Ar. F 161).

δικαίως ἄν τις Εὐριπίδην ἐπαινέσειεν, ὅτι τά τ' ἄλλ' ἦν ἀγαθὸς ποιητής, καὶ τοῦτον τὸν μῦθον προείλετο ποιῆσαι... (Lycurg. 1.100)

One would justly praise Euripides since, in addition to being a good poet in all other respects he also chose to treat this story...

In this phrase as a whole, Lycurgus' diction displays an even more extensive and significant parallel with the Athenian discourses of approbation, the wording of which we find articulated in the highly formulaic language of honorific decrees.[86] These decrees typically recorded 'the decision itself, always expressed by ἐπαινέσαι (plus dative or accusative), and the specific reason (if any) for the commendation'. From the fourth century 'ἐπαινέσαι + accusative is invariable'[87] and the typical extended formulation is 'ἐπαινέσαι + object (accusative) + ὅτι clause'.[88] This construction was common to decrees in the first half of the century, but became rarer over time and by the third century had all but disappeared from Athenian inscriptions.[89]

A decree that grants proxeny and dates to the third quarter of the fifth century offers a useful illustration of the parallels between Lycurgus' language and the inscriptional idiom.[90] Here the *boulē* and the demos of the Athenains have decided:

[...] Κάλλι-
ππον τὸν Θετταλὸν τὸγ Γυρτώνι-
ον ἐπαινέσαι, ὅτι δοκεῖ εἶναι ἀνὴρ ἀγαθὸς περὶ τὴμ πόλιν τὴν Ἀθ-
ηναίων· (κτλ.) (*IG* i³ 92.5–9)[91]

[...] to praise Kallippos the Thessalian from Gyrton,
because it seems that he is a good man
with respect to the city of the Athenians.

The word order of this decree (object accusative + infinitive ἐπαινέσαι) happens to resemble very closely Lycurgus' own appropriation of honorific language:

86 Henry (1983) 1.
87 Henry (1983) 1.
88 Henry (1983) 3.
89 Henry (1983) 3–4.
90 For other decrees that provide good comparisons see e.g. *IG* i³ 73.23–5, from 424/3 BC, with Henry (1983) 3 and and Veligianni-Terzi (1997) A14 on the decree's language; for a later example, see *IG* ii² 110 = Rhodes–Osborne 38, from 363/2.
91 Cf. *SEG* 39.15, Walbank (1978) no. 65, Veligianni-Terzi (1997) A17.

IG i³ 92	Lycurgus 1.100
	δικαίως ἄν τις
Κάλλιππον τὸν Θετταλὸν τὸγ Γυρτώνιον	Εὐριπίδην
ἐπαινέσαι,	ἐπαινέσειεν,
ὅτι	ὅτι
δοκεῖ εἶναι ἀνήρ ἀγαθός	τά τ' ἄλλ' ἦν ἀγαθὸς ποιητής

What is more, and as was often the case in decrees, this proxeny decree describes Kallippos as a 'good man' (ἀνὴρ ἀγαθός) with respect to the city of Athens (περὶ τὴμ πόλιν τὴν Ἀθηναίων). In *Against Leocrates* Lycurgus similarly emphasises how much Euripides has contributed to the 'polis of the Athenians' by virtue of his being a 'good poet'. That characterisation of Euripides appears in a very 'decree-like' position within Lycurgus' sentence. And as we have seen, the concept of the 'good poet' required that the poet in question also be a good man: an *anēr agathos* of the sort that we find praised in the decrees.[92] Lycurgus' phrasing will thus have prompted the jurors to think of Euripides as an 'official' benefactor of Athens, because he had encouraged other citizens to follow the example of Erechtheus' family and so 'to accustom their hearts to loving their fatherland'.[93]

The closest epigraphic comparanda for Lycurgus' construction come from the later fifth century, and so the language may have had an archaising ring for the jurors of Leocrates' treason case. By the close of the third century the formulation ἐπαινέσαι + object (accusative) + ὅτι had ceased to appear in decrees, and as early as the end of the fifth century the abstract noun *andragathia* had largely replaced the adjectival qualification of an honorand as *agathos*.[94] But in at least one document of the

92 Robin Osborne has suggested to me that in ἀγαθὸς ποιητής there may also evoke the phrase ἀγαθὸς πολίτης. In Aristophanes' *Knights*, the Chorus says that one of the Sausage Seller's insults of Paphlagon is a good one. The 'Demos' character then adds – in language reminiscent of official decrees – κἀμοὶ δοκεῖ, καὶ τἄλλα γ' εἶναι καταφανῶς ἀγαθὸς πολίτης (943–4). (The phrase ἀγαθὸς πολίτης does not appear in inscribed documents.)

93 Lycurg. 1.100: συνεθίζεσθαι ταῖς ψυχαῖς τὸ τὴν πατρίδα φιλεῖν.

94 Whitehead (1993) 57; he calls ἀνδραγαθία '*the* cardinal virtue' of Athenian civic life (56).

Lycurgan period we still find the construction ἐπαινέσαι . . . ὅτι. This wording appears in a dedication that was erected in the tribal sanctuary of Cecrops on the Acropolis and which had been made by the ephebes of the Cecropid tribe in 332, at the end of their two-year service.[95] The inscription contains four separate decrees and records the young men's names, along with the honours that they received from their tribe as well as from the Athenian *boulē* and the demes of Eleusis and Athmonon. The portion of the inscription that was sponsored by the deme of Athmonon records that a certain Euphronius proposed to honour the ephebes who were registered in the archonship of Ktesikles. Here the explanatory ἐπειδή-clause justifies the honour by claiming that the ephebes have shown themselves to be well marshalled and willing to do everything that the laws require of them. Further, their overseer, or *sophronistēs*, 'shows that [the ephebes] are obedient and do everything else with love of honour'[96] (ἀποφαίνει αὐτο[ὺς] πειθάρχοντας καὶ τἄλλα πάντα ποιοῦντας φιλοτίμως, 54–5). For these particular reasons, Euphronius was moved to 'praise' and to crown the ephebes with a golden crown, a material recognition of their decorum (κοσμιότης) and orderliness (εὐταξία).

The part of the ἐπειδή-clause that concerns the ephebes' *sophronistēs* also recalls Lycurgus' claim that Euripides would justly be praised for his handling of the story of Erechtheus 'in addition to being a good poet in all other respects' (τά τ' ἄλλ' ἦν ἀγαθὸς ποιητής; compare τἄλλα πάντα in the ephebic inscription).[97] Both Lycurgus and Euphronius identify the praise which they propose as merited on general and specific grounds: Lycurgus begins with a generalising statement in suggesting that Euripides deserves praise in 'all other respects';[98]

[95] *IG* ii^2 1156 = Rhodes–Osborne 89. [96] Trans. Rhodes–Osborne.

[97] Cf. the parallel with Aristotle's identification of Euripides as the 'most tragic' of the tragic poets at *Po.* 1453a28–30: ὁ Εὐριπίδης, εἰ καὶ τὰ ἄλλα μὴ εὖ οἰκονομεῖ, ἀλλὰ τραγικώτατός γε τῶν ποιητῶν φαίνεται. Here, however, the 'τὰ ἄλλα' phrase points to censurable aspects of Euripidean poetic composition.

[98] This sort of (at least initial) vagueness is typical of epigraphic language: see esp. Osborne (1999) 350. Lycurgus almost always uses vague (and perhaps therefore non-controversial) language when characterising the poets he cites: Euripides is ἀγαθός (1.100), Homer σπουδαῖος (102) and the verses of Tyrtaeus are καλά and χρήσιμα (107).

he then moves on to the specific citation of *Erechtheus*. Euphronius, on the other hand, begins with specific praise and ends with the general commendation. Euripides deserves particular praise on account of his depiction of character in the *Erechtheus*, while the *sophronistēs* of the Cecropid ephebes has given particular evidence of the ephebes' obedience. A number of other Athenian honorific decrees construct their approbation as Lycurgus does, using similar formulations to specify both general and specific terms of praise.[99]

Lycurgus was thoroughly familiar with the language of public honours, and we have a handful of inscriptions – of the very many which there must have been – in which 'Lycurgus son of Lycophron of Butadae', is recorded as the mover of public honours for a benefactor of Athens.[100] In his biography of Lycurgus Pseudo-Plutarch even specifically highlights that Lycurgus was responsible for moving a great many proposals (ψηφίσματα) in the Assembly.[101] But as cunning as Lycurgus' appropriation of honorific language in this speech might seem, he was not the first orator to adopt the strategy. In his *Address to Philip* of 346 BC, Isocrates also borrowed from the standardised language of honorific decrees to insinuate that he deserved official public recognition.[102] Isocrates insists that because he has spent his entire life waging war against barbarians to the best of his ability, 'everyone would rightly praise me' (δικαίως ἄν με πάντες ἐπαινοῖεν).[103]

99 See, for example, *IG* ii³ 367, *IG* ii² 554, 670, 715 and 1166; on the tendency see West (1995) 238. The same section of the ephebic inscription (*IG* ii² 1156.58–62) also, like Lycurgus, uses the somewhat dated formulation ἐπαινέσαι . . . ὅτι.

100 These honours are (1) for a son of Eupor-? in *IG* ii³ 329 = Schwenk 15; (2) for an unknown Plataean in *IG* ii³ 345 = Schwenk 36; (3) for Eudemus of Plataea (who gave money for τὸ θέατρον τὸ Παναθηναικόν) in *IG* ii³ 352 = Schwenk 48 = Rhodes–Osborne 94; (4) for managers of the Amphiaraea in *IG* ii³ 355; and (5) a proxeny decree for Sopatros of Akragas = *IG* ii³ 432. Cf. [Plut.] *Vit. dec. or.* 843f–844a for Lycurgus' proposals to award honours to Neoptolemus and Diotimus in 334 BC.

101 [Plut.] *Vit. dec. or.* 842c; Lycurgus was supposedly aided in all of his decree-making by a Euclides of Olynthus, who excelled in these matters. On theatre-related decrees proposed by Lycurgus see pages 106–10.

102 For the date see Markle (1976) 80 n. 1.

103 Isoc. 5.130. Cf. also Ar. *Pax* 1033–6, a passage in which the Chorus likely implies that Trygaeus is also worthy of public honours for his services to the city: τίς οὖν ἂν οὐκ ἐπαινέσει- | εν ἄνδρα τοιοῦτον, ὅσ- | τις πόλλ' ἀνατλὰς ἔσω- | σε τὴν ἱερὰν πόλιν;

There is additionally some small possibility that, long before Lycurgus delivered his speech against Leocrates, Athens had already bestowed official honours upon at least two native poets because of their poetry. Even if the stories about these honours are spurious, both help further to confirm the 'epigraphic' style of Lycurgus' own language. In the first case, the Aristophanic *Vita* provides this account of a decree which the demos supposedly proclaimed in the comic playwright's honour, in the last years of the fifth century:

μάλιστα δὲ ἐπηνέθη καὶ ἐστεφανώθη θαλλῷ τῆς ἱερᾶς ἐλαίας, ὃς νενόμισται ἰσότιμος χρυσῷ στεφάνῳ, εἰπὼν ἐκεῖνα ἐν τοῖς Βατράχοις περὶ τῶν ἀτίμων·
'τὸν ἱερὸν χορὸν δίκαιόν ἐστι χρηστὰ τῇ πόλει ξυμπαραινεῖν.' (*Ran.* 686–7 Ar. T 1.35–9 K–A)

He was extensively praised and crowned with a wreath of sacred olive, which is considered an equal honour as a gold crown, because he had said this in the *Frogs* about the disenfranchised:[104]
'It is right for the sacred chorus to give useful advice to the city.'

This line of the *Frogs* belongs to the *epirrhema* of the play's *parabasis*, and the source of the claim that Aristophanes was honoured in this way is now generally thought to be Dicaearchus, a student of Aristotle's and an early Peripatetic. He is explicitly named as the source for another story which centres on the same Aristophanic passage. At the end of the ancient *hypothesis* to the *Frogs*, the *parabasis* is cited as the specific reason for which the play earned the privilege of subsequent reperformance (as signified here by the verb ἀναδιδάσκω):[105]

(Who would not praise such a man, who endured so many hardships to save the hallowed city?).

[104] The 'disenfranchised' people to whom the Chorus refer were those Athenians who had lost their citizen rights because of their participation in the oligarchic coup of 411.

[105] I do not include here the alleged fifth-century decree which supposedly dictated that anyone who wished to revive an Aeschylean play would be granted a chorus, as I accept the conclusion of Biles (2006–7) that it is a later fiction which may be owed to a fanciful interpretation of Ar. *Ach.* 9–11. Five ancient sources refer to the decree (*Vita Aeschyli* = Aesch. T 1.48–9; Philostr. *VA* 6.11; Σ *ad* Ar. *Ach.* 10; Σ *ad* Ar. *Ran.* 658; Quint. *IO* 10.1.66), but Biles demonstrates that each of these originated from a single report. See Biles (2006–7) 15 on the penchant of later interpreters to elaborate upon and even to invent decrees pertaining to the poets on whose works they commented.

οὕτω δὲ ἐθαυμάσθη τὸ δρᾶμα διὰ τὴν ἐν αὐτῷ παράβασιν, ὥστε καὶ ἀνεδιδάχθη, ὥς φησι Δικαίαρχος. (*Arg. Ran.* 1.39–40 Coulon)

So admired was the play because of its *parabasis* that it was even performed again, as Dicaearchus says.

The presence of a form of ἐπαινέω (ἐπῃνέθη) in the account of Aristophanes' honour has led some to argue that the source used by Dicaearchus was the decree itself.[106] In an elaboration of that idea, Alan Sommerstein has suggested that the official decree will have paraphrased the message of the *parabasis* that it commended. He even offers *exempli gratia* an hypothetical ἐπειδή-clause for the inscription: the demos may have decided to crown Aristophanes 'because he has advised the Athenians that they should live in concord with one another and should restore rights to the disenfranchised' (*vel sim.*).[107] If such a decree ever was passed, and particularly if it did allude to the *parabasis* of the *Frogs* (or to the *Frogs* at all), it will have marked a precedent for the structure of Lycurgus' honorific language in *Against Leocrates*. In terms parallel with the putative decree for Aristophanes, Lycurgus implies that Euripides deserves a decree of his own because of his service to Athens generally, and specifically because of his choice to produce the *Erechtheus*.

In the second case another late source, Pausanias the Lexicographer (2nd century AD) records a decree passed by the Athenians in honour of another of their playwrights – this time a tragedian – during the years of Lycurgus' own career.[108] In his account Pausanias uses the verb δοθῆναι ('it was granted') to mark the decree, an allusion to the standard beginning of inscribed Attic honours (ἔδοξεν τῆι βουλῆι καὶ τῶι δήμωι κτλ.).

Ἀστυδάμᾳ τῷ Μορσίμου εὐημερήσαντι ἐπὶ τραγῳδίας διδασκαλίᾳ Παρθενοπαίου δοθῆναι ὑπ' Ἀθηναίων εἰκόνος ἀνάθεσιν ἐν θεάτρῳ. (Paus. Gr. σ 6 = Astyd. T 2a)

[106] First suggested by Kaibel ap. Kassel–Austin *PCG* III.2.2. On the putative decree see Sommerstein (1993), who proposes that the reperformance of the *Frogs* took place at the Lenaea of 404.

[107] Sommerstein (1993) 465.

[108] On Astydamas' statue see Papastamati-von Moock (forthcoming) 23–33, Ma (2013) 110 and Goette (1999).

For Astydamas the son of Morsimus the Athenians decreed that a statue be erected in the theatre on the occasion of his success in the tragic competition with his *Parthenopaeus*.

Astydamas' *Parthenopaeus* premiered at the Great Dionysia in 340, with the actor Thessalus in the starring role. From inscriptional records we know that Astydamas' *didascalia* that year also included a play called *Lycaon*, in which the actor Neoptolemus played the lead.[109] By naming only the *Parthenopaeus*, however, Pausanias suggests that this was the particular play that won Astydamas the official approbation of the demos. When Lycurgus casts his introduction of Euripides in honorific language, his subsequent citation of the specific *Erechtheus* may have served to align his rhetoric still more forcefully with earlier instances in which the city had issued decrees in honour of its playwrights.[110]

Lycurgus' presentation of Euripides in *Against Leocrates* thus works on multiple fronts to enfold Euripides' poetic legacy into discourses of Athenian civic ideology. In the first place, Lycurgus' selection and framing of the verses serves to render them a poetic near-equivalent of an *epitaphios logos*.[111] But Lycurgus also makes a subtler, more ideological and rhetorically adventurous move to connect Euripides with the official structures of civic life and public praise. By borrowing from the city's honorific language he prompts his audience to agree that Euripides deserved their recognition for the praiseworthy

[109] *IG* ii² 2320.20–2 Millis–Olson = Astydamas T 6. For a discussion of the decree – and the infamous epigram that Astydamas supposedly composed for his honorific statue – see pages 183–8.

[110] For decrees that Greek communities issued in honour of poets (and especially of *poeti vaganti*) during the Hellenistic period see Guarducci (1929). These decrees tend to indicate how the poet has benefitted the city which awards the honour: e.g. 'we find the Delians honouring Demoteles of Andros for poetry on "local myths" and Amphiklos of Chios for poems that "brought lustre to the temple and the Delians"': so Hunter and Rutherford (2009) 3; cf. their discussion at 3–5. See also the case studies of Rutherford (2008) esp. 279–82 and the Appendix at 293–5 (on a decree for Dymas of Iasos issued by the Samothracians) and (2009) 237–40 (on decrees for the poet Aristodama issued by the Aetolian League and Khalaion in Locri). Along the 'wandering poet' model the *Vita Euripidis* records that, before moving to Macedon, Euripides had lived in Magnesia, where he was honoured with proxeny: Eur. T 1 A.6.

[111] Wilson (1996) 314.

service that he performed for the state. Euripides, he implies, should be remembered not only as a poet who was 'good', but also as an exemplary citizen who was above all an *anēr agathos* in the civic sense. His verses embodied and communicated the spirit of his city's institutions, and his praise would therefore 'justly' be articulated in the city's official language of acclamation.

Poetic legislation

When Lycurgus has concluded his presentation of Euripides, he goes on to cite verses of Homer and Tyrtaeus. In both of these instances he again attempts to justify the value of the poetry by first establishing the virtues of the poets. Lycurgus next introduces Homer by connecting him, too, with an Athenian institution. In the case of Homer that institution is the festival of the Great Panathenaea. Lycurgus himself was personally involved in multiple aspects of the planning and organisation of the Panathenaea during his tenure as administrator of the state finances.[112] In *Against Leocrates* he speaks only to one aspect of the festival, namely its rhapsodic competitions in the performance of Homeric verse. Before embarking upon his quotation from Homer he reminds his audience of why their forefathers had legislated (νόμον ἔθεντο) the performance of his poetry:

οὕτω γὰρ ὑπέλαβον ὑμῶν οἱ πατέρες σπουδαῖον εἶναι ποιητήν, ὥστε νόμον ἔθεντο καθ' ἑκάστην πεντετηρίδα τῶν Παναθηναίων μόνου τῶν ἄλλων ποιητῶν

[112] He managed funds for construction on the Panathenaic stadium: cf. the honours that Lycurgus proposed for Eudemus of Plataea, who donated funds for the stadium's construction: *IG* ii³ 352 = Rhodes–Osborne 94 = Lambert 2006 no. 42; see also [Plut.] *Vit. dec. or.* 841d. For the construction of the Panathenaic stadium see Csapo and Wilson (forthcoming) sections I.3–4 and II.3. On reforms of the festival and the Lycurgan programme see also Lambert (2010) 231–2. According to the 'Decree of Stratocles' (*IG* ii² 457, on which see pages 101–2 below), Lycurgus also enhanced the splendour of the Panathenaic procession by arranging for 'gold and silver processional vessels, and gold adornment for one hundred basket bearers (*kanephoroi*)'. For the *kanephoroi* see *IG* ii³ 447.38–9 and Humphreys (2004) 92–3. On Lycurgus' 'adornments' of the Panathenaea and the source of the funding for these see Csapo and Wilson (forthcoming) section II.2.

ῥαψῳδεῖσθαι τὰ ἔπη, ἐπίδειξιν ποιούμενοι πρὸς τοὺς Ἕλληνας, ὅτι τὰ κάλλιστα τῶν ἔργων προῃροῦντο. (Lycurg. 1.102)

For the forefathers understood him to be such an important (σπουδαῖος) poet that they passed a law that, every four years at the Panathenaea, his poetry should be performed by rhapsodes, thereby making a demonstration to all Greeks that they appreciated the noblest sorts of deeds.

The *nomos* to which Lycurgus is referring here is known by modern convention as the 'Panathenaic Rule', or the 'Panathenaic Regulation'.[113] In Plato's *Hipparchus*, Socrates names Hipparchus, 'the oldest and wisest of the children of Peisistratus', as the specific Athenian forefather who was responsible for the custom. Socrates explains that, in addition to the other many and fine works of wisdom that Hipparchus accomplished,

τὰ Ὁμήρου ἔπη πρῶτος ἐκόμισεν εἰς τὴν γῆν ταυτηνί, καὶ ἠνάγκασε τοὺς ῥαψῳδοὺς Παναθηναίοις ἐξ ὑπολήψεως ἐφεξῆς αὐτὰ διιέναι, ὥσπερ νῦν ἔτι οἵδε ποιοῦσιν... (Pl. *Hipparch.* 228b–c)

He first brought the epic poetry of Homer into this land, and compelled the rhapsodes to recite their way through them, each taking up where the other left off, just as they still do today...

While Plato's Socrates describes Hipparchus as having 'forced' or 'compelled' the rhapsodes to recite Homer, in *Against Leocrates* Lycurgus prefers to present the custom as the dictate of a law. That law did not, as Socrates presents it, represent the unilateral decree of a tyrant, but rather was the outcome of a wise decision that had been made collectively by the Athenian ancestors. The interpretation of the poetic past which Lycurgus presents again serves to align the historical values of the forefathers with his own civic vision and cultural agenda.[114]

[113] There is much debate as to how exactly the recitation of Homer proceeded at the Panathenaea; here I am most interested in Lycurgus' stylisation of the law as legislated by the forefathers. On the ancient lore surrounding the introduction of Homeric poetry to Athens and the institutionalisation of its recitation at the Panathenaea see the summary of Nagy (1996) 73–5.

[114] Cf. Ober (2008) 212–13 on debates about codified knowledge (including νόμοι). While 'decision makers' past intentions are not transparent', 'Athenian forensic claims regarding lawmakers' intentions... do have something to tell us about how *later* Athenians interpreted and employed the laws by which they governed themselves'.

Following a brief justification of the ancestors' legislation of the Homeric *nomos*, Lycurgus proceeds to quote six lines from the *Iliad*.[115] In these lines the jurors heard Hector exhorting the demoralised Trojan troops to carry on fighting in defence of their homeland: men who die in battle defending their country are not disgraced, Hector-Lycurgus argues, because in dying they preserve the lives of their wives and children as well as their land and homes. These lines repeat and elaborate, this time from a male warrior's perspective, the sentiments of Praxithea's monologue in Euripides' *Erechtheus*, and so implicitly link Homer's poetic spirit with that of Euripides. When Lycurgus concludes his remarks on Homer he makes yet another appeal to the wisdom and traditions of the Athenian ancestors: because they listened to Homer's words and emulated Hector's deeds they, too, strove for *aretē*.[116] In this account Lycurgus appropriates Homer – the 'poet who educated Hellas'[117] – for Athens, by casting his poetry and its ritual reperformance as uniquely Athenian traditions. Like Euripidean tragedy (ἰαμβεῖα), Homer's epic verses (ἔπη) offer models of heroic behaviour, and the forefathers were wise to legislate that Homer be forever performed and celebrated in their city.[118]

The last poet whom Lycurgus quotes extensively in this section is Tyrtaeus. Lycurgus emphasises that Tyrtaeus, though most famous for his association with Sparta, had in truth been an Athenian by birth.[119] Towards the beginning of Plato's *Laws* the Athenian makes the same claim, with the emphasis reversed: though a native Athenian, Tyrtaeus chose to become

[115] Hom. *Il.* 15.494–9.

[116] Lycurg. 1.104. This passage also recalls the section of Isocrates' *Panegyricus* (from 380 BC) in which he explains that the Athenian ancestors (πρόγονοι) chose to honour Homer with prizes (ἆθλα) because he had praised the Greeks for their expedition against barbarians and so inspired others to emulate their heroic deeds (Isoc. 4.159).

[117] Pl. *Resp.* 10.606e: τὴν Ἑλλάδα πεπαίδευκεν οὗτος ὁ ποιητής.

[118] Homer's importance as a 'teacher' was a commonplace: cf. e.g. Ar. *Ran.* 1034–6, Pl. *Prt.* 325e, *Symp.* 3.5 and Ath. 10.606e (for the same idea in the Roman tradition cf. e.g. Horace *Epist.* 1.2.1–31). On the early view of 'poetry as education' see Nagy (1989) 69–77.

[119] A number of ancient sources attest to Tyrtaeus' Athenian origins, though they give conflicting accounts of how he came to live in Sparta: see Tyrt. T 1–8 Geber.

a citizen of Sparta.[120] Lycurgus, on the other hand, suggests that the Spartans stole Tyrtaeus away from Athens and poses this rhetorical question to the Areopagites:

τίς γὰρ οὐκ οἶδε τῶν Ἑλλήνων, ὅτι Τυρταῖον στρατηγὸν ἔλαβον παρὰ τῆς πόλεως, μεθ᾽ οὗ καὶ τῶν πολεμίων ἐκράτησαν, καὶ τὴν περὶ τοὺς νέους ἐπιμέλειαν συνετάξαντο οὐ μόνον εἰς τὸν παρόντα κίνδυνον, ἀλλ᾽ εἰς ἅπαντα τὸν αἰῶνα βουλευσάμενοι καλῶς. (Lycurg. 1.106)

For what Greek does not know that they snatched Tyrtaeus from our city to be their general, and under his leadership defeated their enemies and established their system of training the young, planning well not only for the present danger, but for the entire future?

He then goes on to credit Tyrtaeus with the Spartans' legendary courage, which is the result of his elegies: by listening to Tyrtaeus' poems the Spartans are educated to be brave.[121] And though the Spartans have no regard for other poetry, they saw fit to make their own law about the poems of Tyrtaeus. Here again it is important that the act of legislation is described with the phrase νόμον ἔθεντο: Lycurgus' claims about poetic laws in this speech help to lay the ideological groundwork – as we shall see shortly – for his own poetic legislation. No other sources for the performance of Tyrtaeus' poetry mention such a law; nevertheless, according to Lycurgus the Spartan *nomos* dictated that, after the Spartan warriors had armed themselves for battle, they must go to the tent of the king to listen to verses of Tyrtaeus so as to be inspired to die for the fatherland.[122] After describing this tradition Lycurgus argues that it would be useful (χρήσιμον) for the jurors to hear some of this inspirational poetry as well. He then proceeds to quote thirty-two lines of Tyrtaean elegy on the nobility of fighting in the front ranks

[120] Pl. *Leg*. 1.629a–c. Here the Athenian also calls Tyrtaeus both wise and good (σοφός ... καὶ ἀγαθός), but later he refers to Homer and Tyrtaeus alike as examples of poets who have 'written bad advice about life and how to live it' (περὶ βίου τε καὶ ἐπιτηδευμάτων κακῶς ... γράψαντας, 8.858e). See Renehan (1970) 226–9 on potential connections between Tyrtaeus' characterisation in *Against Leocrates* and Plato's *Laws*.

[121] Lycurg. 1.107: ὧν ἀκούοντες παιδεύονται πρὸς ἀνδρείαν. Other fourth-century fragmentary sources make the same claim: Aristoxenus F 103.16 Wehrli and Philochorus *FGrH* 328 F216, both preserved *ap*. Ath. 14.630c–f.

[122] On evidence for the written preservation of Tyrtaean poems in Sparta see Millender (2001) 128–30.

and dying for the fatherland, verses which he claims are 'fine and useful for those who wish to heed them'.[123]

It is, then, hardly difficult to make a case for the 'internal' relevance of Lycurgus' entire poetic digression, as well as for its practical importance in the prosecution of Leocrates. Towards the beginning and again at the end of *Against Leocrates*, Lycurgus stresses that his speech contains no irrelevant material.[124] He also encourages the jurors to act in this case as Areopagites must always do, refusing to be convinced by an orator whose words stray from the matter at hand.[125] Although the emphasis that Lycurgus places upon his own commitment to relevance may be largely rhetorical, we should not dismiss his digression upon poetry in attempts to account for the broader strategies of Leocrates' prosecution.[126] As Josiah Ober has argued, fundamental to Lycurgus' rhetorical strategy is an implied 'argument for the instrumental value of common knowledge'.[127] Lycurgus seeks to convince the jurors that Athenians have, and always have had, a shared expectation that citizens will come to the city's aid in times of crisis. The same category of shared expectation, Lycurgus implies, holds that anyone who fails to do so must be punished for the good of the community. Ober further emphasises the importance of Lycurgus' argument that 'Leocrates' departure further endangered the city because it undermined common knowledge among other Greeks regarding the patriotic Athenian commitment to defending their

[123] Tyrtaeus 10 West quoted at Lycurg. 1.108: καλά γ', ὦ ἄνδρες, καὶ χρήσιμα τοῖς βουλομένοις προσέχειν.

[124] Lycurg. 1.11 and 1.149.

[125] Lycurg. 1.13: τοῖς ἔξω τοῦ πράγματος λέγουσιν. In the Athenian homicide courts, nothing 'outside the issue' (ἔξω τοῦ πράγματος) was to be admitted as evidence. On the issue of legal relevance in the homicide courts see Lanni (2006) 96–105.

[126] Rhodes (2004) emphasises the tendency of Athenian orators, perhaps despite appearances, to 'keep to the point' in their speeches. Athenian standards of relevance seem to have allowed for more leeway than our own: see Gagarin (2012) for a review of the issue of juridical relevance in Athenian law and an analysis of relevance in Dem. 18 and Aeschin. 3 (the speeches 'On the Crown').

[127] Ober (2008) 186. Ober's common-knowledge oriented reading of *Against Leocrates* draws heavily on the work of the economist and social scientist Michael Chwe, esp. Chwe (2001), whose research has investigated the social processes by which common knowledge is generated.

territory'.[128] Near the beginning of the speech Lycurgus warns the jurors that,

παρὰ πᾶσιν τοῖς Ἕλλησιν ἔσται λόγος, οἳ ἴσασιν τὰ τῶν προγόνων τῶν ὑμετέρων ἔργα ἐναντιώτατα τοῖς τούτῳ διαπεπραγμένοις ὄντα. (Lycurg. 1.14)

the verdict will be of concern to all Greeks, who know that the deeds of your ancestors stand in total contrast to what has been done by this man.

For Lycurgus it was crucial that the entire Greek world knew how firm Athenians were in their commitment to the city and to their fellow citizens. His transformation of Euripides, Homer and Tyrtaeus into 'witnesses' in this case thus belongs to a strategy of proving both the strength and antiquity of the citizens' devotion to their city's defence.[129] From his perspective, each of these poets offers relevant testimony: their verses prove that ever since the time of the ancestors, common knowledge held that all citizens should be willing to die for their homeland and should never, as Leocrates did, abandon it in the midst of crisis. As he cites these poets' verses, he also assimilates both the poetry and the poets themselves to his idealised vision of the Athenian past. That past had been marked by the valour and patriotic commitment of the Athenian ancestors and forefathers (the πρόγονοι and πατέρες), who from the outset recognised the value of certain poetry to the state.[130] The poetic quotations therefore serve to illustrate historically enduring common values in Athens, and to reinforce Lycurgus' argument that in not upholding those values Leocrates set a dangerous example for the community. By this logic, then, Leocrates

128 Ober (2008) 186. See also Steinbock (2011), who argues in a similar vein that Lycurgus' citation of the ephebic oath and of the historical exampla of King Codrus and King Erechtheus are integral to the argumentation of the speech: together they illustrate the ethos that was instilled into Athenian ephebes – an ethos which Leocrates blatantly violated to the city's harm.

129 See esp. Spina (1980–1) 25 on Lycurgus' presentation of the poets as legal witnesses; Aristotle discusses the strategy: see n. 115 above.

130 On Lycurgus' idealisation of the Athenian past in the speech and the desire that he expresses to return to its values see esp. Salamone (1976); see also Faraguna (1992) 283–4 on the comparable importance that he attributes to the ancestors and the theatre for providing the demos with models of morality. Spina (1980–1) 21 closely connects Lycurgus' use of poetic quotations with his idealised view of the past.

must be prosecuted, so that other Athenians and the rest of Greece might see how the city deals with disloyal citizens.

Nevertheless, in using this speech as an opportunity to erect a kind of pantheon of loosely 'Athenian' poets, Lycurgus also speaks to us about his broader cultural programme for the city and offers a vision for the unity of civic and 'literary' history. Each one of this pantheon's members becomes historically connected with the city of Athens. Euripides' Praxithea is transformed into the speaker of an Athenian *epitaphios logos*. Homer is celebrated as the poet who is rightfully performed, by dictate of the ancestors, at the Great Panathenaea. And though it was the Spartans who codified performance of Tyrtaeus, that great poet of war elegy was an Athenian by birth and at heart. Lycurgus' placement of Euripides at the head of his 'paideutic' poetic canon marks a novel statement about tragedy and about the poet Euripides. By elevating his tragic iambs to the civic status of epic and martial elegy, Lycurgus assigns tragedy to an especially priviliged place in the city's history. And by choosing Euripides as Athenian tragedy's primary and paradigmatic representative, Lycurgus effectively reclaims Greece's most popular tragedian for Athens.

CHAPTER 2

SCRIPTS AND STATUES, OR A LAW OF LYCURGUS' OWN

Lycurgus' use of extended poetic quotations in *Against Leocrates* allows him to present a vision of poetry's importance to the state. The three poets whom he cites each become emblematic of similar patriotic values, but his introduction to Euripides differs from his discussions of Homer and Tyrtaeus on an essential point. In the cases of Homer, whose poetry was performed by rhapsodes in the competitions at the Panathenaea, and Tyrtaeus, whose elegies were regularly recited by Spartans on the eve of battle, Lycurgus uses the phrase νόμον ἔθεντο to describe the processes by which these public recitations had been mandated. He never, on the other hand, mentions any *nomos* (whether in the sense of law or tradition) regarding works by Euripides or by tragedians. But despite his omission of any reference to a 'tragic' law, Lycurgus himself was responsible for an Athenian *nomos* that assured the three great tragedians a very particular (and quite literally iconic) status in the city. No contemporary account has survived to offer an explicit justification for the reasoning behind the law, but the text of *Against Leocrates* provides valuable insight into Lycurgan views about the importance of poetic heritage to the state. The very enactment of the law, when read against the era's shifting theatrical landscape, reveals a desire in Athens to preserve the previous century's tragic scripts. It also, however, speaks to a certain anxiety about the degree to which Attic tragedy – now popular the Greek world over – was receiving due credit as a distinctly Athenian achievement and possession.

Lycurgus and the tragic texts

In the third quarter of the fourth century Athens still enjoyed a strong tradition of dramatic performance, and each year saw a number of new tragedies and comedies premiere at dramatic festivals. As was the case elsewhere in Greece, revivals of tragedies were also regularly staged.[1] The 'Rural' Dionysia celebrated in the Attic demes had likely long served as performance venues for plays that had already competed at the city's major dramatic festivals, the Great Dionysia and the Lenaea.[2] By the time of the trial of Leocrates, 'old tragedy' (παλαιὸν δρᾶμα) had been on the programme of the Great Dionysia for more than half a century.[3] One of our most valuable sources for Athenian theatre history is the combined fragments of the inscribed records of victories at the festival: the *Victorum Dionysiorum Fasti* (*IG* ii² 2318), often simply referred to as the *Fasti*. This inscription was erected as a monument on the Acropolis, and first created sometime between 347/6 and 343/2. A fragment of the *Fasti* indicates that revivals of classical tragedy were first added to the celebrations in 387/6 BC, making this 'the single most important date in the history of fourth-century tragedy'.[4] The first three lines of the record for the year run as follows:

> ἐπὶ Θεοδότου
> παλαιὸν δρᾶμα πρῶτο[ν]
> παρεδίδαξαν οἱ τραγ[ωιδοί]
>
> (*IG* ii² 2318.1009–11 Millis–Olson)

> When Theodotus was archon [in 387/6 BC]
> tragic performers first began also to produce
> old drama.

[1] Biles (2006–7) is persuasive in arguing that the ancient reports of a fifth-century law that instituted reperformances of Aeschylus' plays at the Great Dionysia are mistaken; see page 50 n. 105 above. These reports do, however, suggest a tendency of ancient scholars to connect reperformance with acts of legislation. For a brief survey of the earliest evidence for reperformances of Athenian tragedy (in the fifth and fourth centuries BC) see Nervegna (2007) 17–18.

[2] By the end of the fourth century we have evidence for the celebration of eighteen different 'Rural' Dionysia: see Jones (1999) 127–42; see also esp. Wilson (2010), Paga (2010) and Goette (forthcoming).

[3] The category of παλαιὸν δρᾶμα did not, as Le Guen (2007) 85 n. 3 points out, consist solely of plays by the three tragedians of the 'Lycurgan' canon: παλαιόν simply indicated a play that had already been performed; παλαιὸν δρᾶμα was effectively the 'revival' or 'reperformance' category at the Great Dionysia.

[4] Easterling (1997b) 213.

Another set of inscribed didascalic records happens to survive from the Great Dionysia for the three years just before the Battle of Chaeronea: 342/1 to 340/39. In each of these years a play by Euripides was chosen for the 'revival' portion of the festival programme.[5]

Like the recitations of Homer in Athens and Tyrtaeus in Sparta, the performance of 'old' tragedy had therefore been institutionalised, albeit not by a *nomos*. The momentous addition of *palaion drama* to the programme of the Great Dionysia had perhaps occurred too recently for Lycurgus to attempt to attribute it to the city's forefathers. The *Fasti*, inscribed and on view in the city for more than a decade, credited the practice to *tragōidoi*. But by omitting from *Against Leocrates* any mention of a *nomos* regarding tragic poetry, Lycurgus might have been priming his fellow Athenians to agree that the city was in need of new legislation, of which Lycurgus himself would be the architect.[6] According to Pseudo-Plutarch's *Life of Lycurgus*, one of the many laws that he was responsible for passing in Athens dictated:

> ὡς χαλκᾶς εἰκόνας ἀναθεῖναι τῶν ποιητῶν, Αἰσχύλου Σοφοκλέους Εὐριπίδου, καὶ τὰς τραγῳδίας αὐτῶν ἐν κοινῷ γραψαμένους φυλάττειν καὶ τὸν τῆς πόλεως γραμματέα παραναγινώσκειν τοῖς ὑποκρινομένοις· οὐκ ἐξεῖναι γὰρ <παρ’> αὐτὰς ὑποκρίνεσθαι.[7] ([Plut.] *Vit. dec. or.* 841f)

that bronze statues of the poets Aeschylus, Sophocles and Euripides be erected and that their tragedies be written down and conserved publicly, and that the city's secretary read them out to those acting in them for the purpose of comparison. For it was not allowed for these plays to be performed out of accordance with the official texts.

In the same passage of the *Life* we are told that Lycurgus instituted a competition of comedies at the Chytroi (the 'feast of pots' in honour of the dead) that constituted the third day of celebrations at the Anthesteria – the festival that Thucydides

[5] *IG* ii^2 2320; for an introduction, edition and commentary see Millis and Olson (2012) 61–9.

[6] For the evidence of Lycurgus' legislative activity see Testimonia in Conomis (1970) section III.

[7] On the text of the passage and its implications for our understanding of the transmission of the plays (and their music) in this era see esp. Prauscello (2006) 69–83.

glosses as 'the more ancient Dionysia'.[8] Lycurgus also is said to have legislated for the introduction of cyclic choruses ('no fewer than three') at the Piraeus in honour of Poseidon.[9] Together these laws attest to Lycurgus' commitment to the cultural life of Athens and to the state regulation of the theatre. The law which called for the bronze statues of the three great tragedians and the deposition of their scripts in the archive is however unique within the dossier of Lycurgan legislation, in that it relates not to a festival's organization but to the conservation of cultural patrimony.

At first glance, the law about the tragedians' scripts and statues seems to be directed primarily at ensuring that reperformances of tragedy stay true to the original, or at least to the now state-sanctioned scripts of the tragic playwrights. Yet Pseudo-Plutarch offers no context for the law, nor does he report his source.[10] His text therefore raises a number of questions about the significance of the law and the motivations behind it, as well as about the contemporary state of the dramatic texts and the management of theatrical culture. If accurate, the text implies that actors were playing a leading role in organising their performances of old tragedy: the city official (ὁ γραμματεύς) was to compare or 'collate' (παραναγινώσκειν) the state texts of the tragedies not with, for example, a *chorodidaskalos* or *choregos*, but with the actors themselves.[11] Those actors, it seems, will have already had their own copies of the tragic scripts to compare against those of the state. But the brevity of the account leads to a number of problems of interpretation. For example, we never hear where exactly the state scripts were to be

[8] Thuc. 2.15.4: τὰ ἀρχαιότερα Διονύσια. On the Anthesteria (with mentions of the Chytroi *passim*) see Parker (2005) 290–316.

[9] For Lycurgus' interventions in these festivals see [Plut.] *Vit. dec. or.* 841f and 842a respectively; cf. Csapo and Wilson (forthcoming) section II.3.

[10] This *Life* cites only one source, Dinarchus, at 843a: see Pitcher (2005), who notes that within Pseudo-Plutarch's *Lives* 'explicit citations from other authors are very unevenly distributed' (220).

[11] For the use of παραναγιγνώσκω in fourth-century prose to denote the process of checking copies of documents for accuracy by means of side-by-side comparison see Pl. *Tht.* 172e and Aeschin. 2.135. Thomas (1989) 49 is therefore misleading in suggesting that, because the city's secretary was to read out the texts to actors, 'in effect [the texts'] transmission is oral', with the copy therefore potentially lacking the accuracy 'enforced by learning straight from a written text'.

deposited. In inscribed decrees of the fourth century, provisions that copies of decrees be stored in the Bouleuterion call for their placement 'in the archive' (ἐν τῶι δημοσίωι), and the public archives tend to be referred to as τὰ δημόσια γράμματα.[12] Pseudo-Plutarch's 'in public' (ἐν κοινῷ) does not provide the exact location of the repository where the documents were to be kept. Most likely, the scripts were stored in the same state archive where records of the city's dramatic and dithyrambic competitions were also held; those records were in turn probably the source of the victory information that would come to be preserved on the inscribed *Fasti*.[13]

Other problems raised by the law relate to, for example, the degree to which actors were actually introducing interpolations into the dramatic scripts;[14] the organisation of tragic revivals (and the personnel involved: who selected which plays to revive at the Great Dionysia, or elsewhere?);[15] the nature of venues for performances of old tragedies in the city, the demes and abroad; and the level of agreement among Athenians that a tragic canon existed and was headed by Aeschylus, Sophocles and Euripides. The choice of these three playwrights as Athens' 'official' tragedians could hardly have been an arbitrary one. To be sure, these are the same three who had featured (Sophocles admittedly to a far lesser extent) in Aristophanes' *Frogs* some seventy-five years earlier. Yet the intervening decades allowed the Athenians of 330 the benefit of hindsight that had been unavailable to Aristophanes in 405. Lycurgus' choice of Aeschylus, Sophocles and Euripides served effectively to synchronise the glory days of Athenian tragedy with the years of the city's first empire. Aeschylus, the earliest of the three playwrights, was a great veteran of the Persian

[12] See esp. Shear (1995) 186–7.

[13] On the records of the dramatic and dithyrambic competitions see Sickinger (1999) 42–7 with 209 n. 32 and 134–5. Sickinger postulates that the eponymous archon, who was responsible for organising the Great Dionysia, also kept administrative records of the competitions (43); cf. Millis and Olson (2012) 1.

[14] On which see esp. Garzya (1981) and Page (1934). Page writes that 'The extent and gravity of such interference [i.e. as was made by actors] are incontestably proven by the law of Lukourgos' (18).

[15] Battezzato (2003) examines the law in the light of the avenues of textual transmission in the period.

Wars.[16] Sophocles, the last of the three to die, did so only about a year before Athens fell to Sparta – and lost its empire – at the end of the Peloponnesian War.[17] Together the careers and lifetimes of these playwrights span the three quarters of a century during which Athenian power was at its height. Each was also an Athenian by birth: Aeschylus was from the deme of Eleusis, Sophocles was from Colonus and Euripides was an Athenian from Salamis.[18] The Lycurgan triad was therefore a group that was rooted in an idea and celebration of Athenian identity, as well as in nostalgia for the days of the empire. By this chronology, the Golden Age of Athens exactly and meaningfully corresponded to the Golden Age of Athenian Tragedy.

Thus even if on the surface the Lycurgan law seems most preoccupied with ensuring the 'authenticity' of the tragic scripts that were used in revivals, the law suggests a broader cultural agenda of reaffirming and publicising Athens' status as capital and rightful home of the theatre. As some scholars have emphasised, the passage of this law must have been driven, at least in part, by 'symbolic' intentions – and not merely by concerns over the 'genuineness' of tragic lines.[19] We have already seen how, in *Against Leocrates*, Lycurgus implies a close correlation between the paideutic value of Euripidean tragedies and the Homeric texts. Similarly, the law attributed to Lycurgus effectively proclaimed, as Ruth Scodel words it, 'the tragedians as worthy of regulated performance on the Homeric model'.[20] As Lycurgus himself points out, rhapsodic reperformance of Homer constituted a *sine qua non* of the festival of

[16] Cf. *Vita Aeschyli* T 1 §11 and T 11–15. Aeschylus' epitaph mentions his participation in the Battle of Marathon, but not his career as a playwright: see n. 69 below.

[17] Pausanias effectively synchronises Sophocles' death with the fall of Athens: Paus. 1.21.1–2. Sophocles was known as an engaged citizen who held a number of public offices: Soph. T G (18–27). The *Antigone* supposedly sealed his election to a generalship (a story of questionable truth): *Arg.I.* to Soph. *Ant.* (mss. LA) = T 25.

[18] Salamis was a possession, not a deme, of Attica. For implications of the island's special relationship to Athens for its own theatre festivals see Wilson (2000) 244–5.

[19] Scodel (2007), esp. the claim at 151 that the law saw the tragedians' texts as 'a national treasure, whose value is not limited to the actual use for regulating performances'. See also Dué (2003) and Mossé (1989) 32 for arguments about the law's symbolic significance.

[20] Scodel (2007) 151.

the Panathenaea. A law designed to ensure that the poetry of the three great tragedians would be reperformed in accordance with the 'official' Athenian versions of their works effectively elevated the status of those works to the same level as that of the Homeric poems. Lycurgus' own discussion of poets in *Against Leocrates* moreover clearly lays out his support of state intervention in the promotion and preservation of certain poetry. In the light of the law's reported content, then, it certainly becomes tempting to interpret Lycurgus' expressions of support for the *nomoi* concerning Homer and Tyrtaeus as efforts to justify – whether pre-emptively or retroactively – the *nomos* of his own that was specifically concerned with certain Athenian tragedians and their on-going civic afterlives.[21]

The prescriptions of the law also created a constant opportunity for Athens to consolidate its authority over the tragic texts. Any actor interested in playing in a revival was welcome – and now compelled – to do so, as long as that access was mediated and controlled by the city and the oversight of an official city secretary.[22] And the law's authority only must have increased through the repeated acts of collation: the more actors who came to the archive to check their scripts, the more authority the official Athenian copies would have had. We can only wonder what this process might have looked like, as the secretary perhaps read out dramatic lines and the actor or actors present checked their own scripts (on this occasion would they have 'done the voices' of the tragic characters? Would they have sung through choral parts and characters' monodies?). Perhaps the scene looked more like a modern table-reading, itself a form of dramatic performance. Yet by the law's specifics, the city transformed its regulation and ownership of these texts into a

[21] Scodel (2007) also argues for a strong connection between the Lycurgan law and the rhapsodes' performances of Homer: 'the Panathenaic rule, which similarly governed how a text was to be performed at an Athenian festival, seems the obvious source for Lycurgus' law . . . The enactment of Lycurgus was a Panathenaic rule for the three tragedians' (150); cf. Garzya (1981) 56.

[22] On the office of the γραμματεύς see Pritchett (1996) 19–20: 'Every board at Athens which appears in the epigraphical record was assigned a γραμματεύς' (19). One of the duties of γραμματεῖς seems to have been to read aloud public documents: cf. e.g. Thuc. 7.10 and Arist. *Ath. Pol.* 54.5.

performative act. For an actor to perform a tragic play, he first had to spectate as the city performed its power over the script.[23]

This move to preserve the texts of classical tragedy marked an attempt on the part of men such as Lycurgus to publicise the three great tragedians as unique products of Athens and to affirm that, as such, both the poets and their poetry were inseparable from Athenian institutions and history. The city's theatrical heritage was the city's legal possession, and thus the demos was within its rights to decree that it should be safeguarded in the official archive. As Athenian legislation, Lycurgus' law of course had no formal reach beyond the boundaries of Attica. Nevertheless, the law was certainly tantamount to a powerful symbolic statement. For another example of 'symbolic' Athenian legislation we might look back to the era of the fifth-century Athenian *archē*. The so-called Athenian 'Coinage' or 'Standards Decree' (*IG* i³ 1453) was passed sometime between the 440s and 415 BC, and dictated that the allies of the Delian League must all use only Athenian weights, measures and currency.[24] According to the decree, the only legitimate minting facility was to be the one in Athens: no other silver tetradrachms except those produced in Athens could, under the law, henceforth be used by any of the allied states. As Loren J. Samons notes, however,

> it has become increasingly clear that, whatever the legislation's intent, the Standards decree did not in fact end the minting of coins by all Athens' subjects or bring about the conversion of most allied coins into Athenian owls. Certain states within the empire continued to issue their own currency, and non-Attic coins continued to be used (even if with decreasing frequency) within the empire.[25]

[23] Dué argues that Pseudo-Plutarch's use of the verb φυλάττειν works to communicate the texts' status as 'a possession that the Athenian demos wants to keep and store away . . . in order to regulate and control how that possession is used' (3). This type of regulation, she suggests, will have been akin to the efforts made by certain archaic tyrants, Peisistratus of Athens and Cleomenes of Sparta, to acquire the texts of oracular utterances so as to enhance their own 'wealth, power, and prestige': so Nagy (1990) 158. Yet this comparison is somewhat misplaced, as the Lycurgan law required that the texts remain accessible.

[24] There is currently no consensus as to the date: see the summary of Hadji and Kontes (2003) 263–4. I thank Peter Wilson for suggesting this comparison.

[25] Samons (2000) 330. He goes on to argue that this decree 'arguably had little impact on the way Athenian imperial finance actually functioned'.

Like the Standards Decree, the effect of the Lycurgan law must also have been largely rhetorical: surely not every actor intending to perform a *palaion drama* at a deme festival in, for example, Rhamnus, Eleutherae or Sunium, travelled to Athens to collate his script with the official texts. Nevertheless, this law too marked a declaration of Athenian authority, in this case with respect to cultural patrimony: during the *archē* Athens could make such declarations with consequences for the economy of the Panhellenic world, but now under the terms of the League of Corinth such symbolic legislation was restricted to the borders of Attica and to the commodities of Athenian culture.

This interpretation of Lycurgus' law as a symbolic gesture affirming Athens' control over its classical tragedy is also suggested by the popularity of the Athenian theatre abroad, and especially in Macedon, during this period. Though the law had force solely in Attica, the call for the preservation of the authorised scripts in the city's archive was also effectively a claim of ownership, made at a time when Macedon was the most active agent in the further spread of theatre. By the third quarter of the fourth century Attic tragedy had long enjoyed renown and reperformance in many corners of the Greek world, and the afterlife of classical tragedy looks to have been nowhere so vital as among the Macedonian ruling elite.[26] This popularity can largely be traced in the movements of actors associated with Athens. During the 340s in particular, Athens had repeatedly elected to send its most famous actors on diplomatic missions to Philip II on account of his passion for theatre and goodwill towards actors.[27] Tragic players such as Aristodemus of Metapontum, Neoptolemus of Scyrus, Theodorus, Ischandrus and the former actor Aeschines, as well as the comic actor Satyrus of Olynthus, all found themselves implicated during these years in diplomacy over Athenian and Macedonian

[26] See esp. Csapo (2010) 172–5, Moloney (2003) ch. 4 ('Philip II – Alexander III'), Revermann 1999–2000.
[27] Cf. Aeschin. 2.15–16.

relations.[28] Many of these men had grown famous as players of 'old drama' and especially of plays by Euripides and Sophocles.[29] In order to negotiate on behalf of Athens, the actors – some of whom were foreign born – will have had to be Athenian citizens.[30] That Athens must have been naturalising foreign actors itself stands as testament to the importance both of actors to the city, and of the theatre to international politics.[31]

Philip's own *philanthrōpia* towards actors must also have been a factor in the selection of Athenian envoys to Macedon. The embassy dispatched to Philip in 346 was particularly notable for its inclusion of well-known personalities (such as the actors Aristodemus and Neoptolemus) who were of relative political insignificance.[32] But in diplomatic missions, envoys were often chosen because they held some particular appeal for the people who were to receive them.[33] The celebrity of actors had increased over the fourth century, and famous actors are also likely to have been exceptionally charismatic personalities.[34] In *On the Peace* Demosthenes complains that the Athenians were so captivated by Neoptolemus – whom Demosthenes accuses of having acted in Philip's, and not Athens', best interests – that they showed him as much favour (χάρις) as if the matter were a tragic performance at

[28] On each of these actors see Stephanis (1988) and the prosopographical appendix of O'Connor (1908).

[29] E.g., Neoptolemus performed Euripidean roles in the *palaion drama* section of the Great Dionysia in both 342/1 and 341/0: See Millis and Olson (2012) 66; in *On the False Embassy* Demosthenes claims that Aristodemus and Theodorus often performed Sophocles' *Antigone*: Dem. 19.246; see pages 144–6.

[30] Csapo and Wilson (forthcoming) section 1.4, with notes and bibliography.

[31] Demosthenes implies that Aeschines' trustworthiness as a diplomat was compromised by the skills at dissemblance that he had acquired as an actor: see esp. Easterling (1999) and Duncan (2006) 65–7. He does concede that actors were good choices for diplomats because their profession ensured them safe conduct wherever they went (Dem. 5.6).

[32] Mosley (1973) 59.

[33] Mosley (1973) 44.

[34] On the fame of actors in this period see esp. Easterling (2002) and Lightfoot (2002) 213; see also Csapo (2010) 83–116 and 173 on the preference of Philip II and Alexander to surround themselves with celebrity actors and not famous poets, which perhaps also points to their preference for classical 'revivals' over new plays.

the Dionysia and not the safety of Athens.[35] Neoptolemus was later among the actors who were supposed to perform at the 336 festival in Aegae where King Philip was assassinated.[36] Actors were important tools in diplomacy, but Athens can hardly have been entirely happy to be sharing such valuable theatre resources with the enemy.

Like Philip before him, Alexander the Great was an admirer of Athenian tragedy. He supposedly requested the 'complete works' of Euripides, Sophocles and Aeschylus when he found himself in need of reading material while on campaign in the upper satrapies.[37] Again like his father, Alexander often played host to dramatic performances.[38] Open competition between Athens and Macedon for theatrical resources accordingly grew especially fierce during Alexander's reign. Here we might revisit Plutarch's account of the *choregiai* of the Cypriot kings in his *Life of Alexander*. This anecdote vividly narrates an instance of the theatrical and 'histrionic' rivalry between Athens and Macedon in the 330s. Plutarch portrays Alexander as outdoing the Athenian theatre industry by securing for his own festival Athenodorus, who was already committed to perform at the Great Dionysia of 331 BC.[39] Instead of performing at the Great

35 Dem. 5.7–8.

36 The later anecdotal tradition would have Neoptolemus compare this highly 'theatrical' event with a tragic plot: according to Stob. 4.34.70, when asked what amazed him about the Aeschylus, Sophocles or Euripides he had read, Neoptolemus replied that nothing did (οὐδὲν μὲν τούτων). Rather, he had been amazed by Philip's death in the theatre following the marriage of his daughter and his proclamation as the thirteenth (Olympian) god. On the story see Easterling (1997b) 219.

37 Plut. *Alex.* 8.3: τῶν Εὐριπίδου καὶ Σοφοκλέους καὶ Αἰσχύλου τραγῳδιῶν συχνάς. The 'book-order' would have arrived sometime in the first half of the 330s: the *terminus post quem* is exactly 330 BC, when Alexander left Harpalus (who sent him the books) behind to manage the treasury in Ecbatana. Brown (1967) presents a complex argument that Plutarch's list is mistaken, and that 'Euripides and Euripides alone was on Alexander's list as a tragedian' (361–2). One wonders whether Alexander made this request in the wake of the Athenians' establishment of state copies of works by the same tragedians.

38 See Le Guen (forthcoming), Csapo (2010) 172–5, Moloney (2003) ch. 4 ('Philip II – Alexander III') and Revermann (1999–2000) 455–6.

39 A number of decrees survive that were proposed at the meeting of the Assembly in the Theatre of Dionysus (on which see pages 109–10 below) that followed the celebration of the Great Dionysia in 331; Csapo and Wilson (forthcoming) section II.3 418 suspect that tensions were running high at this Assembly precisely due to Alexander's Phoenician festival.

Dionysia as he (and the Athenians) had expected, Athenodorus was compelled to remain abroad in the retinue of Alexander. Nevertheless,

> ἐπεὶ δ' Ἀθηνόδωρος ὑπὸ τῶν Ἀθηναίων ζημιωθείς, ὅτι πρὸς τὸν ἀγῶνα τῶν Διονυσίων οὐκ ἀπήντησεν, ἠξίου γράψαι περὶ αὐτοῦ τὸν βασιλέα, τοῦτο μὲν οὐκ ἐποίησε, τὴν δὲ ζημίαν ἀπέστειλε παρ' ἑαυτοῦ. (Plut. *Alex*. 29.3)

> when Athenodorus was fined by the Athenians because he had not shown up for the contest of the Dionysia, he asked the king to write on his behalf; [Alexander] did not do this, but rather sent the penalty [to Athens] out of his own pocket.

As Plutarch has it Alexander not only adopted and adapted Athens' choregic practices, but also happily paid to lure away the actors so vital to the city's dramatic industry.[40]

Aeschines' speech *On the False Embassy* offers more reliable evidence for the existence, by at least the late 340s, of fines for actors who failed to fulfil their commitments. Aeschines claims that Demosthenes was so eager for the actor Aristodemus to be a member of the embassy to Philip that he arranged for envoys to go

> ἐπὶ τὰς πόλεις ἐν αἷς ἔδει τὸν Ἀριστόδημον ἀγωνίζεσθαι, οἵτινες ὑπὲρ αὐτοῦ παραιτήσονται τὰς ζημίας. (Aeschin. 2.19)

> to the *poleis* in which Aristodemus was committed to compete [i.e. in theatrical competitions], and ask that he be excused from the fines.

The very existence of fines for actors who failed to perform as they had promised implies that Athens was now more often facing this possibility of losing its theatre industry's personnel to other festivals in Greece and even abroad. As Peter Wilson and Eric Csapo have observed, 'Already by around 340 the city needed to take steps to secure the goodwill – and the very presence at their festivals – of leading actors.'[41] An 'anxiety around the failure to do so' seems evident from certain inscriptions. One key example is *IG* ii^3 423 (*IG* ii^2 429), in honour of an actor.

[40] Wilson (2000) 388 n. 110 observes that the fact that Athenodorus 'had missed the performance at the home of tragedy to appear at Alexander's own festival must have dealt a blow to Athenian pride'.

[41] Wilson and Csapo (2009) 52. On Athenian inscriptions honouring actors in this period see pages 110–11 below.

The inscription was found on the Acropolis and likely dates to the Lycurgan Era (sometime after 336/5).[42] On the basis of comparison with *IG* xiv 1102 (which reads μήτε ἀγῶνα παρ-αλιπών at line 14), Wilson and Csapo have supplemented lines 4–6 of *IG* ii³ 423 to formulate the praise of the unknown actor as follows:[43]

καὶ ουδέπ | [οτε παραλείπων τὸν] ἀγῶνα τὸν. [Δι | [ονυσίων –][44]

and for never having backed out of the competition of the Dionysia.

If the spirit of this supplement is correct, here we have an actor who is singled out with praise for never having reneged on his commitments to the Dionysia – unlike Athenodorus, who 'left by the wayside' the festival in favour of performing for the Macedonians, the enemy of Athens and the cause of the city's devastation at Chaeronea just seven years earlier.

A move on Alexander's part such as the one that Plutarch describes will have sent a powerful message to Athens, letting the city know that it now had to worry about losing top-billed actors, some of the greatest attractions of the Great Dionysia, to Alexander and the Macedonian court.[45] Money was no object for Alexander, and so in order to compete with him the Athenians needed to devise new ways of attracting and retaining the best theatrical talent. Perhaps to combat the Macedonians' efforts on this point, Athens was now also rewarding actors with the kinds of honorific decrees that we shall see later.[46] And even if we cannot be sure of the historicity

[42] Wilson and Csapo (2009) 52–3. In *IG* ii³ Lambert dates the inscription to *c.* 340–320.

[43] Wilhelm (1906) 221; cf. Ghiron-Bistagne (1976) 80–1.

[44] Wilson and Csapo (2009) 52 n. 18 find an earlier comparandum in *IG* ix.1 694, a pre-229 BC inscription from Corcyra which includes information about what happens to the actors' fees 'if someone should leave the *agon*' (ἤ λίπηι τις τὸν ἀγῶνα, line 27; cf. lines 135–6).

[45] Cf. Arist. *Pro.* F 44 on the people's willingness to spend money on watching actors at the Dionysia.

[46] Lambert (2008) 60 notes that in this period there was 'fierce competition to attract international "star" poets and actors, by financial or other incentives', suggesting that the 'prospect of honours' was one of the incentives upon which Athens relied: for a discussion of this dynamic see pages 105–8 below.

of Plutarch's anecdote, the very existence of Alexander's private theatre festivals indicates that Macedon, like Athens, saw tragedy as a critical part of its cultural life.[47] We also know that by the age of Lycurgus and Alexander stories were circulating about Euripides' alleged and self-imposed 'exile' in Macedon at the court of King Archelaus. Those stories belonged to a discourse that, in its fully fledged form, would cast Euripides as a *de facto* Macedonian poet.[48] In the late fifth century King Archelaus of Macedon had managed to woo to Pella some of Athens' best-loved tragic poets, and it may well have seemed to the Athenians that Alexander was now following suit by luring their favourite actors away from the Great Dionysia.[49]

In the light of Athenian drama's success outside of Athens and especially among the ruling elite of the city's most formidable and threatening enemy, Lycurgus' move to preserve the 'official' texts of classical tragedies in the city archive comes to look still more programmatic. Within Athens, the law – like the section of poetic quotations *Against Leocrates* – worked to forge an official connection between old tragedy and the state and to put that tragedy on a par with the Homeric poems. But though enforceable only within Attic boundaries, the law also clearly communicated that Athens alone was the source of, and so remained the ultimate authority for, the plays of Aeschylus, Sophocles and Euripides. These particular tragedians had all been Athenian citizens who were reared in Athens, earned their fame at Athenian dramatic festivals and bestowed their great gift upon Hellas in the Theatre of Dionysus. Like the rhetoric of his oration *Against Leocrates*, Lycurgus' *nomos* concerning the tragedians marked a clear pronouncement that the tragedies of the past had been the product of Athenian citizens

47 As Moloney (2003) has argued, Alexander's theatrical competitions (in Tyre, Susa, Ecbatana, etc.) 'were always symbolic displays of Macedonian power with each emphasising and reflecting a new developing order', as these festivals were typically held in celebration of major Macedonian victories and conquests (115).

48 Hanink (2008).

49 The tragic playwright Agathon also supposedly left Athens for Archelaus' court: Agathon's 'defection' to Macedon has long been suspected as the object of an oblique reference at Ar. *Ran.* 83–5 (where Agathon is said to have gone εἰς μακάρων εὐωχίαν, 85: see the Σ ad loc.); cf. also [Plut.] *Apophtheg. reg.* 177a.

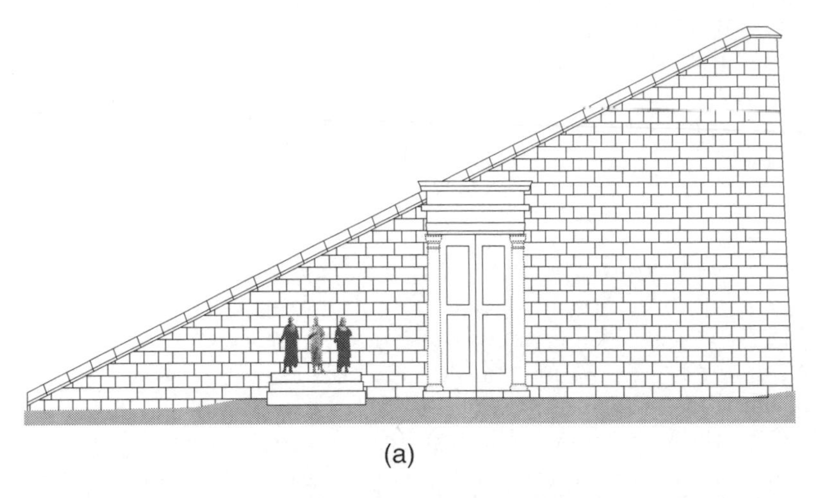

Figure 1a Reconstruction of the eastern *parodos* of the Theatre of Dionysus in Athens with the Lycurgan statue group of tragedians

and values, and so should remain permanently in the protective hands of the state. To Lycurgus' mind the Athenian polis had good historical precedents for creating a law that ensured a well-regulated afterlife for valuable poetry. Just as importantly, his law was a proclamation of the city's sole rights to these artefacts of its heritage.

The Lycurgan statues

The Lycurgan law concerning the tragic texts served to reassert and to proclaim tragedy's fundamental connection to (and possession by) its city of origin, and this message found its clearest expression in the portrait statues effectively commissioned by the law's first clause, 'that bronze statues of the poets Aeschylus, Sophocles and Euripides be erected'.[50] No part of any of the

[50] On the Lycurgan statues in the context of the Theatre of Dionysus see Papastamati-von Moock (forthcoming) and (2007) 312–24, Krumeich (2002), Knell (2000) 139–43 and Hintzen-Bohlen (1997) 39–41; on the statues in the context of the Lycurgan building programme see Hintzen-Bohlen (1997) 95, who also refers to Lycurgus' citation of Euripides in *Against Leocrates*. On 'public honorific portraits' and 'retrospective portraits' in fourth-century Athens see Dillon (2006) 102–6, who notes that 'The Athenians first begin regularly to honor historical figures of the city's illustrious past with retrospective portrait statues in the fourth century' (104).

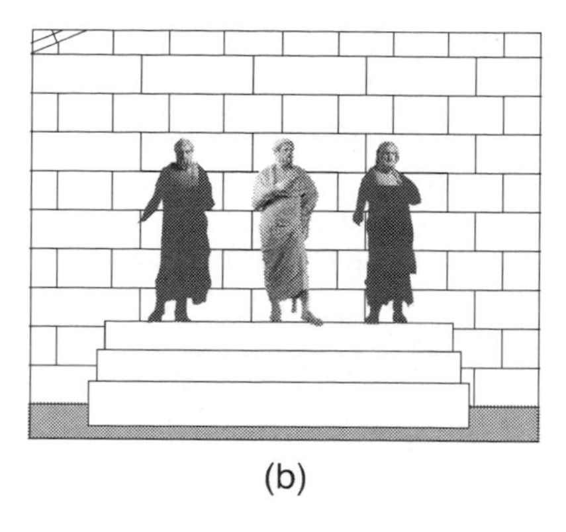

(b)

Figure 1b Reconstruction of the Lycurgan statue group of tragedians (detail of Fig. 1a)

original statues survives, yet a number of Roman pieces have been identified as copies or replicas deriving from the Lycurgan bronzes (see Figs. 2–4 at the end of this chapter). In the cases of Aeschylus and the 'Farnese' Euripides these replicas exist only in the form of herms, but the 'Lateran' Sophocles is a full bodied, larger than life portrait statue which stands at 2.04 metres high without a base.[51] When first completed, the statues of the tragedians were displayed at the eastern *parodos* of the Theatre of Dionysus, set on impressive view before the crowds of Athenian citizens, metics and visiting foreigners who thronged to the theatre for dramatic festivals (see Figs. 1A and 1B for a reconstruction of the sculptural group).[52] These statues long

[51] On the 'Lateran' Sophocles see Papastamati-von Moock (2007) 313–15 with bibliography at 314 n. 158. Dillon (2006) 198 and 207 expresses reservations about the identification of the Lateran Sophocles with the Lycurgan portrait. For the Roman statues identified as deriving from the Lycurgan types see esp. Hintzen-Bohlen (1997) 30–1; on portrait statues of Aeschylus, Sophocles and Euripides in general see Richter (1965) 121–40. Zanker (1995) 56 postulates, on the basis of comparison with Attic grave stelai, that Euripides was depicted in a seated position (as Menander later would be: see pages 236–41 below), though Papastamati-von Moock's (2007) reconstruction (on which my images are based) assumes that all of the tragedians were represented as standing.

[52] Paus. 1.21.2: εἰσὶ δὲ Ἀθηναίοις εἰκόνες ἐν τῷ θεάτρῳ καὶ τραγῳδίας καὶ κωμῳδίας ποιητῶν. Pausanias is not clear as to where exactly 'ἐν τῷ θεάτρῳ' these statues stood, though recent archaeological findings suggest that he will have seen the statues in a slightly different spot than their original installation. Works on the theatre during the Augustan period (which included the installation of a marble *propylon* at the

remained a fixture in the sanctuary's landscape, and Pausanias records seeing them (among those of many 'undistinguished' poets) during his travels through Attica in the second century BC, nearly half a millennium later.[53]

We have seen how Lycurgus' *Against Leocrates* contains a programmatic account of the statesman's view of the relationship between certain poetry and the state. Reflections that he shares elsewhere in the speech upon the Athenian use of portrait statues may also provide insight into his motivations for commissioning the sculptures of the tragedians. At the conclusion of his short encomium of those who died fighting at Chaeronea, Lycurgus informs the jurors that alone of all the Greeks the Athenians know how to honour good men (ἀγαθοὺς ἄνδρας):

> εὑρήσετε δὲ παρὰ μὲν τοῖς ἄλλοις ἐν ταῖς ἀγοραῖς ἀθλητὰς ἀνακειμένους, παρ' ὑμῖν δὲ στρατηγοὺς ἀγαθοὺς καὶ τοὺς τὸν τύραννον ἀποκτείναντας. καὶ τοιούτους μὲν ἄνδρας οὐδ' ἐξ ἁπάσης τῆς Ἑλλάδος ὀλίγους εὑρεῖν ῥᾴδιον, τοὺς δε τοὺς στεφανίτας ἀγῶνας νενικηκότας εὐπετῶς πολλαχόθεν ἔστι γεγονότας ἰδεῖν.[54] (Lycurg. 1.51)

> In the agoras of other cities you will find statues of athletes standing, but you instead have statues of accomplished generals and tyrant-killers, men such as you would not easily find if you searched all of Greece – whereas [statues of] men who have earned wreaths by winning contests are easy enough to see anywhere.

Lycurgus argues that very few men are worthy of statues, and that such honours ought to be reserved for men who had done some great service to the city.[55] Those benefactors are men

eastern *parodos*) likely moved and elevated the statues with respect to their Lycurgan position: Papastamati-von Moock (forthcoming) 47–52. On the original location of the statues see also Papastamati-von Moock (2007) 312–24, with a discussion of the statues as part of Lycurgus' classicising vision at 321–4.

[53] Paus. 1.21.2.

[54] This is a variation upon an established trope; e.g. Isocrates (4.1–2) laments that athletes have been thought worthy of such great prizes (μεγάλων δωρεῶν) when wisdom leads to so many more benefits (cf. Isoc. 15.250 and *Ep*. 8.5; see earlier also Xenophanes F B2 West and Eur. F 282, from the satyr play *Autolycus*).

[55] Lycurgus played an active role in adorning Athens, and particularly the Acropolis, with politically significant statues: Lambert (2010) 261 (with appendix no. 21) discusses Lycurgus' responsibility for the replacement of the Acropolis' golden *Nikai* statues that had been melted down for coins after the Peloponnesian War. Harris

who are *agathoi*, and here we should remember Lycurgus' careful characterisation of Euripides elsewhere in the speech as an *agathos poiētēs*. Like his undertaking to enshrine the texts of the tragedians in a city archive, his initiative to enshrine in bronze the images of the men themselves – a high honour reserved for the city's greatest benefactors – marked a bold move to enfold the legacies of the tragedians into Athenian 'civil religion'.[56] Their scripts now declared sacred, the bronze statue group of the great fifth-century tragedians served to elevate them to the status of civic heroes.

In order for Lycurgus' law to have been passed, the support of the democracy was also required. During this part of the fourth century Athens reserved portrait statues as an honour for individuals who were recognised by a vote of the citizens as having rendered exceptional service to the city. In his discussion of the process by which portrait statues were granted in classical Athens, Jeremy Tanner underscores that

> Honorific portraits were to be awarded only to benefactors of the demos. If a man manifested his good will (εὔνοια) to the demos by performing outstanding services, it was held to be just (δίκαιον) according to the norms of reciprocity which pervaded Greek social life that the demos should respond with a sign of their approval or esteem.[57]

Honorific portrait statues could only be granted by decree of the demos, and an elaborate set of rules was in place which restricted their form and placement within the cityscape.[58] Because of the public approbation tied to these statues, the

(1992) examines the evidence for a Lycurgan inventory of bronze statues on the Acropolis. One wonders how he felt about the installation of an honorific statue of the contemporary tragic playwright Astydamas in *c.* 340 in a position of high honour at the theatre: see pages 183–5 below.

[56] The foundational article on 'civil religion' is Bellah (1967), who focuses on the case of the United States and writes of civil religion (a term that he takes from Locke) as 'a collection of beliefs, symbols, and rituals with respect to sacred things and institutionalized in a collectivity' (8); cf. at 4: the 'public religious dimension is expressed in a set of beliefs, symbols, and rituals that I am calling American civil religion'. Within that 'religion', e.g., Abraham Lincoln is a martyr, Arlington National Cemetery (with its Tomb of the Unknown Soldier) is a sacred site and Memorial Day is a civil-religious holiday (411).

[57] Tanner (2006) 111. On honorific statues in the Hellenistic period see now Ma (2013).

[58] Tanner (2006) outlines the process and restrictions at 109–13. For a list of honorific statues granted to Athenians before 307 BC see Engen (2010) 165 (and see his 164–8

decision to award the honour was also sometimes controversial. Lycurgus himself once brought a suit alleging that Cephisodotus was guilty of a *graphē paranomōn* because he had moved that Demades be honoured with a portrait statue for his role in negotiating both with Philip II after the defeat at Chaeronea and with Alexander in 335.[59] We even have evidence that a similar suit was brought (as a charge of *graphē paranomōn* against Lycurgus himself?) in the case of the statues of the tragedians: the orator Philinus supposedly delivered a speech *Against the Statues of Sophocles and Euripides*. All that we know of Philinus' speech is that part of it contained an account of the invention of the theoric fund as an initiative of Eubulus, whose putative aim in setting up the fund was to ensure that all citizens could attend festivals and that no one would be denied admission for inability to pay.[60] But the title of the speech alone is tantalising on a number of grounds: why, for example, would there have been opposition to the tragedians' statues? And why is the name of Aeschylus missing from the title of the speech (was the decree of a statue for Aeschylus, a veteran of Marathon, less controversial)?[61] In any case, the title marks a rare piece of evidence that the Lycurgan theatre programme was not unanimously supported.

Philinus' suit was evidently unsuccessful, but the controversy is a further reminder of the honorific purpose of portrait statues in this period. It may, moreover, even illuminate Lycurgus' decision to introduce Euripides in *Against Leocrates* with such carefully marked honorific language. As a different *comparandum* for the Lycurgan statues, Christina Papastamati-von Moock – whose work has now revealed the original location of the Lycurgan statues – cites the Monument of Eponymous

on the honour of bronze statues more generally); Engen does not list the Lycurgan statues (or the earlier statue of the tragedian Astydamas, from *c.* 340) among these.

59 Lycurg. 14 fr. 14, see Tanner (2006) 111 and Lambert (2010) 230.

60 Harp. 154 Dindorf (s.v. Θεωρικά). As Csapo and Wilson (forthcoming) section 1.2 397 note, 'it is probably a safe inference that the potted history of the Theoric Fund was relevant to the issue of the statues because Lycurgus was proposing to use theoric money to fund them'; on Eubulus and the theoric fund see their section 1.1.

61 Pausanias thought that he saw an image of Aeschylus at Marathon in the painting of the Stoa Poikile: 1.21.2.

Heroes that once stood in the western part of the agora.[62] This monument, the archaeological remains of which likewise date to about 330 BC, consisted of bronze statues of the ten heroes whose names had been adopted by the Attic *phylai* as part of the Cleisthenic reforms in 508/7. No evidence survives of Lycurgus' own participation in arranging for the construction of this statue group, but in true Lycurgan spirit the Monument of the Eponymous Heroes also put on proud public display some of the city's greatest historical benefactors.[63]

Despite the apparent protestations of Philinus, the tragedians' statues were exhibited at the eastern *parodos* of the Theatre, the structure's principal public entrance. This installation will have occurred as part of the expansion and complete reconstruction of the theatre, a project which began under Eubulus and was not completed until after Lycurgus' death.[64] Perhaps, then, the statues of the three great tragedians were part of a holistic vision for the new stone structure. Later we shall look more closely at the material changes that were being made to the Theatre of Dionysus in this period as well as at other evidence for the symbolic significance that was attributed to the space.[65] Like the deposition of the tragic texts in the state archive, the display of the tragedians' statues served the ideological purpose of tying classical tragedy more closely to Athenian imperatives. Theatregoers were now prompted to associate the poets whose statues they saw with the physical space where, at some point during the festival, they will have seen a revival of an old tragedy (παλαιὸν δρᾶμα), often by one of these very

[62] Papastamati-von Moock (2007) 321–2 with bibliography. On this monument in the context of the Lycurgan building programme see Hintzen-Bohlen (1997) 92.

[63] Papastamati-von Moock (2007) 322: 'Das Monument der Phylenheroen im politischen Zentrum der Stadt einerseits und dasjenige der drei wichtigsten Vertreter des griechischen dramas in ihrem Handlungsumfeld andererseits brachten an traditionsbeladenen Treffpunkten der Stadt in symbolischer Form die ideologische Vision des lykurgischen Programms zum Ausdruck.' *Against Leocrates* also happens to have been delivered in the same year (330 BC) in which Alexander the Great, after his conquest of Persia, supposedly arranged for the bronze statues of Harmodius and Aristogeiton (cf. Plin. *HN* 34.17) to be returned to Athens: Arr. 3.16.8.

[64] See pages 95–103.

[65] Knell (2000) 142–5 discusses the double, i.e. cultural and political, function of the space in this period.

poets. The presence of the statues at the theatre thus only will have enhanced their power to inform and to remind visitors of classical tragedy's inseparability from the city's history. Since January 2012, an image of Papastamati-von Moock's reconstruction of the statue group has been displayed on the explanatory plaque at the archaeological site of the Theatre of Dionysus, at the eastern *parodos* where the statues once stood.[66] In antiquity, however, the statues in and of themselves constituted a kind of didactic display, which for centuries taught travellers to the sanctuary about the playwrights who first made Athens the capital of tragic drama.

If we are to regard the Lycurgan statues, like the new official copies of the tragic scripts, as 'material interventions in social memory',[67] we also need to consider what form those interventions took. In other words, the way in which the Lycurgan statues portrayed Aeschylus, Sophocles and Euripides should also shed light upon the symbolic messages that their images were crafted to send. On the basis of the putative Roman copies and replicas of the Lycurgan originals, it has been argued that the portraits depicted Aeschylus, Sophocles and Euripides above all as model citizens.[68] The statues' position at the entrance to the Theatre of Dionysus left no doubt as to the men's trade, but there is little about the Roman copies to suggest poetry or drama;[69] the full-body Lateran Sophocles, at least, does not portray the playwright as *holding* a scroll or mask.[70] A Neo-Attic relief of Euripides (the 'Apotheosis of Euripides') which may derive from the Lycurgan portrait offers some idea of the alternatives: on the relief Euripides, whose head is also of the

[66] Papastamati-von Moock (2007) figs. 7 and 8; I am grateful to her for confirming this date for me.

[67] Scodel (2007) 151.

[68] On the problems of Roman copies of statues for our knowledge of Greek originals see Ridgway (1984) and Zanker (1995) 9–14.

[69] Zanker (1995) 57, with extended discussion of these statues at 43–57; cf. Knell (2000) 141. We see a similar approach to poets as ideal citizens in the epitaph for Aeschylus (Aesch. T A1.11), which commemorates his ἀλκή in the Battle of Marathon (line 3) but mentions nothing of his craft as a tragedian.

[70] The basket of scrolls is likely a later addition. We find more 'poetic' depictions in the subjects of earlier statues, such as those of Homer, Anacreon and Pindar: see the discussions of Zanker (1995) 14–22, 70–1 and 28 respectively.

'Farnese' (i.e. putatively Lycurgan) type, is seated on a *klismos* chair. Already holding a scroll of poetry, he receives a tragic mask from a female personification of the stage (labelled Skene) while a cult statue of Dionysus presides to the right.[71]

Lycurgus' statues, on the other hand, were designed to show the men as wise and engaged citizens of the illustrious Athenian past. In his discussion of the statues Paul Zanker explicitly connects the physical representation of Euripides with the verbal picture that Lycurgus paints in his speech. Both of these images, Zanker argues, represent Euripides as an exceptional citizen above all else:

> It seems appropriate, in this context, that in his one preserved oration Lycurgus praises Euripides not so much as a poet, but rather as a patriot, because he presented to the citizenry the deeds of their fathers as *paradeigmata* 'so that through the sight and the contemplation of these a love of the fatherland would be awakened in them'.[72]

If analysis of the Lycurgan statues along these lines is accurate, the idea of the tragedians embodied in the Lycurgan statues would certainly have complemented the vision of Euripides that Lycurgus advocates in *Against Leocrates*, a vision that cast the poet as a great and wise citizen whose poetry was the product of his own civic values and a reflection of Athens. The inclusion of Euripides in the company of Aeschylus and Sophocles would also have served to present the three tragedians as a cohesive group who together represented the triumph of fifth-century tragedy.[73] Even if each playwright was portrayed in a slightly different citizen guise ('Sophocles as the citizen who is politically engagé, Aeschylus as the quiet citizen in the prime of life, and Euripides as the experienced and contemplative old

[71] Dillon (2006) 207. The relief, Istanbul Archaeological Museum inv. no. 1242, was found in Izmir and likely dates to the first century BC; see further Richter (1965) 133–40 and Zanker (1995) 52–3, who notes that on many points the relief evokes fourth-century style.

[72] Zanker (1995) 57; he is quoting Lycurg. 1.100: πρὸς ἃς ἀποβλέποντας καὶ θεωροῦντας συνεθίζεσθαι ταῖς ψυχαῖς τὸ τὴν πατρίδα φιλεῖν (the object of these participles is the deeds, πράξεις, of King Erechtheus and his family, deeds which Euripides so finely depicted).

[73] Papastamati-von Moock (2007) 323 describes the statues as representing the ideal of ἰσονομία (das Isonomieideal) of the classical polis.

man', according to Zanker's typology[74]), the display of the statues together at the theatre as a group will have given the impression that these three men together were responsible for one phenomenon, the Golden Age of Athenian Drama.

A tragic canon of Aeschylus, Sophocles and Euripides had already begun to show signs of emergence in 405 BC, at the premiere of Aristophanes' *Frogs*.[75] Yet the decision to put up statues of the three poets together signals a different idea of the group than had been staged in Aristophanes' play. In the *Frogs* the three tragedians bitterly disagreed even after death, but seventy-five years later the Lycurgan statue group presented these men as a harmoniously united front of Athenian citizens, whose individual contributions to the city together marked an exceptional Athenian achievement. By choosing to portray Euripides as an ideal citizen, the commissioner of these statues also effectively glossed over the line of discourse, active at least since the *Frogs*, which had questioned Euripides' civic and democratic loyalties. Lycurgus' temporal distance from the era of Athenian tragedy that had ended (for Aristophanes, at least) with the death of Sophocles was surely a critical condition for the radical reinvention of its most controversial poet: the tragedians' bronze portrait statues were erected at a time when the festival premieres of Euripides' plays were disappearing from the city's living memory. Precisely in the Lycurgan Era Athens' recollection of fifth-century tragedy was transforming from a true 'collective memory' into a primarily 'cultural' one, in that few people still living in this period will have had first-hand experience of the plays' premieres or of the tragedians themselves.[76] At this point of transition, citizens now had the opportunity to romanticise the tragic drama written during its fifth-century empire, and to incorporate that view into larger narratives of their city's past. The very survival of these statues

[74] Zanker (1995) 57; cf. Papastamati-von Moock (2007) 323.

[75] For Aristophanes' role in determining what would come to be the tragic canon see Rosen (2006) and Seidensticker (2002) 526.

[76] Chaniotis (2009) 255: 'The *collective memory* refers to what a community had jointly experienced, i.e., to events of the recent past; by contrast, the *cultural memory* of a community consists of events of the mythical or remote past, the knowledge of which is obscured by time.'

to this day – if only in Roman copies – is a strong testament to the endurance of Lycurgus' vision.[77]

Recalling poets, reinventing Euripides

Pseudo-Plutarch's brief account of Lycurgus' law is unsatisfactory in a number of ways, but when read alongside *Against Leocrates* it provides enormous insight into Lycurgan theatrical ideology. Together the speech and the law herald the politicised reinvention of Athens' 'tragic' past, and signal the advent of Athens' own conception of 'classical' tragedy. Lycurgus' exaltation of tragedy and tragedians seems to run most directly against ideas proposed earlier in the century by Plato's Socrates. Antiquity would remember Lycurgus as thoroughly familiar with Platonic philosophy: the short biography of Lycurgus that appears in the *Lives of the Ten Orators* reports that when Lycurgus first began to study philosophy he became a student (an ἀκροατής) of 'Plato the philosopher'.[78] In his Socratic dialogues, Plato had depicted Socrates as effectively passing a sentence of exile on the mimetic poets, and as singling out Euripides and Homer in particular for banishment from the ideal city. In the *Republic* Socrates' interlocutor Glaucon agrees with him that Euripides is the wisest of the poets and reflects that tyrants are wise to keep company with tragic poets because tragedians such as Euripides praise (ἐγκωμιάζει) the power of tyranny as something godlike (ὡς ἰσόθεον).[79] To this observation Socrates responds that tragic poets cannot be allowed into the utopia, precisely because they praise tyranny. Nevertheless, he continues,

> ἅτε σοφοὶ ὄντες οἱ τῆς τραγῳδίας ποιηταὶ συγγιγνώσκουσιν ἡμῖν τε καὶ ἐκείνοις ὅσοι ἡμῶν ἐγγὺς πολιτεύονται, ὅτι αὐτοὺς εἰς τὴν πολιτείαν οὐ παραδεξόμεθα ἅτε τυραννίδος ὑμνητάς. (Pl. *Resp.* 8.568b)

[77] See Papastamati-von Moock (forthcoming) 47–51 on the care that was taken to preserve and even to restore the statues during the Augustan period.

[78] [Plut.] *Vit. dec. or.* 841b; for other testimonia see Renehan (1970) 219.

[79] Pl. *Resp.* 8.568b. On this passage and its relationship with Plato's *Ion* see Hunter (2012) 99–100.

since they are wise, the poets of tragedy forgive us and those with governments similar to ours for not welcoming them into our state, seeing as they sing the praises of tyranny.

Later in the dialogue Socrates instructs Glaucon that, whenever he should come upon 'praisers' of Homer (Ὁμήρου ἐπαινεταί) who claim that the poet educated (πεπαίδευκεν) Hellas and is worthy of study as a model for life, he should politely concede that Homer is indeed the most poetic and first of the tragedians.[80] Yet Glaucon must also always remember that 'hymns to the gods and encomia of good men are the only poetry to be admitted into the city'.[81] Soon after giving Glaucon these instructions, Socrates goes on to issue a challenge to mimetic poetry to defend itself and to prove that it is worthy of a place in the ideal society:

ὅμως δὲ εἰρήσθω ὅτι ἡμεῖς γε, εἴ τινα ἔχοι λόγον εἰπεῖν ἡ πρὸς ἡδονὴν ποιητικὴ καὶ ἡ μίμησις, ὡς χρὴ αὐτὴν εἶναι ἐν πόλει εὐνομουμένῃ, ἄσμενοι ἂν καταδεχοίμεθα, ὡς σύνισμέν γε ἡμῖν αὐτοῖς κηλουμένοις ὑπ' αὐτῆς· (*Resp.* 10.607c)

but let it be said that, if poetry that is mimetic and meant for pleasure had some good reason for claiming that it ought to exist in a well-governed city, we should happily receive her back, since we admit that we ourselves are enchanted by her.

This challenge is one which is repeated in Plato's final work, the *Laws*.[82] In the *Laws* the Athenian wonders how exactly he might answer the tragedians if they should come begging admittance to the city.[83] He suggests that his fellow hypothetical lawmakers should issue those poets with this response:

[80] For the connotations of 'praise' and 'praiser' in this context see pages 44–5.

[81] Pl. *Resp.* 10.607a: ὅσον μόνον ὕμνους θεοῖς καὶ ἐγκώμια τοῖς ἀγαθοῖς ποιήσεως παραδεκτέον εἰς πόλιν.

[82] Cf. Asmis (1992) 338. See La Spina (1980–1) 33–7 and Renehan (1970) on the relationship between Lycurgus' rhetoric in *Against Leocrates* and certain ideas put forth in Plato's *Laws*.

[83] Pl. *Leg.* 7.817a. On the view of poetry in the *Laws* see e.g. Else (1986) 61–4, Ferrari (1989) 104–9; on tragedy (and passage 817b–d) see Morrow (1960) 374–7, Laks (2010) and Murray (2013). In the *Laws* Tyrtaeus, who is also cited by Lycurgus as an exemplary poet capable of improving the citizens, comes under attack (as Euripides and Homer do) by the Athenian (9.858e, where the poets are compared unfavourably with lawmakers such as Lycurgus of Sparta and Solon).

ἡμεῖς ἐσμὲν τραγῳδίας αὐτοὶ ποιηταὶ κατὰ δύναμιν ὅτι καλλίστης ἅμα καὶ ἀρίστης· πᾶσα οὖν ἡμῖν ἡ πολιτεία συνέστηκε μίμησις τοῦ καλλίστου καὶ ἀρίστου βίου, ὃ δή φαμεν ἡμεῖς γε ὄντως εἶναι τραγῳδίαν τὴν ἀληθεστάτην. ποιηταὶ μὲν οὖν ὑμεῖς, ποιηταὶ δὲ καὶ ἡμεῖς ἐσμὲν τῶν αὐτῶν, ὑμῖν ἀντίτεχνοί τε καὶ ἀνταγωνισταὶ τοῦ καλλίστου δράματος, ὃ δὴ νόμος ἀληθὴς μόνος ἀποτελεῖν πέφυκεν, ὡς ἡ παρ' ἡμῶν ἐστιν ἐλπίς· (Pl. *Leg.* 7.817b–c)

we [i.e. the lawmakers] are ourselves tragic poets, and thus our entire constitution is built as a mimesis of the most beautiful and best life, which we say is really the truest tragedy. You may be poets, but we too are poets of the same things, your rivals and competitors in the finest drama, one which true law alone is able to complete – as is our hope.

Having thus explained that the lawmakers are poets of the truest (and so the finest) tragedy, the Athenian concludes the argument with a reformulation of the challenge that Socrates had put forth in the *Republic*:

νῦν οὖν, ὦ παῖδες μαλακῶν Μουσῶν ἔκγονοι, ἐπιδείξαντες τοῖς ἄρχουσι πρῶτον τὰς ὑμετέρας παρὰ τὰς ἡμετέρας ᾠδάς, ἂν μὲν τὰ αὐτά γε ἢ καὶ βελτίω τὰ παρ' ὑμῶν φαίνηται λεγόμενα, δώσομεν ὑμῖν χορόν, εἰ δὲ μή, ὦ φίλοι, οὐκ ἄν ποτε δυναίμεθα. (Pl. *Leg.* 7.817d)

And so now, O offspring of the delicate Muses, when you have displayed to the rulers first your songs side by side with our songs, if yours should seem the same as ours or better we shall give you a chorus, but if not, o friends, we shall never be able to do so.

Plato is thought to have died in 347 BC, before he was able to complete the *Laws*.[84] Within two decades, Lycurgus would come to the defence of poetry – and of a tragedian – in his *Against Leocrates*.[85] In the speech Lycurgus implies that the same 'Platonic' qualification of the good poet (namely that he is also a good man) does obtain. Nevertheless, he uses that logic to draw conclusions that are different from those of the Platonic Socrates.[86] In explaining how the verses of Euripides, Homer

[84] D.L. 3.37; Stalley (1983) 2–4 summarises the problem of dating the *Laws*.

[85] For the answer to the Socratic challenge that Aristotle seems to offer (an answer of a very different nature than that of his contemporary Lycurgus) see esp. Halliwell (1984) 49. In the *Poetics* Aristotle explicitly (though somewhat enigmatically) states that 'correctness' is not the same thing in public life and in poetry, nor is it the same thing in poetry and in any other art (ὀρθότης οὐχ ἡ αὐτὴ ἐστὶν τῆς πολιτικῆς καὶ τῆς ποιητικῆς οὐδὲ ἄλλης τέχνης καὶ ποιητικῆς: *Po.* 1460b 13–15).

[86] Renehan (1970) argues that Lycurgus knew Plato's *Laws*; for prudent reservations about a direct connection between the texts see Hunter (2012) 28.

and Tyrtaeus provide fine examples of bravery and patriotism, he suggests that these verses could only have been authored by men who were also fine and devoted citizens themselves. Lycurgus is most explicit in reprising Socrates' comparison of poets and lawmakers when he introduces his quotation from Homer. As part of that introduction, he explains that earlier generations were right to pass the law that the rhapsodes recite his poetry at the Panathenaea, because (mimetic) poetry is able to teach things that the laws cannot because of their very nature:

οἱ μὲν γὰρ νόμοι διὰ τὴν συντομίαν οὐ διδάσκουσιν, ἀλλ' ἐπιτάττουσιν ἃ δεῖ ποιεῖν, οἱ δὲ ποιηταὶ μιμούμενοι τὸν ἀνθρώπινον βίον, τὰ κάλλιστα τῶν ἔργων ἐκλεξάμενοι, μετὰ λόγου καὶ ἀποδείξεως τοὺς ἀνθρώπους συμπείθουσιν. (Lycurg. 1.102)

For the laws, because of their brevity, do not teach, but rather order what is to be done, but the poets, by representing human life and picking out the finest of deeds, persuade people with reason and examples.

One of the greatest tasks of a poet, then, is to select (ἐκλέγω) as the objects of their *mimesis* the finest human deeds (τὰ κάλλιστα τῶν ἔργων) – a task at which Euripides, too, was overwhelmingly successful, because he chose (προείλετο) to dramatise the story of Erechtheus' sacrifice.[87]

In using *Against Leocrates* as a platform for suggesting that the poets are complements to, rather than rivals of, the lawmakers, Lycurgus effectively makes an answer on behalf of (certain) poets to the Socratic challenge. For Lycurgus, poets such as Euripides, Homer and Tyrtaeus not only show themselves of equal importance to lawmakers when their works are laid side by side, but they even contribute to the 'poetry' of the state's *politeia* in a way that the lawmakers, who are necessarily restricted by the brevity of their laws, cannot. Euripides was no encomiast of tyrants, nor was he a corrupter of the demos that Aristophanes' 'Aeschylus' had made him out to be in the *Frogs*.[88] To the contrary, he was a poet whose

[87] Lycurg. 1.100. Platos' *Laws* also includes reflections on the 'incompleteness' of laws (esp. at 4.721e): see Renehan (1970) 222–3, who draws a parallel between the need for poetry that Lycurgus expresses and the need for preludes (προοίμια) to the laws that the Athenian claims (at e.g. 4.722c–e).

[88] See esp. Ar. *Ran.* 1010–12, but also *passim* throughout the *agon*.

characters offered *paradeigmata* of noble behaviour to the citizens of Athens. Lycurgus' articulation of this view of poetry might therefore be read metaphorically as a 'recall' of Euripides (and Homer) from the ideological exile that Socrates had imposed upon them in the dialogues. For Plato's Socrates, the tragic poets were by their very nature encomiasts of tyrants. For Lycurgus, citizens needed to have regular contact with certain tragic poetry in order to receive its wisdom and to instil its fine civic values in their hearts.

Within the framework of the Lycurgan cultural programme Euripides becomes the democratic poet *par excellence*. Lycurgus' effort to portray Euripides as an ideal Athenian citizen was thus even more necessary than it first seems. Euripides' reputation as an 'encomiast of tyrants' must have been partially owed to his alleged association with Macedon's King Archelaus.[89] Frustrated with the poor reception that he received in Athens, Euripides is said to have lived out the last years of his life in Macedon at Archelaus' court. Our earliest evidence for the tradition that links Euripides with tyranny is the *Frogs*, where Dionysus makes an uneasy allusion to the tension between Euripidean tragedy and democracy. When 'Euripides' defends his works by claiming that he wrote parts for women and slaves in the spirit of democracy (δημοκρατικὸν γὰρ αὔτ' ἔδρων, 951), Dionysus hints that the subject of Euripides' relationship with the democracy is still a sore one:

> Τοῦτο μὲν ἔασον, ὦ τᾶν.
> Οὐ σοὶ γάρ ἐστι περίπατος κάλλιστα περί γε τούτου.
> (Ar. *Ran*. 952–3)
>
> Let that one go, my friend,
> As your relationship with that topic isn't the best.

For Lycurgus to celebrate Euripides as a paradigm of Athenian patriotism and citizenship, it was especially important that he reinvent the tragedian's reputation for tyrannical sympathies. The Lycurgan Era was a period in which sensitivities to the very prospect of tyranny were running particularly high. Shortly

[89] For the tradition and the testimonia see Hanink (2008) 118–26.

after the city's defeat at Chaeronea, the Athenian *nomothetai* passed a 'law against tyranny' that guaranteed immunity for anyone who killed people who had been plotting to overthrow the democracy and establish tyranny in the city. Two copies of that law were inscribed beneath reliefs of the personified Demokratia crowning the demos, and these stelai were installed at the entrances to both the Ekklesia and the Bouleuterion.[90] Part of Lycurgus' agenda was for Euripides to be remembered as an embodiment of Athenian democratic values, but first Euripides needed the rehabilitation of a positive civic narrative. That narrative is one which Lycurgus masterfully wove into *Against Leocrates*, and which he publicised by means of his law.

Lycurgus' interest in his city's theatrical heritage therefore found expression in his complementary rhetoric and legislation. His highly programmatic presentation of the theatrical past in both of these areas is illuminating of how, during this period, certain members of the Athenian political elite were seeking to entwine the achievements of the theatre with those of the city. In more than one way Lycurgus' constructions of theatre history worked to bring the once controversial Euripides into a new model of 'classical tragedy' and a rubric of three great tragedians. This new model largely glossed over any differences in the poets' personalities and styles, casting them uniformly as ideal Athenian citizens. For Lycurgus, passages of Euripidean poetry such as Praxithea's speech in *Erechtheus* serve as exhortations (much like *epitaphioi logoi*) for citizens to love their country, to be willing to die for it and to celebrate and honour those who had. For this very reason, Lycurgus implies in *Against Leocrates*, Euripides is worthy of the same kinds of honours as those which the city bestowed upon its other benefactors. And in successfully proposing that honorific statues of the three tragedians be set up in the city, Lycurgus gave material expression to that idea.

[90] *IG* ii³ 320, 387/6 BC; originally published by Meritt (1952) 355–9. For more on the inscription see Harding (1985) no. 101.

2 Scripts and statues, or a law of Lycurgus' own

Between the Battle of Chaeronea in 338 and Lycurgus' delivery of *Against Leocrates* in 330 BC, the Macedonians had expanded their empire and also intensified their appropriation of Athenian tragedy by incorporating tragic competitions into the displays of power which marked their victory celebrations.[91] In an era in which actors had more power than playwrights (or so Aristotle laments),[92] Athens' greatest enemy progressed from robbing Athens of its playwrights to luring away the city's most popular actors. An aim of reminding the world of the true home of tragedy – and particularly of Euripides – lay just below the surface both of Lycurgus' law and of his long apology for poetry in *Against Leocrates*. The principal narrative of that speech, we should remember, centres on the defeat at Chaeronea, and as part of that narrative Lycurgus offers his own encomium of the Athenians who died in the battle fighting for the city's freedom from Macedon. In discussing Euripidean poetry Lycurgus implicitly but firmly dispels any notion that Euripides was a friend of tyranny, or was anything but a model Athenian citizen. Lycurgan efforts at 'public relations' on behalf of Euripides, and the attendant transformation of Euripides' public image, lie at the very heart of classical tragedy's emergence in these years as a single and enduring idea.

[91] See n. 38 above. [92] Arist. *Rhet.* 2.1403b21.

Figure 2 Marble portrait statue of Sophocles (the 'Lateran' Sophocles). Putative Roman copy of the 'Lycurgan' original (*c.* 330 BC)

Figure 3 Marble herm of Aeschylus. Putative Roman copy of the 'Lycurgan' original (*c.* 330 BC)

Figure 4 Marble herm of Euripides. Putative Roman copy of the 'Lycurgan' original (*c.* 330 BC)

CHAPTER 3

SITE OF CHANGE, SITE OF MEMORY: THE 'LYCURGAN' THEATRE OF DIONYSUS

In *Against Leocrates* Lycurgus took to the *bēma* and encouraged his fellow citizens to seek patriotic inspiration by looking into certain poetry, and in a similar spirit his legislation invited the city's theatregoers to contemplate statues of great tragic poets. Yet the installation of the tragedians' statues hardly signalled stagnation in Athens' contemporary theatrical life. The Theatre of Dionysus continued to play host to festivals and political assemblies, and its stage showcased a number of new plays every year. A variety of evidence from the Lycurgan Era (and from the second half of the fourth century more generally) also attests to major changes that Greece's premiere theatre was undergoing in terms of its physical structure and management. These changes served to monumentalise the structure both as an historic site and as a grander venue for new production. Foremost among them was the total reconstruction of the Theatre of Dionysus that took place over the course of roughly three decades: Lycurgus' own generation was among the first to attend dramatic festivals in the new and enlarged space. Literary evidence also attests to intense contemporary debates about the significance of the theatre structure and of the Great Dionysia that it hosted. These debates foreground the historic importance of the building and festival but also highlight, as do certain inscriptions from this period, how both were critical to the city on political and economic, and not only cultural, grounds.

The new stone theatre was constructed amidst difficult financial and economic circumstances. In 355 BC, the so-called Second Athenian Empire (or Confederacy) became defunct when Athens conceded independence to the confederate allies that had revolted: Chios, Rhodes, Cos and Byzantium.[1] After this conflict, now known as the Social War, Athens suffered from a general exhaustion of financial resources.[2] Eubulus and his contemporaries were faced with the unenviable task of setting the city back on a path to financial stability and growth, and as part of their efforts to strengthen the economy they recognised the massive potential of the city's dramatic industry.[3] Thus despite the significant monetary challenges, in about 350 BC work began in earnest on the construction of a grand and permanent stone Theatre of Dionysus – the so-called 'Lycurgan' theatre. We now know that the project neither began nor was finished during Lycurgus' tenure as overseer of state finances.[4] Nevertheless, epigraphic evidence indicates that his own efforts to advance the project – and to ensure that the finished product was an elegant monument to Athenian culture – went far beyond his legislation calling for the tragedians' statues. Lycurgus (and his descendants) worked hard and successfully to bind his name to the larger enterprise, the origins of which belonged to the Athens of Pericles.[5]

One of the most prominent ways in which Lycurgus and others encouraged work on the theatre was through the city's system of granting honours. An important strategy was the active encouragement of *epidoseis*, or voluntary gifts to the city. One such category consisted in private contributions made to support the Lycurgan building programme, as part of which work on the Theatre of Dionysus continued apace in the 330s and

[1] The order given at D.S. 16.21–2. The Confederacy was not officially abolished until 338, with the Peace of Demades: Paus. 1.25.3.

[2] Demosthenes (10.37) claims that after the Social War Athenian yearly revenues were just 130 talents. He also discusses the insufficiency of taxes alone to support Athenian expenditures (24.96–7); on the demands placed on statesmen for financing the city see Arist. *Pol.* 1.1259a and *Rhet.* 1359b. Xenophon's pamphlet the *Poroi* (*On Revenue*, likely from the 350s) represents the best surviving compendium of 'fundraising' ideas for Athens.

[3] For work accomplished during Eubulus' administration in this respect see Csapo and Wilson (forthcoming) section I.

[4] See Papastamati-von Moock (forthcoming).

[5] Cf. Csapo and Wilson (forthcoming) section II.1. On Lycurgus' efforts to stylise himself as the 'new Pericles' see esp. Hintzen-Bohlen (1997) 94–5 and Mossé (1989) 25; see also Wirth (1997) for a comparison of the leaders' different regimes.

320s. To finance the building programme, the city urged Athenians and foreigners alike to donate money and resources in exchange for the prospect of public honours.[6] Compared to the value of the benefactions themselves, these honours were of relatively low cost to the city – in some cases the burden on Athens amounted to little more than the price of the awarded crown.[7] But even if the financial costs of bestowing certain honours were relatively low, the Athenians were careful to emphasise that the intrinsic value of their honorific decrees was immeasurably high.[8] Would-be benefactors needed to be persuaded that their donations were worthwhile 'investments' that promised honorific returns of great value. Lycurgus' remarks about Euripides in *Against Leocrates*, his commissioning of the statues of the tragedians and his legislation of official state copies of the tragic texts could only have helped to convince prospective donors of the prestige of the city's theatre and dramatic heritage.

Discourses about the theatre in the Lycurgan Era are closely bound up with the Athenian 'economy of esteem' (or 'economy of honour'),[9] which is often alluded to, invoked and debated in the period's literary and epigraphic sources.[10] During this era the city recognised that an effective way of securing resources, particularly from abroad, was by trading for them with the currency of honours, and the theatre industry was a profitable sector of that trade. The clear importance of honours in the epigraphic record for the Theatre of Dionysus also occasions a closer look at the literary sources for the controversy surrounding Demosthenes' crown, namely Aeschines

[6] Rhodes (2005) 330–1 and 341. On *epidoseis* in this period see also Austin (1994) 549–50.

[7] That is, unless the honours included exemptions from liturgies (*ateliai*): cf. *Against Leptines* (Dem. 20), a response to the proposal by Leptines to eliminate *ateliai*.

[8] For the most expansive elaboration upon this logic see Demosthenes' speech *Against Leptines* (Dem. 20); for a concise ancient account of the Athenian honour system see Arist. *Rhet.* 1361a.

[9] The term used by Brennan and Pettit (2001 and 2004), who argue that, although esteem and honour cannot be bought and sold, these 'non-tradable goods' are still allocated within societies according to specific determinants.

[10] On the symbolic economy of honours in classical Athens see esp. Keim (2011) and Engen (2010).

and Demosthenes' speeches of 330 BC. In these orations, the setting of the proposed crowning for Demosthenes – at the Great Dionysia, in the Theatre of Dionysus – lies at the heart of the conflict. Aeschines and Demosthenes craft their opposing arguments on the basis of shared assumptions about the prestige associated with public honours and the premiere status of the theatre as a venue for crownings. For Aeschines in particular, that status is determined largely by the theatre's venerable past – an idealised past that in this era was also embodied in the statues of the fifth-century tragedians. It is thus an entire constellation of speeches, inscriptions and archaeological remains that illuminates the central importance of the Theatre of Dionysus in this period, an exceptional case study in the literary evidence's power to enhance our understanding of the material record for the Lycurgan programme.

The 'Lycurgan' theatre

During Lycurgus' tenure as administrator of the state treasury, significant pools of financial and human resources were levied and channelled into the cultural life and 'ornamentation' of Athens.[11] Many of these resources were directed towards the augmentation of the city's festal pomp and splendour, as well as to the completion of the most ambitious building programme since the Age of Pericles.[12] Despite Athens' weakened political and economic situation in the mid-fourth century, and particularly in the wake of Chaeronea, the city around the court where Lycurgus, Aeschines and Demosthenes each pleaded their cases in 330 must on many days have resounded with the noise of construction.

The completion of a permanent stone theatre in the sanctuary of Dionysus was one of the most important projects of the mid-fourth century building programme. Before the stone structure was constructed, no permanent theatre structure had

[11] Wilson (2000) 23; Polacco (1990) 174; cf. Lambert (2010).

[12] For an overview see Knell (2000) 15–16; Knell and Hintzen-Bohlen (1997) *passim* contains much information about the individual architectural projects.

stood on the grounds of the sanctuary.[13] Recent work conducted by the Greek Archaeological Service has now radically enhanced our understanding of the architecture and chronology of the late classical, 'Lycurgan', stone theatre. These findings indicate that the transformation was conceptualised and even begun in the later fifth century, as part of Pericles' own building programme. The initial works came to a halt in their early stages, likely due to the drain put on city funds by the Peloponnesian War.[14] Some half century later, Eubulus' financial stewardship of the city saw a general injection of capital into building and beautification projects.[15] Serious building on the theatre also resumed during his administration, in about 350. At roughly the same time that work began again, the victory records of the Great Dionysia (the *Fasti*) were inscribed on white marble and erected somewhere on the Acropolis.[16] The monument that hosted the inscription does not survive, but the inscription's fragments indicate that the records alone spanned an area nearly 9 feet wide and 6 feet tall.[17] The 340s thus witnessed a striking combination of efforts to expand, remodel and embellish the theatre as well as to put the history of that

[13] On fifth-century stone theatres elsewhere in the demes and outside Attica see Moretti (1999–2000) 377–8. Moretti also provides a useful general overview of the fifth-century Theatre of Dionysus.

[14] Papastamati-von Moock (forthcoming) 21; for a more preliminary account see Goette (2007a).

[15] On Eubulus and the theoric fund, likely an important source for the funding of the theatre reconstruction, see most recently Csapo and Wilson (forthcoming) section 1.1; on fifth-century precedents for theoric distributions see Roselli (2009). See Harris (1996) for a reconstruction of Demosthenes' view of the fund and its purposes and management. For opposition to Eubulus' building programme see Dem. 3.21–9 and 13.30 and Allen (2013) 109–10. One thinks of the parallel of opposition to Franklin Delano Roosevelt's Works Progress Administration (the WPA, a New Deal agency) and its building projects during the American Great Depression. The WPA was created by an order of the President in 1935, and its projects included the renovation of one of the United States' first playhouses, the 1736 Dock Street Theatre in Charleston, South Carolina.

[16] Between 347/6 and 343/2 BC: Millis and Olson (2012) 5; see their fig. 1 at 26 for a visual reconstruction of the inscribed portion of the monument. Of the monument's original form Millis (forthcoming) 434 writes: '*IG* ii^{2} 2318 must have been inscribed on the wall of a building or some sort of retaining wall; what this structure was and where precisely it stood on the Acropolis remain unknown.'

[17] 2.7 m by 1.8 m: see Millis (forthcoming) 434. Sickinger (1999) 43 suggests that the inscription may have been designed, at least in part, with an eye to encouraging choregic participation and expenditure.

theatre on display. The capstone of these attempts would come some ten or fifteen years later, when the statues of the three great fifth-century tragedians were set up to adorn the building's eastern *parodos*.

The construction of a stone theatre marked a watershed moment in the evolution both of theatre architecture and of Athens' theatre industry. In the fifth century and the first half of the fourth, during Athenian drama's 'golden age', the theatre space was rectangular in shape and most of the seating was temporary and made of wood.[18] Eric Csapo has made a thorough case as to how this 'seasonal' theatre was managed: prior to the installation of permanent stone seating in the *cavea*, the benches in the Theatre of Dionysus were rebuilt and dismantled for each festival season, as was the case at other early theatres both in Attica and elsewhere in Greece.[19] The job of handling the benches was contracted out by the city to individuals called *theatrones* or *theatropolai*.[20] These positions are not epigraphically attested for the Theatre of Dionysus, but Csapo shows how literary sources and epigraphic parallels provide good evidence that in Athens, too, these were 'figures absolutely central to theatre management and finance'.[21] In return for providing the labour of laying and removing the benches, the contracted lessees had 'the right to collect admission charges, thereby recovering the cost of the lease and chalking up what probably amounted to a handsome profit'.[22]

We have evidence that by 346 a building overseer (*arkhitektōn*) was organising the theatre's seats of honour (the

[18] On new evidence for the wooden seating – *ikria* – see Papastamati-von Moock (forthcoming) 20 with n. 18 and fig. 1.4; cf. Csapo (2007) 98 and Lech (2009).

[19] The theatres at Delphi and Delos seem to represent similar cases: Csapo (2007) 103–4. For evidence relating to the oldest known deme theatres see Paga (2010) 355: the first theatre at Thorikos (late fifth or early fourth century), e.g., 'consisted of a small rectilinear orchestra . . . The natural slope of the hill was most likely used for seating at the time; there are no permanent remains to indicate a cavea during this period, although ephemeral architecture, such as wooden *ikria*, or benches, is possible'.

[20] Csapo (2007) 96–7; cf. 88–9. The term *theatropolēs* is attested once, in a quotation from Aristophanes' lost *Phoenissae* (*PCG* F 575, preserved ap. Pollux 7.199); *theatrones* are attested twice (Theophr. *Char*. 30.6; *P.Oxy.* 4502 lines 39–41); cf. *DFA*² 266.

[21] Csapo (2007) 87.

[22] Csapo (2007) 113.

prohedra) as well as managing the 'general admission' seats, which were sold at the price of two obols per day of performances – roughly the daily wage of an Athenian labourer.[23] These earliest attestations of the *arkhitektōn* coincide nicely with the new archaeological evidence that assigns the beginning of renewed construction of the stone theatre to about 350 BC, and therefore confirm that the new structure inspired new forms of management. And though expensive to build, the stone theatre must have been well worth the investment. A rough calculation that assumes the same 'day rate' seating cost of two obols, a new seating capacity of 16,000 and a five-day festival puts the potential revenue from ticket sales at 160,000 obols, or nearly four and a half talents.[24] With the private *theatrones* out of the picture, this money was retained by the city. Thanks, moreover, to the revenue that the theatre now had the potential to generate, the cost of the entire project could have been recovered in under a decade.[25]

This complete overhaul of the Theatre of Dionysus – an expensive, difficult and multi-decade undertaking – was of enormous significance for both the city and the theatre.[26] The

[23] Csapo (2007) 112; on *arkhitektones* see 108–13: these officials appear to have functioned 'as a combination of the Chairman of the Public Works Dept. and Building Inspector' (108). Cf. also Csapo and Wilson (forthcoming) section I.2. Demosthenes responds to Aeschines' criticism of his granting *prohedria* to the Macedonian embassy of 346 (Aeschin. 3.28) by incredulously asking whether he should have ordered the *arkhitektōn* not to give the ambassadors good seats (θέαν μὴ κατανεῖμαι τὸν ἀρχιτέκτον' αὐτοῖς κελεῦσαι): had Demosthenes not looked after these men, they would have had to watch from the 'two-obol' seats (ἀλλ' ἐν τοῖν δυοῖν ὀβολοῖν ἐθεώρουν ἄν), that is, the 'general admission' seats (Dem. 18.28). Cf. also *IG* ii² 512 (Acropolis, end of the fourth century BC): a certain Paseas is awarded *prohedria*, which is to be arranged for by the *arkhitektōn*: τὸν δὲ ἀρχιτέκτ[ονα κα]- | [τανέμειν τόπον ε]ἰς θέαν (lines 7–8).

[24] Wilson (2008) 93.

[25] Wilson (2008) 93–4. Problematic here are the practicalities of the 'theoric fund' (the θεωρικόν) in this period, whose board of directors enjoyed less power in the Lycurgan Era than in the past thanks at least in part to the limits put on the board's powers by Hegemon in 338 (Aeschin. 3.25). On the fund in the Lycurgan Era see Csapo and Wilson (forthcoming) section II.1 and Faraguna (1992) 187–94; 208–9.

[26] Wilson (2008) 93 calls this a 'magnificent petrification'; cf. Pickard-Cambridge (1946) 141, Csapo (2007) 97 and Knell (2000) 126. Papastamati-von Moock (forthcoming) 34 n. 79 calculates that 6,800 tonnes of Piraeus limestone were needed for the project (the Great Pyramid at Giza required between 5.75 and 6 million tonnes); her article also offers an idea of the architectural and technical complexities of the construction.

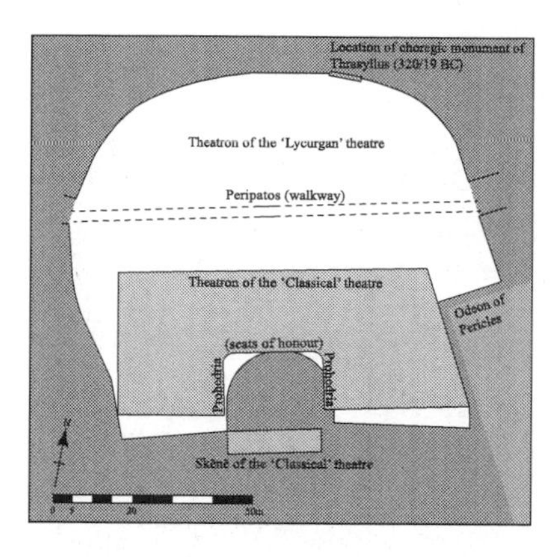

Figure 5 Plan of the 'Lycurgan' Theatre of Dionysus in Athens

restructuring made for a grander and more elegant performance space, but it also greatly expanded the theatre's seating capacity. This increase, surely made with one eye to the theatre's high status as a tourist destination, was due in part to the new building's rounded shape (see Fig. 5).[27] The transformation of the theatre's shape from rectangular to round was also as much of an innovation as the change in its material structure from wood to stone. A curved and so more 'inward facing' design for the *theatron* brought the structure into closer architectural alignment with the banks of seating found in other city meeting places, such as the Tholos, Bouleuterion, Odeon and Pnyx.[28] The change in the shape of the orchestra even seems to have affected choral vocabulary, and perhaps choreography with it: the word *orkhestra* is used of theatrical dancing space only after the emergence of round spaces in theatres during the fourth century.[29]

[27] Pickard-Cambridge's estimate of a new 14,000–17,000 person capacity is still widely accepted: *DFA*² 263. Cf. Csapo (2007) 98–9. Pickard-Cambridge writes at *DFA*² 263 that 'there can never have been 30,000 spectators [as Plato estimates at *Symp.* 175e], and it is best to assume that Plato is influenced by the frequent use of 30,000 as a conventional figure for the population of Athens'.

[28] Cf. Ober (2008) 199–205; a discussion of 'architecture and intervisibility' in Athens in the light of Chwe's (2001) work on inward-facing public spaces.

[29] Bosher (2008–9). The Theatre of Dionysus was also the first theatre in Attica to move to a semi-circular orchestra shape. In the case of rural Attica, for example,

The new archaeological findings reveal that this phase of work on the theatre spanned an entire generation: the building was not completed until 320/19, roughly thirty years after its renovation had recommenced.[30] Already by 340, though, the theatre's new orchestra was complete, and 'construction of the *theatron* along with the retaining walls of the *parodoi* must have been at an advanced stage.'[31] The inscribed victory records for the years 342/1 to 340/39 survive,[32] and show no sign of major disruption to the celebrations of the Great Dionysia. Spectators at the festivals in one or more of those years were likely taking their seats on the banks of the new stone structure. Traditionally, the stone Theatre of Dionysus has been known as the 'Lycurgan' theatre. But if works neither began nor were completed during Lycurgus' administration, what role did he actually play in its construction, and why has he for so long enjoyed sole credit for the project?

The attribution to Lycurgus of the late classical theatre building dates to not long after his death, and ancient sources emphasise Lycurgus' role as the structure's 'completer'. The theatre regularly appears in catalogues of the projects of Lycurgus' own building programme.[33] Pseudo-Plutarch's *Lives of the Ten Orators* reports that Lycurgus, acting in the role of *epistatēs*, or overseer of a public works project, 'completed' (ἐπετέλεσε) the Theatre of Dionysus.[34] The same text

'the four visible and ascertainable deme theatres' (i.e. those at Thorikos, Euonymon, Rhamnous and Ikarion) 'all contain oblong or rectangular orchestras', and each of these except the theatre at Thorikos dates to the fourth century: Paga (2010) 366.

30 Papastamati-von Moock (forthcoming): 320/19 (the archonship of Neaechmus) is the date of the victory commemorated by the choregic monument of Thrasyllos, who was victorious with a men's chorus (from the Hippothontid tribe): *IG* ii² 3056. Parts of its façade would have been transported through openings in an unfinished epitheatron, i.e. the back wall of the theatre behind the uppermost row of seating (the *summa cavea*). The lavishness of the monument suggests the prestige of the Great Dionysia, which would provide a *terminus post quem* for the monument of late spring 319.

31 Papastamati-von Moock (forthcoming) 34.

32 *IG* ii² 2320.

33 On the Lycurgan building programme see Faraguna (1992) 256–79 and Hintzen-Bohlen (1997) 11–73, with parallels to the Periclean programme at 105–35.

34 [Plut.] *Vit. dec. or.* 841d: τὸ ἐν Διονύσου θέατρον ἐπιστατῶν ἐπετέλεσε; cf. Paus. 1.21.16. Pickard-Cambridge (1946) collects the literary testimonia for Lycurgus' completion of the theatre's rebuilding (137). See also the sources gathered in Lambert (2008) 58 n.17.

summarises part of the Decree of Stratocles, the decree of 307/6 by which the Athenians awarded honours to Lycurgus' children:

ἡμίεργα παραλαβὼν τούς τε νεωσοίκους καὶ τὴν σκευοθήκην καὶ τὸ θέατρον τὸ Διονυσιακὸν ἐξειργάσατο. (*Vit. dec. or.* 852c; cf. 841 c–d)

finding buildings half-finished, [Lycurgus] completed the dockyards, the arsenal, and the Theatre of Dionysus.

Fragments of the Decree of Stratocles survive (*IG* ii² 457), and though much of the text is missing we can see that Pseudo-Plutarch followed the document closely in describing Lycurgus' role in the project:[35]

[...] ιὴν δὲ σ-
[κευοθήκην καὶ τὸ θέατρον τὸ] Διονυσιακὸν ἐξηργάσα-
[το τό τε στάδιον τὸ Παναθην]αϊκὸν καὶ τὸ γυμνάσιον τ-
[ὸ κατὰ τὸ Λύκειον κατεσκεύ]ασεν καὶ ἄλλαις δὲ πολλαῖ-
[ς κατασκευαῖς ἐκόσμησεν] ὅλην τὴν πόλιν· [...]
(*IG* ii² 457 fr. b5–9)

[Lycurgus] brought to completion [the arsenal and the Theatre] of Dionysus [and the Panathenaic stadium] and [equipped the Lyceum] gymnasium and [adorned] the entire city with many other [outfittings].

Stratocles' decree for Lycurgus is very fragmentary, but it does clearly preserve the reading of the verb ἐξηργάσατο (from ἐξεργάζομαι, which like ἐπιτελέω in the passage of Pseudo-Plutarch, means 'to finish off'; 'to bring to perfection,' 'to bring [something] to completion').[36] In the interest of heaping high

[35] On [Plut.]'s use of the inscription and for a comparison of his language with that of the decree see esp. Culasso Gastaldi (2003) 60–72 and Faraguna (2003) 487–91. On [Plut.]'s use of documents that attest to the award of the 'highest honours' (μέγισται τιμαί) for Demosthenes and Lycurgus (*Vit. dec. or.* 850f–852e) see esp. Luraghi (2010) 252–6 and Faraguna (2005) 73–5.

[36] In Hyperides' speech *For the Children of Lycurgus*, Hyperides recites this catalogue of Lycurgus' works as a kind of epitaph: τίνα φήσουσιν οἱ παριόντες αὐτοῦ τὸν τάφον; οὗτος ἐβίω μὲν σωφρόνως, ταχθεὶς δὲ ἐπὶ τῇ διοικήσει τῶν χρημάτων εὗρε πόρους, ᾠκοδόμησε τὸ θέατρον, τὸ ᾠδεῖον, τὰ νεώρια, τριήρεις ἐποιήσατο, λιμένας· τοῦτον ἡ πόλις ἡμῶν ἠτίμωσε καὶ τοὺς παῖδας ἔδησεν αὐτοῦ: Hyp. F 118 Jensen. The verb that Hyperides uses of Lycurgus' theatre-work is ᾠκοδόμησε ('to build', 'to build up'; cf. Paus. 1.29.16), which does not offer the same sense of 'bringing to completion' as ἐξεργάζομαι and ἐπιτελέω in the other sources.

praise upon Lycurgus, the Decree of Stratocles surely exaggerates the hand that he had in the various accomplishments which it lists to his credit.[37] The decree was, however, passed only a generation after Lycurgus' death, and its authors must have had compelling grounds for so closely associating him with this particular achievement.

The construction of the new theatre began with a Periclean-Era vision and was well advanced by the time Eubulus left office. Nevertheless, certain distinct aspects of the remodelled theatre can be dated with confidence to the Lycurgan Era.[38] These highly visible and more ornamental aspects of the construction bear the grandiose and 'classicising' touch that was characteristic of Lycurgus' building and cultural programme. The recent archaeological work at the theatre has demonstrated that the installation of the Lycurgan statues at the eastern *parodos* belonged to a larger project that also included the installation of a 'monumental Doric gateway' at the eastern entrance.[39] In Attica similar gateways adorned a number of other high prestige structures, such as the Parthenon, the Propylaea to the Acropolis and the Temple to Demeter at Eleusis. Certain epigraphic evidence to be discussed below also points to the construction of a new stage building, the *skēnē*, during the Lycurgan Era,[40] and attests that Lycurgus had a direct hand in securing funding for this critical part of the larger theatre remodel (see Fig. 6). Even, then, if the new theatre was not

37 Brun (2005); cf. Rhodes (2010) 82, who sees the decree as 'a hagiographic text in which we can see the creation of legend, which has affected the *Lycurgus* in the *Lives of the Ten Orators*'.

38 Papastamati-von Moock (forthcoming).

39 Papastamati-von Moock (forthcoming) with figs. 1.20 and 1.22; she later summarises: 'the gateway and the honorary monument [i.e. of the three tragedians] belong to the same Lycurgan phase which saw the completion of the works in these main entranceways'. She also points out such doors were not purely ornamental: they were necessary to protect the theatrical equipment in the theatre. On ancient Doric doors generally see Büsing-Kolbe (1978) 142–74.

40 On the *skēnē* in the broader context of the Lycurgan building programme see esp. Knell (2000) 127–8 and 136. The Athenians might have preserved the old *skēnē*: Athenaeus 1.19e somewhat dubiously records that the marionetteer Potheinus was allowed to use the stage that Euripides and his contemporaries (οἱ περὶ Εὐριπίδην) had used for their divinely inspired plays. For a discussion of the fifth-century *skēnē* with an emphasis on literary testimonia see Mastronarde (1990).

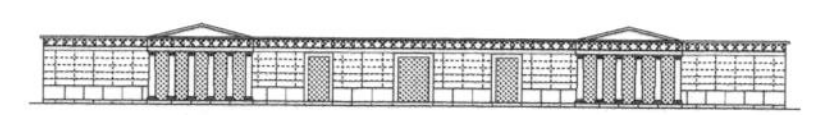

Figure 6 Reconstruction of the 'Lycurgan' *skēnē* at the Theatre of Dionysus in Athens

entirely completed until 320/19 and Lycurgus himself did not truly 'bring it to completion', the finely wrought gateway, the statue group of the tragedians and the new stage building may well have looked like Lycurgus' symbolic finishing touches.

Although he did not live to see the end of construction on the Theatre of Dionysus, his efforts to advance the project and to adorn the space with high profile features helped to link his name in perpetuity with the late classical structure.[41] When the theatre was fully complete, in 320/19, Antipater was Macedonian regent of Athens and the city's democratic constitution no longer held force. It only serves to reason, then, that Lycurgus – the last great leader of the free democracy – should be remembered by his fellow Athenians as the individual responsible for realising the comprehensive redesign and 'petrification' of the theatre. The grandiosity of the Doric gateway and the new stage building, coupled with the memorial of the classical tragedians that now greeted entering spectators, gave material expression to the abstract ideology of the Lycurgan theatre programme. In spirit, then, the new structure and the implicit message that it carried about the centrality of theatre – and theatrical heritage – to the city's cultural life were undeniably 'Lycurgan'.[42]

Honour rolls

As the Theatre of Dionysus continued to evolve, so too did aspects of the festivals that were celebrated there. Ancient

[41] Cf. Csapo and Wilson (forthcoming), who remark that 'the association of Lycurgus with the first stone theatre is a product not so much of faulty scholarship as of the success of the Lycurgan publicity machine' (section II.I) 408.

[42] Papastamati-von Moock (forthcoming) 75–6 emphasises that reference to the late classical theatre as 'Lycurgan', though technically a misnomer, makes sense in the context of Lycurgus' own efforts and policies.

sources credit Lycurgus with a vast increase in Athens' revenues, and his administration's capitalisation upon the economic potential of the city's festivals – the Great Dionysia included – signals further efforts to enfold the city's cultural activities into the economy. The author of the *Lives of the Ten Orators* tells us that one of Lycurgus' great accomplishments was to increase the city's public revenue from sixty to twelve hundred talents.[43] One good example of a Lycurgan creative 'fundraising' initiative linking festivals to the economy was a new scheme to sell the skins (δέρματα) of the animals that were sacrificed at state expense during the city's festivals. This was accomplished through the establishment of the so-called *Dermatikon* Fund, in 335/4 BC.[44] The '*Dermatikon* Accounts' record the revenue earned from the skins for the years 334/3–331/0 and itemise the funds raised at each festival at which skins were sold.[45] Those festivals included the Great Dionysia in the city and the Rural Dionysia in the deme of Piraeus.[46] At the Great Dionysia of 334/3, the *Dermatikon* raised 808 drachmas; the next year it yielded 306 drachmas.[47] Two decades or so before Lycurgus took office, Xenophon had encouraged the city to find new means of generating funds partially so that the festivals might be celebrated with even more splendour.[48] Now more than ever the Athenians were seeing the other side

[43] [Plut.] *Vit. dec. or*. 842f. See Burke (2010) for an analysis of Athens' revenue generation after Chaeronea (which he calls 'an economic bonanza', 411); see also Faraguna (1992) 290–396 and subsequently (2003) 119–24 (with some revisions of his prior conclusions). The numbers in [Plut.] do likely present a biased picture; cf. Oliver (2011) 121. Eubulus, whose influence in the city between 355–42 was comparable to that of Lycurgus in the 330s and 320s, is similarly said to have increased the state's revenue from 130 to 400 talents *per annum* (Dem. 10.37–8).

[44] Cf. Harpocration s.v. Δερματικόν (δερματικὸν ἂν εἴη λέγων ὁ ῥήτωρ τὸ ἐκ τῶν δερματίων τῶν πιπρασκομένων περιγινόμενον ἀργύριον). For an overview of the fund see Mikalson (1998) 26–7.

[45] *IG* ii^2 1496.68–92.

[46] *IG* ii^2 1496.70–1 and 80–1 respectively. See Rosivach (1994) 110, 113 and *passim*.

[47] The most 'profitable' festival for the *Dermatikon* Fund was the festival of Zeus the Saviour, which yielded 1,050 drachmas for skins in 334/3 and 2613 drachmas in 343/2.

[48] Xen. *Poroi* 6.1. Oliver (2011) discusses the *Poroi* as evidence for 'an important and widespread discussion about the Athenian economy' that was already taking place during the 350s and 340s (121).

of that coin: festivals themselves were potential sources of revenue.[49]

Policies that served to increase the magnificence of festivals by exploiting their economic possibilities are clear in the contemporary epigraphic record for the Theatre of Dionysus. Inscriptions indicate that under Lycurgus' aegis private donations, particularly from foreigners, contributed to works on the building.[50] Already the theatre played a role in Athens' honour economy thanks to the practice of *prohedria*: benefactors of the city could be rewarded with illustrious front-row seats at dramatic and choral performances. In the 350s Xenophon had also specifically advocated that the city grant permanent seats in the theatre to well-disposed merchants and ship-owners, for 'if so honoured they would hasten to their *philoi* [i.e. the Athenians] with an eye not only to profit, but also to honour'.[51] But while *prohedria* had long marked a way in which Athens honoured its benefactors, inscribed decrees from the 330s provide a sense of how the theatre building was also directly benefitting from foreign generosity. Non-Athenians were not permitted to serve as *choregoi* for the Great Dionysia, but they could still act as patrons of the Athenian theatre by making a contribution to the building's physical structure.[52]

[49] For a full discussion of festivals in the context of Lycurgan revenue-building initiatives see Csapo and Wilson (forthcoming) section II.

[50] Lambert (2008); Csapo and Wilson (forthcoming) section II.3.

[51] Xen. *Poroi* 3.5: ταῦτα γὰρ τιμώμενοι οὐ μόνον τοῦ κέρδους ἀλλὰ καὶ τῆς τιμῆς ἕνεκεν ὡς πρὸς φίλους ἐπισπεύδοιεν ἄν: for discussion of the passage and the honour of *prohedria* as practised see esp. Engen (2010) 174–5. On *prohedria* generally see Maass (1972) and the overview in *DFA*^{2} 268–70; for the politics of *prohedria* in the new theatre see Knell (2000) 143: the first row contained sixty-seven seats of fine marble reserved for priests of Dionysus, prominent citizens and distinguished guests.

[52] Σ *ad* Ar. *Pl.* 954: a joke in the comic scene is explained by the fact that 'foreigners could not dance in the city [i.e. Great Dionysia] chorus' (οὐκ ἐξῆν δὲ ξένον χορεύειν ἐν τῷ ἀστικῷ χορῷ); the scholiast notes that this was not the case at the Lenaea. Some sources complicate the picture: Dion of Syracuse, e.g., is said to have assumed the responsibilities of *choregos* on Plato's behalf (Plut. *Dion* 17), but we do not hear at which festival. Similarly vague is Lysias' claim (Lys. 12.20) that he and his brother, both metics, had 'performed all choregic duties' (πάσας τὰς χορηγίας χορηγήσαντες); MacDowell (1990) 68 points out that 'we can assume they were only nominated for the Lenaia (and perhaps for local festivals in Peiraieus)'. The only official role played by foreigners at the festival was in the procession with which it opened, where metics apparently participated as tray-bearers: *Suda* s.v. Ἀσκὸς ἐν πάχνῃ (α 4177). On metic

It was not unusual for a polis to exclude non-citizens from choral participation in its festivals. 'Civic purity' however seems to have been more of a concern at the Great Dionysia than at the Lenaea (also celebrated in the Theatre of Dionysus) and at the Rural Dionysia held in the demes.[53] For the Lenaea and certain deme festivals we have a handful of attestations of *choregoi* who were metics, or 'resident aliens'. An Eleusinian decree of the mid-fourth century, for example, informs us that a certain Callimachus successfully moved to award an (extraordinarily expensive) thousand-drachma gold crown to Damasias of Thebes, a metic, for his service as *choregos* at the Dionysia in Eleusis.[54] Choregic participation in the Great Dionysia, on the other hand, was more strictly limited to Athenian citizens. The Aristotelian *Constitution of the Athenians* casts *choregia* at the Great Dionysia as a liturgy reserved for wealthy citizens: one of the first acts of a newly appointed Athenian archon was to select three of 'the richest men of all the Athenians' as *choregoi* for the next festival's tragic contests.[55] Legislation also prevented foreigners from entering the choruses as regular members.[56] These laws were not always upheld, and later we shall hear of how Demades once supposedly flouted them outright. But while some men may have pursued unscrupulous means of including foreigners in their choruses, no evidence survives of a non-Athenian *choregos* at the Great Dionysia.

By the 330s, non-citizens had found other avenues for acting as patrons of the Athenian theatre and so for sharing in the prestige of the dramatic contests. As part of his preparation of *IG* ii³ fascicle 2, Stephen Lambert has gathered and analysed the surviving decrees from the Lycurgan Era (including

liturgies in Athens see Sinclair (1988) 29–30 and Whitehead (1977) *passim*, with 80–2 on the *choregia*.

53 On the interest in maintaining 'civic purity' at festivals see esp. Wilson (2000) 80; for the evidence of the Lenaea and demes see his (2010) 50–1.

54 *IG* ii² 1186 = *IE* 70; see the commentary of Clinton (2008) 2.87–9.

55 Arist. *Ath. Pol.* 56.3: ἐξ ἁπάντων Ἀθηναίων τοὺς πλουσιωτάτους; for discussion see Rhodes (1993) ad loc. and MacDowell (1990) 65–8. The text likely dates to the 330s or 320s: cf. Rhodes (1993) 51–8.

56 See Dem. 21.56–61. For a reconstruction of the process of disqualifying non-Athenian chorus members (as well as the legal background for the exclusion of non-Athenians from choruses) see MacDowell (1990) 276–7.

two proposed by Lycurgus himself) which honour foreigners for their services to the city's drama industry.[57] Most of these inscriptions are badly fragmentary, and Lambert emphasises that the corpus 'acquire[s] significance mainly as a group':

> Apart from one or two earlier outliers honouring poets (no actor seems to have been honoured on an extant Athenian state decree before the 330s), they are the first inscribed decrees to honour foreigners for their services to Athenian theatre and, while there continue to be occasional decrees of this type in the Hellenistic period (though not explicitly for an actor), such decrees never again occur with such frequency.[58]

Inscribed decrees honouring foreigners for services (of any sort) to Athens – which Lambert calls 'potent levers in the honour-driven Greek world of diplomacy' – are the most common type of decree surviving from the Lycurgan period.[59] Among these, the corpus of ten theatre-related documents is third in size only to the honorific corpora concerned with Macedonian affairs (thirty decrees) and the grain trade (twelve decrees).[60] Particularly in the aftermath of Chaeronea, relations with Macedon and repeated food shortages demanded the focus of the city's attention.[61] Perhaps more surprising is that decrees honouring foreign theatre patrons and actors constitute the third most prominent category of inscribed honorific decrees during these years. One of Lambert's conclusions about the inscriptions is that 'Athens deployed the honorific decree to recognise and encourage those who contributed to the maintenance of her status as the greatest theatrical city of Greece.'[62] Particularly when viewed in the light of other Lycurgan Era

[57] Honours were not exclusively bestowed upon foreigners; e.g. *IG* ii^{3} 306 from 343/2 records honours to the Council (βουλή) currently in office: line 2 praises the Council for its work περὶ τὴν ἑορτὴν τοῦ Διονύσου το[ῦ – *vacat* –]; Lambert (2004) 90 restores this to περὶ τὴν ἑορτὴν τοῦ Διονύσου το[ῦ ἐν ἄστει]. Cf. also *IG* vii 4524, from 329/8, which honours the ten *epimeletai* (Lycurgus among them) of the Amphiaraia festival held in Oropus that year. *IG* ii^{2} 2827, a fragment of a dedication to Dionysus (presumably made by a priest of the god) may also have some connection with the Great Dionysia: see Lambert (2004) 110.

[58] Lambert (2008) 57.

[59] Lambert (2006) 115.

[60] Lambert (2008) 60.

[61] The food situation was especially difficult after Philip won control of grain trade routes in the Hellespont: see Oliver (2007) 42–5 and Garnsey (1988) 134–49.

[62] Lambert (2006) 117.

efforts to tie the achievement of the theatre to the unique character of Athens, the honorific decrees speak to the city's eagerness to trade with the valuable currency of its dramatic industry and heritage.

One of the theatre-related inscriptions honours an unknown individual (or a group of individuals) by rewarding him (or them) with exemption from the metic tax because of a donation made toward the Theatre of Dionysus' new *skēnē*.[63] The formulations in the inscription are characteristic of Athenian honorific decrees from this era, and because the stone mentions a metic tax (*metoikion*, 6) it must predate the year 321/0.[64] The *skēnē* referred to in line 3 is thus generally understood to be the new stage building for the 'Lycurgan' Theatre of Dionysus.[65]

[.... ... 13... ...]ΟΣ[....... .. 16... .. ...]
[...... 12... ...]ΙΣΙΟΣ[....... .. 15... ....]
[.. ... 10... .. τὴ]ν σκην[ὴν...... 12......]
[.. ... 10... ..δωρ]εὰς διδ[...... 12......]
[...... 11... ..]ι χρῆσθ[αι...... 12......] (5)
[ἀτέλ-? το]ῦ μετοικ[ίου... ... 11... ..]
[ἐπιμελείσθ]ω δὲ ἡ βου[λὴ τῶν... .. 9. ...]
[.... 8.... ω]ν οἷς ὁ δῆμ[ος... ... 12......]
[.... τὴν δω]ρεάν, ὅπως ἄ[ν...... 12... ...]
[μηδ' ὑφ' ἑνὸς] ἀδικωντα[ι· ἀναγράψαι δὲ τό]- (10)
[δε τὸ ψήφισ]μα τὸν γραπμματέα τῆς βουλῆ]-
[ς καὶ στῆσαι ἐν ἀ]κ[ροπόλει·... .. 10... ..] (*IG* ii[3] 470)

...[since *the honorand(s?)*...are making?] a donation...[towards] the stage building..., they (or he) shall be granted...(5) import (?)...use... exemption (?) from metic tax...and the Council shall take care of the – to whom the People...[has made (10) the grant, so that...(plural) suffer no wrong; and the secretary of the Council shall inscribe this decree and stand it on the acropolis... (Trans. Lambert)

The design and construction of an elaborate new *skēnē* alone will have been an expensive undertaking for the city, as both the stage building itself (with its requisite three doors) and

[63] *IG* ii[3] 470 = Lambert 6. On the *skēnē* in the context of the Lycurgan building programme see esp. Knell (2000) 127–8 and 136.
[64] The *metoikion* is not attested after *IG* ii[2] 545, from 321/0 BC.
[65] Heisserer and Moysey (1986) 177–81. Lambert (2008) accepts this conclusion; the inscription is his no. 6.

two flanking *paraskēnia* (with their Doric colonnades) were also converted from wood into elaborate stone structures (see Fig. 6).[66] Though foreigners, these metics still found a way to enshrine their names on a stele in connection with the Athenian theatre, namely by making what proved to be a 'tax deductible' donation towards the completion of the splendid new stage building.[67]

Another mostly fragmentary decree proposed by Lycurgus himself (*IG* ii³ 345) honours a son of Eudemus of Plataea for an unknown reason, but because the honour was moved at the 'Assembly in the Theatre of Dionysus' (the ἐκκλησία ἐν Διονύσου) of 332/1 his service should have been related to the Great Dionysia.[68] The Assembly in the Theatre was a special assembly held immediately after the conclusion of the festival, and its primary purpose was to address issues that had been raised in the course of the celebrations.[69] Decrees honouring benefactors of the theatre were regularly passed on this occasion. Demosthenes apparently quoted the law that provided for the Assembly to be held the day after the Pandia (which immediately followed the Great Dionysia) in his speech *Against Meidias*. Though probably inserted at a later date, the version of the law transmitted with the speech outlines the purpose of this assembly as one of dealing first with 'sacred' or 'religious' matters (περὶ ἱερῶν), then with complaints and charges (προβολαί) to do either with the festival's procession or with its

[66] There is disagreement as to whether a colonnade also spanned the length of the *skēnē* itself, a view proposed by Dörpfeld in a foundational study of Greek theatre architecture: Dörpfeld and Reisch (1896). Townsend (1986) affirmed the view, and argued that the long colonnade was modelled on the agora's late-Periclean Stoa of Zeus Eleutherios ('the imitation of the 5th-century building had the added advantage of direct association with the age which Lykourgos endeavored to enshrine', 434). Here I follow Papastamati-von Moock (forthcoming) 60–3, who argues against an expansive colonnade in front of the *skēnē*; cf. Moretti (1999–2000) 396.

[67] This system might be viewed as an ancient parallel for today's common practice of naming new theatre wings and auditoria after generous benefactors, and of displaying lists of donors on rolls of honour in the entrances to new buildings.

[68] *IG* ii³ 345 = Lambert 4 = Schwenk 36.

[69] Lambert (2008) 52–5; cf. MacDowell (1990) 226–36. As Lambert (2008) 52 notes, the main literary source for the festival is Dem. 21 *Against Meidias* (esp. 8–12); see also Wilson (1991) 164.

contests.[70] This assembly's very existence speaks to the seriousness with which the festival was taken: matters of praise and blame stemming from it became urgent city business.

The decree honouring the son of Eudemus of Plataea was passed in 331 BC, at the earliest meeting of the Assembly in the Theatre of Dionysus for which we have documentary evidence. Parts of four decrees that were passed at that Assembly survive, one of which also marks the earliest known instance of the city awarding honours to an actor.[71] That inscription records the award of a gold crown to a son of Onoma[?], and grants proxeny to him and to his descendants. Two other inscriptions from the Lycurgan Era also appear to record honours for foreign actors.[72] From at least the 340s Athens had been imposing fines upon actors who broke their commitments to perform at the Great Dionysia;[73] honorific decrees, by contrast, represented a positive incentive for actors to fulfil their obligations. By extending the prospect of official honours to foreign actors, the city must now have been hoping to attract and retain the best talent for its dramatic festivals. The Great Dionysia of 331 was also the same festival for which the actor Athenodorus supposedly broke his commitment to perform, choosing instead to stay with Alexander the Great in Phoenicia.[74] Honours passed for actors at the Assembly in the Theatre in 331 may thus have carried a double message: the city was grateful to the actors who performed, but also upset about those who broke their contracts. In *Against Leptines*, Demosthenes even specifically weighs the value of Athenian public honours against the meaningless rewards of tyrants: he argues that it is far more *kalon* to be judged worthy of civic honours in a city where there is equality amongst citizens than to reap the rewards of sycophancy (κολακεία) at a tyrant's court.[75]

[70] Dem. 21.8; for details see MacDowell (1990) ad loc. The first evidence for the Assembly in the Theatre appears in the mid-fourth century and it is tempting to see its institution as linked to the new stone structure.

[71] *IG* ii³ 344 = Lambert 1. The letters PITHΣ survive in line 10 of the inscription, and have been supplemented to read ὑποκριτής. The four decrees are preserved in *IG* ii³ 344–6 (345 contains two).

[72] *IG* ii³ 423 and 436 = Lambert 8 and 9.

[73] See pages 70–2 above.

[74] Cf. Csapo and Wilson (forthcoming) section II.3.

[75] Dem. 20.15.

Honours and decrees marked the city's end of the bargain in exchange obligations with benefactors, and their purpose extended far beyond the recognition of past generosity. Athens relied on the expectation that the prospect of public honours would exhort individuals to acts of *philotimia*, including financial benefactions, towards the city.[76] The overall number of honorific decrees surged in the third quarter of the fourth century, an increase that has been linked with the appearance in decrees from the 340s of the 'manifesto-clause', or a clear expression of the 'hortatory intention'.[77] The hortatory intention is marked by language expressing hopefulness that others will follow the honorand's example. Inscriptions could even record that an honorific decree was passed not only in recognition of services rendered but also 'in order that in the future, too, all men may show *philotimia*, in the knowledge that the *demos* returns favours to those who do show *philotimia* towards it'.[78] In order to encourage further expressions of *philotimia*, such inscriptions were put on display in high-traffic areas of the city.[79] It is also significant, then, that at least two of the Lycurgan Era theatre inscriptions were inscribed on particularly elaborate stones: *IG* ii³ 345 and 347 constitute examples of the relatively rare class of stelai known as 'document reliefs', or inscriptions adorned by sculpted reliefs.[80] One, a decree honouring the comic poet Amphis of Andros (*IG* ii³ 347), was found in the area of the Asclepion to the northwest of the Theatre of Dionysus. The fragment of the relief depicts the bottom parts of the legs of two males dressed in *himatia*: as Carol Lawton describes, the 'smaller figure undoubtedly represents Amphis, the large figure probably Demos, presenting a crown

[76] Whitehead (1983).

[77] On the 'manifesto-clause' see esp. Whitehead (1983) 62–4 and Henry (1996), who discusses this material in terms of the 'hortative formula' and 'hortatory intention'.

[78] The example given by Whitehead (1983) 63, a translation of *IG* ii² 300.2–5 (now *IG* ii³ 327.20–4 from 336/5 BC).

[79] '[A]n inscription did not merely "record" honours, it commemorated them and *qua* monument it was itself honorific in intention': Lambert (2006) 116.

[80] On *IG* ii³ 345 see page 109 above; *IG* ii³ 347 = Lambert 2 = Schwenk 38. On document reliefs see Lawton (1995), who notes that reliefs are more commonly 'found on honorary decrees than on any other type of document' (5).

to the poet'.[81] The two fragments found on the Acropolis of the inscription for the son of Eudemus of Plataea also indicate that a relief adorned his stele. In this case the figures are not identifiable, but to the left and right we can discern, respectively, the lower legs of a male and those of a female.[82] The prominent display of such document reliefs enshrined the honorands' names in connection with the industry to which they had contributed.

During the Lycurgan Era Athens began to look more to patrons from abroad as potential sources of funding for the city's festivals and drama industry. Despite the fragmentary nature of the epigraphic evidence, the surviving (pieces of) inscriptions imply that some non-Athenians had been convinced that the city's dramatic industry was a worthwhile investment. Lycurgus' own theatre-related legislation also suggests that part of the prestige that was attached to the theatre now derived from its history. While there is little doubt that celebrity actors and contemporary playwrights drew audiences and inspired excitement, the city's decision to preserve the classical tragedians' scripts in the archive proclaimed the importance of fifth-century tragedy to the state, and the bronze statues at the theatre's entrance were a strong advertisement of tragedy's illustrious past. For potential donors who were not Athenian citizens that past was surely part of the incentive to present generosity. Such benefactors were well aware that their largesse could be repaid in the form of public honours, which served not only practical ends (such as exemption from the *metoikion*), but also to bind their names to theatre permanently in the inscribed record. By making a large private donation, a non-Athenian might still significantly contribute to Athens' dramatic festivals and so receive some share of the prestige that was otherwise reserved for citizen *choregoi*.

The theatre and the crown

The construction of the permanent theatre complex marked a period of forward looking change in Athens' theatre industry.

[81] Lawton (1995) 103; cat. no. 45.   [82] Lawton (1995) 103; cat. no. 44.

Together the material and documentary evidence generally attest to a variety of activity around the structure of the Theatre of Dionysus, the home of the dramatic industry and a central space for the performance of Athenian civic identity. It is also in this era that the Sanctuary of Dionysus is first specifically named in decrees as the site where honours are to be posted.[83] Now a site for both assemblies and the display of decrees, the sanctuary had effectively drawn some of the most characteristic aspects of Athenian political life down from the heights of the Pnyx and the Acropolis.

Yet despite the abundance of innovations, the literary record also bears witness to the importance of the theatre as a monument to the city's past. Part of the theatre's cultural significance lay in having been the original performance site of great fifth-century tragedies, including such exemplary works as Euripides' *Erechtheus*. The installation of the bronze statues of the three great tragedians also partially transformed the theatre into a museum of its own history. At the eastern *parodos* the images of Aeschylus, Sophocles and Euripides constituted a 'hall of fame' – a small cycle of *viri illustres* – set on display to remind the entering spectators of the momentous cultural events that the theatre had hosted.[84] These statues also stood as witnesses to the illustrious pedigree of the new performances that the crowds still eagerly came to watch: the great dramatic tradition of the city continued unabated, but with grander facilities (and greater seating capacity) than ever before. At once ancient and entirely new, the Theatre of Dionysus was a space that housed and fused the city's theatrical past and present.

[83] Lambert (2008) 57; cf. 65 n.33 for earlier decrees set up, but without an explicit provision for doing so, at the Theatre of Dionysus. An important example of such a decree is *IG* ii^3 416 (ii^2 410): see Lambert (2003a). Lambert argues, on the basis of an erasure in the decree, that the document was originally meant to be set up at the theatre in the Piraeus. The city saw the Piraeus as a stronghold in the case that Philip should invade Attica after his victory at Chaeronea. The decision to place the decree in the Theatre of Dionysus 'would reflect the dying away of this initial panic, as it became apparent that Philip would not invade Attica' (66). If Lambert's hypothesis is accurate, the display of the decree at the theatre would have served to commemorate, in a high-traffic area, Athens' survival after the battle.

[84] One thinks of the comparison offered by Olympia, which since the sixth century BC had hosted a number of votive statues dedicated by victorious athletes; cf. Paus. 5.21.

But the relationship between past and present in the space was not always an easy one. Conflict as to which era in the life of the theatre – the days of the ancestors or the present day – deserved priority is fervidly attested by Aeschines and Demosthenes' 330 BC speeches 'On the Crown'. Earlier, in 334, Demosthenes had already withstood an attack on the legality of a crown that his cousin Demomeles, along with Hyperides, had proposed for him shortly before the Battle of Chaeronea took place in 338. In that case, Diondas brought the charges against Demosthenes' supporters, charges that Hyperides rebutted on Demosthenes' behalf (fragments of this speech, *Against Diondas*, have recently come to light again thanks to the discovery of the Archimedes Palimpsest). In 330, however, Aeschines assumed the role of prosecutor. He alleged that Ctesiphon's 336 BC proposal for Demosthenes to be crowned in the theatre for his services to Athens was illegal because it violated the city's laws as to which honours could be announced and on which occasions.[85] As Aeschines reports it, Ctesiphon had proposed that:

τὸν κήρυκα ἀναγορεύειν ἐν τῷ θεάτρῳ πρὸς τοὺς Ἕλληνας ὅτι στεφανοῖ αὐτὸν ὁ δῆμος ὁ Ἀθηναίων ἀρετῆς ἕνεκα καὶ ἀνδραγαθίας. (Aeschin. 3.49)

the herald should announce in the theatre, to the Hellenes, that the demos of the Athenians is crowning [Demosthenes] because of his *aretē* and *andragathia*.

But by prescribing that the announcement be made in the Theatre of Dionysus, Ctesiphon had (according to Aeschines) contravened an important law. After bidding the clerk of the court to read out that law, Aeschines offers this summary of the law and assessment of Ctesiphon's violation:

ἀκούετε, ὦ ἄνδρες Ἀθηναῖοι, ὅτι ὁ μὲν νομοθέτης κελεύει ἐν τῷ δήμῳ ἐν Πυκνὶ τῇ ἐκκλησίᾳ ἀνακηρύττειν τὸν ὑπὸ τοῦ δήμου στεφανούμενον, ἄλλοθι δὲ μηδαμοῦ, Κτησιφῶν δὲ ἐν τῷ θεάτρῳ, οὐ τοὺς νόμους μόνον ὑπερβάς, ἀλλὰ καὶ τὸν τόπον μετενεγκών, οὐδὲ ἐκκλησιαζόντων Ἀθηναίων, ἀλλὰ τραγῳδῶν γιγνομένων

85 For an outline of the legal argumentation in this case see esp. Gwatkin (1953). Gwatkin argues for the usual view that Aeschines had the stronger legal case, but this position is challenged by Harris (1994) 59–67.

καινῶν, οὐδ' ἐναντίον τοῦ δήμου, ἀλλ' ἐναντίον τῶν Ἑλλήνων, ἵν' ἡμῖν συνειδῶσιν οἷον ἄνδρα τιμῶμεν. (Aeschin. 3.34)

Listen, men of Athens, how the lawmaker bids that the announcement of someone being crowned by the demos be made before the demos, in the Assembly on the Pnyx, and nowhere else. But Ctesiphon [bids that it happen] in the theatre: not only transgressing the laws, but also changing the location; not when the Athenians are having an assembly, but when the new tragedies are being performed; and not before the demos, but before the Hellenes – so that they might see what sort of man we honour.

Here Aeschines is careful to emphasise the presence of 'all Hellenes' at the Great Dionysia, as spectators of both the contests and the city's folly.[86]

Despite the formidable audience that was present at the Great Dionysia, not all of the honours pronounced on the occasion had been appropriately illustrious. A law regulating the pronouncement of honours is necessary, Aeschines goes on to explain, partially for preventing excessive declarations of minor honours, especially honours conferred by demes, tribes and foreign states – and not by the authority of the Athenian demos. Athenians who were *proxenoi* of other poleis, for example, sometimes arranged to have the foreign honours proclaimed at the festival. In the past, Aeschines claims, the lack of restrictions upon these kinds of announcements had led to a situation in which:

συνέβαινε τοὺς μὲν θεατὰς καὶ τοὺς χορηγοὺς καὶ τοὺς ἀγωνιστὰς ἐνοχλεῖσθαι, τοὺς δὲ ἀνακηρυττομένους ἐν τῷ θεάτρῳ μείζοσι τιμαῖς τιμᾶσθαι τῶν ὑπὸ τοῦ δήμου στεφανουμένων. (Aeschin. 3.43)

it came to be that the spectators and the *choregoi* and the competitors were irritated, and those whose honours were announced in the theatre enjoyed greater honour than those crowned by the demos.

Aeschines' claim here offers a glimpse at the hustle and bustle of the Dionysia, which extended well beyond the official

[86] In Plato's *Symposium* Socrates makes the (likely exaggerated) claim that Agathon's success at the Dionysia had shined forth before 30,000 Greeks (ἐν μάρτυσι τῶν Ἑλλήνων πλέον ἢ τρισμυρίοις, 175e). Ar. *Ach.* 501–8 is the *locus classicus* for a large foreign turnout at the Great Dionysia in the fifth century (this was the occasion by which the allies had to pay their tribute). On foreigners at the Dionysia see esp. Goldhill (1997) 60–1; on 'Athens as tourist attraction' and 'Athens as a city of visitors' see Dougherty (2009) 395–400.

performances, as well as at the recognised Panhellenic significance of the event. Yet some of his other arguments transcend points of strict legality and rely upon an idealised vision of the festival's more remote past. Aeschines plays in his speech on the emotions and the patriotism of the jurors in reminding them of a ritual that was once performed at the Dionysia by the city's ancestors. For him, the Theatre of Dionysus is a site that still harbours the sacred memory of the presentation of war orphans at Great Dionysia of old. By Aeschines' time this tradition had passed out of practice, but in earlier years the children whose fathers had been killed in battle were, upon coming of age, paraded before the city in a ceremony that took place before the start of the tragic performances.[87] Isocrates, in his 355 oration *On the Peace*, had lamented this old tradition as a perverse celebration of the consequences of Athenian arrogance (πλεονεξία).[88] For him the ceremony was, like the parade of surplus allied tribute that also took place at the festival, a testament to imperialist aggression and a justification for the allies' resentment. Aeschines, on the other hand, will regard the custom much more nostalgically. In the second half of his speech he casts Demosthenes' crowning as a civic tragedy with the potential to inspire more tears than any of the dramatic performances that might follow. He asks the jury to forget for a moment that they are in the courtroom and to imagine instead that they are in the Theatre of Dionysus, in the moment just before the herald proclaims Demosthenes' crown.[89] He then requests that the jurors:

> λογίσασθε πότερ' οἴεσθε τοὺς οἰκείους τῶν τελευτησάντων πλείω δάκρυα ἀφήσειν ἐπὶ ταῖς τραγῳδίαις καὶ τοῖς ἡρῳκοῖς πάθεσι τοῖς μετὰ ταῦτ' ἐπεισιοῦσιν, ἢ ἐπὶ τῇ τῆς πόλεως ἀγνωμοσύνῃ. (Aeschin. 3.153)

[87] The parade of orphans took place in a time 'when the city was better governed and had better champions' (Aeschin. 3.155). For the presentation of the war orphans see Arist. *Pol.* 2.1268a8–12 and Pl. *Men.* 248e–249b.

[88] Isoc. 8.82. Isocrates already condemns the custom as a practice of the past: the self-destructively imperialist Athenians of the late fifth century used to bring in the orphans on the occasion of the Dionysia: παρεισῆγον τοὺς παῖδας τῶν ἐν τῷ πολέμῳ τετελευτηκότων (8.82); see esp. Goldhill (1987) 60–1 and Michelini (1998) 123–5. On the speech, Isocrates' critique of Athenian imperialism, see esp. Davidson (1990).

[89] Aeschin. 3.153: γένεσθε δή μοι μικρὸν χρόνον τῇ διανοίᾳ μὴ ἐν τῷ δικαστηρίῳ, ἀλλ' ἐν τῷ θεάτρῳ.

consider whether you think that the relatives of the dead shall shed more tears over the tragedies and the heroic sufferings about to be presented, or over the folly of the city.

What Greek 'educated as a free man' (παιδευθεὶς ἐλευθερίως), Aeschines goes on to ask, would not be aggrieved upon remembering that, during a time 'when the city followed better customs and had better leaders', it was in this very theatre and at that very moment that the herald used to proclaim honours – not for enemies of the city, but for the Athenian children whose fathers had died defending the fatherland?[90] To allow Demosthenes to be crowned in this sacred space at this most meaningful and symbolic point in the festival was tantamount to erecting a monument (τρόπαιον) to the city's defeat, a display to the many Hellenes present of Athens' madness and foolishness.[91] Aeschines finds intolerable the idea that a herald should proclaim honours to Demosthenes – the very man responsible for creating so many orphans at Chaeronea – on the same occasion that had once seen the city proclaim its commitment to honour and to care for the children of the war dead.

This appalling irony is then only exacerbated by the prior conduct that Demosthenes had displayed in the theatre. Not long after making his legal arguments, Aeschines points out another aspect of the farce of Ctesiphon's proposal: Demosthenes had publicly shown his contempt for the theatre by granting *prohedria* to the ambassadors sent by Athens' enemy, King Philip of Macedon, to negotiate peace with the city in 346.[92] Early on a day of performances, Aeschines claims, Demosthenes led the Macedonian ambassadors into the theatre in a manner that caused him to be 'hissed at for his tastelessness and sycophancy'.[93] Aeschines charges that this was the

[90] Aeschin. 3.154–5.

[91] Aeschin. 3.156. By this same logic, Aeschines sees it as reprehensible that Demosthenes was chosen to give the *epitaphios logos* for the dead at Chaeronea: it was precisely Demosthenes who was to blame for escalating tensions with Macedon to the point of Athenian bloodshed: Aeschin. 3.152. For Demosthenes' boast at being chosen (by the demos) over Aeschines to give the funeral oration (Dem. 60) see Dem. 19.285.

[92] On the coincidence of the peace negotiations and the Great Dionysia see Cawkwell (1960) 416–17.

[93] Aeschin. 3.76: συρίττεσθαι διὰ τὴν ἀσχημοσύνην καὶ κολακείαν.

only delegation upon which Demosthenes, a man who fashioned himself as an enemy of both Alexander and Philip, ever granted *prohedria*.[94] His behaviour confirmed that he neither understood nor respected what the Theatre of Dionysus and the festival of the Great Dionysia meant to the city.

To Aeschines' argument that honours awarded by the demos must always be proclaimed in the *ekklesia* and 'nowhere else' (ἄλλοθι δὲ μηδαμοῦ), Demosthenes hyperbolically retorts that he shall pass over the 'countless men' who 'on countless occasions' (μυριάκις μύριοι) have had their honours proclaimed in the theatre.[95] Earlier in his own speech, Demosthenes had reminded the jurors that he counted himself among these myriads. A firm precedent for Ctesiphon's proposal existed in the decree of Aristonicus, thanks to which Demosthenes already had been awarded a crown in the theatre (at the Great Dionysia of 340 BC).[96] Here Demosthenes invokes a clause of the 'Dionysiac Law' (Διονυσιακὸς νόμος) which Aeschines had indeed anticipated that Demosthenes would cite in his own defence.[97] The version of the law that has been transmitted is now known to be a later forgery,[98] but we can infer that part of the actual law to which Demosthenes refers prohibited crowns from being awarded to citizens at the Great Dionysia. This law however allowed for exceptions in special circumstances and only by dispensation of the *boulē*.[99] Demosthenes' claim that myriads upon myriads of honours were regularly announced at the festival is in any case surely exaggerated. The epigraphic

[94] According to Aeschines 3.73, Demosthenes fashioned himself as a hater of Alexander and of Philip, i.e. as μισαλέξανδρος and μισοφίλιππος.

[95] Dem. 18.120. The clause 'and nowhere else' that Aeschines insists upon may have not been in the law at all; cf. Gwatkin (1953) 136. See Lane Fox (1994) 149–54 generally on Aeschines' 'questionable' use of Athenian law.

[96] Dem. 18.83; cf. Yunis (2001) ad loc. This happens to be the same Great Dionysia that saw Astydamas take the prize in tragedy with a slate that included his celebrated *Parthenopaeus* (*IG* ii^2 2320.20–1 Millis–Olson; see pages 184–5 below).

[97] Aeschin. 3.35; cf. Gwatkin (1953) 35. For part of the law (four clauses) see Aeschin. 3.44. Takeuchi (2006) is a full re-examination of the law.

[98] Canevaro (2013) 290–6: the transmitted law is inconsistent with the picture of the Dionysiac Law that the argumentation of Aeschines and Demosthenes otherwise provides.

[99] Cf. Dem. 18.20–1. Demosthenes charges that Aeschines had failed to read the 'excepting clause' of the law.

record is not of enormous help here, as no surviving inscription after 393/2 or before 319/8 carries the provision that honours were to be announced at the festival,[100] and all of the surviving fourth-century decrees which stipulate conferral of honours at the Great Dionysia are in honour of non-Athenians.[101] But despite the silence of the record, it is clear that Demosthenes and Aeschines' arguments rely on the same premise: the Great Dionysia, especially in the moments before the premiere of new tragedies, was an occasion on which all of Greece paid close attention.

In rebutting Aeschines, Demosthenes also spends considerable efforts upon outlining the benefits that the city reaps from the public awards of honours. He especially underscores the importance of the present-day festival to the city's objective of encouraging *philotimia*. He reminds the jurors that the purpose of crowning someone in the theatre is to encourage as many people as possible to do good (ποιεῖν εὖ) for the state, and goes on to berate Aeschines for failing to understand this:

ἀλλὰ πρὸς θεῶν οὕτω σκαιὸς εἶ καὶ ἀναίσθητος, Αἰσχίνη, ὥστ' οὐ δύνασαι λογίσασθαι ὅτι τῷ μὲν στεφανουμένῳ τὸν αὐτὸν ἔχει ζῆλον ὁ στέφανος, ὅπου ἂν ἀναρρηθῇ, τοῦ δὲ τῶν στεφανούντων εἵνεκα συμφέροντος ἐν τῷ θεάτρῳ γίγνεται τὸ κήρυγμα; οἱ γὰρ ἀκούσαντες ἅπαντες εἰς τὸ ποιεῖν εὖ τὴν πόλιν προτρέπονται, καὶ τοὺς ἀποδιδόντας τὴν χάριν μᾶλλον ἐπαινοῦσι τοῦ στεφανουμένου· (Dem. 18.120)

But by the gods are you so tactless and oblivious, Aeschines, that you are incapable of comprehending that the crown is equally desirable to the man who is crowned, wherever it should be proclaimed, but that the proclamation is made in the theatre in the interest of those doing the crowning? For everyone who hears it is thereby encouraged to do good deeds for the city, and it is really the men awarding the crown whom the people praise rather than the one receiving it.

For Demosthenes, a crown conferred in the theatre before a crowd of potential future benefactors (citizens and foreigners alike) had an effect similar to that of the erection of

[100] See the chronological list of all known such decrees in Wilson and Hartwig (2009) 22.

[101] Cf. Yunis (2001) 179, *ad* Dem. 18.120: 'no extant fourth-century inscription directs that a crown bestowed by the demos on a citizen be proclaimed in the city theater'; see too Harris (1995) 144–5.

honorific stelai. A quarter-century earlier, in his speech *Against Leptines*, Demosthenes had taken pains to describe how stelai preserving records of honours serve as models or examples (παραδείγματα) of the rewards awaiting potential benefactors of the city.[102] In *On the Crown*, he specifically argues that the proclamation of honours in the theatre encourages the spectators 'to do good deeds for the polis'.[103] In a study of proclamations of honours at tragic competitions, Paola Ceccarelli has stressed that 'the moment chosen for the announcement would be among those the polis and the honorand considered most important'.[104] Demosthenes' own words suggest that, to his mind, Athens' most prestigious and therefore most visible moment for crownings was precisely the Great Dionysia. Aeschines, in attempting to justify the rationale for the Dionysiac Law against crownings of citizens on this occasion, also acknowledges the prestige of those moments when he laments that in the past 'those whose honours were announced in the theatre enjoyed greater honour than those crowned by the demos', that is, in the Assembly on the Pnyx.[105]

In his study of the Athenian institution of the *choregia*, Peter Wilson has proposed that we view the *choregia* as 'a kind of paradramatic performance taking place alongside, and in intimate relation to, the institutionally recognised forms of dramatic performance in the polis'.[106] In their speeches 'On the Crown', Demosthenes and Aeschines both emphasise the spectators' scrutiny of the 'performers' (the demos and the honorands alike) of crownings in the Theatre of Dionysus. These events, too, should be read as occasions of 'paradramatic performance' at the festival.[107] But while both orators regard the Theatre of Dionysus as an incomparably high-profile space

[102] Dem. 20.64; see esp. West (1995) on Demosthenes' citations of honorific decrees in the speech. For another near contemporary source on the potential of decrees to encourage foreign benefaction see Xen. *Poroi* 3.11.

[103] Dem. 3.18: εἰς τὸ ποιεῖν εὖ τὴν πόλιν προτρέπονται.

[104] Ceccarelli (2010) 102; see also Wilson (2009) and Wilson and Hartwig (2009).

[105] Aeschin. 3.43.

[106] Wilson (1996) 85–6 and (2000) *passim*.

[107] Chaniotis (2007) 54–9 describes crownings in terms of 'theatre rituals' and discusses the 'staging instructions' for these rituals that are present in the epigraphical formulae.

for the announcement of honours, Demosthenes insists that the city most needs the gaze of spectators upon contemporary benefactors because the sight of the honorands will encourage others to emulate their deeds. Only a few months before the crown trial, Lycurgus had argued that the citizens would profit from 'looking into' certain tragic poetry. For Demosthenes, on the other hand, the models offered by men such as himself provided the most important exempla of patriotism and the best sources of encouragement towards *philotimia*. And while Lycurgus implied that certain 'old' tragedies were capable of exhorting the citizens to patriotism, Demosthenes looked instead to the 'hortative' power of the new decrees that were pronounced in the moments before new tragedies premiered.

Demosthenes' arguments evidently proved compelling, and Aeschines' failure to convince the jury of the illegality of Ctesiphon's decree was so spectacular that he was forced to leave Athens. Nevertheless, Aeschines' own speech serves as an important illustration of yet another construction of the theatrical space in this period and affords a glimpse at how some Athenians might have understood the theatre's present importance in terms of its past. For Aeschines, the theatre had been hallowed by its service as the site of a venerable old custom, the parade of the war orphans. In *Against Ctesiphon* his most direct appeal to the past is activated by his request that the jury, just for the moment, imagine themselves (γένεσθε ... τῇ διανοίᾳ) in the theatre.[108] This invocation of the theatre should be contextualised within an Athenian oratorical habit that emerges precisely in the second half of the fourth century, namely the strategy of appealing to public buildings as symbols of events and institutions that belonged to the past and which had shaped Athenian history.[109] In *Against Leocrates* Lycurgus also built his case partially by relying upon the jurors' sentimental attachments to the physical structures of the city: when Leocrates abandoned Athens, Lycurgus claims, he showed no pity for the vulnerability of the city's walls, harbours and the

[108] Aeschin. 3.153.
[109] Liddel (2007) 156, with n. 70 on bibliography on Athenian buildings in oratory; cf. also Hobden (2007).

temples of Zeus 'Soter' and Athena 'Soteira'.[110] Aeschines had even criticised precisely this kind of rhetorical strategy in *On the False Embassy*. There he charged that the prosecution's 'rhetors' had skirted the real issue of the safety of the state by diverting the jury's attention:

ἀποβλέπειν δὲ εἰς τὰ προπύλαια τῆς ἀκροπόλεως ἐκέλευον ὑμᾶς, καὶ τῆς ἐν Σαλαμῖνι ναυμαχίας μεμνῆσθαι, καὶ τῶν τάφων τῶν προγόνων καὶ τῶν τροπαίων. (Aeschin. 2.75)

[the opposition] instructed you to gaze upon the Propylaea of the Acropolis, and to remember the sea-battle at Salamis and the tombs and monuments of our forefathers.[111]

But despite his earlier dismissal of this sort of appeal, in *Against Ctesiphon* Aeschines refers to a handful of Athenian architectural landmarks – and above all to the Theatre of Dionysus – as he repeatedly grafts the past onto the present.[112] He also effectively elevates both the Theatre of Dionysus and its greatest annual festival to the status of Athenian *lieux de mémoire*: 'sites' that 'had become a symbolic element of the memorial heritage'.[113] The texts of the three great tragedians might have found their protector in Lycurgus, but here in *Against Ctesiphon* Aeschines fashions himself as guardian of the Theatre of Dionysus, in the face of its own form of potential corruption.

The competing discourses of past and present that surface in the speeches from the crown trial are symptomatic of a tension inherent within the Lycurgan theatre programme as a whole. More than ever Athens looked to and idealised its past, but at the same time the city needed innovation to secure its future. This combination of pressures is nowhere so palpable as in the evidence for contemporary changes to and conversations about the physical theatre space. During the third quarter of the fourth century, the Theatre of Dionysus was made new in a

110 Lycurg. 1.17 and 1.143; cf. Liddel (2007) 157.
111 On Aeschines' negotiation of past and present in this passage see Hobden (2007) 496.
112 Hobden (2007) 500, with 496–7 on Aeschines' hypocrisy.
113 Nora (1996) xvii.

number of ways. By the Lycurgan Era it was largely embodied in a new stone building, the construction of which had inspired new strategies of finance and management. New methods of encouraging (or at least rewarding and commemorating) foreign 'investment' in the structure had been developed, yet these innovations were attended – perhaps even guided – by a fundamental concern for preservation of the site's 'classical' legacy. The Lycurgan statues of Aeschylus, Sophocles and Euripides marked a novel use of the theatre's space, but behind that novelty lay a desire to communicate an idealised version of the Athenian past. And though the city now bestowed honours upon certain non-citizens who contributed to the theatre and festivals, no foreigner was allowed to participate in the festival's choruses as either choreute or *choregos*. Athens may have been encouraging certain types of foreign involvement in the financing of its theatre industry, but the persistent concern for 'civic purity' at the Great Dionysia meant that, regardless of who gave money or came to watch, this festival was – like classical tragedy and its most famous poets – an Athenian product and possession.

Against this ideological backdrop we can better understand the implications of a transgression that, according to Plutarch's *Life of Phocion*, Demades made shortly after Athens lost independence to Macedon. The truth behind Plutarch's anecdote is again doubtful, but once more we may recognise through it his astuteness as a reader of the complexities and conflicts of Athenian theatrical history. In the *Life of Phocion* Plutarch's character sketch of Demades, the Athenian statesman and orator, serves largely as a foil for his presentation of the honest Phocion, whose staunch loyalties to Athens in the face of Macedonian rule eventually cost him his life.[114] Demades, like his political rival Lycurgus, took a strong interest in Athens' theatre: he is named as the proposer of two of the ten decrees in the corpus of theatre-related inscriptions from the Lycurgan Era. From Plutarch, however, we hear that Demades once scorned the civic sanctity of the Great Dionysia by illegally leading

[114] See esp. Brun (2000) 169.

a chorus of 100 foreigners into competition. What is worse, knowing the penalties that he would incur for doing so, he came to the festival prepared with enough money to pay the enormous fines (100,000 drachmas, a staggering sixteen and two-thirds talents).[115] Plutarch uses this anecdote largely to draw a contrast between Demades and the poor but virtuous Phocion: Demades 'prided himself on his wealth and on his contempt for the laws which enabled him to acquire it'. This wealth, he tells us, had come to him in great part from Antipater, who had been named the Macedonian regent of Athens following Alexander the Great's death.[116] By using extravagant sums of money that he had acquired in betraying the interests of Athens, Demades deliberately chose to flout a law that was intended to protect the Athenian character of the Dionysia. Even worse, he did so at a time when the city was newly under Macedonian rule and the festival's integrity was most under threat.[117]

This story about Demades shows certain thematic points of contact with Plutarch's story of Alexander's festival in Phoenicia, the festival at which Alexander is said to have happily paid the fine that Athens charged the actor Athenodorus for failing to appear on their own stage.[118] Here too Macedonian wealth and arrogance are the vehicles by which the Great Dionysia is compromised, and in both cases the vulnerable Athenian theatre is a metonymy for the vulnerable city. Despite the lack of further or better historical evidence for these stories (neither of which is told by any other writer), Plutarch's inclusion of them within his accounts of Macedonian–Athenian interactions in the 330s and 320s reveals his sense of how Macedon had sought

[115] 'Demades thus succeeded in turning the punishment for one transgression into the occasion of another': so Wilson (2000) 168.

[116] Plut. *Phoc.* 30.

[117] A more detailed picture of Demades' role in the theatrical sphere is to be desired. Though Plutarch depicts him as flouting the sanctity of Athens' most important theatrical festival, we do know that Demades was somehow engaged in the city's theatre industry thanks to the record of two theatre-related inscriptions (Lambert 3 and 7) that were proposed by him. As Lambert (2008) observes, 'There may have been not only a greater rivalry between these two political giants of the 30s and 20s [i.e. Lycurgus and Demades], but also a greater coincidence of purpose across a wider range of policy spheres than is sometimes recognised' (57).

[118] Plut. *Alex.* 29.3.

both to undermine and to appropriate the status of the Athenian theatre. That status was determined by past accomplishments, but also by the industry's present significance to the city and its widespread fame abroad. With the anecdote about Demades' *choregia*, Plutarch again puts his finger on fourth-century Athenian anxieties about retaining control over the city's theatre industry and heritage. As critical complements to the archaeological and epigraphic records, the contemporary literary texts also reveal a Lycurgan circle attempting by means of rhetoric and 'rhetorical' actions to preserve and to assert possession over the city's theatrical traditions, and especially over the scripts and playwrights of fifth-century tragedy. Nevertheless, the combination of Macedon's wealth with the theatrical passions of its kings meant that Athens could not be sure of retaining control over its dramatic industry, even at home in the Theatre of Dionysus.

PART II

READING THE THEATRICAL HERITAGE

CHAPTER 4

COURTROOM DRAMA: AESCHINES AND DEMOSTHENES

The years of the Lycurgan Era saw an unprecedented partnership of innovation and retrospection in Athens' cultural economy as well as major civic initiatives directed at the theatrical heritage. Classical tragedy was coming to be defined, idealised and even commoditised in spaces and conversations throughout the city: in the court, at the Assembly and in the Theatre of Dionysus. The annual celebration of the Great Dionysia, with its combination of revivals, debuts and preplay ceremonies remained an occasion for the city's self-performance before thousands of spectators. Certain tragedies and tragedians of the past also now occupied a highly visible and 'official' space in the city's landscape and cultural memory. Each of the various pieces of evidence for the Lycurgan theatre programme that we have seen thus far contributes to a colourful and complex picture of the fifth-century theatre's status in the fourth-century city. The sum of this evidence indicates that the 330s saw the idea of classical tragedy concretised in Athens, as certain citizens engaged in legal and even legislative efforts to affirm the city's exclusive rights to this cultural patrimony.

In the first part I outlined as fully as possible our evidence for the 'Lycurgan' vision for Athens' theatre industry and theatrical heritage. This second part will expand the dossier by turning to literary texts of a wider chronological horizon and to the contemporary writings of Aristotle. I shall be concentrating primarily upon fourth-century discussions of Athenian tragedy in further attempts to trace and to contextualise the significance of the Lycurgan theatre reforms. Each of the new sets of texts either sheds light upon or is illuminated by the Lycurgan measures to define, repackage and promote classical tragedy. These texts offer valuable insight into the kinds of debates that, primarily during the 340s and 330s, took place in

Athens and touched upon the role of classical tragedy in civic and everyday life. Many of my earlier arguments relied upon a combination of material and literary evidence, but here I shall be focusing primarily on the surviving literary witnesses.

The texts represent three very different types of 'literature': oratory, comedy and Aristotelian treatise. A number of common themes nevertheless run through these varied corpora. For example, they all bear witness to the increase of the celebrity and star power of fourth-century actors.[1] Aeschines' own erstwhile career as an actor is often the subject of Demosthenes' rhetorical sneers, but at the same time Demosthenes' speeches paint our most vivid literary picture of acting and performance repertories in the mid-fourth century. The comic fragments also contain allusions to contemporary actors, and we even have notice of a comedy by Antiphanes entitled *Tritagonistēs*, the name for a third actor in a troupe. Works by Aristotle also contain various remarks and *obiter dicta* on the subjects of actors and acting;[2] oftentimes these consist in complaints about the excessive power and arrogance that Aristotle felt characterised the actors of his time.

Another theme that these texts share is the ongoing development of theatrical repertories and a dramatic canon. From our sources we can begin to make out which greatest hits of fifth-century tragedy were enjoying the liveliest afterlives in reading and revival. The contemporary evidence suggests that the corpus of classical tragedy had already begun to take steps towards its modern shape by at least the mid-fourth century.[3] For example, and as we shall be seeing shortly, Demosthenes' *On the False Embassy* implies the existence of debates over the appropriate parameters of the emerging canon. The Euripidean tragedies which are most frequently satirised in the fourth-century comic fragments are the plays best attested by the

[1] On actors in the fourth century see esp. Csapo (2010) 85–7 (on the profession from *c.* 370–300 BC); Garland (2004) 107–8 (an account of actors' celebrity in the period); Easterling (2002); and Ghiron-Bistagne (1976) 154–61. See also Le Guen (2001) vol. II.9–11 on the fourth-century background for the formation of associations of 'artists of Dionysus' in the third century, on which see also pages 231–4 below.

[2] See Sifakis (2002) for a synthesis and analysis.

[3] On tragic repertories in the fourth century see esp. Easterling (1997b) 214–20.

papyrus fragments, which marks further evidence for the early popularity of specific plays.[4] A number of the tragic quotations that occur in fourth-century comedy belong to the few classical plays for which we also have a relatively substantial fourth-century tradition, such as Euripides' *Orestes* and Sophocles' *Antigone*. It is also surely no coincidence that, whenever a tragedy is explicity mentioned more than once in the *Poetics*, its name also appears on the roster of Greek tragedies that has survived to the present day. Together all of these observations speak strongly to the fourth century's importance in determining the survival (or disappearance) of the fifth-century plays.

In homing in on these particular witnesses, we shall also notice the conspicuous absence of Aeschylus from moments of tragic citation and discussions of tragic plays. Before the Lycurgan law, Aeschylus' status as a fixture in the classical canon seems to have been in doubt: although some evidence does persist for the continued performance of (parts of) the *Oresteia* in the mid-fourth century,[5] Aeschylus' name is largely missing from our extant literary testimonia. Lycurgus' project to rehabilitate Euripides evidently went hand in hand with an effort to reinvigorate the legacy of Aeschylus, the great playwright and – importantly for Lycurgus' agenda – the heroic veteran of Marathon. From the modern perspective, a perspective very much shaped by Aristophanes' *Frogs*, it is certainly surprising that in the decades before the law Athens seems to have been on the brink of enshrining only a pair, rather than a triad, of great fifth-century tragedians.[6]

In a path-breaking piece on Attic tragedy in the first half of the fourth century, Patricia Easterling emphasised that despite our modern tendency to focus on fifth-century tragedy and to see that period as the genre's golden age, 'the fourth century was a time of extraordinary vitality in the theatre'.[7] This conclusion, I wish to emphasise, is roundly affirmed by all of the sources that I shall be discussing. The fourth-century theatre continued in a largely unbroken line from the days of Sophocles

[4] Arnott (1996) 63. [5] See page 160 below. [6] Cf. Scodel (2007) 131.
[7] Easterling (1993) 562; cf. Le Guen (1995).

and Euripides, and in later antiquity the fourth-century tragedians, too, were perceived as belonging squarely to Athens' tragic heyday. One strong witness to this is Plutarch's treatise *de gloria Atheniensium*: Plutarch observes that the city of Athens still offers sacrifices to the gods because of the city's celebrated military victories, and 'not because of the victories of Aeschylus or Sophocles'. In the next sentence he adds that the polis of Athens (rightly) does not mark the day when Carcinus ('the Younger') fared well with his *Aerope*, or Astydamas with his *Hector*, but rather the day of the Athenian victory at Marathon.[8] For Plutarch at least, these two famous fourth-century tragedians are comfortable representatives of 'classical' tragedy. Even in the *Poetics* Aristotle uses examples from the tragedies of his own time – including plays by Carcinus and Astydamas – to illustrate general observations about the dramatic form. Over the pages that follow we shall be catching a number of glimpses at the successes and reputations of tragedy's fourth-century playwright celebrities.

Nevertheless, strains of classicism undeniably pervade the sources for the theatre in the literary documents of the later fourth century. The only tragedians whom orators cite in the surviving speeches are Sophocles and Euripides; the fourth-century comic poets hardly mention their tragic counterparts and contemporaries in the surviving fragments; and despite Aristotle's attempts at a 'universal' account of tragedy in the *Poetics* he, too, repeatedly shows himself to be under the spell of the classical past. The theatrical discourses that can be detected in the Athens of the mid-fourth century are to a large extent classically oriented and classicising. With respect to Aristophanes and his audiences, however, one critical difference is worth emphasising. Few of the jurors who heard Aeschines and Demosthenes plead their cases, or of the spectators at comic plays by Antiphanes, or of the students who attended Aristotle's lectures, would ever have witnessed the premiere of a play by any of the fifth-century tragedians.

[8] Plut. *Mor.* 349e.

Tragedy on trial

Earlier we saw that the Theatre of Dionysus and the pre-play ceremonies of the Great Dionysia become points of ideological dispute in the trial surrounding Demosthenes' crown. Yet the 'crown' speeches of 330 by no means mark the first encounter between Aeschines and Demosthenes, nor even their first clash over the relationship between the theatre and the city. Three earlier orations survive as artefacts of their enmity: Aeschines' *Against Timarchus* (from 346/5)[9] and Demosthenes and Aeschines' speeches *On the False Embassy* (from 343/2).[10] In both of these cases Aeschines was charged with treason for allegedly accepting, while in the diplomatic service of Athens, bribes from King Philip. The first time that he was prosecuted, by Demosthenes and Timarchus, Aeschines successfully deferred the charge by attacking Timarchus' fitness to act as a prosecutor. Alleging that Timarchus had acted as a male prostitute, Aeschines claimed that he had forfeited his citizen rights to participate in public life. A few years later, Demosthenes and Aeschines would go head to head when Demosthenes reprised the treason charge and both orators delivered their orations *On the False Embassy*. The speeches from that case, like the speeches *Against Ctesiphon* and *On the Crown*, record precious evidence for the afterlife of fifth-century tragedy and speak to the intertwining of theatrical patrimony and civic discourses in the third quarter of the fourth century. Here, however, the theatre-related arguments centre on certain dramatic poetry and the appropriateness of its citation in the courtroom, rather than upon the significance of the Great Dionysia and the Theatre of Dionysus.

The trials of Timarchus and of Aeschines took place in the decade before the Battle of Chaeronea and the arrival of Lycurgus as overseer of state finances. We have already seen that this,

[9] The trial almost certainly took place during the archonship of Archias (346/5); Harris (1985) has proposed the summer of 346 as the most probable season. On the controversy over the date see MacDowell (2000) 21.

[10] MacDowell (2000) 22 with n. 64: 'probably before the end of 343'.

the era of Eubulus' administration, also saw a number of initiatives related to the theatre industry.[11] In roughly 350 works had begun afresh on the Theatre of Dionysus, and shortly thereafter the victory records of the Great Dionysia, the *Fasti*, were first inscribed on the Acropolis (between 347/6 and 343/2).[12] Thus just as the theatre building was undergoing full renovation, the city chose to highlight the importance of its theatrical past by means of a monument to the Great Dionysia's long and continuous tradition. Coincidentally, the case against Timarchus and the trial of Aeschines for his 'false' embassy fall exactly within the possible date range for the inscription of the *Fasti*. Perhaps not coincidentally, however, speeches from these trials are the first that we know of to include citations of tragic poetry. During these years – the years of Eubulus' tenure and Alexander the Great's childhood – Athens' theatrical past was becoming ever more a part of public discourse. And importantly, Aeschines and Demosthenes' orations provide hints at the kinds of debates about tragic poetry and performance that were taking place in Athens shortly before Lycurgus launched his own theatre programme.

Euripides, as wise as any other poet

Aeschines had been a tragic actor before he earned fame on the political stage.[13] Demosthenes seizes every rhetorical opportunity afforded by Aeschines' former career, and even alludes to a handful of roles that Aeschines had played – poorly, he claims – on the stage. These include Creon in Sophocles' *Antigone*,[14] Cresphontes (likely in Euripides' *Cresphontes*) and Oenomaus in Sophocles' *Oenomaus*;[15] in *On the Crown* Demosthenes also accuses Aeschines of having once mutilated the first

[11] For an overview see Csapo and Wilson (forthcoming) section 1.

[12] See Millis (forthcoming) 434 n. 26 for the evidence that the monument was located on the Acropolis.

[13] The evidence for Aeschines' acting career (most of which comes from the speeches of Demosthenes) is collected by Stephanis (1988) no. 90. Demosthenes' invective against Aeschines on account of his former acting career only intensifies in *On the Crown*: see Harris (1995) 30.

[14] Dem. 19.246–7.

[15] Dem. 18.180.

line of Euripides' *Hecuba*.[16] In *On the False Embassy* he even alleges that the spectators used to hiss Aeschines out of the theatre when he performed the 'misfortunes of Thyestes and the men in Troy'.[17] Demosthenes presents Aeschines as a generally incompetent actor, but it is striking that the specific plays that he names are all by either Sophocles or Euripides. As a result, whenever he mentions a particular part or performance that Aeschines botched he is also prompting the members of the jury to see him as having disgraced a classic of Athenian drama.[18] And at a number of turns, Demosthenes links these theatrical failures with Aeschines' civic shortcomings: one of his strategies in *On the False Embassy* is to tie Aeschines' status as a third-rate actor to his third-rate performance as a citizen. Both in life and on the stage Aeschines has proven a mere parroter of lines; having already shown himself incapable of performing the great works of the Athenian theatre he now performs the ideals of Athenian citizenship equally poorly.

Given Aeschines' former career, it is perhaps fitting that he is the first Athenian orator whom we know of to have used poetic citations in court. In *Against Timarchus* he does so to make disparaging claims about Timarchus, Demosthenes' political ally and fellow prosecutor. Aeschines uses poetry to cast Timarchus' own sexual behaviour as shamefully remote from the paradigms of honourable love that are provided by the 'good and useful poets'.[19] In the corpus of ancient oratory the speech is second only to Lycurgus' *Against Leocrates* for its quantity of quoted poetic verse. Like Lycurgus, Aeschines is also sure to prepare the jurors to accept the validity and

[16] Dem. 18.267; the line in the play is uttered by the ghost of Polydorus. Here Demosthenes asks the court-secretary to read out to him τὰς ῥήσεις ἃς ἐλυμαίνου, 'the speeches which you [i.e. Aeschines] mangled'. The first is the opening line of Eur.'s *Hec.*, the second is from an *adespoton* play (*adespota* F 122). Demosthenes then weaves into his prose the beginning of an iambic trimeter (κακὸν κακῶς σε); Pontani (2009) 404 argues that the fragment belongs to comedy and cites a loose parallel with Ar. *Eq.* 2–3. See also Rowe (1966) 402.

[17] Dem. 19.337.

[18] On Demothenes' strategy of tying the duplicitousness nature of Aeschines to his acting career see, e.g., Dorjahn (1929), Rowe (1966), Dyck (1985), Easterling (1999), Duncan (2006) 58–89 and Pontani (2009).

[19] Aeschin. 1.141: ἀγαθοὺς καὶ χρηστοὺς ποιητάς.

importance of his poetic 'witnesses'. When he argues for a critical distinction between being in love with those who are beautiful and chaste and behaving licentiously, he anticipates that a certain general speaking for the defence will cite the examples of Harmodius and Aristogeiton and Achilles and Patroclus.[20] These models will be invoked, he claims, to convince the jurors that Timarchus' own sexual behaviour had noble precedents.[21] To pre-empt the defence's expected strategy Aeschines declares that he too shall bring poetry to bear on the case:

ἐπειδὴ δὲ Ἀχιλλέως καὶ Πατρόκλου μέμνησθε καὶ Ὁμήρου καὶ ἑτέρων ποιητῶν, ὡς τῶν μὲν δικαστῶν ἀνηκόων παιδείας ὄντων, ὑμεῖς δὲ εὐσχήμονές τινες προσποιεῖσθε εἶναι καὶ ὑπερφρονοῦντες ἱστορίᾳ τὸν δῆμον, ἵν' εἰδῆτε ὅτι καὶ ἡμεῖς τι ἤδη ἠκούσαμεν καὶ ἐμάθομεν, λέξομέν τι καὶ ἡμεῖς περὶ τούτων. (Aeschin. 1.141)

But since you bring up Achilles and Patroclus and Homer and other poets, as if the members of the jury had no experience of education, and you act as if you were so refined, looking down in your knowledge upon the people, we shall also say a bit on this matter so that you may know that we too have already heard and learned a little something.

This passage has been read as evidence of the principal peril faced by orators who quoted poetry, namely the risk of appearing elitist.[22] Aeschines' rhetoric serves at once to accuse the defence of literary pretension and to defend himself preemptively from any similar charge.[23] Aeschines takes on an especially didactic tone in this section of the speech (1.142–53) by quoting extensively from poetry but also by submitting polemical interpretations of the poets' intended meanings.[24] He describes Homer, for example, 'whom we count as among the oldest and wisest of the poets',[25] as having intentionally concealed (ἀποκρύπτεται) the erotic dimension of the relationship between Achilles and Patroclus, 'reckoning that the great

[20] The published version of Aeschines' speech may however reflect Aeschines' own *a posteriori* knowledge of the case that had been made by the defence.

[21] Aeschin. 1.131–2.

[22] Ford (1999) 250–5; cf. Ober (2001) 202–5, Garland (2004) 20 and Scodel (2007) 135–6.

[23] See esp. Hunter (2012) 25 and Ford (1999) 252 on the passage.

[24] On this strategy's appearance in fourth-century oratory see esp. Ford (1999).

[25] Aeschin. 1.142: λέξω δὲ πρῶτον μὲν περὶ Ὁμήρου, ὅν ἐν τοῖς πρεσβυτάτοις καὶ σοφωτάτοις τῶν ποιητῶν εἶναι τάττομεν.

extent of their goodwill towards each other would be evident to educated members of the audience'.[26] But though Aeschines focuses primarily on quotations from the *Iliad* which 'prove' the skill and dignity with which Homer represented Achilles and Patroclus, in the same section of the speech he also marshals to the attack two passages of Euripidean tragedy.

After the discussion of Homer, Aeschines calls to witness Euripides, whom he had already briefly cited (alongside Hesiod) on the nature of rumour.[27] As a preface to this longer quotation, Aeschines, like Lycurgus will later do, first issues something of a character reference for the poet:

ὁ τοίνυν οὐδενὸς ἧττον σοφὸς τῶν ποιητῶν Εὐριπίδης, ἕν τι τῶν καλλίστων ὑπολαμβάνων εἶναι τὸ σωφρόνως ἐρᾶν, ἐν εὐχῆς μέρει τὸν ἔρωτα ποιούμενος λέγει που·

> Ὁ δ' εἰς τὸ σῶφρον ἐπ' ἀρετήν τ' ἄγων ἔρως
> ζηλωτὸς ἀνθρώποισιν, ὧν εἴην ἐγώ.
> (Eur. F 672) (Aeschin. 1.151)

Euripides, who is as wise as any of the poets, and who understood that chaste love is one of the most beautiful things there is, presents such love as something to be prayed for when he says somewhere:

> Love that leads to self-restraint and to virtue
> is sought by men in whose number I would like to
> belong.

Lycurgus' introduction of Euripides in *Against Lycurgus* will be richer in its allusive and rhetorical strategies, yet Aeschines' characterisation of Euripides as 'as wise as any of the poets' is also remarkable, not least for the source of the quotation. The two verses come from Euripides' lost *Stheneboea* (from before 422 BC)[28] and belong to the prologue that Bellerophon delivers at the start of the play.[29] In the prologue Bellerophon

[26] Aeschin. 1.142: ἡγούμενος τὰς τῆς εὐνοίας ὑπερβολὰς καταφανεῖς εἶναι τοῖς πεπαιδευμένοις τῶν ἀκροατῶν. On Aeschines' tendentious interpretation of the Homeric text see Ford (1999) 252–3.

[27] Aeschin. 1.129.

[28] Eur. F 663 and 665 were parodied in Ar. *Ves.* (at lines 1074 and 111–12 respectively; in both instances the scholia identify Eur. *Sthen.* as the play of reference); see Collard, Cropp and Lee (1995) 79–89.

[29] Eur. F 661.24–5.

explains how Stheneboea, the wife of his host Proteus, has been attempting to persuade and to trick him into sleeping with her. Bellerophon there differentiates, as Aeschines aims to do here, between the kind of love that destroys and the chaste sort of love that is described in the tragic lines.

From a surviving *hypothesis* to the lost play we know that, when Stheneboea proved unsuccessful in her attempt at seduction, she claimed that Bellerophon had tried to rape her. In the fifth century Aristophanes had not failed to see the parallels between Euripides' Stheneboea and the Phaedra of his *Hippolytus*. In the *Frogs* the Aristophanic Aeschylus contrasts the types of people whom he and Euripides portrayed in their plays, boasting first that his own 'mind created' (ἡμὴ φρὴν . . . ἐποίησεν) paragons of valour such as Patroclus and Teucer. He declares:

> ἀλλ' οὐ μὰ Δί' οὐ Φαίδρας ἐποίουν πόρνας οὐδὲ Σθενεβοίας,
> οὐδ' οἶδ' οὐδεὶς ἥντιν' ἐρῶσαν πώποτ' ἐποίησα γυναῖκα.
> (Ar. *Ran.* 1043–4)

> But by God I never portrayed whores, Phaedras or Stheneboeas,
> nor does anyone know of any lustful woman I depicted.

In Aristophanes' *Thesmophoriazusae* the principal female character, Mica, also alludes to Euripides' *Stheneboea*, in a monologue detailing Euripides' slanders of women. Mica complains that now, thanks to Euripides, if a wife so much as drops something around the house her husband suspects that she has been distracted by distress over an illicit love. Her husband asks her, 'On whose account was the pot broken? Surely for your Corinthian guest' (403–4). A scholion indicates that this phrase comes 'from the *Stheneboea* of Euripides'. In a fragment of Euripides' play, Stheneboea's nurse claims that whenever her mistress realises that she has dropped something, she declares 'to the Corinthian guest!' (τῷ Κορινθίῳ ξένῳ) – that is, Bellerophon.[30]

[30] F 664. The phrase would become famous: see Collard, Cropp and Lee (1995) ad loc. A further reference to *Stheneboea* appears in the *lekythion*-scene of the *Frogs* (1217–19 = F 666.1–3), where its first lines are quoted.

In Aristophanes' comedies, then, *Stheneboea* stands as a kind of byword for Euripides' tendency to stage sexual scandal and so to set bad examples for the citizens. Aristophanes' Aeschylus and Mica provide two different and distinctly gendered accounts of the nature of the damage that Euripides has caused: 'Aeschylus' charges that his plays have encouraged immoral behaviour on the part of Athenian women, while Mica laments that they have drawn husbands into constant suspicion of their wives. Given the apparent notoriety of *Stheneboea*, it was perhaps wise for Aeschines not to mention the play as the source of his quotation. When he introduces the tragic verses without attribution, saying only that Euripides 'says somewhere' (λέγει που) that the love which leads to self-restraint is desirable, his vague phrasing serves to imply that he wears his learning lightly, but it also enables him to gloss over the infamous source of the quotation.[31] Aeschines' introduction of the lines with his affirmation that Euripides understood the importance of chaste love also works to dispel any negative associations that his audience may have had with Euripides, associations that were due in part to Aristophanic depictions.[32] That introduction also, however, underscores what Aeschines hopes to present as the inherent authority of Euripidean verse: with Euripides as the source of a sentiment, Aeschines implies, who could possibly argue?

But Aeschines does still more to commend Euripides. In his later discussion of lines from Euripides' *Phoenix*, he actively champions the morality of the poet. This positive view is presented in rhetorical terms that are closely aligned with the

[31] Cf. Wilson (1996) 314–15; see also Pontani (2009) 412, who suggests that Aeschines' invocation of *Stheneboea* would prompt Demosthenes to respond with rhetoric that also drew upon the terms of the *Frogs*' critical discourses (at Dem. 19.243–50): see further below. Aeschines may have simply pulled the quotation from an anthology: F 665–8 and 671 are all preserved by the gnomological tradition.

[32] In the *Clouds*, for example, Strepsiades presents the Euripidean *rhēsis* that his son performs, about an incestuous brother and sister – certainly a case of 'unchaste' love – as all too typical (Ar. *Nub.* 1371–2). Aristophanes' negative characterisations of public figures could be potent and enduring: Plato's Socrates suggests that the slanderous representation of him also in Aristophanes' *Clouds* contributed to his prosecution (Pl. *Ap.* 18c–d). For comedy's influence on the biographical tradition for Euripides see Lefkowitz (1981) 88–9.

defence that 'Euripides' makes of his own poetry in the *Frogs*. Now Aeschines makes no attempt to hide the source of his Euripidean citation:

πάλιν τοίνυν ὁ αὐτὸς ἐν τῷ Φοίνικι ἀποφαίνεται, ὑπὲρ τῆς γεγενημένης αὐτῷ πρὸς τὸν πατέρα διαβολῆς ἀπολογούμενος, καὶ ἀπεθίζων τοὺς ἀνθρώπους μὴ ἐξ ὑποψίας μηδ' ἐκ διαβολῆς, ἀλλ' ἐκ τοῦ βίου τὰς κρίσεις ποιεῖσθαι· (Aeschin. 1.152)

Again the same poet declares [his views] in the *Phoenix*, when he is defending him [i.e. Phoenix] against the slander of his father, and teaching people to form their judgements on the basis not of suspicion and slander, but rather of the man's life.[33]

Following this introduction Aeschines goes on to quote nine lines of the *Phoenix* (which premiered sometime before 425 BC)[34] to the effect that a man is rightly known by the company he keeps.[35] Here again the 'wise' Euripides is presented as having offered valuable lessons to the citizens through his poetry: it is he, and not the character in the play, who defends (ἀπολογούμενος) the unjustly accused Phoenix; in doing so Euripides also attempts more generally to 'disaccustom' (ἀπεθίζω) people from relying on rumour in their judgements of others. Aeschines then paraphrases the *Phoenix* quotation, adapting its lessons to the courtroom setting. He goes so far here as to assimilate the historical figure of Euripides entirely to the speaker of the verses, as Euripides himself is the subject of every underlined phrase in the Greek below:

σκέψασθε δέ, ὦ Ἀθηναῖοι, τὰς γνώμας ἃς ἀποφαίνεται ὁ ποιητής. ἤδη δὲ πολλῶν πραγμάτων φησὶ γεγενῆσθαι κριτής, ὥσπερ νῦν ὑμεῖς δικασταί, καὶ τὰς κρίσεις οὐκ ἐκ τῶν μαρτυριῶν, ἀλλ' ἐκ τῶν ἐπιτηδευμάτων καὶ τῶν ὁμιλιῶν φησι ποιεῖσθαι, ἐκεῖσε ἀποβλέπων πῶς τὸν καθ' ἡμέραν βίον ζῇ ὁ κρινόμενος, καὶ ὅντινα τρόπον διοικεῖ τὴν ἑαυτοῦ οἰκίαν, ὡς παραπλησίως αὐτὸν καὶ τὰ τῆς πόλεως διοικήσοντα,

33 In Euripides' version Phoenix refused his mother's pleadings that he sleep with his father's mistress; she nevertheless accuses him of rape: see the summary of Collard and Cropp (2008) 405–6.

34 Ar. *Ach.* (425 BC) contains a reference to the raggedy costume of Euripides' Phoenix (Euripides offers Dicaeopolis τὰ [τρύχη] τοῦ τυφλοῦ Φοίνικος, 421; cf. below). That it is Phoenix – the tragic *victim* – who lends his name to the title of the play may have meant that it was less hazardous for Aeschines actually to name this tragedy.

35 F 812. The lines are likely spoken by the centaur Chiron, who healed Phoenix after he was blinded by his father King Amyntor (Apollod. 3.175; Propertius 2.1.60): cf. Collard and Cropp (2008) ad loc.

καὶ τίσι χαίρει πλησιάζων· καὶ τελευτῶν οὐκ ὤκνησεν ἀποφήνασθαι τοιοῦτον εἶναι οἷσπερ ἥδεται ξυνών. (Aeschin. 1.153)[36]

Consider, then, Athenians, the sentiments (γνῶμαι) which the poet lays out. He says that he has already acted as judge in many matters, just as now you are jurymen, and he says that he makes his judgements not on the basis of witnesses, but on the basis of the accused's habits and the company that he keeps. He judges by considering how the man leads his everyday life, how he administers his own household – since he is likely to manage himself and the affairs of the polis in essentially the same way – and with which people he is happy to associate. And finally it does not pain him to declare that he is 'the same sort of man as those whose company he enjoys'.

When in *Against Leocrates* Lycurgus introduces his own quotation of Praxithea's speech from *Erechtheus* he too consistently emphasises Euripides' good judgement, in this case his good judgement as a poet: Euripides 'made' Praxithea's speech (πεποίηκε); he portrayed her nobly (ἐποίησε); and in doing so he 'displayed' (ἐνδεικνύμενος) an important lesson for Athenian citizens.[37] In *Against Timarchus* Aeschines had gone even further in presenting the words of one of Euripides' characters as the wise words of Euripides himself, that is, as authentic artefacts of the poet's own experience, virtues and teachings.[38] In Euripidean tragedy, and as Glenn Most has noted, older characters tend to ground the authority of their gnomic pronouncements in the body of experience which they have gained in the course of their lives.[39] This is precisely the type of Euripidean character into which Aeschines here transforms the poet himself: a man made wise by experience and years, who has 'already acted as judge in many matters'.

[36] Aeschines' phrase τοιοῦτον εἶναι οἷσπερ ἥδεται ξυνών hearkens back to the final sentiment of the *Phoenix* quotation: ὅστις δ' ὁμιλῶν ἥδεται κακοῖς ἀνήρ, | οὐ πώποτ' ἠρώτησα, γιγνώσκων ὅτι | τοιοῦτός ἐστιν οἷσπερ ἥδεται ξυνών (Eur. F 812 lines 7–9).

[37] Lycurg. 1.100–1; cf. page 39 above.

[38] The ancient practice of inferring information about a poet from his verses, the so-called 'Chamaeleontic Method' is detailed at Arrighetti (1987), esp. 141–59 and 177–80. Chamaeleon, an early 'literary biographer', claimed that 'the tragic poet attributes to his heroes what he himself used to do' (ἃ δ' αὐτὸς τραγῳποιὸς ἐποίει, ταῦτα τοῖς ἥρωσι περιέθηκε, F 26 Wehrli); cf. Satyrus F 6 fr. 39.9 Schorn = Aristophanes fr. 694 K–A with Schorn (2004) 272–8 and Arrighetti (1964) 124–5.

[39] Most (2003) 149; cf. Arist. *Rhet.* 2.1395a on the attribution of *gnōmai* to old and experienced people.

Having thus established Euripides' moral authority, Aeschines concludes his long section of poetic citations with an injunction to the jurors: 'and so it is right that you apply Euripides' reasoning also in the case of Timarchus'.[40] In the *Frogs* 'Euripides' defended his own poetry's capacity precisely to prompt the citizens to logical 'reasoning' (*logismos*). In the midst of the agon there with 'Aeschylus', 'Euripides' offers contrasting characterisations of Aeschylus' and his own disciples. When Dionysus observes that one of Euripides' pupils, Theramenes, always knows how to escape trouble, Euripides replies with this account of the 'practicality' of his own dramatic composition:

τοιαῦτα μέντοὐγὼ φρονεῖν
τούτοισιν εἰσηγησάμην,
λογισμὸν ἐνθεὶς τῇ τέχνῃ
καὶ σκέψιν, ὥστ' ἤδη νοεῖν
ἅπαντα καὶ διειδέναι
τά τ' ἄλλα καὶ τὰς οἰκίας
οἰκεῖν ἄμεινον ἢ πρὸ τοῦ
κἀνασκοπεῖν·
(Ar. *Ran.* 971–8)

Well I instructed these people to think carefully about such things, having added rational reasoning to the art form, and critical thought too, so that now [the citizens] have become perceptive about everything, and among other things they manage their homes better than they used to, before they examined things closely.

In this final appeal to the practical benefits of Euripidean *logismos* in general and the *logismoi* of the *Phoenix* passage in particular, Aeschines' rhetoric echoes the language of Euripides' 'own' self-presentation in the *Frogs*.[41] In the comedy 'Euripides' stood by his choice of bringing 'everyday matters' (οἰκεῖα

[40] Aeschin. 1.153: οὐκοῦν δίκαιον καὶ περὶ Τιμάρχου τοῖς αὐτοῖς ὑμᾶς Εὐριπίδῃ χρήσασθαι λογισμοῖς.

[41] Elsewhere in Aeschines' speeches λογισμός tends to mean a financial account (three times at 3.59–60), a 'reckoning' as in a determination of judgement (3.170) or an 'account' of something that has transpired (2.130). On one occasion in *Against Timarchus* the word's meaning is closer to its sense here: Aeschines reports that Demosthenes told Pyrrandrus that the truth defeats all human 'calculations' (οὕτως ἰσχυρόν ἐστιν ἡ ἀλήθεια, ὥστε πάντων ἐπικρατεῖν τῶν ἀνθρωπίνων λογισμῶν, 1.84). On λογισμός in Dem. 18 see Todd (2009) 170.

πράγματα, *Ran.* 959) into his plays – matters with which the people were familiar and so could understand.[42] Aeschines, like Aristophanes' Euripides, also views Euripidean reasoning as a 'transferable skill', with equal applications on the stage and in everyday life.

Demosthenes and the voice of the *Frogs*

On certain grounds the presentation of Euripides in *Against Timarchus* accords well with the introduction that Lycurgus would give Euripides some fifteen years later in *Against Leocrates*. For Aeschines and Lycurgus alike, Euripides is a font of moral insight and a poet whose verses are a result and reflection of his own sage character. Lycurgus will differ from Aeschines in taking elaborate pains to identify that character with the Athenian polis, but in *Against Timarchus* Aeschines offers us an idea of how Euripidean poetry could already be regarded as a repository of wisdom. Aeschines' account and use of Euripides nevertheless proved provocative enough for Demosthenes to issue a response, albeit a few years later, when he finally gained an occasion to reply to Aeschines in *On the False Embassy*. There he makes no comments about Euripides when he repeats the *Phoenix* quotation; in this respect as well as others his methods of poetic quotation differ from those of Aeschines and Lycurgus. Demosthenes never, for example, quotes from Homer; he also deploys all eight of his poetic quotations as part of direct attacks upon Aeschines.[43] Thus while Aeschines attempts to use poetry as proof and poets as witnesses, Demosthenes' own verse citations always mark personal counter-attacks in response to those moves: he sets out to prove that he can beat Aeschines at his own game. Accordingly, within the Demosthenic corpus poetry appears exclusively in the speeches delivered against Aeschines: *On the False Embassy* and *On the Crown*.

[42] On this passage and the concept of οἰκεῖα πράγματα (a phrase that has important implications for the characterisation of Euripides' poetic style) see Hunter (2009) 17–20.

[43] Cf. Pontani (2009) 402.

On the False Embassy is Demosthenes' only speech that contains an extended discussion of multiple poetic quotations, and there he offers the jury passages from Hesiod, Euripides, Sophocles and Solon.[44] His citations of Hesiod and Euripides are particularly unusual, in that he does not quote their poetry for the wisdom that it contains. Instead, Demosthenes effectively quotes Aeschines' own recitations of verses by these poets in *Against Timarchus*. Not only does Demosthenes charge that Aeschines had included poetry in his case because he could not provide actual witnesses (οὐδένα μάρτυρα ἔχων, 19.243), he also argues that Aeschines erred in choosing which poetry to recite. To illustrate, he first repeats Hesiod's lines on the nature of rumour,[45] claiming that in reality they condemn Aeschines himself: 'all these men say that you got money out of the embassy, so that indeed it is also true in your case that "no rumour which many people spread dies completely"'.[46] He likewise repeats the final three lines of Aeschines' nine-line quotation of the *Phoenix*, on how a man is like the company he keeps, claiming that 'these iambics now also apply to my case against you'.[47] Only afterwards does he attempt to top Aeschines by offering his own selections of poetry – verses from Sophocles' *Antigone* and Solon's elegiac poem on *eunomia* (F 4 West) – as examples of passages which his opponent ought to have had in mind and taken to heart.[48]

Demosthenes' criticisms of the Euripidean citation begin with the claim that these were lines that Aeschines had 'gathered up and recited' (συλλέξας ἐπέραινεν, 19.245). Once more he turns Aeschines' own words against him, claiming that 'though he calls others logographers (λογογράφοι) and sophists (σοφισταί), he will be shown to be deserving of those names himself' (19.246). Demosthenes then offers this explanation as to why Aeschines' invocation of the *Phoenix* was a mark of poor judgement:

[44] Dem. 19.243–55. [45] Hes. *Op*. 763–4.
[46] Dem. 19.243. [47] Dem. 19.246.
[48] Dem. 19.247 with Soph. *Ant*. 175–90; Dem. 19.255 with Solon 4 West. On the 'competition in quotation' between Aeschines and Demosthenes in these speeches see Scodel (2007) 137–9.

ταῦτα μὲν γὰρ τὰ ἰαμβεῖ' ἐκ Φοίνικός ἐστιν Εὐριπίδου· τοῦτο δὲ τὸ δρᾶμ' οὐδεπώποτ' οὔτε Θεόδωρος οὔτ' Ἀριστόδημος ὑπεκρίναντο, οἷς οὗτος τὰ τρίτα λέγων διετέλεσεν, ἀλλὰ Μόλων ἠγωνίζετο καὶ εἰ δή τις ἄλλος τῶν παλαιῶν ὑποκριτῶν. (Dem. 19.246)

These iambic verses [i.e. which Aeschines cited in *Against Timarchus* and Demosthenes has just repeated] are from the *Phoenix* of Euripides. But neither Theodorus nor Aristodemus, actors for whom [Aeschines] often played the third part, has ever acted it; rather it was Molon and some other of the olden-day actors who competed with it.

Modern scholars often discuss how Demosthenes insults Aeschines here by labelling him a 'tritagonist', the third and so least important actor in a troupe.[49] This comment is valuable as an insight into the sociology of actors and acting, but perhaps still more important is Demosthenes' characterisation of the *Phoenix* as an unpopular play. For him, the authority of that play's verses is undermined by the realities of (non-)performance: *Phoenix* was a play with little place in contemporary repertoires. It had only been performed by actors of old, the *palaioi hypokritai*.

Molon, the 'olden-day' actor whom Demosthenes claims acted in *Phoenix*, is likely the Molon who is mentioned briefly in Aristophanes' *Frogs*.[50] Towards the play's beginning, Dionysus recounts to Heracles how he became overcome with longing for Euripides while reading the *Andromeda*. Heracles responds by asking how great Dionysus' longing was (πόθος; πόσος τις;), and Dionysus replies that it was small – Molon-sized.[51] Theodorus and Aristodemus, on the other hand, were two of the best-known actors of Demosthenes and Aeschines' time

[49] The bibliography is large; on the term as applied to Aeschines see esp. Dorjahn (1929), Ghiron-Bistagne (1976) 158–60, Duncan (2006) 65–7 and 78–9 and MacDowell (2000) 289 *ad* 200; on the word 'tritagonist' (τριταγωνιστής) see Todd (1938) and Csapo and Slater (1995) 222–3.

[50] For the testimonia to Molon's career see Stephanis (1988) no. 1738.

[51] Ar. *Ran*.55: σμικρός, ἡλίκος Μόλων. According to a scholiast and loc., Didymus noted that there were two famous Molons – one an actor, the other a thief – and that the Molon mentioned in *Frogs* was the thief; Timachidas, however, identified him with the actor (ὁ ὑποκρίτης). Timachidas of Rhodian Lindus (late second–early first century BC) also compiled the 'Lindian Chronicle' and was responsible for a commentary on Aristophanes; see Ziegler (1936).

and both are well attested in epigraphic and literary sources.[52] In making a distinction between earlier and contemporary actors, Demosthenes implies that Aeschines has made sophistic recourse to an out of the way play. His failure to be in touch with this aspect of the city's culture is, Demosthenes implies, further evidence of his weaknesses as a citizen.

But in spite of Demosthenes' characterisation of the play as obscure, *Phoenix* does have traceable reception in antiquity.[53] In Aristophanes' *Acharnians*, Dicaeopolis refuses to borrow the clothing of 'blind Phoenix' from Euripides' wardrobe of old tragic costumes.[54] The fourth-century tragedian Astydamas wrote a *Phoenix* (T 5d), as would Ennius.[55] And although we have no evidence of specific reperformances of the play, the case is the same for the majority of fifth-century tragedies that *have* survived. But even if the *Phoenix* was not altogether forgotten after its fifth-century premiere, Demosthenes here adopts a strategy of casting the play as not well known to the jurors. Aeschines' hunting down of quotations from such a recherché source was therefore the pretentious move of a sophist and logographer.

Already we have seen how Aeschines' 'recommendation' of Euripides in *Against Timarchus* recalls aspects of the defence the 'Euripides' lays out in the *Frogs*. Filippomaria Pontani has also convincingly argued that Demosthenes' strategies in this portion of *On the False Embassy* evoke aspects of Aristophanes' play:

[T]here is at least a chance that the link between our speech [i.e. Dem. 19] and the *Frogs* goes beyond the narrow boundaries of the obvious affinities

[52] The testimonia are gathered at Stephanis (1988) nos. 1157 and 332, respectively; cf. MacDowell (2000) 210 and 305. For Theodorus see also *SEG* 34 174.4.

[53] This is particularly because the blinding of *Phoenix* by Amyntor appears to have been a Euripidean innovation that subsequently became a fixture of the myth: cf. Jouan and van Looy (2002) 316 (cf. e.g. Men. *Sam.* 498–500 = their T iiib; *AP* 3.3 = T iiic; Apollod. 3.3.18 = T iiid); on the afterlife of *Phoenix* see their discussion at 314–18. On the Euripidean innovations to the story of Phoenix see Σ *ad* H. *Il.* 9.448 and 553 (T iia–b).

[54] Ar. *Ach.* 421–2. Cf. Telò (2007) 110–12, on an allusion to *Phoenix* in Eupolis' late fifth-century comedy the *Demes*.

[55] Jocelyn (1967) 389–90 detects traces of Euripides' treatment in the Ennian fragments.

between comedy and oratory, and that Demosthenes' strategy of reference to Euripides and Sophocles somehow rests on an Aristophanic background.[56]

In support of this argument he gathers seven pieces of circumstantial evidence.[57] These include, besides Demosthenes' reference to Molon, certain key points of diction. Pontani notes, for example, that when Demosthenes re-introduces the *Phoenix* quotation:

ἔτι τοίνυν ἰαμβεῖα δήπου συλλέξας ἐπέραινεν ... (Dem. 19.245)

Then what is more he recited iambic lines that he had collected ...

The verb ἐπέραινεν appears in its rare meaning of 'to recite', 'a use which occurs in the same scene [i.e. the great contest] of the *Frogs*'.[58] There, 'Euripides' and Dionysus both use the verb in commands. Euripides does so in ordering Aeschylus to 'get on with reciting' (πέραινε, 1170) the first lines of the *Choephori*, which he had begun to deliver in order to disprove the allegation that he composed abstruse opening scenes. Later, when Euripides mocks Aeschylus' lyric passages for all sounding the same, he begs that Dionysus stay to hear some more of his parodies. Dionysus responds by bidding Euripides, again with the injunction πέραινε, to carry on with his act of caricaturing Aeschylean songs.[59] The verb is common in fifth-century poetry, but it only appears some ten times within the entire Demosthenic corpus. In most cases Demosthenes uses it to mean 'accomplish' a task that one has set his mind upon,[60] or else to 'run through', 'address' a point or even to 'strive after accomplishing' something.[61] His use of the word in *On the*

[56] Pontani (2009) 413. [57] Pontani (2009) 410–11.

[58] At *Ran.* 1170 and 1284; Pontani (2009) 411.

[59] Ar. *Ran.* 1284: ἴθι δή, πέραινε. When Demosthenes uses the verb with the sense of 'to recite' the usage itself is strictly speaking closer to what we find in fragments of his contemporary Antiphanes, where περαίνω means something closer to 'recite poetry' or to 'sing a song': his *Agroikos* begins (F 1) with a character reciting lines of poetry (= Soph. F 754); when someone asks what this is (τί λέγεις;) he responds: τραγῳδίαν περαίνω Σοφοκλέους (line 6; see page 173 in the next chapter). In another of his plays (F 85) one character asks another not to sing (περάνης) one of those old-fashioned (ἀπηρχαιωμένων) songs, such as the 'Telamon' or the Paean or the 'Harmodius'.

[60] E.g. Dem. 2.13 and 18.149, 34.2 and 35.3; cf. Aeschines 2.66.

[61] Dem. 4.28 and 23.9 respectively.

False Embassy, where the verb takes on its relatively rare meaning of 'recite' or 'get on with reciting', may therefore faintly evoke the many interrupted and failed acts of poetic recitation that we find in the *Frogs*.

Yet Pontani's suspicion that 'Demosthenes' strategy of reference to Euripides and Sophocles 'somehow rests on an Aristophanic background' is even better supported by two other instances of shared diction. The first point of contact comes through the verb συλλέγω. When in *On the False Embassy* Demosthenes says that Aeschines recited *iambeia* which he had 'collected' or 'assembled' (συλλέξας), his use of συλλέγω recalls the image of the verse-gathering Euripides that appears twice in Aristophanes.[62] The first occurrence is in the *Acharnians*, which took the comic prize at the Lenaea of 425 BC: when Dicaeopolis there tries to persuade Cephisophon to let him into the house to see Euripides, Cephisophon tells him that Euripides, though inside, is not really 'in'.[63] Dicaeopolis asks how that can be, and Cephisophon explains:

> ὁ νοῦς μὲν ἔξω ξυλλέγων ἐπύλλια
> οὐκ ἔνδον, αὐτὸς δ' ἔνδον ἀναβάδην ποεῖ
> τραγῳδίαν. (Ar. *Ach*. 398–40)

> His mind is not in, but outside gathering
> up little verselets; he however is inside, sat up,
> composing a tragedy.

Aristophanes' *Peace* (421 BC) also contains a similar description of poetic activity. When Trygaeus' servant asks him whether he encountered anyone on his travels in heaven, Trygaeus responds that he saw no one but the souls of two or three dithyrambic poets. The servant asks what those poets were doing up there, and Trygaeus responds that they were

[62] The word συλλογή, or gathering, which later also had the meaning '(literary) anthology'. For evidence of 'anthologising' – that is, gathering up poetic excerpts – in the fourth century, see e.g. Isoc. 2.44 (*Ad Nicoclem*) and Pl. *Leg*. 7.811a. For the development of poetic anthologies see Hunter and Russell (2011) 15–16.

[63] Ar. *Ach*. 396: οὐκ ἔνδον ἔνδον ἐστίν.

ξυνελέγοντ' ἀναβολὰς ποτώμεναι
τὰς ἐνδιαεριαυρονηχέτους τινάς.
(Ar. *Pax*. 830)

flying about, gathering up lyrical preludes[64]
that were floating around in the gentle breezes.

But when a similar image is used of Euripides the tone becomes more sharply critical; no longer is the poet who 'gathers' his verses one who is harmlessly away with the fairies. During the contest of the *Frogs* an enraged Aeschylus lunges at Euripides (only to be restrained by Dionysus), charging:

ὦ Κρητικὰς μὲν συλλέγων μονῳδίας,
γάμους δ' ἀνοσίους εἰσφέρων εἰς τὴν τέχνην, –
(Ar. *Ran*. 849–50)

O you collector of Cretan songs,
who introduced unholy unions into our art form –

In the eyes of 'Aeschylus', Euripides' poetic gatherings are far from innocuous: they are at the heart of the citizen-harming immorality of his plays. The insult that the image implies is only reinforced when Aeschylus indignantly responds to the accusation from Dionysus that he, too, is a 'gatherer' who 'collected' (συνέλεξας) the songs of rope-winders at Marathon and imported them into his tragedies.[65] Aeschylus defends himself in part by tendentiously substituting a form of the verb φέρω for Dionysus' συλλέγω:

ἀλλ' οὖν ἐγὼ μὲν εἰς τὸ καλὸν ἐκ τοῦ καλοῦ
ἤνεγκον αὔθ', ἵνα μὴ τὸν αὐτὸν Φρυνίχῳ
λειμῶνα Μουσῶν ἱερὸν ὀφθείην δρέπων·
(Ar. *Ran*. 1298–1300)

No, rather I brought them from a fine source to
a fine place, so as not to seem to be culling the
same sacred meadow of the Muses as Phrynichus.[66]

[64] Cf. LSJ s.v. ἀναβολή II.1: an ἀναβολή is a striking up or prelude to singing on the lyre, and hence comes to mean a 'rambling dithyrambic ode' (*LSJ* cites s.v. Ar. *Av*. 1385 with *Pax* 830 and Arist. *Rh*. 1409b25).

[65] Aeschylus likewise accuses Euripides of being a 'chat-gatherer' (στωμυλιοσυλλεκτάδης) at *Ran*. 841.

[66] In Aristophanes' *Birds* (lines 748–50) Phrynichus is compared to a bee who gathers nectar for his honey-sweet songs: on the image see Sommerstein (1996) *ad* Ar. *Ran*. 1299–1300.

Phrynichus' own action of 'culling' or 'plucking' (δρέπω) is here similar to Euripides' habitual 'gathering'. In the next lines, 'Aeschylus' contrasts himself with 'Euripides' on this very point, claiming that Euripides is happy to take *his* honey from any source at all (ἀπὸ πάντων): the songs of prostitutes and the *skolia* of Meletus, as well as Carian *aulos*-melodies, dirges and dances.[67]

When Demosthenes uses a form of συλλέγω to characterise Aeschines' 'collecting' of poetic quotations, the charge carries the same notes of disparagement: Aeschines, too, gathered his verses without regard for their origin, or for their appropriateness to his own argument. Demosthenes' depiction of Aeschines as a 'collector' of verses à la Euripides therefore implicitly assimilates him to the negative figure of the indiscriminate poet who gathers his *epyllia* from any and every source. For Demosthenes and Aristophanes' Aeschylus alike, such poets are heedless of whether their sources are 'fine' ones that promise to improve the citizen body. The obscurity and infelicity of the tragic passage that Aeschines hunted down and gathered up thus not only confirm his sophistry but also points to the potential malignance of his influence upon the demos.[68]

We should of course be wary of drawing too direct or firm a line between the *Frogs* and these passages of Demosthenes, or of seeing Demosthenes' strategy in his speech as absolutely hinging upon allusions to the play or upon his assimilation of Aeschines to the Aristophanic Euripides.[69] Yet even if the success of Demosthenes' argument did not depend upon the audience's recognition of any comic allusions, it is certainly striking how often both he and Aeschines employ critical vocabulary that is for us first attested in the Aristophanic corpus, and most

[67] Ar. *Ran.* 1301–11. Lucian's *The Dead Come to Life, or the Fisherman* makes an explicit connection between gathering literary verses or sayings and (a bee's) gathering flowers (*Pisc.* 6). Meleager used similar wordplay when, in the proem to his *Garland*, he compared the poets whose verses he had collected to flowers (*AP* 4.1). Aristotle (e.g.) uses ἀνθολογέω of bees gathering flowers at *Hist. an.* 8.628b.

[68] Demosthenes comically inverts the imagery in *On the Crown*, where he mocks Aeschines for having 'gathered' not verses, but rather the figs, grapes and olives thrown at him by spectators (18.262).

[69] Cf. Pontani (2009) 413.

prominently in the *Frogs*.[70] The persistence of that vocabulary is also attended by the persistence of certain critical views and categories. For Demosthenes, Aeschines' rhetoric shared negative and destructive qualities similar to those which Euripidean poetry was said to have displayed, and put the demos at risk on similar counts. Within the same oration his use of βλάπτω, 'to harm', also evokes discussions staged in the *Frogs* about tragedy's potentially damaging effects upon the morality of the spectators:

ἃ μὲν πολλάκις ἠγωνίσω καὶ ἀκριβῶς ἐξηπίστασο, ὑπερέβης, ἃ δ' οὐδεπώποτ' ἐν τῷ βίῳ ὑπεκρίνω, ταῦτα ζητήσας ἐπὶ τῷ τῶν πολιτῶν βλάψαι τιν' εἰς μέσον ἤνεγκας. (Dem. 19.250)

The [lines] which you competed with many times and knew by heart [i.e. the lines from *Antigone*] you passed over, but those lines which you have never in your life performed – these you hunted down and used to harm one of the citizens publicly.

Aeschines' own recitation of Euripidean verse 'harmed' a citizen, just as Euripides' Stheneboeas had, according to the Aristophanic Aeschylus, 'harmed' the entire polis.[71] The distinction of poetry that 'harms' – a concept which first surfaces for us in the *Frogs* – would go on to have a long and productive afterlife in ancient literary criticism, where forms of the verb βλάπτω often appear as moral-evaluative terms.[72] At the end of the fifth century Euripidean verse was represented as corrupting and harming the citizen body; now some sixty years later someone who failed to handle his quotations correctly could be accused of just the same thing.

A firm farewell to Sophocles

Demosthenes is nevertheless not content simply to make a rebuttal of Aeschines' choice of quotation. To prove himself

[70] Hunter (2009) 2 outlines the importance of the *Frogs* as the first site of attestation for a number of antiquity's most persistent critical terms and conceits.

[71] At *Ran*. 1049 Euripides asks Aeschylus καὶ τί βλάπτουσ', ὦ σχέτλι' ἀνδρῶν, τὴν πόλιν ἁμαὶ Σθενέβοιαι; Aeschylus responds that those 'Stheneboeas' have led well-born women to commit suicide by hemlock because of their shame.

[72] Hunter (2009) 25–9.

the superior Athenian citizen he next offers his own more fitting quotation, from a truly important and well-known play by the Athenian playwright *par excellence*. The last piece of evidence that Pontani assembles in arguing for a connection between *On the False Embassy* and the *Frogs* is that 'Just like Aristophanes, Demosthenes too stages a comparison between Euripides . . . and an earlier tragedian: Sophocles' *Antigone* is quoted extensively (vv. 175–90) in 19.247.'[73] Demosthenes' mention of *Antigone* does imply an agonistic comparison of the tragedians, but equally important is the manner in which he presents this specific play. His characterisation of *Antigone* and its afterlife marks a valuable testimonium for tragic repertoires in the mid-fourth century. Even if *Phoenix* was a better known play than Demosthenes would have the jurors believe, his efforts to contrast its fame with that of *Antigone* are an early witness to discussions about the idea and ideology of an Athenian tragic canon.

Demosthenes claims that, as opposed to Euripides' *Phoenix*, Sophocles' *Antigone* had a secure place amongst the contemporary popular repertoire of classical tragedy.[74] The *Phoenix* may have only been performed by actors of a bygone era,

Ἀντιγόνην δὲ Σοφοκλέους πολλάκις μὲν Θεόδωρος, πολλάκις δ' Ἀριστόδημος ὑποκέκριται. (Dem. 19.247)

but the *Antigone* of Sophocles has been performed many times by Theodorus, and many times by Aristodemus.

Other contemporary sources confirm that *Antigone* was both well known and well regarded in this period. A fragment by the comic playwright Antiphanes reworks lines 712–14 of *Antigone* into a kind of drinking song.[75] Aristotle also refers to the play on a handful of occasions. In the *Poetics* he mentions Creon's failed attempt to kill Haemon and subsequent flight as an

[73] Pontani (2009) 412.

[74] None of these performances is epigraphically attested, but Aristodemus did act in Astydamas' *Antigone* at the Dionysia of 342–1 (*IG* II^2 2320.6 Millis–Olson), the year after the speeches on the 'false' embassy.

[75] Antiphanes *adesp.* F 228; see page 173.

example of 'intending to perform an action with full knowledge but not carrying it out';[76] in the first book of the *Rhetoric* he twice uses lines from the play to illustrate the existence of the 'common law' (ὁ κοινὸς νόμος, or a law κατὰ φύσιν) which can sometimes be an 'unwritten law' (ἄγραφος νόμος).[77] In *Rhetoric* III he then raises Antigone's final speech as an example of a case in which a non-credible moral purpose is explained;[78] he also expresses approval of Sophocles' portrayal of Haemon.[79] Aristotle's citations of the play are not tantamount to confirmation of a lively reperformance tradition, but their frequency suggests that he expected his audience to be familiar with the characters and plot. Moreover, some scholars have detected evidence for fourth-century performances of *Antigone* embedded in the transmitted texts of other plays. Certain passages of Aeschylus' *Seven Against Thebes* and Euripides' *Phoenissae* are often thought to have been interpolated by later actors, whose purpose in modifying the plays will have been to render their narratives more compatible with the celebrated story of Sophocles' *Antigone*.[80]

In *On the False Embassy* Demosthenes claims that Aeschines should have known Sophocles' play, or at least parts of it, very well: as tritagonist in the troupe of Theodorus and Aristodemus, the role of Creon fell to him.[81] Demosthenes reminds the jury that Creon's part contains:

πεποιημέν' ἰαμβεῖα καλῶς καὶ συμφερόντως ὑμῖν πολλάκις αὐτὸς εἰρηκὼς καὶ ἀκριβῶς ἐξεπιστάμενος παρέλιπεν. (Dem. 19.246–7)

verses that are finely constructed and profitable for you [to hear], which, though [Aeschines] recited them many times and knew by heart, he left out.

[76] Arist. *Po.* 1453b–1454a.

[77] At *Rhet.* 1.1373b11–12 he cites Soph. *Ant.* 456–7; at 1.1375b1–2 he cites *Ant.* 456 and 458, though 458 differs slightly from the transmitted text of the play.

[78] Arist. *Rhet.* 3.1417a28–32.

[79] Arist. *Rhet.* 3.1417b20 and 3.1418b32.

[80] For a summary of the arguments see Scodel (2007) 144–5; Taplin (2010) 33–5. Taplin argues that the Sophoclean version of Antigone's story would, by the fourth century, have come to represent the 'vulgate', or standard, narrative of the myth (33).

[81] There is some question as to whether the part of Creon actually fell to a 'tritagonist': see Easterling (2002) 338 n. 41 and MacDowell (2000) 305.

He then goes on to order the clerk to recite a passage from Creon's 'ship of state' speech (*Ant.* 175–90), in which Creon explains how he finds despicable the man who, when responsible for guiding an entire city, does not pursue the best counsels but keeps silent out of fear. Here Creon also pronounces that he hates anyone who counts a friend as more important than his country.[82] Despite the value of Creon's words, 'Creon-Aeschines' (ὁ Κρέων Αἰσχίνης) never repeated them to himself, either during the 'false' embassy or in the presence of the jurors when he delivered *Against Timarchus*. Instead, he ignored the wisdom of the lines when he chose to rank his own relationship with King Philip of Macedon above the interests of Athens: 'having bid a firm farewell to the wise Sophocles',[83] Aeschines remained silent about the imminent (and disastrous) Macedonian invasion of Phocis, which he had known to be on the horizon.

Like the character of Creon in Sophocles' *Antigone*, Demosthenes suggests, Aeschines steered his city towards ruin. Demosthenes' naming of 'Creon-Aeschines' implies an association between Aeschines (an ally, to Demosthenes' mind, of Macedonian tyrants) and the figure whose downfall *Antigone* charts. Yet Demosthenes does see the lines uttered by Creon as containing good advice for Athenian citizens, an apparent contradiction that has troubled some scholars. Part of Demosthenes' disparagement of tritagonists such as Aeschines is his sarcastic claim that their 'honour' (*geras*) is to play the part of tyrants and sceptred kings.[84] Sarah Ferrario, for example, accounts for Demosthenes' ostensible approval of a tyrant's words by arguing that, because Athenian practices of commemoration had evolved, *Antigone* 'may have been received by fourth-century audiences as a much less contentious play'. Because some of the tension between private and public modes of memorialisation had dissipated by Demosthenes' time, the

[82] Martin (2009) 64–5 argues that in invoking the example of Creon, Demosthenes is insinuating that Aeschines, too, is an 'upstart'.

[83] Dem. 19.247: ἐρρῶσθαι πολλὰ φράσας τῷ σοφῷ Σοφοκλεῖ. Demosthenes' use of the verb ἐρρῶσθαι implies that Aeschines issued a disrespectful 'farewell'.

[84] Dem. 19.247.

argument runs, Creon could now be seen as 'a spokesman of good political advice' even if he still appeared villainous on a private level.[85]

There is, however, a simpler explanation as to how Demosthenes could have argued for the wisdom of a tyrant's words. For Demosthenes, those words did not truly belong to Creon, but rather to the 'wise Sophocles' – the poet to whom Aeschines had chosen to bid a firm farewell. When Aeschines and Lycurgus quote lines from tragedy, they too appeal to the moral authority of the tragedian and not of the fictional speaker of the lines. Lycurgus praises Euripides for the decisions that he took in composing the patriotic speech of Praxithea, while Aeschines had gone even further in effacing any distinction between the speaking 'I' of the verses from *Phoenix* and the man who composed them. Demosthenes' accusation that Aeschines has taken his leave of the 'wise Sophocles' likewise implies that the poet, and not the character, is the source of the lines' wisdom. Thus Sophocles himself, not the tyrant Creon, is the voice that proves superior to Aeschines and to the poetry that he made the mistake of invoking.

In the *Frogs* Dionysus had declared Aeschylus victor of the contest, an outcome which the chorus goes on to justify with the claim that 'Aeschylus' has proven himself sensible (εὖ φρονεῖν, 1485) and wise (συνετός, 1490).[86] In *On the False Embassy* Euripides loses yet again to a 'wise' opponent (τῷ σοφῷ Σοφοκλεῖ) because his words are determined to carry less weight. Demosthenes' rhetoric in the speech serves to recast Aeschines' earlier quotation from *Phoenix* as a frivolous excerpt, whose verses belonged to a little-performed play and so were 'gathered up' from obscurity. In contrast, Sophocles' *Antigone* was well known – and rightfully so, since certain of its lines contained insights that every Athenian citizen should internalise. Unlike his colleagues Euripides and Aeschylus, Sophocles suffered no criticism at all in the *Frogs*. But Demosthenes, in fixing himself at the helm of a Sophoclean victory, again presents a vision of

[85] Ferrario (2006) 82, 106.

[86] For recent discussions of the play's puzzling resolution see Hunter (2009) 36–8 and Halliwell (2011) 138–54.

classical tragedy that corresponds to the 'Aeschylean' position in the play. When, near the end of the *Frogs*, Aeschylus vacates the Underworld's Chair in Tragedy, he asks Pluto to hand it over to Sophocles for safekeeping, on the grounds that Sophocles is second to him in wisdom.[87] Before he departs for the upper world, Aeschylus also asks Pluto to ensure that Euripides never sit on the throne – not even accidentally.[88] Sophocles' own metaphorical defeat of Euripides in *On the False Embassy* thus also has precedent in the final ranking of the three tragedians, as determined by the final decision of Dionysus and Aeschylus' choice of his successor. The moment of that choice is the point at which the curtain of the *Frogs* effectively falls.

Demosthenes never gave up his attempts to portray Aeschines as an Athenian citizen unworthy of the name. In *On the Crown* he would defend his own election to deliver the funeral oration for the dead of Chaeronea by contrasting the sincerity of his own grief for the fallen Athenians with the disingenuousness of Aeschines, who had also hoped to give the speech. The people, Demosthenes claims, thought that the man who praised the dead's *aretē* should not be the same one who had shared a roof and poured libations with the enemy; nor did they reckon that the chosen speaker should be a man who had celebrated in song, together with the Macedonians, the calamities suffered by Greeks. Moreover,

> μηδὲ τῇ φωνῇ δακρύειν ὑποκρινόμενον τὴν ἐκείνων τύχην, ἀλλὰ τῇ ψυχῇ συναλγεῖν, τοῦτο δ' ἑώρων παρ' ἑαυτοῖς καὶ παρ' ἐμοί, παρὰ δ' ὑμῖν οὔ. διὰ ταῦτ' ἔμ' ἐχειροτόνησαν καὶ οὐχ ὑμᾶς. (Dem. 18.287–8)
>
> nor did they want someone who would lament for their fate [only] with his voice, as an actor, but rather someone who was also aggrieved in his soul. They saw this quality in themselves and in me, but not in you. That is why they voted for me and not for you.

In the next section of the speech, Demosthenes instructs the clerk to read out the epitaph that the polis had inscribed on

[87] Ar. *Ran*. 1519: σοφίᾳ κρίνω δεύτερον εἶναι.

[88] At the beginning of *Frogs* Heracles also expresses a preference for Sophocles and asks Dionysus to bring *him* back to life since he is better than Euripides. Dionysus agrees, but claims that he first wants to test Iophon (Sophocles' son) to see what he can do without the help of his father (Ar. *Ran*. 76–9).

the monument to the Chaeronea dead.[89] By the sincerity of the epigram's sentiments, the jurors are to realise the full extent of Aeschines' crimes against the city. In both this passage of *On the Crown* and the section of poetic quotations in *On the False Embassy*, Demosthenes presents Aeschines as capable only of perfunctory recitation, whether of an *epitaphios logos* or of tragic lines. He has no sincere connection with or understanding of the words that he utters – or would have uttered, had he been chosen to deliver the funeral oration. Every move that Aeschines makes to speak about Athens and its past, be it putting himself forward as a candidate for the Chaeronea speech or quoting lines from Euripides, is a reflection of his insincere and hypocritical engagement with the institution to which the words and ideas belonged.[90] Aeschines cites tragedy but does not understand which tragedians tragedies or verses are really worth quoting, and a similar irony marked his aspirations to deliver the *epitaphios logos* for the dead of Chaeronea when he had no regard for or grasp of what their sacrifice had meant.[91]

As Lycurgus does in his *Against Leocrates,* both Aeschines and Demosthenes appeal to classical tragedy for purposes specific to their speeches in ways that also happen to shed light on the contemporary status of fifth-century tragedy. These speeches show just how much classical tragedy could matter to constructs of Athenian citizenship and identity. It is particularly telling that, though Demosthenes criticises the specifics of Aeschines' 'dramatic' strategy, he does not call into question the status of tragedy as a showcase for Athenian morals. Instead, his criticisms centre upon how Aeschines has failed truly to understand the institution, and sought out lines from a little-performed play when the famous lines of the much-performed *Antigone* would have served him much better. This

[89] The transmitted text of this epigram is likely spurious: see Yunis (2001) ad loc. with bibliography.

[90] Cf. Scodel (2007) 139 on the relationship between Aeschines' failures as an actor and as a citizen.

[91] See also Demosthenes' criticisms (Dem. 19.252) of Aeschines' invocation of Solon (Aeschin. 1.25–6), with discussion at Tanner (2006) 122–3.

indictment of Aeschines' choice of play is also a first telling sign that some fifth-century plays had come to be (or could be) regarded as more obscure than others. Demosthenes' argumentation, tendentious though it may be, perhaps offers an early preview of the kinds of discourses that attended the emergence of a tragic canon, the processes of reduction that would leave us with only the small sampling of fifth-century tragedies that we have today. *Antigone* is alive and well, but few fragments of *Phoenix* remain. Demosthenes' assimilation of Aeschines to the Aristophanic Euripides on account of the harm that he has caused the demos also helps to highlight the radicalism of the Lycurgan reinvention of Euripides as an ideal citizen, only a decade or so later. Lycurgus' account of the poet in *Against Leocrates* would mark the first presentation of Euripides that collapsed and dispelled with the old Aristophanic battle lines. And with the eventual installation of the Lycurgan statues, all three of the great tragedians would soon stand on equal footing alongside each other, in a display of unity that no character in the *Frogs* – not even Dionysus– ever imagined possible.

CHAPTER 5

CLASSICAL TRAGEDY AND ITS COMIC LOVERS

In the decade before the Lycurgan Era, terms of tragic criticism that are first attested in the *Frogs* resurface with rhetorical flair in the improbable setting of the Athenian courtroom. Less surprisingly, Aristophanes' legacy is still more palpable in the comic fragments from roughly the same period. One theme which proves especially persistent in these fragments is the zeal of theatrical spectators.[1] In the fifth century, Aristophanes' portrayals of ardent fans of tragedy had caricatured the enthusiasm of an engaged and opinionated theatre-going public. Certain passages of his comedies offer some indication as to the fiercely loyal followings that tragedians could inspire in their own lifetimes. In the *Clouds*, for example, Strepsiades claims that the clash with his son Pheidippides over their tragic tastes – the father on the side of Aeschylus, the son in the camp of Euripides – grew so heated that it came to blows.[2] And though passionate lovers of tragedy were sometimes the subject of comic satire, they must have immensely enjoyed a production such as the *Frogs*. James Porter has discussed how an important aspect of the 'classicism' of the *Frogs*[3] – and one of the ways in which the play fulfils a 'fantasy of classicism' – is the sensory experience that its performance will have afforded. Because the contest-scene is set in Hades, spectators who, like the play's Dionysus, longed for the tragedians of the past had the opportunity to 'see' those poets and even to hear the sounds of 'their' voices. Thus in a way the *Frogs* made going to the

[1] Cf. also Knöbl (2008) 63–5.

[2] Ar. *Nu.* 1373–6. On the fifth-century fans of tragedy see Rosen (2006). For an important survey of the evidence for Euripides' wild popularity outside of Athens see Bing (2011).

[3] The play 'is retrospective, tinged with nostalgia, venerating, canonizing, and so on': so Porter (2006) 301.

theatre 'like going to a museum, only the museum here is so to speak coming to its audience, live'.[4]

Later comic poets, as we shall see, also showed a lively interest in staging passionate appreciation of tragedy, and wrote still more serious cases of tragedy-mania into their own productions. A number of comic poets also continued in the earlier traditions of parodying tragic verses, reworking tragic scenes and revisiting 'tragic' myths. Particularly in the early part of the century, writers of comedy had a taste for plots which satirised the traditional myths that had often been, and certainly still were, the subjects of tragedy.[5] In some cases these mythological plays will have been parodies or 'spin-offs' of the more famous tragic treatments: Donald Mastronarde has identified more than twenty-five 'Euripidean titles that occur as titles of comedies in the late fifth and in the fourth century'.[6] Some of these, he notes, are also known titles of plays by multiple tragedians, although there are a few instances in which a particular tragic scene of reference can be identified. A fragment of Alexis' *Agonis* (F 3), for example, suggests that the play included a takeoff on the 'madness' scene in Euripides' *Orestes* (the lines include a comic adaption of *Or*. 255),[7] and the fragment of Timocles' *Orestautocleides* (F 25) implies parody of the famous image at the start of Aeschylus' *Eumenides*.[8]

[4] Porter (2006) 302. Phrynichus' *Muses* took second place at the Lenaea in 405, the year that the *Frogs* was victorious, and seems also to have depicted an Underworld competition between deceased tragedians. Aristophanes' *Gerytades* also staged a meeting between living poets and ones in the Underworld; on similar comic plots see Young (1933). Aristophanes was not the only fifth-century comic playwright in dialogue with tragedy; recent studies by e.g. Bakola (2010) and Miles (2009) have highlighted the tragic allusions of Cratinus and Strattis respectively. Aristophanes' level of engagement nevertheless appears to have been exceptional: see Silk (1993).

[5] On mythical parodies in comedy see e.g. Webster (1970) 82–97, Nesselrath (1985) and (1990) 188–231, Casolari (2003) and Cusset (2003) 31–5; on Antiphanes see Vuolo (1985) and Mangidis (2003). Shaw (2010) argues for an important relationship between mythological comedies and tragedians' satyr plays.

[6] Mastronarde (2010) 5–6 n. 18.

[7] See Arnott (1996) ad loc. Alexis also wrote an *Orestes* (F 171) and a *Seven Against Thebes* (F 83); F 63 of his *Banished Man* (Εἰσοικιζόμενος) also contains a citation of Euripides' *Telephus*: see Cusset (2003) 47–8.

[8] The Aeschylean scene was famous and is depicted on an Apulian bell-krater dated to the 360s (Saint Petersburg State Hermitage Museum 349) and kalyx-krater from the 350s (Boston MFA 1976.144); see esp. Taplin (2007) 64–6 and Giuliani (2001).

In Timocles' version, the sleeping Furies who surround Orestes at Delphi were re-imagined as courtesans slumbering around the figure of Autokleides.[9] Antonis Petrides has recently discussed such instances of 'intervisuality' between moments of later comedy and famous scenes of fifth-century tragedy, particularly with reference to Menander. He argues, for example, that the opening tableau of Menander's *Perikeiromenē* may have recalled the opening of Aeschylus' *Niobe*, a visual echo that will have cast an arrestingly funereal ambience over the comic scene.[10] Comic playwrights also continued to borrow from tragedy's repertoire of theatrical devices. Comedy might contain prologues delivered by gods, messenger speeches, references to the tragic *deus ex machina* and *ekkyklema*, tragically influenced recognition scenes and even overt allusions to plots, *personae* and other speeches of specific classical plays.[11]

Unsurprisingly, there is a correlation between the tragedies whose comic parodies and allusions we can identify and those which enjoyed a vibrant afterlife more generally. Euripides' *Orestes* and *Medea* are two of the tragedies most often parodied or otherwise alluded to by fourth-century comedians and are also two of the three plays (along with Euripides' *Phoenissae*) which are best attested on papyri.[12] We know that *Orestes* was reperformed in Athens in at least 340 BC,[13] and that the stories of Orestes and Medea were both popular subjects of new tragedy: Theodectes wrote an *Orestes*, Carcinus the Younger wrote an *Orestes* and *Medea*; a *Medea* is also documented for

[9] Autokleides was notorious for pederasty (Aeschin 1.52); on the parody see Constantinides (1969) 59–60 and Sidwell (1996) 194–5, who dates Timocles' play to the 350s or 340s (*contra* Webster (1970) 63).

[10] Petrides (2010).

[11] As relatively little Middle Comedy survives, the bulk of the evidence for these comes from New Comedy: see esp. Cusset (2003), Gutzwiller (2000), Hunter (1985) 130–4 and Katsouris (1975).

[12] Arnott (1996) 63; cf. Carrara (2009) 585–93 for an overview of papyrological evidence on the early diffusion of these plays. For the malleability of the Medea story (particularly with regard to the fate of the children) in the fourth century see Taplin (2010) 29–31; the evidence comes primarily from vase painting.

[13] *IG* ii^2 2320.21 Millis–Olson; see also page 131. Arnott (1996) 54 admits that it is tempting to date the *Agonis* to not long after this revival.

the fourth-century tragedians Theodorides and Dicaeogenes.[14] Identifiable citations of Sophocles in fourth-century comedy also tend to come from plays with otherwise robust indirect traditions. Antiphanes F 231 contains a parodic adaptation of lines from *Antigone*, and a papyrus (first century AD) preserves part of a comic speech in which the titan goddess Rhea borrows tragic diction from *Oedipus at Colonus* to complain about her husband Chronus:

'τί οὖν ἐμοὶ τ̣ῶ̣ν̣ σ̣[ῶν μέ]λει;' φαίη τις ἂν
ὑμῶν. ἐγὼ δ' ἐρῶ [τ]ὸ Σοφοκλέους ἔπος·
'πέπονθα δεινά'. (κτλ.) (*adespoton* F 1062)[15]

'So what's it to me?', one of you might ask.
I shall speak the phrase of Sophocles:
'I have suffered terrible things.'

The phrase πέπονθα δεινά is uttered by Oedipus at line 892 of *Oedipus at Colonus*.[16] Admittedly, little firm evidence survives for the indirect tradition of *Oedipus at Colonus* in the fourth century, although an Apulian kalyx-crater from the 340s depicts a scene that may well have been designed to evoke one of its scenes.[17] The first *hypothesis* to the play also claims that it had been one of the admired or 'wondrous' ones (τῶν θαυμαστῶν), and a scholion to line 900 refers to an opinion on the text that had been issued by Praxiphanes, a philosopher and student of Theophrastus.[18] The tragedy also plays an important role in the later (though probably invented) biographical tradition surrounding Sophocles, according to which he defended

[14] Carcinus' *Medea* is mentioned at Arist. *Rhet.* 2.23.1400b. Dicaeogenes supposedly wrote a *Medea Metapontion* (T 1a). On such 'spin-offs' of classical tragedies see Hall (2007) 279–81.

[15] The lines were once assumed to belong to Philiscus' *Dios Gonai* (cf. *ad* Philiscus *215 in *CGFPR*) but there is no strong evidence for the attribution. On the fragment see esp. Xanthakis-Karamanos (1994), who argues for a 'Middle' comic classification.

[16] Earlier in the play (at 595) Oedipus had also declared πέπονθα, Θησεῦ, δεινὰ πρὸς κακοῖς κακά. Austin *ad adesp.* F 1062 cites a number of similar locutions found elsewhere in both tragedy and comedy; Xanthakis-Karamanos (1994) 339 finds the phrase 'too commonplace to show convincing dependence on Sophocles', but Rhea explicitly states that she is quoting [τ]ὸ Σοφοκλέους ἔπος.

[17] Easterling (2006) 8, with bibliography. The vase is in the Geddes Collection in Melbourne (A5:8). See also Nervegna (forthcoming) 181–3 on the fourth-century tradition for the play.

[18] Σ *ad* Soph. *OC* 900 = Praxiphanes F 23 Wehrli.

himself against his son's accusation of senility by offering lines from the play as evidence of his lucidness.[19]

Poets of fourth-century comedy may have drawn at least some of their tragic quotations from anthologies that contained tragic excerpts. One joke which possibly signals the circulation of anthologies in at least the early third century BC occurs in Act 3 of Menander's *Aspis*, where the frenzied character Daos lets forth a torrent of tragic *sententiae*, including lines from Euripides' *Stheneboea*, Chaeremon's fourth-century *Achilles Thersitoktonos* and Aeschylus' *Niobe*.[20] At a certain point Smikrines interrupts this flood of quotations to ask: 'Are you gnomologising, you horrible wretch?' (γνωμολογεῖς, τρισαθλία; 414). Daos replies nonsensically with what is probably another borrowed piece of tragic diction (ἄπιστον, ἄλογον, δεινόν–, 415). Yet given the sheer variety of comic allusions – verbal and visual alike – to tragedy, it seems unlikely that classical drama had become merely a source of tired maxims and ethical models.[21] To be fair, later comedians do not seem to have directly interrogated or challenged the earlier tragedies' content, form or moral effects on the demos in the same way as their predecessors had done. But tragic production (of both new plays and revivals) continued with vigour, and experiences of tragedy in the mid- to later fourth century were by no means restricted to encounters with the *written* scripts, whether in their entirety or as excerpted in anthologies.

One particular aspect of comedy's relationship with tragedy in this period has received relatively little attention, though it will provide us with an important context for the Lycurgan theatre programme. Comic playwrights of the mid- to late fourth century often (humorously) depicted the relationships

[19] See Soph. T 81–84a. On the play's tradition in antiquity see esp. Easterling (2006) 6–11; on its role in the Sophoclean biographical tradition see Hanink (2010a) 55–62.

[20] Eur. F 666.1, Chaer. F 2 and Aesch. F 154a15 respectively, at Men. *Aspis* 407–13. On the scene see Gutzwiller (2000) 130; on tragedy and the *Aspis* see ibid. 122–33. The line from Eur. *Stheneboea* also appears at Ar. *Ran.* 1217 and is cited by Arist. *Rhet.* 2.1394b2; see further Gomme and Sandbach (1973) ad loc. for other witnesses to the lines quoted by Daos.

[21] *Pace* Slater (1985) 103.

that everyday people had with what by now had become 'classical' tragedy.[22] The fragments contain a number of instances of tragic citation by decidedly non-elite (and likely non-literate) characters such as parasites and cooks, whose knowledge of the tragic texts is hardly to be understood as particularly literary or intellectual. And comic titles such as *Philotragoidos* (*The Tragedy Lover*) and *Phileuripides* (*The Euripides Lover*) indicate that the comedians were also portraying characters who were precisely that: lovers of tragedy, and of Euripides most of all. Significantly, nearly every identifiable tragic reference in these comic fragments is to a member of the great triad, most often Euripides. It would, of course, be far more difficult to identify allusions in comic fragments to lost tragedies, whether of the fifth century or of more recent vintage. Yet, and as we shall see, the patterns of tragic engagement that we do find suggest that later comic playwrights remained preoccupied with the tragic poets and plays of the fifth century.

However absurd and exaggerated comic instances of tragic reception may be, they leave us with an impression of just how much Athenians of the fourth century lived with and among classical tragedy.[23] Here I shall be exploring ways in which fifth-century tragedy's continued importance to the cultural landscape manifested itself on the comic stage during roughly the lifetimes of Lycurgus, Demosthenes, Aristotle and Alexander the Great. I shall also be looking ahead to the fragments of 'New Comedy', which I define as comedy written after the fall of Athens to Macedon in 322. These fragments show some continuity with the 'Middle Comedy' plays in terms of comic bits and themes; they also attest to the long shadow that classical tragedy cast over every aspect of Athens' dramatic industry.[24] Admittedly, some of the plays whose

[22] Knöbl (2008) observes that 'Euripides appears in the fragments of Old and Middle Comedy as the author of texts which serve as a point of reference for jokes, quotations, and wordplays' (54).

[23] On the picture of daily life in Athens afforded by the fragments of 'Middle Comedy' see Nesselrath (1997).

[24] On the problems of drawing a clear line between 'Middle' and 'New' comedy see esp. Csapo (2000) and Sidwell (2000).

fragments I consider may have premiered in cities and communities outside of Athens. Ioannis Konstantakos has recently discussed how, during the fourth century, the 'pan-Hellenization' of the Athenian comic theatre changed what he calls the 'working conditions' of comic playwrights, many of whom will have written for venues beyond Attica.[25] As the century progressed, playwrights may have felt an ever increasing need to appeal to wide audiences, and references to classical tragedy in new comic productions were certainly a safe bet: Euripides was a household name throughout the Greek world and spectators nearly anywhere could have enjoyed allusions to him.[26] Nevertheless, many of the new plays were presumably set and/or produced in Athens, where the annual theatre festivals still, for the moment, reigned supreme.[27] We might note that, whether by coincidence or by design, the intrigue of every surviving comedy by Terence – who owed a great debt to his Greek models – unfolds in Athens.[28] In the later fourth century Athens remained at the heart of the genre, and the fragments highlight various roles that classical tragedy could be imagined as playing in the everyday life of the polis. They also, tellingly, reveal a desire to keep the theatrical past strong in the fabric of the present-day city. The shape of that desire – and of Athens' *pothos* for old tragedy – provides an important backdrop for the construction and celebration of the city's theatrical heritage during the Lycurgan Era.

[25] Konstantakos (2011), esp. 9–18. He points out that each of e.g. Antiphanes' reported 260 plays could not have first been produced at the Great Dionysia or the Lenaea, even over the course of his many-decade career (14–15), but a number of these could have premiered at celebrations of the Dionysia in the Attic demes: on these see esp. Paga (2010), Wilson (2010) and Goette (forthcoming); see too Csapo (2010) 89–95 on the early spread of the theatre within the Attic demes.

[26] For a history and critique of the 'internationalization' theory of fourth-century comedy (which has been thought to explain its lack of local politics and personal abuse) see Csapo (2000) 126–8.

[27] Konstantakos (2011) 11–12: in the fourth century, 'Athens has become the central theatrical metropolis that feeds the life of other Greek cities'; cf. Csapo (2000) 127: 'Athens remained the privileged venue for any ambitious dramatist'.

[28] On comedies not set in Athens see Roselli (2011) 142–4, with reference to the international audiences of the Attic drama.

(Classical) tragedy for the masses

Later comic poets followed in the footsteps of their fifth-century predecessors by making explicit references to well-known tragic poets, but these references are of a different spirit than the sort that we find in Aristophanes, whose lampoons of the fifth-century tragedians were potent enough to influence poets' enduring biographical traditions.[29] By contrast, the fourth-century fragments suggest that the later comic poets had little interest in the tragedians' personal lives and histories. Instead these fragments demonstrate a greater engagement with the tragedians' status as authors of works that were highly recognisable, at least in name or in outline, to the majority of the public. Rather than satirise the old poets and poetry anew, comic playwrights now parodied and poked fun at the excesses of classical tragedy's admirers and crafted various situations in which comic characters (mis)appropriated tragic verses to their own ends.

Fourth-century comic poets did not, however, limit their literary engagements to tragic poets. We know of six plays called *Sappho* (by Amipsias, Antiphanes, Amphis, Ephippus, Timocles and Diphilus) and of an *Archilochus* by Alexis; in Diphilus' *Sappho* the poets Archilochus and Hipponax appeared onstage, apparently as Sappho's lovers.[30] Somewhat surprisingly, no fragment points directly to a tragedian's eponymous play. Euripides is the most frequently recurring personage among the surviving comedies of Aristophanes (he appears in the *Acharnians*, *Frogs* and *Thesmophoriazusae*; he also is said to have featured in the lost *Proagon*),[31] but the later fragments

[29] See esp. Lefkowitz (1981) 88–9 and Roselli (2005) 1–28. Cf. also the comment of the biographer Chamaeleon of Heracleia (41 Wehrli, cf. Ath. 21e), a student of Aristotle's who wrote a number of works on lives of poets (see esp. Podlecki (1969) 120–4.): 'The comic poets are reliable on the subject of the tragedians' (παρὰ δὲ τοῖς κωμικοῖς ἡ περὶ τῶν τραγικῶν ἀπόκειται πίστις). Besides the Lycurgan 'three', Aristophanes' characters refer on multiple occasions to e.g. the fifth-century tragedians Carcinus, Melanthius, Philocles, Theognis, Morsimus, Morychus, Xenocles and Agathon (see the testimonia in Snell *TrGF* I).

[30] Diphilus F 70–1; see Brivitello (1998) and Dover (1978) 174 on Sappho 'on the stage'.

[31] See the Σ *ad* Ar. *Ves*. 91.

seem to offer only one good possibility for his reappearance on the comic stage. This unique case is the *Dionysius* of Eubulus (active *c.* 380–*c.* 335 BC),[32] a play that may have depicted a meeting of the minds between Euripides and the Sicilian tyrant-tragedian Dionysius of Syracuse, and to which we shall return.[33]

Comic commentary on classical tragedians does not resurface for us until Menander's generation of comic poets. The two extant cases both involve Euripides, and both occur in the fragments of Diphilus, traditionally one of the three great poets of New Comedy and a near-contemporary of Menander and Philemon.[34] In Diphilus' *Synoris* (a comedy named after a courtesan) someone makes a pun on 'Euripides' as the name of both the tragedian and a lucky throw in a game of dice.[35] A woman (Synoris herself?) expresses her hope of throwing a 'Euripides', but her opponent (Speaker B) retorts that this is unlikely, given Euripides' notorious hatred of women:

(B) οὐκ ἄν ποτε
Εὐριπίδης γυναῖκα σώσει'. οὐχ ὁρᾷς
ἐν ταῖς τραγῳδίαισιν αὐτὰς ὡς στυγεῖ;
τοὺς δὲ παρασίτους ἠγάπα. (Diphilus F 74.3–6)

Euripides would never save a woman! Don't you see
how he shows his hatred for them in his tragedies?
But he loved parasites.

To illustrate the point, the speaker quotes three verses, supposedly by Euripides:

λέγει γέ τοι·
ἀνὴρ γὰρ ὅστις εὖ βίον κεκτημένος
μὴ τοὐλάχιστον τρεῖς ἀσυμβόλους τρέφει,
ὄλοιτο, νόστου μή ποτ' εἰς πάτραν τυχών. (Diphilus F 74.7–9)

[32] On the chronology see Hunter (1983) 7–10.

[33] See the text and commentary of Hunter (1983).

[34] Nesselrath *DNP* s.v. Diphilus.

[35] Ap. Ath. 6.247b–c. See the discussion of Knöbl (2008) 61–3, with explanation of the 'Euripides' dice roll (a very high roll, and likely a pun on εὖ ῥίπτω).

As he says:
'For if any rich man fails to support at least three
people who don't contribute to the dinner expenses,
might he perish and never return to his fatherland!' (Trans. Olson)

In reality these verses are a mishmash of genuine Euripidean lines from two different plays, coupled with what is likely a comic invention. The first line belongs to Euripides' *Antiope* (F 187.1) and the third is line 535 of *Iphigenia in Tauris*, but the second (underlined above) should probably be understood as a humorous segue contrived by Speaker B for his or her own purposes. Synoris(?) does find the 'quotation' as a whole dubious and asks 'where is that from, by the gods?' (πόθεν ἐστὶ ταῦτα, πρὸς θεῶν?). Her friend responds with mild exasperation:

(B) τί δέ σοι μέλει;
οὐ γὰρ τὸ δρᾶμα, τὸν δὲ νοῦν σκοπούμεθα (Diphilus F 74.10–11)

What do you care?
It's not the play, but the thought, that we're considering.

The joke here on Speaker B's pseudo-literate recourse to the authority of Euripidean verse will be revisited below, but it is worth dwelling for a moment on the details of the brief sketch of Euripides that the character offers. By Diphilus' era Euripides' misogyny was an old and well-worn trope; it had been at the heart of the plot in Aristophanes' *Thesmophoriazusae* and was lamented by the sex-striking women of *Lysistrata*.[36] But rather than newly interrogate or reconstruct this aspect of the received Euripidean persona, Diphilus' Speaker B treats it as a piece of common knowledge, expressing only mock surprise at Speaker A's hopes that a 'Euripides' might assist her.

On the other hand, the notion that Euripides had been especially fond of parasites, or semi-professional flatterers with notoriously voracious appetites, is not attested before Diphilus.

[36] *Lys.* 283–4 (= Eur. T 108a) and *Lys.* 368–9 (= Eur. T 108b). See also F *adesp.* 1048 (= Eur. T 111b), which has been preserved on an ostracon (Pack^2 2721) νὴ τὸν Δία τὸν μέγιστον, εὖ γ' Εὐριπίδης | εἴρηκεν <εἶναι> τὴν γυναικείαν φύσιν | πάντων μέγιστον τῶν ἐν ἀνθρώποις κακῶν; on Euripides' misogyny see also Satyrus' *Vita Euripidis* (F 6 fr. 39 col. x Schorn = Eur. T 110). For Aristophanes' influence upon this aspect of Euripides' reputation see Rosen (2006) 44–5.

The conceit appears in another fragment of his from a comedy called the *Parasite*. In these lines a parasite appropriates poetry which he claims is by the 'golden' Euripides, at the beginning of a speech about the troubles caused by a hungry stomach:

εὖ γ' ὁ κατάχρυσος εἶπε πόλλ' Εὐριπίδης·
'νικαῖ δὲ χρεία μ' ἡ ταλάιπωρός τε μου
γαστήρ.'[37] ταλαιπορότερον οὐδέν ἐστι γὰρ
τῆς γαστρός ... (Diphilus F 6.1–4)[38]

Golden Euripides said many fine things on the subject:
'Poverty and my miserable belly are defeating me.' For nothing is more miserable than the belly ...

This character's claim that Euripides 'said many things' (εἶπε πολλά) on the problem of the stomach serves to cast Euripides as a parasite *avant la lettre*, and so to make an anachronistic assimilation of Euripides to the parasite stock-character type that was popular in fourth-century comedy.[39] The conceit of Euripides-as-parasite would later rematerialise with some regularity in imperial Greek literature, where Euripides is often portrayed as a parasite upon his patron, King Archelaus of Macedon. In Lucian's dialogue *On Parasites* the character Simon lists for Tychiades a number of historical examples of 'philosophers eager to play the part of the parasite'.[40] When Tychiades asks Simon about his sources for Plato's sponging off the Sicilian tyrants (Simon's first and most extensive example), Simon lists precedents of intellectuals who were parasites of kings. Euripides appears among them: 'Euripides acted as

[37] Eur. F 915, which Casaubon emended to νικᾶι δὲ χρεία μὲν κακῶς τε οὐλομένη | γαστήρ.

[38] Ap. Ath. 10.422b–c. Cf. Theopompus F 35 (from the comedy *Odysseus*, quoted ap. Ath. 4.165b), where to have a 'Euripidean breakfast' means to eat someone else's food; cf. Knöbl (2008) 59. The complaint about the *gastēr* that is attributed to Euripides does recall Odysseus' comments on his own hunger at H. *Od.* 215–21; see esp. Pucci (1987) 181–208. On the motif of the 'tyranny of the belly' in Middle Comedy see Arnott (1996) 613–14.

[39] The earliest attestations of the word occur at Pl. *La.* 179c (as a verb, παρασιτεῖ) and in the comedy *Hymenaeus*, by Araros the son of Aristophanes (Araros F 16). On the figure of the parasite see Nesselrath (1990) 309–17 and Webster (1970) 64–7; cf. also Arnott's (1996) commentaries on Alexis' *Parasite* and *Helmsman*. In the latter a character identifies a type of parasite as the kind seen in comedy: this type is κοινὸν καὶ κεκωμῳδημένον (Alexis F 121.2).

[40] Luc. *Par.* 31: Φιλοσόφους παρασιτεῖν σπουδάσαντας; cf. ibid. 36.

parasite to Archelaus until the day he died.'[41] On the other hand, in the pseudo-Euripidean *Epistles* 'Euripides' denies that he ever behaved that way, and complains at one point that his patron has been feasting him more lavishly than he likes – hardly the grievance of a parasite.[42] Plutarch and Aelian both also report pithy quips that Euripides allegedly made at lavish banquets hosted by Archelaus.[43]

Diphilus' representation of Euripides as a parasite might also be read as a kind of comic twist on the Platonic notion that Euripides was an 'encomiast' of tyrants.[44] Earlier we saw how in *Republic* 8 Socrates and Glaucon could agree that Euripides 'sings the praises of tyranny as something godlike' (ὡς ἰσόθεόν ... τὴν τυραννίδα ἐγκωμιάζει, 568b). Their observation is easily translatable in comic terms to a view of Euripides as a typical 'flatterer', or *kolax*. This particular breed of parasite made frequent appearances on the later fourth-century stage, and *Kolax* was the title of plays by at least Philemon and Menander.[45] But the comic reinterpretation of Euripides' character 'type' could also owe something to the representation of Euripidean tragedy in Aristophanes' *Frogs*, where both 'Aeschylus' and 'Euripides' agree that Euripides depicted common characters, as opposed to the more noble ones (γενναίους, 1019) portrayed by Aeschylus. Pluto's slave claims that Euripides has earned an enormous following in Hades amongst the many 'thieves and pickpockets and father-beaters and burglars' (772–3), and 'Aeschylus' accuses him of having brought

41 Luc. *Par.* 35: Εὐριπίδης μὲν γὰρ ὅτι Ἀρχελάῳ μέχρι μὲν τοῦ θανάτου παρεσίτει. On Euripides' appearance in the passage see Nesselrath (1985) 384–6. A similar list of historical parasitic relationships (which does not include Euripides) occurs at Pl. *Ep.* 2.311b.

42 [Eur.] *Ep.* 5.1: εἱστία με λαμπρότερον ἢ ἐμοὶ φίλον ἦν ἑκάστης ἡμέρας. In the collection's paraenetic letter 'Euripides' also recommends that Archelaus keep poets and artists at his court and not associate with 'flatterers and buffoons' (κολάκων καὶ βωμολόχων, 4.4). On the parasite theme in the *Epistles* see Hanink (2010b) 551–5.

43 Eur. T 79a–d (= Ael. *VH* 13.4, [Plut.] 177a, Plut. 770c, Plut. *Alc.* 1.5). The anecdotes all illustrate Euripides' desire for Agathon.

44 Knöbl (2008) 56–60 links the Euripidean parasite theme in comic fragments to the tradition that Euripides had a number of collaborators who helped him with his plays: 'Euripides was thus imagined as dependent on the helping hands of others' (59).

45 For an overview of this stock type see Wilkins (2000) 71–86.

civic-duty evaders, commoners, rogues and scoundrels onto the stage (1014–15). In his own defence, 'Euripides' maintains that by giving equal parts to women and slaves (949–51) he acted democratically.[46] The appropriation of Euripides by Diphilus' parasite thus also develops and extends these more cynical views of Euripides' 'democratic' appeal: the Aristophanic Aeschylus will have been little surprised to see Euripides hailed as a spokesman of spongers.[47]

Other comic fragments also play upon the idea of pseudo-literate (mis)quotations of classical tragedy, as well as with the misplaced literary pretensions of improbable characters. A handful of these occur within the fragments of Antiphanes, an enormously productive poet of Middle Comedy whose career spanned much of the fourth century.[48] Antiphanes often parodied the affectations of literary culture and his surviving fragments contain more direct references to tragedians than those of any other fourth-century poet but for Menander.[49] A scene from Antiphanes' *Traumatias* (*The Wounded Man*) features, like the dice scene of Diphilus' *Synoris*, an instance of comically confused Euripidean quotation.[50] Here one character encourages another to indulge in sympotic conversation and song. He orders:

παραδίδου δ' ἑξῆς ἐμοὶ
τὸν ἀρκεσίγυιον, ὡς ἔφασκ' Εὐριπίδης. (Antiphanes F 205.7)

Thereafter give me
the 'limb-strengthening' [wine], as Euripides called it.

[46] Ar. *Ran.* 952: δημοκρατικὸν γὰρ αὔτ' ἔδρων.

[47] Cf. Dover (1993a) *ad* Ar. *Ran.* 952: 'In comedy, anything that made life easier for the mass of the population could be called "democratic", e.g. the provision of brothels (Philemon F 3) or free clothing for the poor (*Ec.* 411–21).'

[48] On the chronology of Antiphanes' career – in the course of which he wrote about 260 plays – see Konstantakos (2000): it likely began between 388/7–385/4 (i.e. twenty years after his birth in the 93rd Olympiad: so *Suda* α 2735 = Antiphanes T 1) and ended with his death around 310, or even later.

[49] On Antiphanes and literary culture see Vuolo (1989). Antiphanes' most famous fragment on tragedy, from his play *Poiesis* (F 189, ap. Ath. 6.222a–223a), contains a meditation on the advantages that tragic playwrights enjoy over comic ones (tragic playwrights are handed their material by mythology, whereas comic playwrights must be inventive): see the recent discussions of Cusset (2003) 42–6 and Taplin (2010) 28; 33.

[50] F 205 ap. Ath. 13.446a. *Traumatias* is also the title of plays by Alexis and Philocles.

Like the incredulous character from *Synoris*, the man's friend is sceptical of his literary sources:

(B.) Εὐριπίδης γὰρ τοῦτ' ἔφασκεν; (A.) ἀλλὰ τίς;
(B.) Φιλόξενος δήπουθεν. (A.) οὐθὲν διαφέρει,
ὦ τἄν· ἐλέγχεις μ' ἕνεκα συλλαβῆς μιᾶς. (F 205.8–10)

(B.) Euripides really said that? (A.) Who else?
(B.) Philoxenus, I think. (A.) It doesn't matter,
my friend. You're hassling me because of a single syllable.

Exactly what Speaker A means by 'one syllable' is obscure,[51] but it is clear that the fragment represents another instance in which a comic bit hinges upon a posturing character's ignorant attempt at a Euripidean reference. Here we also see two poets of the past confused under a heading of loosely defined classicism: whether Speaker A's citation comes from Euripides or Philoxenus (a younger contemporary of Euripides who was famous for his avant-garde dithyrambs), we are to understand the poetic language as having an air of the classical past – and so of erudition, however feigned – about it.

Allusions to Sophoclean verse occur in similarly low-brow contexts in two other fragments attributed to Antiphanes. One of these, from the *Agroikos* (*The Rustic*),[52] contains an instance of gastronomic pseudo-citation similar to those uttered both by Speaker B in *Synoris* and by the Euripides-'quoting' parasite of Diphilus' *Parasite*. These lines are spoken by a cook who is about to prepare a banquet and is describing the menu that he has planned:[53]

καὶ πρῶτα μὲν
αἴρω ποθεινὴν μᾶζαν, ἣν φερέσβιος
Δηὼ βροτοῖσι χάρμα δωρεῖται φίλον·
ἔπειτα πνικτὰ τακερὰ μηκάδων μέλη,
χλόην καταμπέχοντα, σάρκα νεογενῆ. (Antiphanes F 1.1–5)

51 Lamagna (2004) suggests that there is a joke on Philoxenus' name and the word φιλόκενος.

52 One *Agroikos* is listed for Antiphanes in *PCG*, though Konstantakos (2004) has argued that he wrote at least two plays on the theme.

53 On the figure of the 'boastful chef' in Greek comedy see Wilkins (2000) 387–407 and on this fragment Dobrov (2002) 189–90.

And first of all
I'm fetching a luscious barley-cake, which Deo,
the giver of life, grants mortals as a welcome source of joy.
Then tender smothered goat-haunches,
new-born flesh clad in greens. (Trans. Olson)[54]

The cook's addressee is justifiably perplexed and asks him what he is going on about (τί λέγεις;); the cook responds that he is 'reciting a tragedy of Sophocles' (τραγῳδίαν περαίνω Σοφοκλεόυς).[55] It may be the case that the cook has been citing or adapting genuine tragic verses which have not survived. Yet it is also possible, as Konstantakos has suggested, that he was simply 'parodying tragic style in general and attributing his paratragic piece to a well-known poet, in order to pose as a connoisseur of literature'.[56] In either case, part of the joke must again rest in this character's absurd attempts to elevate his work with high literary quotation, a move not unlike the one that Diphilus' parasite makes as he seeks to dignify his plight by citing Euripides as a respectable precedent.

Like both fragments of Diphilus, Antiphanes' lines mark an instance of comic transposition of classical tragedy to a paradigmatic fourth-century comic scene, namely one centred on food.[57] The fragments of Antiphanes also contain another instance of such 'gastronomic' appropriation of tragedy, since in an *adespoton* play an anonymous drinker invokes and adapts lines of Haemon's great speech in *Antigone* into a kind of drinking song.[58] The Sophoclean borrowings are underlined below:[59]

[54] On the cook's 'description of food in elevated poetic style' see Konstantakos (2004) 29.

[55] Antiphanes F 1.6. We might remember that λέγειν is also the verb typically used of 'quoting' poetic verses: see e.g. Diphilus F 74 above and page 36.

[56] Konstantakos (2004) 29.

[57] For an overview of the broad topic of food in Greek comedy see Wilkins (2000) 52–102.

[58] On the use of tragic language in 'gastronomic' situations in Middle Comedy see Arnott (1996) 20–1.

[59] Cf. Soph. *Ant.* 712–4: ὁρᾷς παρὰ ῥείθροισι χειμάρροις ὅσα | δένδρων ὑπείκει, κλῶνας ὡς ἐκσῴζεται, | τὰ δ' ἀντιτείνοντ' αὐτόπρεμν' ἀπόλλυται.

ὁρᾷς παρὰ ῥείθροισι χειμάρροις ὅσα
δένδρων ἀεὶ τὴν νύκτα καὶ τὴν ἡμέραν
βρέχεται μέγεθος καὶ κάλλος οἷα γίνεται,
τὰ δ' ἀντιτείνονθ' {οἱονεὶ δίψαν τινὰ
ἢ ξηρασίαν ἔχοντ'} αὐτόπρεμν' ἀπόλλυται. (Antiphanes F 228.3–7)

Look at the trees along torrent streams
that stay moist all day and night;
how large and beautiful they grow!
But those that resist are destroyed root and branch. (Trans. Olson)

In this case the character does not explicitly name his tragic source: the verses may have been either famous or at least 'tragic'-sounding enough to achieve paratragic effect without any specific mention of their author or play.[60]

Antiphanes offers yet a more pointed take on misplaced literary pretension in his *Carians*.[61] The previous fragments have provided glimpses of comic situations in which characters seek to fit tragedy to their decidedly low-brow purposes. In this fragment of the *Carians*, on the other hand, we hear about a *sophos* – a man who fancies himself a serious intellectual – who is unashamed to dance with cringeworthy flamboyance:

οὐχ ὁρᾷς ὀρχούμενον
ταῖς χερσὶ τὸν βάκηλον; οὐδ' αἰσχύνεται
ὁ τὸν Ἡράκλειτον πᾶσιν ἐξηγούμενος,
ὁ τὴν Θεοδέκτου μόνος ἀνευρηκὼς τέχνην,
ὁ τὰ κεφάλαια συγγράφων Εὐριπίδῃ. (Antiphanes F 111)

Don't you see the
pansy dancing with his hands? He's not ashamed–
the man who explains Heracleitus to everyone,
and is the only person able to make sense of Theodectes' art[62]
and the author of summaries of Euripides. (Trans. Olson)

Kephalaia, or 'summaries' of tragedies, were perhaps similar to the transmitted tragic *hypotheses*, and these lines suggest that

[60] The same lines were also parodied by Eupolis: F 260.23–5 = *CGFP* *97. On the fourth-century tradition for *Antigone* see pages 152–6 above and Taplin (2010) 33. On the originality of Sophocles' treatment of the myth see Griffith (1999) 6–12.

[61] *Carians* was also the name of a tragedy by Aeschylus (Aesch. F 99–101).

[62] On Theodectes – a famed orator, tragedian and associate of Aristotle's – see pages 199–200 below.

the writing of them was culturally marked as the kind of business in which dignified and learned men engaged. Rather than contrast a comic character with pretensions of literary sophistication, here the comedy lies in the embarrassing display of the literary sophisticate who behaves like a buffoon.

Fragments such as these point to a number of comic scenarios in which classical tragedy is invoked in the midst of everyday situations. These fragments do not, like the plays of Aristophanes, seem to question the value, quality or even morality of the classical tragedies (or tragedians) themselves. Instead, the comic playwrights take for granted that their audiences already recognise the authority and prestige of Euripidean tragedy. This set of fragments also illuminates how the use of classical tragic citations might contribute to the construction of different comic stock types: the greedy parasite, the inebriate and the *sophos*.[63] With this in mind, we might briefly return to Demosthenes' speech *On the False Embassy* and his criticisms of Aeschines' choice, in *Against Timarchus*, to quote from Euripides' *Phoenix*. According to the picture that Demosthenes paints, Aeschines, like a number of characters in fourth-century comedy, has misplaced literary pretensions that have led him to recite 'gathered-up' verses of Euripides in an inappropriate context. With the help of the comic fragments, we can identify yet another facet of Demosthenes' own 'comic' strategy: he aligns Aeschines with characters such as the parasite or heavy drinker of the stage, that is with characters whose absurd quotations of tragedies only make their literary airs more outrageous.[64] A dramatic parallel even exists for Demosthenes' scoffs at Aeschines' days as a third(-rate) actor, or *tritagonistēs*: a play with precisely that title is attested among the works of Antiphanes.[65] No tritagonist is actually

[63] Theophrastus' *Characters* helps to illuminate the categories, as 'Comedy furnishes much the same cast of players' as the *Characters*: so Diggle (2004) 8. Theophrastus devotes a section to the κόλαξ (§2), as well as to other comic stock types such as the ἄγροικος (§4).

[64] Rowe argues correctly, though more generally, that Demosthenes seeks to cast Aeschines as 'the incongruous imposter, the *alazôn* of the comic stage': (1966) 406.

[65] F 207, ap. Ath. 14.643d–e. See Nesselrath (1990) 287 n. 53 on 'Middle' comic references to the theatre industry.

mentioned in the one fragment that survives,[66] though it is easy enough to imagine that the title character was a tragic actor who miserably and comically failed – as Demosthenes alleges that Aeschines had – to do justice to his material.

In a study of 'play and playwright references' in (mostly) post-Aristophanic comedy, Niall Slater has observed that when characters from later comedy quote from fifth-century tragedy 'Any tension between the sentiment expressed and the comic context . . . makes us laugh at the character quoting, not the tragedian quoted'.[67] In these fragments it is generally the case that the malapropistic allusions to classical tragedy cause the allusion maker to appear (even more) ridiculous. These instances, particularly the case of the dancing *sophos*, all importantly presume classical tragedy's status as a constituent of and even metonymy for 'high' literary culture. For the playwrights, misappropriation of that culture is a means of drawing attention to the ridiculous pretensions of the 'low' character who evokes it. The quantity and quality of these passages also suggest that audiences were expected to have enough of a sense of Sophoclean and Euripidean tragedy to recognise – if not necessarily to identify precisely – tragic citation and its comic irony. For the spectators to laugh at appropriations of the classical tragedies, they first had to take for granted the cultural prestige of Athens' tragic heritage.

Longing for tragedy

References to classical tragedy in mid- to late fourth-century comedy extend beyond instances of (pseudo-)citation. Euripides 'himself' may even have appeared, in Aristophanic fashion and possibly *redivivus*, among the *dramatis personae* of Eubulus' *Dionysius*. The fragment that contains lines plausibly uttered by Euripides is preserved by a scholion to line 476

[66] The fragment consists in a speech praising the superiority of the dithyrambist Philoxenus (πολύ γ' ἐστὶ πάντων τῶν ποιητῶν διάφορος | ὁ Φιλόξενος, 1–2) over contemporary poets. On the play see Fongoni (2005), with discussion of the play's title at 92 and of the 'classical' status of the earlier dithyrambists at 97–8.

[67] Slater (1985) 103.

of Euripides' *Medea*. This note draws attention to the excessive sibilance of the line and quotes four satirical verses by Eubulus on the subject of Euripides' apparently notorious sigmatism.[68] The first two of these lines parody sigma-heavy Euripidean verses,[69] but the next contain what may be a complaint uttered by Euripides about the would-be *sophoi* who mock him:

[καὶ][70] τοῖς ἐμοῖσιν ἐγγελῶσι πήμασιν
τὰ σῖγμα συλλέξαντες, ὡς αὐτοὶ σοφοί. (Eubulus F 26.3–4 = F 27 Hunter)

having gathered up the (my?) sigmas they mock me for my woes,
so that they might be *sophoi*.

The Dionysius of Sicily after whom Eubulus named his play was famed as an aspirational tragedian of little skill and thin skin who nevertheless managed to secure a win at the Lenaea of 367 with his *Ransom of Hector*.[71] If these two lines of Eubulus' fragment do belong to Euripides it is indeed, as Richard Hunter has remarked, 'tempting to imagine a scenario in which he came back from Hades to protest that such a λωβητὴς τέχνης [a degrader of the craft] as Dionysius had enjoyed the dramatic success which he himself had notoriously failed to win'.[72] It is certainly attractive to imagine that Euripides

[68] A trait also parodied by the fifth-century comedian Plato in his *Heortae* (F 29). On Euripides' reputation for sigmatism in antiquity see Clayman (1987) 69–70 and Hunter (1983) *ad* Eubulus F 26. On Eubulus' engagement with Euripidean tragedy more generally see Cusset (2003) 35–43.

[69] ἔσωσά σ' ὡς ἴσασ' ὅσοι, an abbreviated version of Eur. *Med.* 476, and παρθέν' εἰ σώσαιμί σ', ἕξεις μοι χάριν, a slight alteration of Eur. F 129, from *Andromeda*: see Hunter (1983) ad loc.

[70] Richard Hunter has suggested to me that this καί may belong to the scholiast, who intended to indicate that he was citing two separate fragments, i.e. F 26 and 27 Hunter.

[71] Dionysius was said to have sent Philoxenus to the quarries for scorning his tragic efforts (Luc. *Ind.* 15 = Dion. trag. 76 T 11; Plut. *Alex. fort.* 334c = 76 T 13; *Suda* φ 397). He was also famed for having died of joy at the news of his victory at the Lenaea, a victory that supposedly fulfilled an old prophecy that he would die 'when he had beaten his betters', Diod. 15.7.3.5 = Dion. trag. 76 T 1. Cicero implies that opinions of his work were generally low, *Tusc.* 5.22.63 = Dion. trag. 76 T 7. On Dionysius' literary career, his harsh treatment of the poets hosted at his court and the comic roots of the 'hostile' ancient accounts of him see esp. Sanders (1987) 1–40.

[72] Hunter (1983) ad loc. Euripides won four times at the Great Dionysia in his lifetime and once after his death (*Suda* ε 3695.5 = Eur. T 3), while Sophocles supposedly won eighteen times (*Suda* σ 815 = Soph. T 2). See however Stevens (1956) 91–2 on

'himself' appeared onstage in Eubulus' play, but even if he did not the reference in the lines to Euripidean poetry must somehow have served to contrast Dionysius' feeble dramatic aspirations with Euripides' far-reaching fame. Dionysius was later remembered for having been a pathetically zealous admirer of Euripides, and the *Vita Euripidis* cites the third-century Peripatetic biographer Hermippus of Smyrna as the source for this story:

Διονύσιον τὸν Σικελίας τύραννον μετὰ τὴν τελευτὴν τοὺ Εὐριπίδου τάλαντον τοῖς κληρονόμοις αὐτοῦ πέμψαντα λαβεῖν τὸ ψαλτήριον καὶ τὴν δέλτον καὶ το γραφεῖον, ἅπερ ἰδόντα κελεῦσαι τοὺς φέροντας ἐν τῷ Μουσῶν ἱερῶι ἀναθεῖναι ἐπιγράψαντα τοῖς αὐτοῦ <καὶ> Εὐριπίδου ὀνόμασι. (Eur. T 1.3.4 = Dion. trag. 76 T 10 = Hermippus F 84 Bollansée)

After Euripides' death Dionysius the tyrant of Sicily sent a talent to his heirs to purchase his lyre and writing-tablet and pen, and when he saw these things he ordered the people who procured them for him to dedicate them in the temple of the Muses, having had them inscribed with both his and Euripides' names.

Peter Bing has discussed how this anecdote, in its presentation of Euripides as *xenophilōtatos*, 'much loved by foreigners', well captures Euripides' reception in antiquity: Euripides inspired zealous devotees abroad as well as second-rate imitators.[73] Even in Hermippus' prose account, Dionysius' adulation of Euripides takes a humorous turn in the excesses to which it supposedly ran.[74]

Obsession with Euripides and Euripidean tragedy ranks second after semi- and pseudo-citation as the most common tragic subject of fourth-century comic fragments. Lyric poets such as Sappho and Archilochus may have been popular characters in comedies, but again the comic playwrights seem to have

modern under-estimations of Euripides' success on the basis of comparison with Sophocles and the story of Euripides' alleged Macedonian 'exile'.

73 Eur. T 1.3.4: διὸ καὶ ξενοφιλώτατον κεκλῆσθαί φασι διὰ τὸ μάλιστα ὑπὸ ξένων φιλεῖσθαι; Bing (2011) 1.

74 A similar anecdote about Dionysius and Aeschylus appears in Luc. *Ind.* 15 (Dion. trag. 76 T 11): Dionysius became so fed up with Philoxenus' inability to contain his laughter at his tragedies that he acquired Aeschylus' writing tablet in the hopes that by using it he too would be inspired (ἔνθεος). He only managed to write things that were even more laughable (μακρῷ γελοιότερα).

been interested less in the tragedians themselves than in the fervour of their fans. Alexis, whose first recorded victory is for the Great Dionysia of 347, wrote a *Philotragoidos*,[75] and plays entitled *Phileuripides* are attested for both Axionicus and Philippides.[76] Nothing is known about the life of Axionicus, although his fragments and other surviving titles (e.g. *The Tyrrhenian*, *Philinna* and *The Chalchidian*) seem to have a certain 'Middle' comic flavour.[77] Philippides, by contrast, was a productive poet of New Comedy whose career is well attested. His *Phileuripides* will have been composed and staged in the post-Lycurgan period during which Athens was under Macedonian rule.[78] Given the popularity of Euripides amongst the Macedonian elite, it is easy to imagine that its members were familiar with Euripidean devotees – and perhaps were even counted among them.[79]

In the late fifth century, Aristophanes' comedies implied that Euripides had inspired licentious sexual behaviour in the women of Athens. In the *Frogs*, 'Aeschylus' condemns Euripides for his 'Phaedras and Stheneboeas' (1043) while the Mica of the *Thesmophoriazusae* laments that Euripides 'taught' (ἐδίδαξεν) Athenian men to suspect their wives of affairs (399–405).[80] In the fragments of fourth-century comedy, the erotic charge of Euripidean verse becomes reconfigured, with desire transferred from the corruptible wives of Athens to fans of Euripides (his 'groupies', if such a concept is possible when the object of admiration is dead) who longed for the poet himself. No Euripides-related fragment of Philippides' *Euripides Lover* survives, but two tantalising fragments remain of

[75] Arnott (1996) remarks ad loc.: 'A unique title, but several characters in Menander could be described as φιλοτραγῳδοί: Daos at *Asp.* 407ff., Syros . . . and Onesimos at *Epitr.* 325ff., 1123ff. respectively.' The sole surviving fragment is a gnomic line, possibly a tragic citation: σοφοῦ γὰρ ἀνδρὸς τὰς τύχας ὀρθῶς φέρειν (F 254; on tragic verses which contain similar sentiments see Arnott (1996) ad loc.). For Alexis' entry in the Great Dionysia of 348/7 see *IG* ii² 2318.1474 Millis–Olson = Alexis T 6. He is said to have been Menander's uncle: *Suda* α 1138 = T 1; cf. T 2.

[76] Quoted by Pollux at 9.38.

[77] On Axionicus see Nesselrath (1990) 245–8.

[78] For more on Philippides see pages 241–2.

[79] See esp. Revermann (1999–2000) and Hanink (2008).

[80] Here ἐδίδαξεν may pun the verb's meanings of 'to teach' and 'to direct' (a play); in theatre inscriptions the verb 'specifically refers to the "director of the chorus"': Csapo (2010) 91.

Axionicus' earlier treatment.[81] Fragment 4 consists in an eighteen-line monody, possibly a parody of Euripidean lyric, that is sung by a chef who is deliberating on how a 'fish' ought to be 'cooked' (Athenaeus mysteriously informs us that this fish is a cipher for an orator named Callias).[82] A clearer connection with Euripides is evident in F 3 of the play, in which we hear of a couple who are so mad or 'sick' about Euripidean lyric that all else has become unbearable:

οὕτω γὰρ ἐπὶ τοῖς μέλεσι τοῖς Εὐριπίδου
ἄμφω νοσοῦσιν, ὥστε τἄλλ' αὐτοῖς δοκεῖν
εἶναι μέλη γιγγραντὰ καὶ κακὸν μέγα. (Axionicus F 3)[83]

They are both so mad for Euripidean songs
that all others seem to be songs of
the *gingras*, and terribly awful.

Axionicus' use of the verb νοσέω, 'to be ill', here has the effect of transforming Euripidean verse into a sickness, and even a pathology.[84] This conceit, too, can be traced as far back as the description of the god Dionysus' longing for Euripides at the beginning of Aristophanes' *Frogs*. In the first scene of the *Frogs*, Dionysus informs Heracles that he has been doing very badly ever since, while reading Euripides' *Andromeda*, a sudden pang of longing desire – *pothos* – overtook him:[85]

καὶ δῆτ' ἐπὶ τῆς νεὼς ἀναγιγνώσκοντί μοι
τὴν Ἀνδρομέδαν πρὸς ἐμαυτὸν ἐξαίφνης πόθος
τὴν καρδίαν ἐπάταξε πῶς οἴει σφόδρα. (Ar. *Ran.* 52–4)

And as I was reading the *Andromeda* on the ship
a sudden longing struck my heart so badly.

81 See Scharffenberger (2012) for a discussion, text and commentary.

82 The lines appear ap. Ath. 8.342a–b, in a section about famous men who had a weakness for fish; on the fragment see Nesselrath (1990) 245–6.

83 Ap. Ath. 4.175b, amidst a discussion of the γίγγρας, a shrill-sounding pipe supposedly used by the Phoenicians in lamentations for Adonis.

84 On the conceit see Bing (2011), with further amusing anecdotes of Euripides provoked illness. Knöbl (2008) 63 suggests that this may also be a comic inversion of the idea that Euripides' own 'new music' was unbearable.

85 On the sense and significance of *pothos* in this passage see Halliwell (2011) 101–6. Sfyroeras (2008) offers an interpretation as to why it was the *Andromeda* that provoked Dionysus' longing.

When Heracles fails to take Dionysus' problem seriously, Dionysus pleads with him:

μὴ σκῶπτέ μ', ὦδέλφ'· οὐ γὰρ ἀλλ' ἔχω κακῶς·
τοιοῦτος ἵμερός με διαλυμαίνεται. (Ar. *Ran.* 58–9)

Don't mock me, brother, for I'm doing very badly.
Such is the desire that is driving me mad.

Dionysus soon attempts to explain his problem to Heracles by means of a gastronomic analogy, of which Diphilus' parasites would surely approve: he tells him that his longing is like the longing that one feels when overcome with a sudden desire for soup. The explanation leads Heracles to grasp the problem perfectly. This, Dionysus continues, is the way that his longing for Euripides is 'devouring' him.[86] Dionysus' characterisation of his own desire thus foreshadows both the erotic as well as gastronomic dimensions of Euripides' comic reception in the fourth century.

This comic conceit of longing for Euripides may even be traceable to the kind of erotic longing that had been portrayed by Euripides. Extreme levels of desire were, at least for Aristophanes' characters, a hallmark of Euripidean tragedy.[87] In perhaps the most famous expression of desire for the tragedian, one comic character goes so far as to claim that he would be willing to kill himself just to see the great tragedian in Hades – if there could be any assurance that he would still have his wits about him when dead. The fragment is by Philemon, an older contemporary of Menander and a playwright whose first victory fell late in the Lycurgan Era, at the Great Dionysia of 327.[88] Its verses are preserved both towards the end of Euripides' *Vita* and as a stand-alone epigram in the *Palatine Anthology*.[89] The *Vita* establishes the assumption that it was Philemon himself (rather than one of his characters) who loved Euripides to such an extreme:

[86] Ar. *Ran.* 66–7: τοιουτοσὶ τοίνυν με δαρδάπτει πόθος | Εὐριπίδου. Later, when Dionysus cites some examples of Euripidean verse at Heracles, Heracles asks him if 'these really please you'. Dionysus replies that he is 'beyond crazy' about them: μάλλὰ πλεῖν ἢ μαίνομαι (103).

[87] Cf. Scharffenberger (2012) 161.

[88] *FGrH* 239 B7 = Philemon T 13.

[89] *AP* 9.450; the verses are introduced as στίχοι, οὓς εἶπεν Φιλήμων εἰς Εὐριπίδην.

οὕτω δὲ αὐτὸν Φιλήμων ἠγάπησεν ὡς τολμῆσαι περὶ αὐτοῦ τοιοῦτον εἰπεῖν:
εἰ ταῖς ἀληθείαισιν οἱ τεθνηκότες
αἴσθησιν εἶχον, ἄνδρες, ὥς φασίν τινες,
ἀπηγξάμην ἄν, ὥστ' ἰδεῖν Εὐριπίδην. (Eur. T 1.4.3 = Philemon F 118)

Philemon loved [Euripides] so much that he dared to say this about him:
If it were really true as some people say, men,
That the dead still have feeling,
I would have hanged myself to see Euripides.

These lines have enjoyed a measure of modern fame thanks to their radical interpretation in Nietzsche's *Birth of Tragedy* (*Die Geburt der Tragödie aus dem Geiste der Musik*). In a section in which Nietzsche describes the death of Athenian tragedy – the genre's 'suicide' at the hands of Euripides – he contends that it was in Attic New Comedy that 'the degenerate form of tragedy lived on as a monument of its exceedingly painful and violent death'.[90] Viewed from this perspective, Nietzsche argues, Philemon's desire begins to make sense, because it can be understood as an expression of the passionate fondness (*die leidenschaftliche Zuneigung*) which the poets of New Comedy felt for the great tragedian.

Although we cannot equate the feelings of Philemon (and still less of all of his comedy-writing colleagues) with a desire expressed by one of his characters, from at least the *Frogs* onward an unhealthy obsession with Euripides became commonplace in representations of tragic reception. In the *Frogs* the various lowlifes of Hades were said to 'have gone crazy for [Euripides] and reckoned him the wisest' (ὑπερμάνησαν κἀνόμισαν σοφώτατον, 776) when they heard his antilogies, 'twistings' and strophes.[91] A significantly later source, Plutarch's *Life of Nicias*, also provides an imaginative description of the Euripides mania that allegedly was current in the poet's own lifetime. Plutarch records that the Sicilians yearned

[90] 'In ihr [*sc.* New Comedy] lebte die entartete Gestalt der Tragödie fort, zum Denkmale ihres überaus mühseligen und gewaltsamen Hinscheidens' (§11, trans. Kaufmann (2000) 76).

[91] On the passage see Rosen (2006) 34–6; Hunter (2009) 10–17; Halliwell (2011) 108–9. Roselli (2005) even sees the story from the *Vitae* that Euripides' mother was a vegetable-seller (T 1 IA 1) as highlighting 'the poet's tragic style as more in tune with Athenian popular culture' (38).

for the poetry of Euripides more than anyone else outside of Hellas proper and construes this yearning just as the god Dionysus had described his own desire: as *pothos*.[92] Many of the Athenians who managed to return home from the Sicilian Expedition, Plutarch relates, expressed immense gratitude to Euripides because his poetry had saved their lives. Some had been released from slavery because they were able to sing Euripidean lyrics for their masters and some who had wandered Sicily reciting his verses were offered food and water by locals desperate to hear the latest of his work.[93] There is no telling as to how accurate a picture Plutarch paints, but the story does attest to the persistence of Euripides' reputation as a poet who inspired a remarkably loyal following. And while our sources never forthrightly explain what, exactly, motivated this kind of fanaticism, a fragment of an unknown play by Aristophanes' son Nicostratus may offer some insight into the mentality of Euripides' most loyal followers:

'οὐκ ἔστιν ὅστις πάντ' ἀνὴρ εὐδαιμονεῖ.'
νὴ τὴν Ἀθηνᾶν συντόμως γε, φίλτατε
Εὐριπίδη, τὸν βίον ἔθηκας εἰς στίχον. (F 27)

'No man is happy in every way.'
By Athena, most beloved Euripides,
you summed up life in a line.[94]

Despite the comic genre of these fragments, they also contain traces of Euripides-mania as a more sober sentiment. For these comic characters the power of Euripidean poetry was seductive and great: sadness, madness, illness and desire were all potential effects produced by their confrontations with the classical.

The 'Astydamas epigram' in context

At least one tragic poet of the fourth century, a dramatic colleague of comedians such as Antiphanes, is said to have

[92] Plut. *Nic.* 29.2: ἐπόθησαν αὐτοῦ τὴν μοῦσαν οἱ περὶ Σικελίαν. The principal speaker in Satyrus' biography of Euripides claims that the Athenians only learned to appreciate Euripides thanks to the Sicilians and Macedonians: F 6 fr. 39 col. 19 Schorn.
[93] Plut. *Nic.* 29.2–4. [94] Cf. Philippides F 18.

resented the status and following that the earlier tragedians had achieved. Astydamas 'the Second', who was active between 373/2 and at least 340 BC, evidently begrudged tragedians of the past for their untouchable standing in the minds of the people. Astydamas himself belonged to a long and distinguished line of tragedians (Aeschylus was his great-great-great uncle)[95] and earned enormous success in the family trade. Diogenes Laertius however mentions with indignation the honorific bronze statue that the Athenians awarded him. This notice occurs in an account of the life of Socrates, among a list of other injustices (besides the execution of Socrates) which the Athenians committed against intellectuals:

καὶ γὰρ Ὅμηρον, καθά φησιν Ἡρακλείδης [= F 169 Wehrli], πεντήκοντα δραχμαῖς ὡς μαινόμενον ἐζημίωσαν, καὶ Τυρταῖον παρακόπτειν ἔλεγον, καὶ Ἀστυδάμαντα πρότερον τῶν περὶ Αἰσχύλον ἐτίμησαν εἰκόνι χαλκῇ. (D.L. 2.43)

For they fined Homer, as Heraclides says, fifty drachmas for being a madman, and they said that Tyrtaeus was deranged, and they honoured Astydamas with a bronze statue before [they honoured] the tragedians of Aeschylus' era.

A more fleshed-out version of the story behind Astydamas' statue is given by Pausanias the Lexicographer (second century AD) in his *Collection of Attic Words* (Ἀττικῶν ὀνόματων συναγωγή):

Ἀστυδάμᾳ τῷ Μορσίμου εὐημερήσαντι ἐπὶ τραγῳδίας διδασκαλίᾳ Παρθενοπαίου δοθῆναι ὑπ' Ἀθηναίων εἰκόνος ἀνάθεσιν ἐν θεάτρῳ. (σ 6 = Astyd. T 2a)

For Astydamas the son of Morsimus the Athenians granted that a bronze statue be erected in the theatre on the occasion of his success in the tragic competition with his *Parthenopaeus*.

We know from the didascalic records that Astydamas won with *Parthenopaeus* at the Great Dionysia in 340, during the administration of Eubulus and a good decade or so before the Lycurgan decree that provided for statues of Aeschylus, Sophocles and Euripides.[96] In his account Pausanias goes on to say that

95 For the genealogy of the family (whose patriarch was Euphorion) see Sutton (1987) 12–13. On Astydamas and the honorific statue that the Athenians awarded him see pages 183–8.

96 *IG* ii^2 2320.22–3 Millis–Olson = Astydamas T 6 = DID A 1.292.

Astydamas composed this boastful epigram (ἐπίγραμμα ἀλαζονικόν) for his statue's base:

> εἴθ' ἐγὼ ἐν κείνοις γενόμην, ἢ κεῖνοι ἅμ' ἡμῖν
> οἳ γλώσσης τερπνῆς πρῶτα δοκοῦσι φέρειν,
> ὡς ἐπ' ἀληθείας ἐκρίθην ἀφεθεὶς παράμιλλος·
> νῦν δὲ χρόνῳ προέχουσ', ὧι φθόνος οὐκ ἕπεται.[97]
>
> If I had lived in their day, or they in mine,
> those men who seem to carried off the first prizes in eloquence,
> then I will have been judged on fair grounds as their competitor.[98]
> But they have the advantage of time, where envy does not follow.

Astydamas here complains of having no chance at 'fair' competition with deceased predecessors – competition of the sort that the *Frogs* stages between the dead Aeschylus and Euripides. From another source we hear that, precisely because of the arrogance that it betrayed, the Athenians did not in the end allow the lines to be inscribed. Did Astydamas really think that he could ever equal the great tragedians of the past – the rivals whom he surely meant by the men 'who carried off the first prizes in eloquence'?[99]

If truly of mid-fourth century origin, the epigram attributed to Astydamas marks an early moment of conscious 'epigonality' or belatedness in classical literature. Like the fifth-century epic poet Choerilus who, in the proem to his *Persica* (*SH* 317), expressed yearning for the days when the 'meadow' of epic remained untouched, Astydamas bitterly contrasts the 'then' and 'now' (Choerilus' κεῖνον χρόνον ... νῦν) of literary

[97] *AppAnth.* 43. The text reproduced is Page's, at *FGE* 33–4.

[98] Page (1981) explains that ἀφεθεὶς παράμιλλος is 'the language of the stadium. ἄφεσις is the start of a race, the man who is παράμιλλος is "competing side-by-side"' (34).

[99] Zenob. 5.100 = Astyd. T 2b: οἱ [*sc.* the Athenians] δὲ ἐψηφίσαντο ὡς ἐπαχθὲς αὐτὸ μηκέτι ἐπιγραφῆναι. On the Athenians' injunction against the epigram's inscription see most recently Papastamati-von Moock (forthcoming) 58–9 and Goette (1999) 23; on the epigram in the context of Astydamas' career see Xanthakis-Karamanos (1980) 23. See too Biles (2011) 22–3 on the Astydamas epigram's 'competitive poetics'.

production and opportunity.[100] Yet as opposed to Choerilus (or at least to his poetic persona) the 'I' of the Astydamas epigram hardly feels that the potential for original poetic production has dried up. Instead, his epigram laments that the modern tragedian has little hope of earning recognition on the scale which the lavishly praised classical poets still enjoy, because the new poet's successes will always be mitigated by the rivalrous envy (*phthonos*) of his contemporaries and competitors – or even by his own envy of the earlier tragedians.[101]

The impossible standard of achievement set by ancestors also weighed upon other individuals of Astydamas' time. In *On the Crown* Demosthenes insists that his politics and principles are the same as those of the illustrious men of history (τῶν τότ' ἐπαινουμένων ἀνδρῶν), even if Aeschines charges that he is entirely unlike those men (λέγεις ὡς οὐδὲν ὅμοιός εἰμι ἐκείνοις ἐγώ, 18.317–18). Still, Demosthenes continues, comparison with the past is unfair. He asks Aeschines whether *he* can really be compared to such men, or if any living orator can be. Given the impossible standards which the earlier generations set, the answer is clearly 'no'. Demosthenes continues,

ἀλλὰ πρὸς τοὺς ζῶντας, ὦ χρηστέ, ἵνα μηδὲν ἄλλ' εἴπω, τὸν ζῶντ' ἐξέταζε καὶ τοὺς καθ' αὑτόν, ὥσπερ τἄλλα πάντα, τοὺς ποιητάς, τοὺς χορούς, τοὺς ἀγωνιστάς. ὁ Φιλάμμων οὐχ ὅτι Γλαύκου τοῦ Καρυστίου καί τινων ἑτέρων πρότερον γεγενημένων ἀθλητῶν ἀσθενέστερος ἦν, ἀστεφάνωτος ἐκ τῆς Ὀλυμπίας ἀπῄει, ἀλλ' ὅτι τῶν εἰσελθόντων πρὸς αὐτὸν ἄριστ' ἐμάχετο, ἐστεφανοῦτο καὶ νικῶν ἀνηγορεύετο. καὶ σὺ πρὸς τοὺς νῦν ὅρα με ῥήτορας, πρὸς σαυτόν, πρὸς ὅντινα βούλει τῶν ἁπάντων· (Dem. 18.318–19)

Instead, my good man (I shall call you nothing else), compare a living man with the living, the men of his own time, just as one does in all other fields: with poets, choruses and athletes. Philammon, for lack of being as strong as Glaucus of Carystus and other combatants who had come before him,

[100] See MacFarlane (2009) for a recent reading of *SH* 317 which argues that the proem represents a rhetorical move to prepare the audience for Choerilus' own innovations.

[101] Astydamas' complaint may have some support in Aristotle: in ch. 18 of the *Poetics* Aristotle claims that a poet of his own day must be good at every part of tragedy, given the harshness of the spectators (νῦν συκοφαντοῦσιν τοὺς ποιητάς). In the past tragedians excelled at particular aspects of tragedy, but now the people demand that a single tragedian exceed all the combined talents of his predecessors (ἑκάστου τοῦ ἰδίου ἀγαθοῦ ἀξιοῦσι τὸν ἕνα ὑπερβάλλειν, Arist. *Po.* 1456a6–7).

did not leave Olympia without his crown. But because he fought best against the men who fought against him, he was crowned and proclaimed victor.[102] Likewise, evaluate me against the orators of today – against yourself, against whomever you please.[103]

Here Demosthenes is far more careful than Astydamas to deflect any charge of *hubris* in stressing that no man of the present day can hope to clear the bar set by the politicians, orators, poets, choruses or athletes of the past. No living orator should have pretensions of being more skilled than Antiphon, just as no tragic poet should ever be expected to outdo Sophocles.[104] There is, however, an irony to the case of Astydamas: despite the impossibility of competing with the past, Diogenes Laertius grumbles that in one respect Aeschines did best his predecessors: Astydamas' was the first statue of a tragic poet to grace the Theatre of Dionysus. A statue base dating to the period and inscribed with part of Astydamas' name (though certainly no epigram) has been discovered in the theatre.[105] This statue was erected in a highly visible position, built into the retaining wall of the new stone theatre's western *parodos*. A decade or so later, the Lycurgan group of the fifth-century tragedians would come to grace the opposite part of the structure as the dominating visual image at the eastern entrance.

In his discussion of the Astydamas epigram, Denys Page issued a prudent reminder that 'it would be an act of blind faith to accept the truth of the tale or the authenticity' of the poem.[106] Nevertheless, the sentiment which the verses express does seem to square with the fanaticism for classical tragedy

[102] For Philammon, who won the boxing at Olympia in 364, see Golden (2004) s.v. Philammon.

[103] I am grateful to Peter Wilson for drawing this passage to my attention.

[104] Aeschines would respond that *aretē* is the only true standard by which men are measured (Aeschin. 3.189).

[105] *IG* ii² 3775 = T 8b: Ἀστυ[δάμας. On the 'Astydamas base' and its significance for our understanding of the 'Lycurgan' theatre see Papastamati-von Moock (forthcoming) 23–33. The statue is not mentioned by Pausanias (the Periegete), who noted that most of the statues in the theatre were of comedians and tragedians of little importance (αἱ πολλαὶ τῶν ἀφανεστέρων, 1.21.1).

[106] Page (1981) 33.

that Astydamas will have seen depicted on the comic stage during his own lifetime. The sources for the epigram even claim that Astydamas' jealousy itself became a motif on the comic stage. Lexicographical and encyclopaedic texts preserve the story of the epigram under the lemma 'you praise yourself' (Σαυτὴν ἐπαινεῖς).[107] The sources all record that 'the saying came about thanks to the comic poets' and name Philemon as the principal culprit. The relevant verse by Philemon is preserved by Zenobius and Athenaeus (1.33f):

σαυτὴν ἐπαινεῖς ὥσπερ Ἀστυδάμας, γύναι. (Phil. F 160)

You praise yourself, woman, just like Astydamas.

If Astydamas' epigram marks a lament about the untouchable status of classical tragedy among his contemporaries, part of what he was responding to may have been the kind of popular adoration – however absurd in its manifestations – of fifth-century tragedy that the comic playwrights had come so often to caricature.

To save the city

At the end of the *Frogs* Dionysus offers 'saving the city' as his reason for his descent to Hades in search of a *dexios* poet. 'I came down here for a poet', he informs Euripides, 'so that the city can be saved and stage its choruses.'[108] Dionysus tells the two tragedians that whichever of them gives the best advice about Athens will be the one that he takes back. He begins by asking Euripides and Aeschylus their opinions about the problem of Alcibiades, but is satisfied with the answer of neither. He then moves on to pose the challenge more directly: Aeschylus and Euripides must each give their opinion as to how the city can find salvation (σωτηρία, 1435–6).[109] The expectation that Athens might by saved by a resurrected tragic poet remains in

[107] Zen. 5.100; Phot. σ 502; *Suda* σ 161. In Paus. Gram. the lemma (σ 6) is σαυτὴν ἐπαινεῖς ὥσπερ Ἀστυδάμας, γύναι.

[108] Ar. *Ran.* 1419: ἵν' ἡ πόλις σωθεῖσα τοὺς χοροὺς ἄγῃ.

[109] On the theme of the salvation of Athens in Aristophanes' comedies see Storey (2012) esp. 303–4.

force until the end of the play, when Dionysus finally chooses Aeschylus as the city's best hope.

In the latter part of the Peloponnesian War and during the years that followed the loss at Chaeronea we find repeated evidence of the city turning to the classical tragedians in the hopes of a kind of 'salvation'. Dionysus does this explicitly in the *Frogs*, but the idealising nostalgia of the Lycurgan theatre programme also suggests that later citizens were optimistic that trading on the cultural capital afforded by the tragedy of the past had the potential to improve the outlook for the city's future. In Aristophanes' play Dionysus sought to bring a tragedian back from the dead so as to save the city during the Peloponnesian War. In the 330s we find the same tragedians at the heart of a theatre programme whose aim, in a way, was to 'save' the city by promoting literary and cultural history in the face of Macedonian expansion. Aristophanes fulfilled a 'tragic' longing by putting the tragedians themselves onstage and back in the gaze of the theatre-going public. Lycurgus did much the same, though with far more material permanence, by calling for the three tragedians' portrait statues to be erected in the space that had witnessed the first performances of their plays.

The comic longing for tragedy that was staged by the poets of fourth-century comedy helps us to understand better the more general, and more serious, nostalgia on the part of men such as Lycurgus for the days when Athenian hegemony – economic, political and cultural – was in all ways more assured. Against the comic backdrop, the Lycurgan-Era efforts to give definite shape to the theatrical past (in the form of the bronze statues and the archived scripts) and also to invest in the theatre's future seem to mark the city's attempts to act concretely upon its *pothos*, and on an enormous scale at that. Throughout the century spectators had the opportunity to view comic representations of this tragic longing, which often were performed in the same theatrical space in which the seeds of fanaticism had first been planted. By the time of the New Comic playwrights and comedies such as Diphilus' *Phileuripides* (likely an early third-century production), spectators filing in and out of the

Theatre of Dionysus will have been used to gazing upon larger-than-life representations of the men who were the objects of comic nostalgia. Even if the comedy of the fourth century seems to have been more interested in poking fun at tragedy's 'maddening' effects upon individuals than in interrogating and unpacking its moral effects on the city as a whole, this interest suggests that fifth-century tragedy's status as classic was dear to the population at large. The tragedy of the past was a subject that seems never to have worn thin, even as the fifth-century 'golden age' became an ever-more distant horizon.

CHAPTER 6

ARISTOTLE AND THE THEATRE OF ATHENS

Representations of tragic nostalgia persisted on the comic stage over the course of the fourth century, but the more serious work of preserving Athens' theatrical heritage also took place under the administrations of Eubulus and Lycurgus. Aristotle, too, took part in the efforts to consolidate and to archive the record of the city's dramatic competitions. In 335 BC, towards the beginning of Lycurgus' stewardship of the city's finances, Aristotle returned to Athens from Macedon. During this, his 'second Athenian period', he began assembling and organising the historical records of dithyrambic and dramatic victories at Athenian festivals. His research into the history of those competitions yielded at least three works, according to the catalogue provided by Diogenes Laertius: one book of *Victories at the Dionysia* (Νῖκαι Διονυσιακαὶ α´), one book *On Tragedies* (Περὶ τραγῳδιῶν α´) and a *Didascaliae* (Διδασκαλίαι α´).[1]

Of the *Victories* and *On Tragedies* we know nothing except the titles. The *Didascaliae* will have documented similar, yet more complete, information as the inscribed *Fasti* (*IG* ii² 2318), erected on the Acropolis not long before (sometime between 347/6 and 343/2). A later inscribed Athenian monument, known as the *Didascaliae* (*IG* ii² 2319–2323a; *SEG* XXVI 203), probably offers a better idea of what Aristotle's work included. The inscription recorded the results of tragedy and comedy at both the Great Dionysia and the Lenaea, reporting not only victorious poets and plays but also the ranking and plays of the second- and (when relevant) third-place playwrights.[2] The

[1] D.L. 5.26 *opera* 135–7; see *DFA*² 71. Hesychius of Miletus identifies the *Nikai* as one book of *Victories at the City Dionysia and Lenaea*, *op.* 126 listed ap. Rose (1886) 15, who also collects the fragments of Aristotle's *Didascaliae* (F 618–30). See also Reisch (1903) cols. 396–9.

[2] See Millis and Olson (2012) 61 and generally their ch. 2 on the *Didascaliae*.

monument of *Didascaliae* was likely inscribed in the first part of the third century BC, and its authors may even have profited from Aristotle's research in addition to the city's records.[3] Aristotle's own foray into Athenian festal and literary history was long ago linked by Werner Jaeger with the 'state reform of the theatre' that occurred in the 330s, the same reform that led to Lycurgus' establishment of state copies of plays by the three great tragedians.[4] The assembling of historical records and of the fifth-century tragedians' scripts marked two major and roughly contemporary efforts to collect, and in different ways to monumentalise and to preserve, Athenian dramatic history. During these same years Aristotle was also working on drama from another angle, as he refined and lectured on the theories of tragic poetry. Aspects of those theories are preserved for us today in the *Poetics*.[5]

No account of classical tragedy in Lycurgan Athens could pass over the substantial contributions of Aristotle, which mark a unique addition to our picture of the role that the city's classical heritage now occupied in the greater Greek imagination. Aristotle's works provide our most thorough picture of any single individual's conceptualisation of the imaginary space that the theatre occupied. From his corpus, two themes of great importance for our purposes emerge. One is the more antiquarian side of Aristotle's interest in tragedy, as manifested in his efforts to assemble didascalic records, his use of biographical anecdotes about the tragedians, his interest in the historical evolution of tragedy (particularly in ch. 4 of the *Poetics*) and his emphasis on the primacy of Sophocles and Euripides within the tragic tradition. The other is the 'universalising' view of tragic drama that he takes in the *Poetics*, where he presents the genre

[3] Millis (forthcoming) 436 n. 39; see also Sickinger (1999) 42–8 on Athens' public records of festival victories.

[4] Jaeger (1923) 348–9. On the relationship between Aristotle's works and the inscribed Athenian dramatic records see Blum (1991) 24–43.

[5] On the date of the *Poetics* see the synthesis in Halliwell (1998) 324–30. Halliwell argues that the *Poetics* contains aspects of a poetic theory which Aristotle began to develop before 347 (during the 'first Athenian period'), but that the form in which it survives is most likely 'to represent the first book of a treaty used for instruction in the full course of study and enquiry offered in the Lyceum during the last decade and a half of Aristotle's life' (330).

as a global art form unbound to any single period or place.[6] Still, even as Aristotle sets out in the *Poetics* to outline a general theory of tragedy (and not of Athenian, or even of 'Greek', tragedy),[7] he consistently draws his conclusions from a mental repertory of primarily fifth-century Attic plays.[8]

Aristotle's historically orientated interest in tragedy, particularly as represented by his own compilation of didascalic records, chimes well with what we have seen of Lycurgan-Era attempts to evaluate, inventory and conserve the achievements of the Athenian past. On the other hand, his omission from the *Poetics* of any discussion of tragedy's connections to Athens also reflects the longstanding and well-established popularity of Attic tragedy in the Greek world at large. The tragic examples adduced in the *Poetics* are drawn entirely from the works of tragedians who competed in Athens at the Great Dionysia. But as Edith Hall has importantly pointed out, the *Poetics* contains no discussion of either the 'civic context' of the festival or the tragic genre's particular connection to the Athenian polis.[9] Aristotle's account of tragic drama should therefore be read as a kind of alternative to the Lycurgan vision, which rooted tragedy deeply in Athens and Athenian values. Herein lies the apparent contradiction of Aristotle's efforts: his archival work on the city's dramatic history fits well within the context of Lycurgan theatre initiatives, yet nowhere does the *Poetics* grant that tragedy was the product of an extraordinary moment in Athens. The view of tragedy as a 'universal' phenomenon, almost completely deracinated from Athenian soil, marks exactly the view that Athenians such as Lycurgus must have been hoping to correct with their various efforts to reclaim the city's tragic patrimony.

Here I shall be reading Aristotle with an aim of reconstructing the space that Attic tragedy and tragedians occupied in his own thought. By retreading the well worn paths of the *Poetics* and the *Rhetoric* with an eye to the broader theatrical

[6] Cf. Arist. *Po.* ch. 9; on Aristotle and the 'universality' of poetry see esp. Heath (2009) and (1991).

[7] See esp. Heath (2009) 473–4. [8] Cf. Heath (2009) 473. [9] Hall (1996).

landscape, we stand to gain a wider perspective on the co-existence of tragic drama's past and present in the third quarter of the century. Most importantly, Aristotle's remarkably non-Athenian account of Athenian tragedy provides crucial insight into the urgency of the Lycurgan theatre programme and its efforts to ensure that tragedy be recognised as uniquely, autochthonously, Athenian.

The lives of tragedians

Aristotle's works contain a small scattering of tales about renowned literary figures of the past, and his lost *On Poets* appears to have combined aspects of the literary criticism found in the *Poetics* with a more generally anecdotal approach to, or at least interest in, literary history.[10] The *Poetics*, on the other hand, is relatively free of anything like literary biography: apart from two *bon mots* which are attributed to Sophocles and Agathon,[11] we hear nothing of the tragedians themselves but only of their plays, poetry and innovations with respect to the genre.[12] There is therefore little indication, whether in the *Poetics* or elsewhere, that Aristotle actively sought to infer information about the lives of poets from their works.[13] One version of the widely popular inferential method of literary biography is exuberantly staged in the *Frogs*, where Aristophanes' caricatures of Euripides and Aeschylus are drawn

[10] On Aristotle and literary anecdotes see Huxley (1974), on his *On Poets* see esp. Janko (1991) 51–9. On Aristotle 'the biographer' see Arrighetti (1987) 170–6, which focuses on the figure of Solon in the *Constitution of the Athenians*.

[11] By Agathon at *Po.* 1456a23–5 and by Sophocles at *Po.* 1460b32–5; see below.

[12] E.g. Aeschylus added the second actor to tragedy and reduced the role of the chorus; Sophocles introduced the third actor and set-painting (σκηνογραφία): *Po.* 1449a15–19 (on problems with these claims see e.g. Glucker (1969) and Brown (1984)); Agathon is said to be the first to use the chorus for 'interludes' (ἐμβόλιμα): *Po.* 1456a30. At *Po.* 1449a37–b1 Aristotle claims that tragedy (as opposed to comedy) has always been taken seriously, and thus its transformations (μεταβάσεις) and the poets responsible for them have not been forgotten (οὐ λελήθασιν). For Aristotle's potted history of tragedy in *Poetics* ch. 4 see esp. Lord (1974) and Cantor (1991) (attempts to understand Aristotle's account), Scullion (2002) 102–10 (a critique of the argument's historicity), Depew (2007) (on Aristotle's differentiation in ch. 4 of Dionysiac genres).

[13] For an account of this method and a number of case studies see Lefkowitz (1981).

largely from their tragic styles.[14] For Aristotle, however, the personal lives and characters of the poets look to have been incidental to the nature and quality of their literary production.

The anecdotes about tragedians which the Aristotelian corpus does preserve reflect more of a general interest in the literary figures of the past. Aristotle tends to use stories about celebrated poets in much the same way that he uses aspects of mythology (and even of particular tragedies) as specific instances which speak to the validity of general observations. For instance, in the *Nicomachean Ethics* he exemplifies his notion of 'actions completed in ignorance' with the example of Aeschylus' involuntary revelation of the Mysteries.[15] Soon after he illustrates another type of ignorant action, this time with the mythological story of Merope: 'someone might mistake [his/her own] son for an enemy, as Merope does'.[16] Little practical difference separates his didactic use of an episode from the myth of Merope or from the (life-)story of Aeschylus.

Two other anecdotes told by Aristotle recount events in the life of Euripides. In the *Politics* we hear that a certain Decamnichus once led an attack on King Archelaus of Macedon because the King had handed him over to Euripides for flogging.[17] The story serves to exemplify the general observation that people who have suffered corporal punishment often seek revenge on those responsible. The other story occurs in a chapter of the *Rhetoric* (3.15) which catalogues a number of ways in which a defendant might counter a false accusation (διαβολή). Euripides' defence of himself against Hygiaenon

[14] On inferential biography see page 141 n. 38 above.

[15] A case of 'not knowing that something was secret', οὐκ εἰδέναι ὅτι ἀπόρρητα ἦν, 3.1111a9–10. Aeschylus was supposedly tried before the Areopagus for revealing secrets of the Eleusinian mysteries (Aesch. T 93–4; see Gagné (2009) 218–21 with bibliography); he defended himself by claiming that he said 'whatever came to his lips', a statement which then became proverbial: see Plato *Resp.* 8.563c and Plut. *Amat.* 763c.

[16] Arist. *NE* 3.1111a13: οἰηθείη δ' ἄν τις καὶ τὸν υἱὸν πολέμιον εἶναι ὥσπερ ἡ Μερόπη. This may be a reference to Euripides' *Cresphontes*, which Aristotle refers to by the shorthand ἐν τῶι Κρεσφόντῃ at *Po.* 1454a5–7.

[17] Euripides had been angry with Decamnichus for remarking upon his bad breath: Arist. *Pol.* 5.1311b33–4.

in an *antidosis* case demonstrates the principle of appeal to a former verdict: on the stand Hygiaenon had argued that Euripides revealed his fundamental impiety (ἀσέβεια) when he celebrated perjury in what became a famous line of *Hippolytus*: 'My tongue swore, but my mind is unsworn.'[18] To this accusation Euripides is said to have retorted that

> αὐτον ἀδικεῖν τὰς ἐκ τοὺ Διονυσιακοῦ ἀγῶνος κρίσεις εἰς τὰ δικαστήρια ἄγοντα· ἐκεῖ γὰρ αὐτῶν δεδωκέναι λόγον, ἢ δώσειν εἰ βούλεται κατηγορεῖν. (Arist. *Rhet.* 3.1416a)
>
> [Hygiaenon] was wrong to bring verdicts from the agon at the Dionysia into the courtroom, for he [i.e. Euripides] had already given an account of those things there [i.e. at the Dionysia], or would give one if [Hygiaenon] should wish to make a charge against him.

The *hypothesis* to Euripides' *Hippolytus* informs us that the 'verdict' already reached at the festival had in fact been in the playwright's favour: in the year that Euripides competed with the play, 428 BC, he took first prize.[19]

Aristotle does not present any of these stories as specifically bearing on the poetry which the playwrights composed, and the very existence of a distinction between a poet's works and his life and character (a distinction not often found in other biographical accounts of the tragedians) seems to be part of the point of Euripides' response to Hygiaenon. Nevertheless, Aristotle does not use stories from the lives of any contemporary poet in such an exemplary way: Antiphon 'the poet', a contemporary of Plato's, is the latest tragedian (and the only one apart from Aeschylus and Euripides) who earns any biographical mention.[20] The poets who are the subjects of anecdotes are presented as immediately recognisable historical figures, and Aristotle's interest in their lives reflects an interest in the 'particulars' of tragic history that may have been more

[18] Eur. *Hipp.* 612: ἡ γλῶσσ' ὀμώμοχ', ἡ δὲ φρὴν ἀνώμοτος.

[19] *Arg.Eur.Hipp.* = DID C 13. The line quickly became notorious: cf. Ar. *Th.* 275–6; *Ran.* 101–2 and 1471; Pl. *Tht.* 154d. On its *fortuna* see Avery (1968), esp. 22–5; on trials in which Euripides was either prosecutor or defendant see Cagnazzi (1993).

[20] A story about Antiphon's execution by Dionysius of Syracuse appears at *Rhet.* 2.1385a9 (= Antiphon T 1). Aristotle refers to Antiphon's *Andromache* (*EE* 7.1239a39) and *Meleager* (*Rhet.* 2.1399b25).

fully developed in his work *On Poets*. In the *Poetics* itself he suggests that biographical anecdotes are precisely the purchase of the historian: in chapter 9 he explains that it is history (ἡ ἱστορία) and not poetry which aims at representing 'particulars' (τὰ καθ' ἕκαστον): an example of a 'particular' being 'what Alcibiades did or experienced'.[21] What Aeschylus, Euripides and even Antiphon 'did and what they experienced' was now, then, a matter of (literary) history – but not one which bore on literary criticism, whose object for Aristotle would be the identification and critique of poetic universals.

Aristotle on fourth-century tragedians

Although Aristotle's works contain no biographical information about any tragedian after Antiphon, he alludes in other ways to a handful of contemporary (or nearly contemporary) tragic poets.[22] Within the corpus, most often in the *Poetics* and *Rhetoric*, he discusses and quotes from four tragedians of roughly his own day: Astydamas II, Theodectes, Carcinus II ('the Younger') and Chaeremon. Aristotle evidently assumed that his audience had some knowledge of their works, as his references presuppose basic acquaintance with the plots of their plays: each of these poets is, in Patricia Easterling's words 'mentioned familiarly'.[23] External evidence also indicates that these four poets were well-known figures in their own right. Carcinus and Astydamas both repeatedly won first prize at the Great Dionysia; Chaeremon is the only tragedian whose verses are identifiably satirised and quoted in surviving fourth-century comedy; and Theodectes not only produced tragedies but was also a prominent rhetorician and a member of Aristotle's circle in Athens.[24] The sketches below offer an overview of what we

[21] Arist. *Po.* 1451b11: τί Ἀλκιβιάδης ἔπραξεν ἢ τί ἔπαθεν.
[22] On Aristotle as a source for fourth-century tragedy see esp. Karamanou (2011), Xanthakis-Karamanos (1980) 24–5 and Webster (1958).
[23] Easterling (1993) 563.
[24] See esp. Easterling (1993) 565 on the vitality of the theatre industry in fourth-century Athens, particularly with regard to the 'continuing prestige of the competition for new plays, and the productivity and fame of some of the fourth-century dramatists'.

know about these four tragedians. In each case, the abundance of non-Aristotelian testimonia for these poets attests to their fame and success, and so to the vibrancy of new tragic production in Athens during these decades.

Astydamas II

In the light of the fame that Astydamas II enjoyed both in his own lifetime and after, it is surprising that Aristotle only clearly refers to him once in his surviving works, in the *Poetics*.[25] Astydamas was a prolific tragedian and the *Suda* (α 4265) records the name of seven of his tragic plays as well as a satyr play, *Herakles Satyrikos*. His career spanned from 373/2 until sometime after 340 (in 341 he won at the Great Dionysia with *Achilles*, *Athamas* and *Antigone*; in 340 he won with *Parthenopaeus* and *Lycaon*),[26] and he was considered important enough in later generations to have the year of his first victory recorded in the *Parian Chronicle*.[27] Earlier we saw that he was the first tragedian to be honoured with a portrait statue in Athens on account of the success of his *Parthenopaeus*.[28] Yet the single reference which Aristotle makes to Astydamas occurs only in passing. In the *Poetics* he explains that characters in a tragedy may do 'a horrible deed' outside the drama (as in Sophocles' *Oedipus Tyrannus*), or they may do it

> ἐν δ' αὐτῇ τραγῳδίᾳ οἷον ὁ Ἀλκμέων ὁ Ἀστυδάμαντος ἢ ὁ Τηλέγονος ὁ ἐν τῷ Τραυματίᾳ Ὀδυσσεῖ. (Arist. *Po.* 1453b33–4)

> in the tragedy itself, as Astydamas' Alcmeon does, or Telegenus in the *Wounded Odysseus*.

Only one line of Astydamas' *Alcmeon* survives (F 1c ap. Stob 2.15.1), though the myth would suggest that in it Alcmeon

[25] At Arist. *Po.* 1453b33. The phrase λόγχην ἣν φοροῦσι Γηγενεῖς at 1454b22 has been thought a quotation from an *Antigone* either by Euripides (Janko (1987) and Lucas (1968) ad loc.) or Astydamas (Webster (1954) 305–7).

[26] *IG* ii² 2325.5–7 and 22–4 Millis–Olson.

[27] *FrGH* 239 A71. The last tragedian mentioned on the marble before Astydamas is Sophocles (for his death in 407/6: entry 64). There is considerable confusion in the ancient sources about Astydamas I and II (father and son), most of which has been sensibly untangled by Capps (1900) 41–5.

[28] See pages 51–2 above.

unknowingly killed his mother. The *Wounded Odysseus* which Aristotle mentions has been identified with Sophocles' *Odysseus Akanthoplex* (Soph. T 453–61a) in which Odysseus is killed by Telegonus, his son by Circe. Aristotle's one reference to Astydamas serves (as is often the case in the *Poetics*) to illustrate a more general point, in this case about actions that happen 'within the drama itself', with double reference to a well-known fifth-century play and to a more contemporary tragedy. The strategy of using examples from both fifth- and fourth-century plays in support of a single observation is key to the programme of the *Poetics*, and we shall be returning to it below.

Theodectes

Of the four later tragedians, Aristotle refers most often to the work of Theodectes of Phaselis (in Lycia),[29] who was likely born around 390 BC and probably died in Athens not long before 334.[30] Aristotle's fondness for Theodectes may be partially explained by the two's alleged personal relationship: in addition to being a successful tragedian, Theodectes was a philosopher and by some accounts close friend of Aristotle's.[31] The *Suda* (θ 138) records that he composed fifty plays and took first prize at the Great Dionysia seven times, and a surviving didascalic inscription attests that he

[29] See *DNP* s.v. 'Theodektes' and Theodectes 72 T 1–17 in *TrGF* vol. I. On Theodectes' tragic output see esp. Xanthakis-Karamanos (1980) 53–8 and 63–70; Theodectes' poetry is now best known for F 6, in which a shepherd describes letter shapes likely in imitation of Eur.'s *Theseus* (F 382) and/or Agathon's *Telephus* (F 4).

[30] For the chronology see Capps (1900) 40–1. We have notice of an epitaph: 72 T 2 = *GV* 547. According to [Plut.] *dec. or. vit.* (T 7) and Paus. 1.37.4 Theodectes had a memorial statue on the Sacred Way. The *terminus ante quem* for his death is provided by a story in Plutarch: when Alexander the Great passed through Phaselis (in 334/3) he garlanded a statue of the deceased Theodectes in honour of the association they had once had on account of Aristotle and philosophy (Plut. *Alex.* 674a = T 4). Capps (1900) 40 however places his death date shortly after 350 BC.

[31] On Theodectes and Aristotle see esp. T 11–13 (11 and 13 suggest that the two had a very close personal relationship: 13 = Ath. 13.566d compares Aristotle's affections for Theodectes to Socrates' for Alcibiades). At *Rhet.* 3.1410b2 Aristotle refers to a Θεοδέκτεια and Diogenes Laertius mentions a τέχνης τῆς Θεοδέκτου συναγωγή (5.34). [Plut.] *Vit. dec. or.* tells us that he came to tragedy after philosophy: he is called Θεοδέκτης ὁ Φασηλίτης ὁ τὰς τραγῳδίας ὕστερον γράψας (837c).

won a victory soon after 372, not long after Carcinus and Astydamas' earliest first prizes.[32] Aristotle mentions seven of Theodectes' tragedies in eight references scattered across four different works: these are to *Philoctetes* (*EN* 1150b9), *Helen* (*Pol.* 1.1255a37), *Alcmeon* (*Rhet.* 2.1397b3), *Ajax* (*Rhet.* 2.1399b28 and 2.1400a27), *Orestes* (*Rhet.* 2.1401a33), *Tydeus* (*Po.* 1455a09) and *Lynceus* (*Po.* 1455a37); these references also provide lines of his *Helen*, *Alcmeon* and *Orestes*. Only two of Aristotle's allusions to Theodectes occur in the *Poetics*, and half of these appear in *Rhetoric* 2, as part of the discussion of common enthymemes. Theodectes' *Lynceus* was evidently well enough known that Aristotle could mention it without naming Theodectes as the playwright.[33] If Theodectes had really been a member of the Lyceum we might reasonably imagine that Aristotle's pupils there were familiar with his work.

Carcinus 'the Younger'

Carcinus II also belonged to a family of tragedians. His father Xenocles was one of the three playwright sons of the poet Carcinus (I) who are repeatedly mentioned in Aristophanic comedy.[34] The *Suda* (κ 394) records that Carcinus II had his *floruit* (ἤκμαζε) in the 100th Olympiad (380/79–377/6 BC) and won eleven victories;[35] according to Diogenes Laertius (2.63) he also spent time in Syracuse at the court of Dion, who died in 357/6. Together with Astydamas, Carcinus appears to have been the best known tragedian of the century. In Menander's *Aspis* Daos would quote a line that he attributes to Carcinus as part of his torrent of tragic quotations.[36] Aristotle refers to

32 *IG* ii² 2325A.45 Millis–Olson.

33 Arist. *Po.* 1452a27; Theodectes is named in connection with *Lynceus* at 1455b29.

34 See Olson (1997) on Carcinus I and Sutton (1987) 17–18 on the 'family of Xenotimus' (the father of Carcinus I). The family was from Thorikos.

35 One of these, won shortly before 372 BC, may be recorded in *TrGF* vol. I DID A3a 43, from *IG* ii² 2325.

36 Men. *Asp.* 415–18 = Carcinus F 5a. A papyrus (Louvre *Antiquités egyptiennes* inv. E 10534, second century BC) also happens to preserve lines of Carcinus' *Medea* with musical notation: see West (2007).

at least five of Carcinus II's plays: a *Medea* (*Rhet.* 2.1400b28), *Oedipus* (*Rhet.* 3.1417b18), *Alope* (*EN* 7.1150b10), *Thyestes* (*Po.* 1454b23) and likely an *Amphiaraus* (*Po.* 1455a26–9), though only two of these references (to *Thyestes* and *Amphiaraus*) occur within the *Poetics*. In the *Poetics* his *Amphiaraus*, or at least a play about Amphiaraus, becomes the subject of Aristotle's one concrete criticism of staging: because Carcinus failed to 'visualise' (to put 'before his eyes', πρὸ ὀμμάτων) the action of his play as he was composing it, he made the staging mistake of having the seer Amphiaraus emerge from a shrine in an improbable way. As a result the spectators were annoyed and the play was a flop.[37] With the exception of this anecdote about a failed production, Aristotle uses examples from Carcinus II's plays solely to illustrate aspects of plot design or strategies of rhetorical argument.

Chaeremon

Chaeremon was a renowned tragedian, though he is mistaken for a comic playwright by the *Suda* (χ 170).[38] Some of his plays enjoyed an afterlife on the stage and works of his were also parodied in later comedy and excerpted in literary anthologies. Evidence for reperformance of his work comes from a Hellenistic inscription found near the theatre at Arcadian Tegea.[39] The inscription records the plays, all of them revivals, for which an unknown actor (who was also a prize-winning boxer) won the acting competition. Five of the actor's seven victories were with three different Euripidean tragedies: *Orestes*, which he performed at the Great Dionysia, as well as a *Heracles* play

[37] Arist. *Po.* 1455a28–9: ἐπὶ δὲ τῆς σκηνῆς ἐξέπεσεν δυσχερανάντων τοῦτο τῶν θεατῶν; for an analysis of the passage and hypotheses as to Carcinus' staging mistake see Green (1990).

[38] On Chaeremon see esp. Snell (1971) 158–68 and Collard (1970); on Aristotle's allusions to him see Webster (1954) 303.

[39] *IG* v 2.118 = DID B 1; the inscription likely dates to between 190 and 179 BC: see Le Guen (2007) (a fresh reappraisal of the entire inscription). On the inscription cf. also Revermann (1999–2000) 462–5, Xanthakis-Karamanos (1980) 7, Snell (1971) 159. The *Suda* also attributes to him a *Thersites*, which Snell identified with the *Achilles* of this inscription and so with the *Achilles Thersitoktonos* mentioned at Stob. 1.6.7. A line of the play is quoted at Men. *Asp.* 411.

and the *Archelaus*. But one of the actor's wins was with Chaeremon's celebrated *Achilles*, perhaps *Achilles Killer of Thersites* (*Thersitoktonos*), at the Naia festival in Dodona.

The *Suda* attributes eight plays to Chaeremon (though we have evidence for at least nine); this list includes the problematic *Centaur* mentioned twice by Aristotle (*Po.* 1447b21–2 and 1460a2) but omits the *Dionysus* that is cited at *Rhet.* 2.1400b25. Differences of opinion persist as to the genre of the *Centaur*: was it a tragedy, a satyr play or not a dramatic work at all?[40] Aristotle calls it a 'composition in a mix of all metres'[41] and emphasises the oddity of Chaeremon's choice to blend trimeters with tetrameters within it: for any other poet to do this would be quite unusual (ἀτοπώτερον 1460a2). Aristotle may nevertheless have had works such as the *Centaur* in mind when in the *Rhetoric* he named Chaeremon, 'precise in the manner of a logographer', together with the dithyrambist Licymnius as among the popular poets who are good for reading – the *anagnōstikoi*.[42] Poetry that was 'suited for reading' (though surely not precluded from oral performance) stands for Aristotle in contrast with 'agonistic' pieces, which were meant to be performed. He explains that agonistic works are most appropriate for interpretation by actors and as such he classes them as *hypokritikōtata*.[43] Though the nature of the *Centaur* remains mysterious Aristotle is explicit that it was not the kind of composition that Sophocles or Euripides would ever

[40] Possibly a tragedy: Snell (1971) 168; a satyr play: Else (1968) 54–60, followed by Collard (1970) 28, Cipolla (2003) 276, with commentary on the surviving fragments at 307–12; not a drama at all: Ford (1988) 303–5 (on the basis of *Rhet.* 3.1413b Ford concludes that the *Centaur* 'belongs in the category of ῥαψῳδία, distinct from drama in its performance because it lacked the metrical and musical variety requiring a professional singer', 304). Athenaeus calls the work a 'polymetric drama' (δρᾶμα πολυμέτρον, 13.608e).

[41] Arist. *Po.* 1447b22: μικτὴ ῥαψῳδία ἐξ ἁπάντων τῶν μέτρων.

[42] Arist. *Rhet.* 3.1413b12–13; Chaeremon is ἀκριβὴς . . . ὥσπερ λογογράφος.

[43] On the ἀναγνωστικοί see Zwierlein (1966) 128–34 and Handley (2002) 167–9; for the role that they have played in scholarly narratives of fourth-century theatrical decline see esp. Le Guen (1995) 70. Chaeremon F 14b (incert., preserved only on papyrus by *P.Hib.*2.2234 = Pack² 6) is an acrostic poem – the earliest known – whose first letters spell out Chaeremon's name (ΧΑΙΡΗΜ . . .), a gimmick hard to catch in performance: cf. Ford (2003) 18. Chaeremon was one of the 'cherished' poets among readers: see Cope and Sandys' (1877) discussion of the verb βαστάζεσθαι (βαστάζονται δὲ οἱ ἀναγνωστικοί) *ad Rhet.* 3.1413b.

have undertaken.[44] Aristotle's comments upon Chaeremon are exceptional, for he never otherwise indicates that contemporary tragedians have influenced or innovated with respect to the genre.

Each of these four playwrights was a star in his own time, and an inscription such as we have from Tegea for the boxer-actor indicates that their plays even entered into the repertories of successful professional actors.[45] Centuries later, Plutarch would identify two plays that premiered and took the prize in this period – Carcinus II's *Aerope* and Astydamas' *Hector* – as part of the heyday of Athenian tragic production.[46] Altogether, the Aristotelian corpus contains about a score of references to sixteen plays by this set of tragedians. Not even half of these references occur in the *Poetics*, where each of the contemporary tragedians is mentioned at least once and we can securely identify references to six of their plays (Chaeremon's *Centaur*, Carcinus' *Thyestes* and the Amphiaraus play, Astydamas' *Alcmeon* and Theodectes' *Tydeus* and *Lynceus*). Nevertheless, and with the single exception of his critique of Carcinus' staging, Aristotle does not express critical judgements in the *Poetics* about more recent tragic plays. Instead he tends to mention them only briefly and so as to illustrate aspects of character or plot device such as a type of recognition or reversal.[47] This contrasts starkly with the cases of Sophocles and Euripides, about whose plays he offers detailed aesthetic and structural judgements. With, moreover, the possible exception of Chaeremon, none of these later tragic poets is credited with a lasting innovation in the form, style or content

[44] On Chaeremon's 'unconventional' poetry – Athenaeus calls him ἐπικατάφορος ἐπὶ τὰ ἄνθη (13.608d) for his many descriptions of flowers – see further Lorenzoni (1994) and Collard (1970) 23–8.

[45] Meritt (1938) 116–18 restored the name of Astydamas as the author of a *Hermes*, which may have been victoriously staged in a competition of 'old' satyr drama in Athens in 251/0.

[46] Plut. *Mor.* 349e, *de gloria Atheniensium*. The reference occurs in a section in which Plutarch also names Aeschylus and Sophocles to the same effect.

[47] At *Po.* 1454b24 Aristotle does class the recognition in Carcinus' *Thyestes* as of the least artful type (it is ἀτεχνότατη).

of tragic poetry or performance. In the *Poetics* the latest poet said to have introduced a significant change to tragedy (albeit a change for the worse) is Agathon, whom Aristotle identifies as the first tragedian who gave his choruses only *embolima*, or songs 'thrown in' between episodes and having little to do with the action of the play.[48] For Aristotle, poets were now working within a tradition whose parameters were already fixed.

Facts and figures

More references to fourth-century tragedy and tragedians appear in the *Rhetoric* than in any other of Aristotle's works, the *Poetics* included. The *Rhetoric* contains ten mentions of newer tragedy as opposed to the eight of the *Poetics*: in the *Rhetoric* seven of those references occur in chapter 2.23 (which spans sections 1397a–1400b),[49] and another appears very shortly afterwards.[50] This particular chapter is dedicated to various strategies of rhetorical proof, or enthymemes, which Aristotle often illustrates with examples from speeches as recorded by historiographers.[51] No overlap occurs between the fourth-century plays which are mentioned here and those in the *Poetics*, which itself attests to the breadth of fourth-century plays with which Aristotle was familiar. Aristotle's tragic references in the *Rhetoric* illustrate modes of logical argumentation (we might also think back to the anecdote about Euripides' *antidosis* trial), while the citations and plays that he picks out in the *Poetics* serve to clarify his points about construction of plot, character, etc.

The same section of the *Rhetoric* contains relatively few references to works by the great fifth-century tragedians who so dominate the *Poetics*, where Aristotle mentions Aeschlyus a handful of times and Sophocles and Euripides on tens of

48 Arist. *Po.* 1456a30.

49 To Antiphon's *Meleager* (1379b13 and 1399b26), Carcinus' *Medea* (1400b28); to a play by Chaeremon that is likely his *Dionysus* (1400b25); to Theodectes' *Alcmeon* (1397b3) and *Ajax* (1399b26 and 1400a28).

50 At Arist. *Rhet.* 1401a36, a reference to Theodectes' *Orestes*.

51 Such speeches include Astydamas' *Messianicus* (1397a), and speeches by Iphicrates against Harmodius (1397b) and Aristophon (1398a).

occasions.[52] In *Rhetoric* 2.23 only Sophocles and Euripides appear, and four of their plays are named or cited: Sophocles' lost *Teucer* and *Tyro*[53] and Euripides' *Trojan Women* and lost *Thyestes*.[54] This single chapter of the *Rhetoric* thus cites later tragedians twice as often as their great fifth-century predecessors.[55] Aeschylus, we might note, is once again absent from a fourth-century source that is otherwise rich in testimonia for tragedy. The relative prominence of fourth-century tragedy in this chapter of the *Rhetoric* may be partially explained by an observation that Aristotle makes in the *Poetics*: while the 'old' poets made their characters speak 'in a civic' or 'statesman-like way' (πολιτικῶς), modern-day tragedians craft their characters to speak 'rhetorically' (ῥητορικῶς).[56] But Aristotle may also have felt more at liberty to quote from contemporary tragedy in the *Rhetoric* because there, as opposed to in the *Poetics*, an account of tragedy's universal essence is not at stake.

In the *Poetics* the allusions to fourth-century tragedy almost always occur in the company of references to plays by either Sophocles or Euripides. Theodectes' *Lynceus* is cited together with Sophocles' *Oedipus Tyrannus* as an example of a plot that features a reversal of fortunes (περιπέτεια, 1452a24–7); Astydamas' *Alcmeon* is mentioned in the same breath as Sophocles'

[52] See the calculations at Green (1994) 50: in the *Poetics* 'Aristotle refers to five plays of Aeschylus, twelve of Sophocles, and twenty of Euripides.'

[53] At Arist. *Rhet.* 1398a4 (cf. 1416b1) and 1400b18 respectively.

[54] At Arist. *Rhet.* 1397a17–19 (Eur. F 396) and 1400b23–4 respectively. In 1400b lines from Sophocles, Euripides and Chaeremon (his *Dionysus*) are noted for drawing attention to characters' aptronyms.

[55] I.e. nine fourth-century references (= seven plus two mentions of Antiphon), as opposed to four fifth-century ones. Sullivan (1933–4) 70 has counted twenty-two total references to Euripides in the course of the work, all but two of which are favourable (on Aristotle's estimation of Euripides see further below).

[56] Arist. *Po.* 1450b7–8: οἱ ἀρχαῖοι πολιτικῶς ἐποίουν λέγοντας, οἱ δὲ νῦν ῥητορικῶς. See esp. Xanthakis-Karamanos (1979a) and Le Guen (1995): 69–70 on this passage and the perceived influence of rhetoric upon fourth-century tragedy. Cf. also Hunter (2009) 43 on Dio's later 'recasting' of this aspect of Aristotle's model (at Dio 52.10–11). The *Poetics* and *Rhetoric* contain a number of cross-references to each other: Aristotle refers his reader to the *Rhetoric* for e.g. a discussion of διάνοια at *Po.* 1456a35, and to the *Poetics* at *Rhet.* 3.1404a39 (a recusal from discussing poetic style), 3.1404b7 (referring to the *Po.*'s discussion of poetic 'ornamentation', κόσμος) and 3.1405a6 (referring to the *Po.*'s discussion of metaphor).

Wounded Odysseus (1453b33–4) as an example of a tragedy in which the crucial deed happens within the play (at 1453b31 *Oedipus Tyrannus* is named as a play in which the action occurs 'outside the drama'); Carcinus II's *Thyestes* and Sophocles' *Tyro* are both cited for their employment of 'recognition by signs' (star-shaped birthmarks in *Thyestes* and a necklace in *Tyro*: 1454b23–5); and Theodectes' *Tydeus* is listed among other plays (Aeschylus' *Libation Bearers*, Euripides' *Iphigenia in Tauris* and an unknown *Sons of Phineus*) in which a recognition comes about 'as a result of inference' (ἐκ συλλογισμοῦ).[57] Only Theodectes' *Lynceus* is cited independently to exemplify a general concept, namely dramatic 'resolution'.[58] In the *Poetics* the citation of fourth-century tragedy almost always serves to support a point that can also be, and indeed is, made with a fifth-century example.

This tendency of Aristotle's to use examples from fifth- and fourth-century tragedy alongside each other serves an important and even programmatic purpose within the *Poetics*. The method serves to imply that the plays of Astydamas and Sophocles, Theodectes and Euripides, all participated in the same single genre of tragedy.[59] Even if that genre had evolved and seen a number of innovations since it first diverged from the dithyramb (cf. *Po.* ch. 4), its essential and optimal features – the kinds of features which are both described and prescribed in the *Poetics* – had and would remain constant. Towards the beginning of the work Aristotle explains that, after undergoing a number of transformations the development of tragedy 'came to a halt' when the form at last realised its true nature.[60] The unique *physis* of tragedy, the distinct essence of the genre, is what allows Aristotle to assign to the form its own definition. Tragedy, for Aristotle, is famously a

[57] Arist. *Po.* 1455a3–10.

[58] I.e. λύσις: Arist. *Po.* 1455b29–32, cf. Karamanou (2007).

[59] On Aristotle's notion of tragedy as universal genre see n. 6 above; Donini (1997) examines his view that poetry (as opposed to history) is about universals (Arist. *Po.* ch. 9, esp. at 1451b).

[60] Arist. *Po.* 1449a14–15: καὶ πολλὰς μεταβολὰς μεταβαλοῦσα ἡ τραγῳδία ἐπαύσατο, ἐπεὶ ἔσχε τὴν αὑτῆς φύσιν.

μίμησις πράξεως σπουδαίας καὶ τελείας μέγεθος ἐχούσης, ἡδυσμένῳ λόγῳ χωρὶς ἑκάστῳ τῶν εἰδῶν ἐν τοῖς μορίοις, δρώντων καὶ οὐ δ'ἀπαγγελίας, δι' ἐλέου καὶ φόβου περαίνουσα τὴν τῶν τοιούτων παθημάτων κάθαρσιν. (Arist. *Po.* 1449b24–8)

representation of a serious, complete action which has magnitude, in embellished speech, with each of its elements [used] separately in the [various] parts [of the play]; [represented] by people acting and not by narration; accomplishing by means of pity and terror the catharsis of such emotions. (Trans. Janko)

Despite the century or so that separated them, Carcinus' *Thyestes* and Astydamas' *Alcmeon* were just as much 'tragedies' in accordance with this definition as Aeschylus' *Libation Bearers* and Sophocles' *Oedipus* (sc. *Tyrannus*). In the *Poetics* Aristotle reinforces his essentialist view of tragedy as a genre that, once perfected, transcended space and time – and Sophocles and Euripides – each time that he sets examples from fifth- and fourth-century tragedy alongside each other when exemplifying his observations.

Sophocles and Euripides

Aristotle's account of tragedy attempts to define and to describe tragedy as a universal genre, yet even so the names and works of Sophocles and Euripides dominate the pages of the *Poetics*. Not only does Aristotle uphold Sophocles' *Oedipus Tyrannus* as the finest kind of tragedy, but near the outset of the *Poetics* he also implies that 'Sophocles' is sufficient as a synecdoche for all of tragic drama. After explaining the nature and varieties of mimesis in *Poetics* ch. 2, Aristotle goes on to chart the relationship between epic, tragedy and comedy as follows:

τῇ μὲν ὁ αὐτὸς ἂν εἴη μιμητὴς Ὁμήρῳ Σοφοκλῆς, μιμοῦνται γὰρ ἄμφω σπουδαίους, τῇ δὲ Ἀριστοφάνει, πράττοντας γὰρ μιμοῦνται καὶ δρῶντας ἄμφω. (Arist. *Po.*1448a25–8)

in one way Sophocles is the same kind of 'representer' as Homer, since they both represent dignified people, but in another respect [he is like] Aristophanes, in that they both represent people *doing* things.

In this passage Homer's name evokes epic, Aristophanes' name stands as a metonym for comedy and the name of Sophocles embodies tragedy. This implicit identification of Sophocles as the tragedian *par excellence* reprises a tradition whose origins may yet again be traced back at least to the end of the fifth century. At the close of the *Frogs*, 'Aeschylus' leaves Hades' Chair in Tragedy to Sophocles, who never comes under critical fire in the course of the play.[61] The recently deceased Sophocles is also praised in another comedy that premiered at the festival. In Phrynichus' comedy *Muses*, which placed second after the *Frogs* at the 405 Lenaea, it looks as if the Muses themselves judged an Underworld competition between (tragic?) poets. Only snippets of the play survive, but in the longest fragment (quoted in an argument to Sophocles' *Oedipus at Colonus*), a speaker declares that Sophocles, a fortunate and *dexios* (lucky; clever) man, is blessed because he 'composed many and fine tragedies' (πολλὰς ποιήσας καὶ καλὰς τραγῳδίας) and died peacefully.[62] Even in the fifth century, Sophoclean tragedy appears to have been largely beyond reproach.

In the fourth century, Plato's Socrates had also adduced Sophocles as the model of a competent tragedian. During a discussion in the *Phaedrus* about the nature of technical expertise, Socrates asks Phaedrus what would happen if someone were to go to Sophocles or Euripides and claim that he knew how

> περὶ σμικροῦ πράγματος ῥήσεις παμμήκεις ποιεῖν καὶ περὶ μεγάλου πάνυ σμικράς, ὅταν τε βούληται οἰκτράς, καὶ τοὐναντίον αὖ φοβερὰς καὶ ἀπειλητικὰς ὅσα τ' ἄλλα τοιαῦτα, καὶ διδάσκων αὐτὰ τραγῳδίας ποίησιν οἴεται παραδιδόναι; (Pl. *Phdr.* 268c–d)

> to make long speeches about small matters and very short speeches about big ones, and pitiable sayings when he wanted, and also conversely frightening and threatening ones, and he thought that by teaching these things he was imparting the art of composing tragedy.

Phaedrus responds that they would surely laugh at him, and Socrates goes on to conjecture that *Sophocles would say* (he

[61] Ar. *Ran.* 1518–19: τοῦτον γὰρ ἐγὼ σοφίᾳ κρίνω δεύτερον εἶναι.
[62] Phrynichus F 32, from Arg. II in Soph. *OC*.

does not repeat the name Euripides) that this man exhibited the first steps towards tragedy, but not the tragic art itself.[63] We have also already seen Aristotle's contemporary Demosthenes appear as a champion of Sophocles and his poetry in *On the False Embassy*, where he argues that Aeschines would have done better to reflect upon verses from *Antigone* than to quote lines that he had gathered up from a comparatively obscure Euripidean play. In these texts Sophocles repeatedly stands for the epitome of Athens' fifth-century tragic achievement.

Sophocles also clearly emerges as the preferred tragedian of Aristotle, who in the *Poetics* only ever criticises him on two minor counts. Haemon's failure to kill Creon despite his resolution to do so in *Antigone* represents the worst kind of action,[64] and *Electra* is somewhat marred by the 'improbability' of the Pedagogue's account of Orestes' death at the Pythian Games.[65] Elsewhere in Aristotle's works, however, *Antigone* is mentioned in an explicitly favourable light and other aspects of Sophoclean characterisation receive high praise. For example, in Book 7 of the *Nicomachean Ethics* Sophocles' Neoptolemus is called especially commendable (ἐπαινετός) because he abandons the schemes of Odysseus in favour of helping Philoctetes.[66]

Euripides endures far more criticism in the *Poetics,* though he takes the prize for being the tragedian to whom Aristotle most often refers.[67] Aristotle prefers that the tragic chorus 'be a part of the whole and be involved in the action not as in

[63] Pl. *Phdr*. 269a: ὁ Σοφοκλῆς τὸν σφίσιν ἐπιδεικνύμενον τὰ πρὸ τραγῳδίας ἂν φαίη ἀλλ' οὐ τὰ τραγικά. Cf. Xen. *Mem*. 1.4.2–3: when Aristodemus 'the Little' is asked which wise men he admires, he answers Homer for epic, Melanippides for dithyramb, Sophocles for tragedy, Polycleitus for sculpture and Zeuxis for painting.

[64] I.e. 'to be about to act with full knowledge but not to do it', τὸ . . . γινώσκοντα μελλῆσαι καὶ μὴ πρᾶξαι: Arist. *Po*. 1454b38.

[65] The Pythian Games did not exist in the heroic age depicted by tragedy, cf. *Po*. 1460a31–2.

[66] Arist. *EN* 7.1146a19; cf. 1151b18.

[67] On the Euripidean 'defects' criticised in the *Poetics* (and the long-lasting influence of the criticism) see Mastronarde (2010) 2; see further Zagdoun (2006), who sees conflict between Aristotelian theory and the reality of a single playwright's *oeuvre* as inevitable (774). Sullivan (1934) points out that Aristotle takes a more favourable view of Euripides in the *Rhetoric* than he does in the *Poetics*.

Euripides but as in Sophocles',[68] and is more impressed by Sophocles' portrayals of people 'as they should be' than by Euripides' habit of portraying people 'as they are'.[69] He also disapproves of the excess villainy of character on display in Euripidean plays such as *Orestes*, *Melanippe the Wise* and *Iphigenia in Aulis* (each contains an 'example of unnecessary wickedness of character')[70] and he criticises the device (μηχανή) by which Euripides provides for Medea's escape.[71] On the other hand, Euripides' *Iphigenia* (sc. *in Tauris*) is praised on many counts,[72] and Aristotle commends how his plays often end 'in misfortune' (εἰς δυστυχίαν).[73] On account of that tendency he declares that:

ὁ Εὐριπίδης, εἰ καὶ ἄλλα μὴ εὖ οἰκονομεῖ, ἀλλὰ τραγικώτατός γε τῶν ποιητῶν φαίνεται. (Arist. *Po.* 1453a29–30)

Euripides, though he does not manage [his plots][74] well in other respects, appears to be the most 'tragic' of the poets.

Elsewhere Aristotle voices a number of criticisms of Euripides' work, but this statement and the frequency with which Aristotle mentions him are both indicative of Euripides' foremost position within the Aristotelian framework for tragic drama. And despite the considerable differences that Aristotle sees between Sophocles and Euripides, this was the pair of playwrights who to his mind best illustrated and most embodied the genre. Aristotle surely expected his audience to be familiar

68 Arist. *Po.* 1456a26–7: καὶ μόριον εἶναι τοῦ ὅλου καὶ συναγωνίζεσθαι μὴ ὥσπερ Εὐριπίδῃ ἀλλ' ὥσπερ Σοφοκλεῖ; Mastronarde's (2010) discussion at 145–52 is especially useful.

69 See esp. Arist. *Po.* 1460b34 (the distinction is attributed to Sophocles) with 1448a15; 1454b8; 1461b11–13.

70 Arist. *Po.* 1454a28–9: παράδειγμα πονηρίας μὲν ἤθους μὴ ἀναγκαίας.

71 Arist. *Po.* 1454b1.

72 E.g. it showcases the best kind of action/incident (Arist. *Po.* 1455a18), the best type of recognition (1455a18) and is a strong example of a play with a 'universal' plot (1455b2). On Aristotle's use and account of the play see Belfiore (1992); for an attempt to make sense of why Euripides' *IT* and Sophocles' *OT*, Aristotle's two 'favourite' plays, have such different plot structures see White (1992).

73 Arist. *Po.* 1453a23–6.

74 Cf. Lucas (1968): 'οἰκονομεῖν is the regular word in the scholia for management of plot, etc.' (ad loc.).

with the works of these poets, and perhaps selected his concrete examples from their works for that very reason. Nevertheless, hindsight confirms that his selection only served to concretise a view of tragedy according to which Sophocles and Euripides were its most pre-eminent and quintessential representatives.

Classical versus contemporary

Euripides and Sophocles are the indisputable stars of the *Poetics*, but even as Aristotle lectured on poetry at the Lyceum the life of Athens' theatre and festivals remained vibrant around him. His allusions to contemporary tragedies stand as some of our most direct witnesses to the continued importance of new productions, and the *Poetics* provides some idea of how Aristotle understood tragic style and theatrical practice – if not the essence of tragedy – as having changed since the end of the fifth century. His own mental periodization of the genre appears to be organised roughly into three eras of tragedians:

1 'the first poets' (οἱ πρῶτοι ποιηταί, *Po.* 1450a37);
2 the 'old' poets (οἱ ἀρχαῖοι, 1450b7); and
3 the poets of the 'present day' (οἱ νῦν, 1450b8).[75]

In the table below I organise his observations about the habits of contemporary and earlier tragedians under the 'old' versus 'present-day' rubric of *Poetics* ch. 6. In broad strokes, this table suggests an image of the general differences that Aristotle perceived between tragic drama of his own time and that of the period which Sophocles had epitomised. Since Sophocles' generation tragedy had undergone no fundamental or essential changes in its nature, but on more minor points Aristotle evidently perceived a contrast:

[75] See Kitto (1966) 114–16, who synthesises Aristotle's criticisms of contemporary tragedy.

	THE OLD POETS (οἱ ἀρχαῖοι)	THE CONTEMPORARY POETS (οἱ *νῦν*)
Competence in a specific part of tragedy (*Po.* 1450a36–7)	Better at diction (λέξις) and character (ἦθος) than plot construction (τὰ πράγματα συνίστασθαι)	Implies that there has been improvement in plot construction
Nature of characters' speech (*Po.* 1450b7–8)	Characters speak 'civically' or 'politically' (πολιτικῶς)	Characters speak 'rhetorically' (ῥητορικῶς)
Source of tragic plots (*Po.* 1453a17–22)	Used 'whichever myths they fancied' (τοὺς τυχόντας μύθους ἀπηρίθμουν)	'Nowadays the finest tragedies are constructed around a few "Houses"' (*νῦν* δὲ περὶ ὀλίγας οἰκίας αἱ κάλλισται τραγῳδίαι συντίθενται); e.g. those of Alcmeon, Oedipus, Orestes, Meleager, Thyestes and Telephus
Role of the chorus (*Po.* 1456a25–32)	Part of the action (as in Sophocles, not as in Euripides)	Reduced to interludes, *embolima* (thanks to Euripides and Agathon)
Creative power (*Rhet.* 2.1403b21)	Playwrights more powerful than actors	Playwrights less powerful than actors

It is difficult to tell where Aristotle will have classed Euripides between the 'old' and the more 'modern' tragedians.[76] Tragedy had been perfected in the hands of Sophocles thanks largely to

[76] See Hunter (2009) 43 for how, centuries later, Dio Chrysostom would also contrast early and later phases of tragic composition. In the oration Dio also explicitly separates Euripides from the category of ἀρχαῖοι when he expresses the wish that no clever critic pass judgement on him for preferring Menander to Old Comedy and Euripides to the 'old tragedians': καὶ μηδεὶς τῶν σοφωτέρων αἰτιάσηταί με ὡς προκρίναντα τῆς ἀρχαίας κωμῳδίας τὴν Μενάνδρου ἢ τῶν ἀρχαίων τραγῳδων Εὐριπίδην (Dio 18.7).

his introduction of the third actor and set painting;[77] Sophocles should therefore probably be assigned to the last generation of the 'old' poets. But Euripides' innovations draw him closer (for better or worse) to the playwrights who were currently active. In the *Poetics* Aristotle identifies Euripides as responsible for beginning to diminish the role of the chorus, a decline which Agathon then supposedly advanced.[78] In the *Rhetoric*, however, Euripides is praised for being the first to compose eloquent poetry out of ordinary language.[79] For Aristotle, Euripides seems to stand at the threshold of the old and present generations of tragic poets: Sophocles was the final piece of the puzzle in developing the essence (*physis*) of tragic poetry and performance, and Euripides begins the line of poets whose heirs were active when Aristotle was setting down his ideas about drama.

The distinctions that Aristotle makes between the characteristics of current tragedies and the drama of the earlier era may reflect an increased attention paid by playwrights to their protagonists. Within his own schema he identifies character as second to plot among the components of tragedy,[80] but he also implies that individuals, rather than events, are the true core of tragic *mythoi*. For example, his list of the 'few Houses' (ὀλίγας οἰκίας) which usually supply the plots for the finest of new productions is in reality a list of individuals from mythology: Alcmeon, Oedipus, Orestes, Meleager, Thyestes and Telephus.[81] The titles attested for plays from this

[77] Arist. *Po.* 1449a18–19, cf. 1449a14–15.

[78] Arist. *Po.* 1456a30. The role of the fourth-century tragic chorus is not well understood. There is some evidence that choral lyric was increasingly being seen as 'optional'; e.g. a papyrus fragment of Astydamas' *Hector* (*P.Hib.* 2.174 = Astydamas F 1) reads simply ΧΟΡΟΥ ΜΕΛΟΣ ('choral song') in place of an ode: cf. on this case Taplin (2009a) 258 and more generally Revermann (2006) 281, Pöhlmann (1977) and Taplin (1976). Capps (1895) argued on the basis of theatre architecture that the chorus must have continued to engage directly with actors in the *orkhestra* throughout the fourth century.

[79] Arist. *Rhet.* 3.1404b24: ἐκ τῆς εἰωθυίας διαλέκτου.

[80] Arist. *Po.* 1450b38–9: ἀρχὴ μὲν οὖν καὶ οἷον ψυχὴ ὁ μῦθος τῆς τραγῳδίας, δεύτερον δὲ τὰ ἤθη.

[81] Arist. *Po.* 1453a17–22. Cf. the catalogues of tragic protagonists in two fragments of mid to late fourth-century comedies: Antiphanes' *Poetry* (F 189.5–12) and Timocles' *Women at the Dionysia* (F 6.9–16). Both lists share with Aristotle's

period (as preserved epigraphically and by the indirect tradition) also indicate that these tragedians almost always named their plays after the main character and not after the chorus, as was common in the fifth century (e.g. *Suppliants*, *Women of Trachis*, *Phoenecian Women* etc.). Aristotle's complaints about the diminished role of the chorus also belong to his account of the increased emphasis on main characters. Powerful actors hungry for the spotlight will have been inclined to revive plays with significant protagonist roles, and a large and active choral presence had the potential to divert audience attention from a single star of the stage.[82] Aristotle did not favour this shift in the power dynamics of performance and complains about the vanity of actors,[83] the excesses of their influence upon tragic production[84] and their habit of pandering to the audience.[85]

Some of Aristotle's remarks in the *Poetics* even reflect and illuminate the realities of contemporary performance. The *Poetics* supports documentary evidence that the format of tragic competitions at the Great Dionysia had changed since the days when Sophocles and Euripides were among its regular competitors. The near wholesale omission of satyr play from the discussion in the *Poetics* may reflect the elimination of that genre from the old four-play entry slate (i.e. a

the names of Alcmeon and Oedipus. Aristotle also mentions a number of plays that participate in his own catalogue: an *Alcmeon* by Astydamas and Theodectes (*Po*. 1453b33 and *Rhet*. 2.1397b3 respectively), an *Oedipus* by Carcinus II (*Rhet*. 3.1417b18.), an *Orestes* by Theodectes (*Rhet*. 2.1401a; Aphareus likely placed third with an *Orestes* in 341: cf. Millis and Olson (2012) 67.13), a *Meleager* by Antiphon (*Rhet*. 2.1379b13 and 2.1399b26) and a *Thyestes* by Carcinus II (*Po*. 1453b23). He omits mention of only a *Telephus*, but the *Suda* (κ 1730) attests one for the fourth-century tragedian Cleophon (the poet mentioned at *Po*. 1448a12, and perhaps at 1458a20).

[82] There is evidence that actors in revivals sometimes appropriated for themselves lines that had originally belonged to the chorus: see Falkner (2002) 353, on a scholion to Eur. *Med*. 520–1.

[83] Cf. Arist. *Pol*. 7.1336b 27–31: the actor Theodorus, whom we have already encountered (pages 68 and 145), would never let anyone appear on stage before him (Aristotle also mentions Theodorus at *Rhet*. 2.1404b22).

[84] Arist. *Rhet*. 2.1403b31: μεῖζον δύνανται νῦν τῶν ποιητῶν οἱ ὑποκριταί.

[85] Arist. *Pol*. 8.1341b8–18. The fourth-century audience was not forgiving: Aristotle claims that when acting is bad some members of the audience turn their attention to snacking (*EN* 10.1175b).

tragedian's *didascalia*).[86] In the fifth century, tragedians had competed with a 'three-plus-one' set of plays (three tragedies followed by a satyr play).[87] The nearly complete didascalic records which survive for 341–339 BC indicate that the dramatic portion of the festival now kicked off with a single satyr play (in 340 BC Timocles – who placed second in the tragic competition – offered a *Lycurgus*), which was then followed by a piece of *palaion drama*.[88] The *Poetics* would lead us to believe that Aristotle's tastes in tragedy were conservative, but even here evidence for the continued vitality (and evolution) of Athens' theatre industry occasionally breaks the surface.

Where is the polis in the *Poetics*?

If the *Poetics* reflects aspects of changes to Athenian theatrical practice since the fifth century (such as the increased influence of actors, the introduction of the *palaion drama* category and the severance of satyr play from the standard tragic *didascalia*), it also reveals certain shifts of focus with respect to earlier tragic criticism. As compared with the earlier discussions of tragedy in Aristophanes' *Frogs* and Plato's *Republic*, Aristotle's account of tragedy in the *Poetics* seems strikingly apolitical. Nowhere does he discuss the genre's relationship with Athens or with the old debates about the effects of tragic plays upon (Athenian) citizens. In *Poetics* ch. 25 Aristotle even explicitly states that 'correctness' is not the same thing in public life and in poetry,[89] and this claim is the first piece of evidence

[86] Aristotle remarks only in passing that tragedy developed out of satyric compositions, ἐκ σατυρικοῦ: *Po.* 1449b20.

[87] The formulation of Easterling (1997b) 40. Satyr plays do not seem to have ever been offered at the Lenaea, and Euripides' *Alcestis* marks at least one exception made in the fifth century to the standard *didascalia*: see Slater (2005) and Marshall (2000).

[88] *IG* ii^2 2320, on which see esp. Millis and Olson (2012) 61–9. The actor Neoptolemus won with Euripides' *Iphigenia* [*in Tauris*?] in 341, with *Orestes* in 340 and with an unknown play of Euripides in 339. That only two tragedians' entries (as opposed to three) are recorded for these years does not necessarily mark a dramatic change to the festival programme, which as Millis and Olson (2012) observe was relatively flexible (2).

[89] Arist. *Po.* 1460b13–4: οὐχ ἡ αὐτὴ ὀρθότης ἐστὶν τῆς πολιτικῆς καὶ τῆς ποιητικῆς. Lucas (1968) ad loc.: 'πολιτική includes both public and private morality. The

that Hall marshals in drawing the conclusion that 'There is indeed no *polis*, concrete or abstract, to be identified in Aristotle's *Poetics*.'[90] In constructing this argument, Hall emphasises three striking silences in the *Poetics*. Aristotle issues no comment upon:

> the political nature of the context of tragic performances at the City Dionysia; the patently Athenian content and latent Athenocentric import of many of the plays; and the civic-didactic function of tragedy, whose consumer in other Athenian authors is especially a *citizen*, and specifically a citizen of the Athenian democracy.[91]

Hall further contends that Aristotle's account of tragedy suppresses the Athenocentrism of the many (fifth-century) tragedies that had some connection to Athens (whether they were set there, featured an Athenian character or resulted in an Athenian aetiology). Aristotle's narrative overlooks the 'particularly patriotic function of tragedy' that is implied by the Aeschylus of the *Frogs* as well as by Lycurgus himself, who in *Against Leocrates* saw a primary virtue of Euripidean tragedy as its power to inspire Athenian citizens to do great deeds on behalf of their country.[92] For Hall, Aristotle's agenda in composing the *Poetics* 'seems to have involved the complete erasure from tragedy of even the abstract idea of the *polis* as an institution – whether Athenian, democratic, or otherwise'.[93] Yet we have already noted on many occasions that Attic tragedy had become immensely popular throughout Greece by the eras of

independence of poetic ὀρθότης suggests the existence of a set of purely aesthetic values, but they are recognized, if at all, only by implication'. In Arist. *EN* 6.9, εὐβουλία (the ability to take good counsel) is described as a form of 'correctness' (δῆλον ὅτι ὀρθότης τις ἡ εὐβουλία ἐστίν, 1142b8–9), and the idea in the *Poetics* seems to be that one does not hold poetry to the same moral standards that one holds to decision making and behaviour in the real world. The sophist Prodicus had been renowned for teaching ὀρθότης ἐπῶν, or the precise use of words (and discernment between synonyms); on Ar. *Ran.* 1181 in this intellectual context see esp. Dover (1993a) 29–32. On Plato's *Ion* as foreshadowing the argument in this passage of Aristotle see Hunter (2011) 28–40. Hall (1996) writes of the *Poetics* passage: 'Thus, finally, albeit in the context of epic rather than tragedy, Aristotle explicitly cuts the umbilical cord which has tied poetry so firmly to the city-state in all previous literary criticism' (302).

90 Hall (1996) 306. See Heath (2009) 460–70 on the passage, with a critique of Hall (1996) at 470.

91 Hall (1996) 296. 92 Hall (1996) 299. 93 Hall (1996) 301.

Aristotle and Lycurgus.[94] If Athenian drama was a truly Panhellenic phenomenon, its enjoyment even a marker of 'Hellenic' identity, what need was there actively to 'erase' Athens from an equation from which it was already by many accounts absent?

In arguing for Aristotle's suppression of the polis-related dimensions of tragedy, Hall points out that Aristotle does address the 'civic performance context' of tragedy in other works of his.[95] This however is only partially true. Aristotle does discuss the Athenian Great Dionysia in the *Constitution of the Athenians*, where we hear a good deal about the festival and its management with respect to, for example, the theoric and stratiotic funds (43.1 and 47.2) as well as the role of the archon in assigning *choregoi* to tragic poets and overseeing the pre-festival procession at (56.2–3).[96] Nevertheless, no comment of his explicitly connects tragedies or tragic performance with a specifically Athenian civic context. Nor does he give any indication that the Athenian Great Dionysia differed in any meaningful way from the 'Rural' Dionysia of the Attic demes, or even from those celebrated elsewhere in Greece (he explicitly mentions Dionysia held in Piraeus and Salamis,[97] as well as farther afield: in Lesbian Antissa, Caria, Elis and on Delos).[98] If it is the case, then, that there is no polis in the *Poetics* we must also grant that there is no poetry in the *Politeia*.

Hall's influential discussion has provoked a number of responses, each of which grants that Aristotle's interest in tragedy was not at all a 'political' or polis-oriented one. Page DuBois, who emphasises Aristotle's Macedonian origins, maintains that his 'attitudes toward Athenian tragedy . . . must be located within a belated and antidemocratic situation'.[99]

94 Pages 69–174 esp. 95 Hall (1996) 298.

96 On these passages see Rhodes (1993) ad loc.

97 *Ath. Pol.* 54.8; on the Dionysia festivals celebrated in the demes see esp. Whitehead (1986) 212–22 and Wilson (2010) 279–302.

98 Arist. *Oec.* 1347a 26 and 1351b37; *Mir.* 842a26; and *Ath. Pol.* 56.3 respectively. Aristotle tells of how the Antissans raised money for the festival which they had come to celebrate extravagantly (λαμπρῶς). At his *NE* 1123a24 we hear that in Megara comic *choregoi* bring their chorus members onstage in purple.

99 DuBois (2004) 67.

Aristotle's failure to grasp the religious and ritual aspects of fifth-century tragedy will have resulted primarily from this 'belatedness': he was already 'remote from the richest and most productive moment of Greek tragic production'.[100] Jennifer Wise, too, explains the absence of a 'civic aspect' from Aristotle's account of tragedy by his temporal distance from the fifth-century productions, and regards his theories as heavily conditioned by contemporary (re)performance practices. For Wise, the tragedies that had once 'bristl[ed] with political significance' were now being staged 'in decontextualised, heavily excerpted form'. As a result, Aristotle is likely

> to have mistaken these works for what they had indeed become for the actors who remounted them: an Everyman's Library of 'greatest tragic hits', a storehouse of politically neutral scenes and monologues to select from in pursuit of an acting award.[101]

And yet, and as Malcolm Heath has argued, we should have had no *a priori* expectation of finding a polis in the *Poetics*. Aristotle was interested primarily in describing the universal properties of tragic poetry, and not in historicising its development in a political or ethnographic way. He was well aware that tragedy was not 'an exclusively Athenian phenomenon', as we know from his reference to Peloponnesian claims on tragic drama's invention.[102] It was nevertheless Athens that gave rise to the single tragic tradition that, as Oliver Taplin has detailed, enjoyed early and wide diffusion in Greece.[103] In the fifth century Athenian tragedians were called to the courts of foreign monarchs (Aeschylus to Hieron's court in Sicily and Euripides to Archelaus' court in Macedon), and Plato's Laches could observe that Athens was the city in which aspiring poets always

[100] DuBois (2004) 65.

[101] Wise (2008) 400. For a response to this aspect of Wise's discussion see Hanink (2011) 321–4, which outlines aspects of the arguments presented here; see then Wise's (2013) rebuttal.

[102] Arist. *Po.* 1448a34–5.

[103] Taplin (1999). Hall (2007) 272–3 discusses the widespread diffusion of Athenian tragedy by 380 BC. For an illuminating case study in its dissemination (through text as well as image) see Giuliani (2001).

dreamt of one day competing.[104] The Athenian plays and playwrights were the best known throughout Greece, and therefore provided the handiest repertory from which Aristotle could draw his examples, examples whose primary function was to illustrate universal theories and observations.

Given the international character that Athenian tragedy had attained, the fact that Aristotle fails to discuss its Athenian 'particulars' comes to look less surprising – and is even arguably to be expected. What for us looks like a suspicious oversight in the *Poetics* is in reality a symptom of Attic tragedy's success abroad, success that had been set in motion when Aeschylus first landed in Sicily and perhaps even earlier.[105] And it is precisely tragedy's popularity outside of Athens, a circumstance that is reflected in – but was neither created nor anticipated by – the *Poetics*, which provided much of the impetus for the Athenian theatre initiatives. That Aristotle could even think of producing an account of tragedy that entirely disregarded its relationship with the city that reared Sophocles and Euripides – the *only* city that could have done so – must have been deeply troubling to Lycurgus and his like-minded fellow citizens.

In the 330s, Lycurgus' challenge was one of somehow counteracting any notion that the form brought to its peak in Athens was either a 'Greek' accomplishment or a universal idea. He and Athenians like him therefore set out to construct a theatre programme that did nothing if not assert the city's sole claims to classical tragedy's origins and inheritance. That programme was only made more pressing by tragedy's fame amongst the Macedonians, the greatest enemy of Athens and a people whose passion for (and competition with) the Athenian theatre we have encountered here at nearly every turn. Ironically, then, Athens' very absence from Aristotle's *Poetics* provides unparalleled insight into the rationale behind the

[104] Pl. *La.* 183a7–b2. Hall (1996) 304 cites the passage as evidence for Athens' 'virtually complete monopoly over the generation of tragedy', but Heath reminds us that 'this passage surely presupposes that there *are* opportunities to produce tragedy in other cities' (2009) 472.

[105] Kowalzig (2008) 142 describes Aeschylus' arrival in Sicily as 'Athenian tragedy's disembarkation on the island'.

programme which set out to ensure that Athens and tragedy be forever linked. The establishment of 'official' texts of tragedy, the deposition of those texts in the state archive, the 'monumentalisation' of the Theatre of Dionysus, the display of the inscribed *Fasti* and the commissioning of portrait statues of the three great tragedians all belonged to that effort.

Both aspects of Aristotle's twofold interest in tragedy – an interest that is historical and even antiquarian in nature, but also invested in the 'universals' of the genre – should therefore be contextualised in the practical realities of the theatre and the discourses of theatrical heritage. His many references to contemporary tragedy, especially in the *Rhetoric*, attest to the vitality of the 'new' theatre industry in Athens as well as to the renown of present-day poets. And yet the *Poetics*, with its 'praise of classical tragedy on every page',[106] highlighted and perhaps even helped to consolidate the primacy of Sophocles and Euripides. Aristotle's own work specifically on the history of Athenian tragedy in its Athenian context is evidenced by his compilation of *Victories at the Dionysia* and *Didascaliae*. We can now readily understand these titles against the backdrop of other efforts that were being made in this part of the century to take stock of Athens' cultural heritage. Nevertheless, the arresting absence in the *Poetics* of the Athenian polis should be seen as good evidence of the success with which other Greek poleis and communities had developed their own relationships with the Attic theatre. Despite that theatre's perceived acme in fifth-century Athens, it was now indeed 'universal', at least in its proven appeal throughout Greece. The challenge that Lycurgus faced was immense, and the fact that today we still, despite the immeasurable influence of the *Poetics,* speak primarily of 'Athenian' and 'Attic' tragedy speaks loudly to the success of his initiatives.

[106] Webster (1954) 307.

EPILOGUE: CLASSICAL TRAGEDY IN THE AGE OF MACEDON

On the 28th of the Macedonian month of Daesius (traditionally reckoned as 11 June) in 323 BC, Alexander the Great died in Babylon after succumbing to a violent and mysterious fever.[1] He left no heir apparent, and Athens saw in this turn of events an opportunity to recover the city's freedom from Macedon and to re-establish primacy in Greece. Led into battle by the general Leosthenes, the Athenians along with the Aetolians and other allies went to war against Antipater, the Macedonian whom Alexander had named General of Europe (στρατηγὸς τῆς Εὐρώπης).[2] Just a year or so later the Lamian or 'Hellenic' War ended when, following a decisive Macedonian victory at the Battle of Crannon in Thessaly (on 5 September 322), Athens sent an embassy that included Phocion and Demades to Antipater to sue for peace.[3] Antipater was said to have acted 'humanely' (φιλανθρώπως) towards the Athenians in allowing them to keep their city and possessions, though his terms demanded an end to the Athenian democracy and the establishment of oligarchic rule. Under the new regime, only citizens who possessed more than 2,000 drachmas enjoyed full franchise.[4] After three decades of manoeuvring the Macedonians had at last conquered Athens; 322 BC accordingly marks the conventional beginning of the Hellenistic period in the city.

By this point Lycurgus had already died of natural causes, in 325/4.[5] In the wake of the Athenian defeat at Crannon,

[1] The principal Greek sources are Plut. *Alex.* 75–6 and Arr. *Ana.* 7.25–8; on the day of Alexander's death see Depuydt (1997).

[2] Diod. Sic. 18.12.1. The other allies are listed at Diod. Sic. 18.11.

[3] Diod. Sic. 18.18.1–3. On the Lamian War see esp. Schmitt (1992).

[4] Diod. Sic. 18.18.4.

[5] He did not live to see the 'Harpalus affair' of 324. The *Suda* s.v. Λυκοῦγος (λ 825) details that he died of disease; Pausanias (1.29.15–16) records that his tomb lay along the road that led from Athens to the Academy.

Demades successfully moved that a death sentence be passed upon Demosthenes *in absentia*. After being apprehended by an associate of Antipater's, Demosthenes committed suicide in 322 at the temple of Poseidon in Calauria.[6] Aristotle died the same year of natural causes at Chalcis in Euboea, where he had fled fearing for his life after news of Alexander's death reached Athens in 323.[7] With the exception of Aeschines (who had left Athens in 330, following his defeat by Demosthenes in the case 'On the Crown') all of this story's main characters – Lycurgus and Demosthenes, Alexander and Aristotle – died before they could witness Antipater's installation of oligarchy in Athens.

With hindsight it appears that the Athenian defeat in the Lamian War also marked a new era for the city's theatre. In 322/1 BC, at either the first Lenaea or Great Dionysia after the war, Menander – aged only about twenty – first entered the comic competitions.[8] Menander would not win his first victory until about 316/5, supposedly with his celebrated *Dyscolus*.[9] By that time Athens was already operating under another new regime. After a brief interlude of restored democracy, in 317 Cassander (the son of Antipater) defeated Polyperchon, the successor whom his father had named instead of himself, and appointed Demetrius of Phaleron *epimeletēs* or 'caretaker' of the city.[10] Demetrius' administration of Athens lasted for ten years, until Demetrius Poliorcetes 'liberated' the city in 307.[11] Scant epigraphic evidence survives for Athens' dramatic festivals during the decade of Demetrius of Phaleron's rule (the *Decennium*): we have the fragmentary didascalic inscription *IG*

[6] On the death of Demosthenes see Plut. *Dem.* 29 – a highly 'theatrical' account which tells of a dream that Demosthenes had on the eve of his death in which he was acting (and lost) in a tragic competition. Cf. Philochorus *FGrH* F 164 ap. [Plut.] *Vit. dec. or*. 846e–847b.

[7] On the sources for Aristotle's 'flight from Athens' in 323 and death in 322 see Chroust (1973) 145–54.

[8] Men. T 3 and 49. Menander was born in 342/1 (*IG* xiv 1184 = T 2). There is chronological confusion in the ancient sources for Menander's dates: for a reasoned attempt at disentangling these see de Marcellus (1996).

[9] Men. T 50 (*Arg. Dysc.*); the *Parian Chronicle* (*FGrH* 239 B140 = Men. T 48) gives the year of his first victory 'in Athens' as 316/5.

[10] For an accessible account of the period 322–307 in Athens see Williams (1983).

[11] On the ancient testimonia for Demetrius' *Decennium* see SOD T 17–20; the most comprehensive modern account is O'Sullivan (2009a).

2323A, which preserves outcomes of the comic contests at the Great Dionysia for 313/2 and 312/1.[12] The only oddity in this document is the notice that Ameinias, who placed third with his *Woman Who Ran Away* (*Apoleipousa*), was awarded a chorus though only an ephebe.[13] The literary accounts, by contrast, attest to notable peculiarities surrounding at least one of the festivals that was celebrated in Demetrius of Phaleron's Athens.

In 309/8 Demetrius himself held the archonship and so was responsible for organising both the Great Dionysia and the Panathenaea.[14] According to the historian Duris of Samos (as cited by Athenaeus), during the procession of Demetrius' Great Dionysia a chorus sang lines by Seron of Soli that had been composed in his honour and which compared his glory to that of the sun.[15] Demochares, a contemporary of Demetrius, was also scandalised by other personal touches that Demetrius put on the festival.[16] Demetrius reportedly felt no shame (οὐκ αἰσχύνεσθαι) that

> κοχλίας αὐτομάτως βαδίζων προηγεῖτο τῆς πομπῆς αὐτῷ, σίαλον ἀναπτύων, σὺν δὲ τούτοις ὄνοι διεπέμποντο διὰ τοῦ θεάτρου ... (Polyb. 12.13.11 = Demochares *FGrH* 75 F 4)

a [mechanical] snail which walked on its own led his procession, excreting slime, and in addition to this donkeys were sent through the theatre.[17]

[12] See Millis and Olson (2012) 70–5 and O'Sullivan (2009a) 117 and 171. The *Parian Chronicle* also records that in the archonship of Theophrastus (313/2) the tragedian Sosiphanes competed (*FGrH* 239 B15 = DID D I B15).

[13] *IG* ii² 2323A.12–13 Millis–Olson (and see their note ad loc.); Ameinias T 2. Menander is also remembered for having entered the comic competitions while an ephebe: see de Marcellus (1996).

[14] O'Sullivan (2009a) 273 raises the possibilities that Demetrius had wanted to be archon in this year because there was a Panathenaea, and that Cassander himself may have visited Athens for one or both of these festivals. For the testimonia to Demetrius' archonship see SOD T 23a–e.

[15] Duris of Samos *FGrH* 76 F 10 ap. Ath. 12.542e, a discussion of Demetrius' personal extravagances. See O'Sullivan (2009a) 213; see also her p. 300 on the comparison that this account invites with that of the ithyphallic hymn sung for Demetrius Poliorcetes cf. 291/0 (in Duris *FGrH* 76 F 13).

[16] On Demetrius' organisation of the Great Dionysia see O'Sullivan (2009a) 182, 193 n. 83, 220, 273.

[17] On this passage see Walbank (1967) ad loc., who notes that 'Such processions as this are a great feature of the Hellenistic courts' (359).

If the story of the mechanical snail is true, one can only imagine the horror with which Lycurgus, Demosthenes and Aeschines alike would have responded at seeing such a grotesque animatronic display at the Great Dionysia. The snail may even have left its trail of slime in a path that passed by the eastern *parodos* of the Theatre of Dionysus, before the statues of the great tragedians.

An account of the management and organisation of the Great Dionysia during Demetrius' *Decennium* nevertheless remains difficult, given the scarcity of material and its apparent inconsistencies. For although Polybius-Demochares' account points to a lavishness of expenditure on the festival in 309/8, other evidence suggests that Demetrius frowned upon the excessive displays of wealth that had traditionally characterised the Athenian *choregia*. Plutarch, in his *de gloria Atheniensium*, cites a Demetrius (likely of Phaleron) as having called the dedicatory tripod of a victorious *choregos* not a dedication marking victory (οὐκ ἀνάθημα τῆς νίκης) but rather a 'last libation of squandered livelihoods and a cenotaph of forsaken estates'.[18] This pronouncement has been read as coherent with other sumptuary legislation enacted by Demetrius, which included the curbing of extravagant funerary monuments.[19] And yet elsewhere within the Plutarchan corpus (in the *Precepts of Statecraft*) we hear that spectacles designed to please the people were among the 'public acts' (πολιτεύματα) of Pericles and Demetrius alike.[20] Perhaps then Demetrius' policies favoured a 'centralisation' of expenditure, and a turn away from competition between wealthy individual Athenians for choregic prestige.[21]

The decades that followed the Lycurgan Era in Athens saw continued changes to the dramatic landscape of the city, many

[18] Plut. *Mor.* 349e: ἐπίσπεισμα τῶν ἐκκεχυμένων βίων καὶ τῶν ἐκλελοιπότων κενοτάφιον οἴκων.

[19] O'Sullivan (2009a) 177–8; Wilson (2000) 272.

[20] Plut. *Mor.* 818c–d. See O'Sullivan (2009a) 172–3, who uses the passage to argue against the view that Demetrius' reforms were in line with Aristotle's criticism of the wasteful extravagance of festival liturgies (at e.g. Arist. *Pol.* 6.1321a).

[21] On Demetrius' reforms in the context of the theatre industry see Csapo and Wilson (2010) 84.

of which marked further progressions of the changes that were taking place in the third quarter of the fourth century. Here I shall sketch some of those developments (i.e. the elimination of the *choregia* in Athens, the appearance of the *technitai* of Dionysus, the rise of 'New Comedy' and the advent of Alexandria as the centre of Greek learning) which occurred between the death of Alexander and the height of the Alexandrian library. In each of these areas we can detect changes whose clearest beginnings lie in Lycurgan Athens. Those years had seen the development of rhetoric that aimed to bind classical tragedy to Athens but also the foundation, in 331, of the city of Alexandria – the future home of the Lycurgan texts. Over the next half century, Athens' theatrical heritage would become still more central to the workings of the contemporary industry, as the city became ever more identified with the achievements of its playwrights and its gift of theatre to Greece. What follows is only a survey; a detailed study of drama in these years remains to be desired not least because of the radical relocation of the centre for the texts' preservation from Athens to Alexandria.

The Athenian institution of the *agonothesia*

One of the most important, and yet most difficult, problems in the theatre history of early Hellenistic Athens is the reform of the *choregia*, or rather its replacement by the new institution of the *agonothesia*. For centuries wealthy Athenian liturgists had spent vast sums of money in the hopes of earning the prestige that attended victory in a contest at the Dionysia. After the change, however, a single elected *agonothetēs* was responsible for co-ordinating choruses on behalf of the state. This individual may also have discharged some of the duties (such as the preparation of the Dionysia's *proagon*, at which the titles of the upcoming plays were announced) that had once belonged to the brief of the archon.[22] Modern scholarship long attributed this reform to Demetrius of Phaleron on the basis of a body

[22] Wilson (2000) 272.

of relatively thin evidence.[23] In addition to the testimonium for Demetrius' likening of choregic tripods to cenotaphs of squandered estates, that evidence includes a handful of inscriptions from the years immediately before and after his rule. The last case of a truly choregic inscription relating to the Great Dionysia dates to about 320/19 (and to 317/6 in the demes), the year that saw the final completion of the 'Lycurgan' Theatre of Dionysus, whereas the first agonothetic inscription does not appear until just after Demetrius' *Decennium*, in 307/6.[24]

In recent years significant challenges have been raised to the narrative that attributed this reorganisation to Demetrius' regime. In the light of a previously overlooked inscription that honours a non-Athenian named Nicostratus for his ambition and services regarding the Dionysia,[25] Peter Wilson and Eric Csapo have argued that the transition from *choregia* to *agonothesia* may have begun prior to 318, when it happens that a non-Athenian named Nicostrastus also served as a special *epimeletēs* of the festival. Nicostratus' tenure may have been a sort of 'trial run' of the new position, which would eventually be held by the *agonothetēs*.[26] Lara O'Sullivan has now also suggested the possibility that the *agonothesia* was created after the Antigonids 'liberated' Athens in 307/6. She argues that its introduction will have been 'compatible with the ideals of the Athenian democrats of 307/6 because it is consistent with the earlier policies of Lycurgus',[27] who had undertaken the restructuring of festivals on many fronts. Though the details of these

[23] Wilson and Csapo (2009) 49; for a summary account of the standard narrative of the reform and the principal bibliography see pp. 47–9. For a reading of the reform against Demetrius of Phaleron's other policies see esp. Mikalson (1998) 55–8.

[24] See Wilson and Csapo (2009) 48 and Csapo and Wilson (2010) 86–90; the last clear cases of choregic inscriptions relating to the Great Dionysia are *IG* ii² 3055 and 3056; the last deme inscription is from Aixone (*IG* ii² 1200), though Wilson and Csapo here point out that *SEG* XXXVI 186, also from Aixone, likely dates to 313/12. Summa (2003) collects the epigraphic documents for the transition to the *agonothesia*. For a timeline of the evidence for the reform see Csapo and Wilson (2010) 103.

[25] *IG* ii³ 473 (= Lambert 10). The fullest critical edition is found at Wilson and Csapo (2009) 52–3.

[26] Wilson and Csapo (2009); Csapo and Wilson (2010) 90–8.

[27] O'Sullivan (2009a) 173. For the argument for an Antigonid reform see 173–6.

accounts differ, both allow that choregic reform began pre-318 and was fully realised in about 307/6, only after a gradual process of transition. Surely such a radical change could not have been implemented overnight: as Wilson and Csapo remind us, the replacement of the *choregia* with the *agonothesia* 'involved the substantial transformation of a major cultural and socio-political institution that had operated effectively in more or less the same form for some two hundred years'.[28]

Of particular interest to the problem is *IG* ii² 3073 (from 307/6), the earliest epigraphic evidence for the institution of the *agonothesia*. The inscription appears on the monument dedicated by the *agonothetēs*, who until recently was thought to be Xenocles of Sphettos. Xenocles was one of Athens' richest and most prominent citizens, a close associate of Lycurgus and the man who succeeded him upon his death as administrator of the city's treasury.[29] Stephen Lambert has now argued that the first line of the dedicatory inscription should instead be supplemented with the name of Xenocles' brother, Androcles.[30] Whichever of the brothers served, the monument that he dedicated afterwards was an elegant and grand memorial to his office: the structure stood over four metres high and served as a stately gateway into the Sanctuary of Dionysus.[31]

This *agonothetēs* was responsible for overseeing all of the contests at the year's festival (unlike the *choregoi* of the past who worked with single playwrights), and the inscription provides a record of victories for the entire dramatic section of the programme:[32]

[28] Wilson and Csapo (2009) 68.

[29] On the many dedicatory displays of wealth made by Xenocles and Lycurgus see Mikalson (1998) 34–6, Habicht (1988), Ampolo (1979) and Davies (1971) no. 11234.

[30] Lambert (2003b).

[31] For a description see Korres (1983); see also Lambert (2003b) 99 and Wilson (2000) 273. Goette (2007b) 141 writes of the monument: 'To my knowledge, this is the first example of an architectural form whose later examples are known as "triumphal arches" or "honorary gates"'; for a reconstruction see his fig. 13.

[32] Whether the festival was the Lenaea or the Great Dionysia remains unclear; see Wilson (2000) 381 n. 38 for the controversy. The Dionysia does seem more probable, given the particular status of the festival in this period and the fact that the lavish choregic monuments of the previous decades (those of Lysicrates, from 335/4 and Nicias and Thrasyllus, from 320/19) all mark victories at the Great Dionysia.

ὁ δῆμος ἐ[χορήγει ἐπ' Ἀναξι]κράτους ἄρχοντος.
ἀγωνοθέ[της Ξενοκλῆς Ξ]είνιδος Σφήττιος.
ποιητὴς τραγωιδοῖς ἐνίκα [Φανόστρατο]ς Ἡρακλείδου Ἁλικαρνασσεύς.
ὑποκριτὴς τραγωιδοῖς ἐνίκ[α Ἱερομνήμ]ων Εὐανορίδου Κυδαθηναιεύς.
ποιητὴς κωμωι[δ]οῖς ἐνί[κα Φιλήμω]ν Δάμωνος Διομειεύς.
ὑποκριτὴς κ[ωμωδοῖς ἐνίκα Κάλλιπ]πος Καλλίου Σουνιεύς. (*IG* ii² 3073)

The demos was the *choregos* during the archonship of Anaxikrates.
The *agonothetēs* was Androcles son of Xeinis, from Sphettos.
The poet who won for tragedy was Phanostratus son of Heracleides, from Halicarnassus.
The actor who won for tragedy was Hieromnemon son of Euanorides, from Kydathenaion.
The poet who won for comedy was Philemon son of Damon, from Diomeia.
The actor who won for comedy was Kallippos son of Kallias, from Sounion.

Although this monument stood most impressively as a testament to the involvement and investment of the *agonothetēs* in the competitions (and to his expenditure on the monument itself), the phrase 'the demos was the *choregos*' is of enormous consequence for how we understand the relationship between the city of Athens and its theatre during this period. Throughout I have argued that the Lycurgan Era in Athens was marked by attempts – many of them spearheaded by Lycurgus himself – to reclaim Athenian tragedy for Athens and to entwine the city's theatrical heritage with broader narratives of Athenian history. Those aims were accomplished in part by the presentation of the tragedians' accomplishments as a collective achievement of the demos. Xenocles' (or Androcles') monument belongs to the first year of yet another restored democracy in Athens, whose champions used the figure of Lycurgus 'as something of a figurehead and rallying point'.[33] It is also to 307/6 that the Decree of Stratocles, the highly encomiastic decree that granted posthumous honours to Lycurgus, dates. Xenocles – Lycurgus' successor in the administration of state finances – had himself been closely allied with Lycurgus in terms of both politics and cultural ideology.[34] What clearer

33 O'Sullivan (2009a) 174, cf. 175.
34 Work remains to be done on Androcles' own career and political leanings; for a sketch see Lambert (2003b) 100 and 104–5, who draws attention to the need for a careful rereading of Dem. 35, a speech written for him.

way, then, for the city to assert ownership of the theatre (and of its classical heritage) than to make the entire demos of Athens the festival's collective *choregos*?

The phrase 'the demos was the *choregos*' (ὁ δῆμος ἐχορήγει) continues to appear in agonothetic inscriptions until the second century.[35] Robert Parker has argued that 'the ideal expressed in the phrase was little more than pseudo-populist rhetoric',[36] largely because the *agonothetēs* will have topped up the festival's budget with money from his own funds.[37] The formulation comes to look even more superficial when we consider the possibility that members of the Macedonian ruling elite may on some occasions have served as *agonothetai*: Plutarch reports that Phocion persuaded Nicanor, a general of Cassander, to show great generosity to Athens in the capacity of *agonothetēs*.[38] On its own terms, though, the rhetoric of the claim that 'the demos was the *choregos*' raises significant questions regarding the image that the city wanted to present of its relationship with the theatre. The attribution of festival sponsorship to the whole of the demos marks an extreme but logical extension of the Lycurgan-Era discourses that had emphasised the city's sole rights to its dramatic industry and heritage. Those discourses, we have seen, worked to link the name of the state as closely as possible with the traditions of its theatre. Read in retrospect, some of Lycurgus' own words in *Against Leocrates* even seem to foreshadow this movement towards state sponsorship and organisation of dramatic festivals. Near the end of the speech Lycurgus claims that he 'particularly resents' (μάλιστ' ἀγανακτῶ) when defendants present to the jurors catalogues of

[35] Cf. e.g. *IG* ii² 3074, 3076, 3079, 3081, 3083, 3088 (the last secure attestation, from about 175/4).

[36] Parker 1996: 268. Wilson (2000) 273 observes that, because 'the lustre of agonistic victory cannot belong to the demos and as such', the *agonothetēs* was 'the real inheritor of the classical *khoregos*' prestige'. See also Wilson and Csapo (2009) 70–1 for the possibility that the rhetoric 'may well express the new democracy's desire to usurp the role of *khoregoi*, already diminished and compromised by an oligarchic ἐπιμέλεια τῶν ἀγώνων'.

[37] Cf. the honorific decree from 283/2 for the comic poet Philippides (discussed further below), who had served as *agonothetēs* in the previous year: Philippides is praised for giving of his own funds (ἐκ τῶν ἰδίων, *IG* ii² 657.40).

[38] Plut. *Phoc.* 21.3; see Wilson and Csapo (2009) 68.

the liturgies which they have performed for Athens.[39] According to Lycurgus, these kinds of liturgies – including brilliant choregic productions – are not undertaken in the interest of the city or the people. Instead the liturgist alone enjoys his crown, and his success benefits no one but himself.[40]

Although other motivations may have been involved, in the light of the arguments that I have presented here it is tempting to read the institution of the *agonothesia* as Athens' last great attempt in the fourth century to maintain its status as Greece's uncontested capital of theatre. A generation earlier, the citizens of Lycurgus' era had voted to deposit the scripts of the three great tragedians in the city's archive; they had also resolved that any actor intending to perform one of these plays must check his own copy against the official exemplar, which was to be read out by a city secretary. According to Pseudo-Plutarch's account, this law further stipulated 'that it was not allowed for these plays to be performed out of accordance with the official texts'.[41] The law marked a great ideological statement, but like the claim that 'the demos was the *choregos*' in the agonothetic inscriptions that statement must have been primarily a rhetorical one. Attic tragedy was out of Athenian hands, especially as dramatic festivals were cropping up throughout Greece (and beyond) in the last decades of the fourth century. While on campaign Alexander the Great had put on a number of theatrical performances and competitions (and surely did so without any thought for the Lycurgan law);[42] in his *Life of Alexander* Plutarch even claims that Alexander summoned an unbelievable 3,000 'theatre professionals' (τεχνῖται; see below) to participate in the festivals that he held in Ecbatana during the period when Hephaestion grew fatally ill.[43] In a series of

[39] Lycurg. 1.39. For an especially blatant example of the strategy that Lycurgus dislikes see Lys. 21.1–6.

[40] Lycurg. 1.139: ἐπὶ τούτοις γὰρ αὐτὸς μόνος στεφανοῦνται, τοὺς ἄλλους οὐδὲν ὠφελῶν. Nevertheless, as Wilson (2000) 269 observes 'There is no sign that, at the level of civic policy, Lykourgos acted upon this argument by curtailing the actions of the *khoregoi*.'

[41] [Plut.] *Vit. dec. or.* 841f.

[42] On these see esp. Csapo (2010) 172–8 and Le Guen (forthcoming).

[43] Plut. *Alex.* 72.1.

studies on the Hellenistic theatre, Brigitte Le Guen has also collected a large dossier of evidence for the dramatic festivals that came into existence in Greece during the Hellenistic period.[44] The Great Dionysia in Athens remained an integral part of the city's fabric in the late fourth and early third centuries,[45] but after the death of Alexander the theatre became still more international, an institution unto itself which Athens had no hopes or means of regulating.

The Artists of Dionysus and the Athenian 'metropolis'

From the first decades of the third century we have further and even more explicit evidence of the theatre's confirmed international status. That evidence comes in the form of the inscriptions which testify to the activity of Greece's theatrical guilds, the 'Artists' (τεχνῖται) of Dionysus. The earliest known reference to *technitai* (if not yet to a formal actors' association) appears in Aristotle's *Rhetoric*: Aristotle remarks in passing that some people call actors 'flatterers [or 'parasites'] of Dionysus (διονυσοκόλακας) but that they call themselves 'artists' (τεχνῖται).[46] The first epigraphic mention of theatrical *technitai* does not appear for another forty years or so (*c.* 294–288 BC), when a long inscribed document records the attempts of four Euboean cities to organise theatre festivals for which they have contracted the services of 'artists', or theatre professionals.[47] We then have two decrees from roughly a decade later which mention specific chapters of the guild of 'the *technitai* of Dionysus' (οἱ περὶ τον Δίονυσον τεχνῖται). A decree that likely dates to about 280 records privileges awarded by the

[44] Le Guen (1995) 64–6; (2010) with a comprehensive table at 501–4. See esp. Fantuzzi and Hunter (2004) 432–7 and Le Guen (2007) for overviews of new tragic production in the Hellenistic period.

[45] See in particular Wilson and Hartwig (2009) on the many inscriptions which attest to the continued proclamation of honours for the city's benefactors before the competition of new tragedies at the festival (their Appendix I records fifteen such instances between 319/18 and the middle of the third century BC).

[46] Arist. *Rhet.* 3.1405a23–4. Cf. [Arist] *Pr.* 956b11, perhaps from the end of the fourth century, on negative stereotypes about the 'artists'. On the term 'flatterers of Dionysus' see esp. Ceccarelli 2004.

[47] *IG* xii.9 207 = Le Guen 1; cf. Csapo–Slater III.162.

Delphic Amphictyony to the *technitai* from the Isthmus (i.e. Corinth) and Nemea,[48] while the first reference to an Athenian association appears in an inscription of 279/8 or 278/7, a decree which lists the privileges that have also been granted by the Amphictyony to the *technitai* of Athens.[49]

Although Athenians constituted one of the first – if perhaps not the very first – chapters of the guild, they do not play an especially large or distinguished role within the corpus of early inscriptions attesting to *technitai*.[50] Much later, towards the end of the next century (117/6 BC), a lengthy decree of the Amphictyony would claim that the Athenians' chapter had been the first and remained the foremost association thanks to Athens' status as the birthplace of the theatre.[51] This inscription was cut into the south face of the Athenian treasury at Delphi and confirms the rights of the Athenian *technitai*, who are characterised as the legitimate heirs of a long and illustrious Athenian tradition of bequeathing cultural gifts upon Greece. The inscription refers to Athens as the 'mother city' – the *mētropolis* – of the theatre, which is itself named as the greatest of the city's many contributions to Hellas:

> ... πρῶτός τε πάντων, συναγα<γ>ὼν τεχνιτῶν σύνοδον
> [καὶ ἀγωνιστῶν, θ]υμελικ[οὺς καὶ σκ]ηνικ[οὺ]ς ἀγῶνας ἐποίησεν, οἷς καὶ
> συμβαίνει μαρτυρεῖν μὲν τοὺς πλείστους τῶν ἰ-
> [δίων τῆς πόλεως] ποιητῶ[ν, αὐτὴν] δὲ καὶ τ[ὴ]ν ἀλήθειαν ἐμφανῶς δεικνύειν,
> ὑπομιμνήσκουσαν ὅτι μητρόπολίς ἐστι τῶν
> [δραμάτων ἁπάντων, τ]ρα[γωιδίαν κ]αὶ κωμωι[δ]ίαν εὑροῦσά τε καὶ αὐξήσασα
> [κτλ.] (*FdD* 3.2.69 lines 16–19)

[48] *FdD* III 1.55 = Le Guen 17. Le Guen gives the date as '*ca* 280? ou 247?'; see her discussion of the date: (2001) I.129–30; cf. Csapo–Slater IV.38.

[49] *IG* ii² 1132 = Le Guen 2; cf. Csapo–Slater IV.39.

[50] For the controversy over whether the Athenians had formed the first such guild see also Le Guen (2001) I.5–6; see esp. her 14–16 on the Athenian 'branch' of the association.

[51] *FdD* III 2.69 = Le Guen 11. The copy of the decree found on the Athenian Acropolis is *IG* ii² 1134. This emphasis on the primacy of Athens in terms of both its theatrical tradition and its association of *technitai* is puzzling in the light of the other epigraphic documents: as Le Guen (2001) I.14 writes, 'Si l'on en jugeait par le nombre des témoignages qui nous sont parvenus sur l'association athénienne au IIIᵉ s., on aurait bien du mal à y reconnaître la confrérie née, semble-t-il, pour défendre haut et fort la primauté culturelle de l'ancien centre politique du monde grec.'

...and first of all [gifts], [Athens] assembled a guild of *technitai*
and competitors, and established thymelic and scenic competitions, as
the majority of the city's
own poets bear witness, and she herself [i.e Athens] manifestly declares the
truth in
reminding [the world] that she is the *mētropolis* of
all drama, because she invented and fostered both tragedy and comedy...
(etc.)

This decree of the Amphictyony has rightly been characterised as a 'hymne sans musique ni chanson': in strikingly hymnic fashion it sings the praises of Athens as both mother and birthplace of Greece's entire theatrical tradition.[52]

Lycurgus *redivivus* would certainly have been pleased to see these words inscribed on the Athenian treasury in the Panhellenic sanctuary of Delphi, a monumental affirmation on view to all Greece of the 'theatrical' vision that he and other contemporaries of his had worked so hard to propagate. Nevertheless, from other inscriptions it also becomes clear that these artists had come to conceive of their enterprise, and of the theatre itself, as an institution that was not just international, but even 'supranational' in character.[53] In the words of Jane Lightfoot, these associations 'characterised themselves as cities – corporations based in cities... but distinct and exclusive, cities existing for the sake of citizens with itinerant careers'.[54] Like independent cities, the *technitai* 'appoint their own financial, religious, diplomatic, and legislative officials'; they also 'issue their own decrees, patterned on the civic model'.[55] Thus despite Athens' best efforts at the close of the fourth century, already by the

[52] Le Guen (2001) II.97; see her edition and commentary at II.92–8. She highlights the wistfulness of the inscription, which seems to want to see the Athens of the present day as the great imperial power of the past: 'Il est en effet assez piquant de constater que ce décret reprend les thèmes mis en avant par les Athéniens, lorsqu'ils pouvaient encore prétender à l'hégémonie' (2.97).

[53] For the use of this term see esp. Šarnina 1987.

[54] Lightfoot (2002) 222; see her discussion at 222–4. For a comprehensive study of the *technitai* and their development, organisation and finances in the Hellenistic period see Aneziri (2003).

[55] Lightfoot (2002) 222. See also the discussion of Le Guen (2001) II.77–84, who calls the associations 'cities in miniature' and discusses them under the rubric of 'un État dans l'État'.

early decades of the third the city seems to have wielded little power over the theatre industry at large. An epitaph for Euripides attributed to Adaeus, a Macedonian epigrammatist perhaps of the late fourth century, even articulates a poetics of the theatre's new supranationalism. Here the epigrammatist concedes that Euripides' physical tomb (τάφος) lies at the Macedonian spring of Arethusa, but argues that his real monument lies elsewhere:

> σοὶ δ' οὐ τοῦτον ἐγὼ τίθεμαι τάφον, ἀλλὰ τὰ βάκχου
> βήματα καὶ σκηνὰς ἐμβάδι σειομένας.[56]
> (Adaeus 3.15–16 *GP* = *AP* 7.51 lines 5–6)
>
> However, I do not consider this your tomb, but rather the stages of
> and scene-paintings of Bacchus that quake with the step of buskins.

In these verses the city of Athens has been all but erased from Euripides' biography. And despite the passing (albeit striking) mention of implied Macedonian claims to 'ownership' over the poet, Adaeus goes still further in arguing that he is now the true possession only of 'theatre' itself.[57]

Menander's Dionysia

By the end of the fourth century the theatre had fully flowered as an international institution, but even after the Macedonian takeover of Athens in the aftermath of the Lamian War the Great Dionysia continued to have a high-profile role in the local politics of the city.[58] The Assembly in the Theatre (ἐκκλησία ἐν Διονύσου) continued, at least at first, to be held immediately following the festival's celebration. An inscription attests to the assembly after the Great Dionysia of 322/1, the first to be celebrated since the Macedonian conquest

[56] Con. Hartung: πειθομένας codd.

[57] For further discussion and contextualisation of the epigram see Hanink (2010a): 53–5.

[58] For signs of New Comedy's own engagement with politics see esp. Lape (2004) 40–67 and Major (1997).

and possibly the same occasion that saw Menander's comic debut.[59] The next known theatre assembly inscription dates to the year of the briefly restored democracy (and the war with Cassander) in 318/7.[60] Soon afterwards Demetrius of Phaleron was installed as *epimeletēs*, and (according to the *Parian Chronicle*) Menander took his first victory at the Great Dionysia of 316/5.[61] No mention of the *ekklēsia* surfaces again until the next century, in a record of the theatre assembly of 282/1.[62] The evidence is meagre, and though we must of course be wary of *argumenta ex silentio* this may be a reflection of the assembly's transformation, or even elimination, in the hands of these decades' various Macedonian regents and kings.[63]

We do however know that honours for benefactors of Athens continued to be announced before the contest of new tragedies. In some cases these honours will have been bestowed upon allies of the ruling Macedonians, who certainly recognised the historical prestige of the occasion and appropriated the forum to their own political ends.[64] On the whole and apart from the introduction of the *agonothesia*, the Great Dionysia of early Macedonian Athens seems to show structural continuity with the festival of the Lycurgan Era. The evidence for the dramatic

59 *IG* ii³ 384 = *Agora* 16.95(1). Demades may have been responsible for a motion passed at the meeting, cf. line 9, which is heavily restored: [Δημάδη]ς Δημέ[ου Παιαν-ιεὺς εἶπεν].

60 *Agora* 16.105(3). 61 *FGrH* 239 B140 = Men. T 48.

62 *Agora* 16.181; see below.

63 The politics of the period surely affected the festivals in other and unknown ways: see esp. O'Sullivan (2009b) on the evidence that, in 302/1, Menander's *Imbrians* was pulled from the Great Dionysia (or even that the whole festival was cancelled) at the behest of the tyrant Lachares, briefly ruler of Athens, and about whom little is known. The evidence is from *P.Oxy.* 10.1235, which claims that in the archonship of Nicocles the *Imbrians* was slated for performance at the Dionysia but that either the play or the festival 'did not happen because of Lachares' (οὐκ ἐγένετο δ[ὲ διὰ] | τὸν Λαχάρην, lines 9–10). This has typically been read as an indication that the *entire* Dionysia 'did not happen', but O'Sullivan prudently sees this 'as a claim that must be regarded at best with suspicion' (79).

64 See e.g. Walbank (1990) 445–6, on *IG* ii² 309 and 552. Cf. the further discussion in Wilson and Hartwig (2009) 22 n. 36; see also their Appendix 1 on the evidence for the announcement of honours before the *agon* of new tragedies in the last decades of the fourth century.

landscape in this period nonetheless becomes entirely dominated by notices of comic production. These years marked the great height of New Comedy: Menander had been born in 342/1, and as a child he will have witnessed the progression of Lycurgus' theatre and other reforms. He was therefore also among the first young generation of theatregoers to know the theatre as the home of statues of the great fifth-century tragedians, and to have grown up with productions of 'old' (*palaion*) comedy on the programme of the Great Dionysia.[65] Menander and his fellow playwrights must have been highly conscious of Athens' theatrical past, memorials of which were now built into the structure of the city's dramatic festivals and into the physical theatre. The other two members of antiquity's great New Comic triad, Philemon of Syracuse and Diphilus of Sinope, were both non-Athenians who were older than Menander but active in roughly the same period.[66]

Menander died in 291/0. Not long after his death a portrait statue of him was erected at the eastern *parodos* of the Theatre of Dionysus, next to where the Lycurgan group of the three great tragedians also stood. In the second century AD Pausanias described the contemporary assortment of statues in the area as follows:

εἰσὶ δὲ Ἀθηναίοις εἰκόνες ἐν τῷ θεάτρῳ καὶ τραγῳδίας καὶ κωμῳδίας ποιητῶν, αἱ πολλαὶ τῶν ἀφανεστέρων· ὅτι μὴ γὰρ Μένανδρος, οὐδεὶς ἦν ποιητὴς κωμῳδίας τῶν ἐς δόξαν ἡκόντων. τραγῳδίας δὲ κεῖνται τῶν φανερῶν Εὐριπίδης καὶ Σοφοκλῆς. (Paus. 1.21.1)

At the theatre in Athens there are statues of tragic and comic poets, many of them undistinguished; apart from Menander none of the comic poets is famous. But for tragedy there are statues of the illustrious Euripides and Sophocles.[67]

[65] These had been instituted in 339 BC: *IG* ii^2 2318.1565–6 Millis–Olson.

[66] See Rusten (2011) 660 on the dates of Diphilus; Webster (1970) 152 posited 360–295 as the dates of his life. According to the *Suda*, Philemon 'had his *floruit* during the rule of Alexander the Great, a little before Menander' (ἤκμαζεν ἐπὶ τῆς Ἀλεξάνδρου βασιλείας, βραχεῖ Μενάνδρου πρότερος, *Suda* φ.327 = Philemon T 1).

[67] On the honorific statues that came to grace the south slope of the Acropolis see Ma (2013) 105–6. Dio Chrysostom (31.116) had complained of a slovenly and unpleasant poet whose statue had been installed next to that of Menander.

A base of 'pentelic' marble that has been identified with this statue of Menander was discovered in 1862, near the place where it would originally have stood outside the theatre.[68] This base, which alone stands 1.08 metres tall, is inscribed with the name ΜΕΝΑΝΔΡΟΣ; in smaller letters below the names of the sculptors, Cephisodotus and Timarchus, are recorded (Κηφισόδοτος Τίμαρχος ἐποίησαν).[69] These artists were sons of the famous Praxiteles, and Pliny the Elder lists their names among sculptors whose *floruit* was in the 121st Olympiad – the same Olympiad in which Menander died.[70] The current consensus thus holds that the statue was erected shortly after his death, in about 290.[71]

In a comprehensive re-analysis of the evidence for the Menander base and statue, the original location at the Theatre of Dionysus and the historical and cultural circumstances that surrounded the statue's installation, Christina Papastamati-von Moock has made a number of observations which shed light on how this physical addition to the theatrical landscape marked a new configuration of Athenian dramatic history (for a reconstruction of the statue in its original position at the theatre see Fig. 7).[72] The base of the statue indicates that Menander was depicted in a seated pose, which in the late fourth century had become a standard way of representing intellectuals.[73] But this position was not only suggestive of Menander's own 'philosophical' qualities: his seat may have recalled the front-row *prohedra* seats in the Theatre, the 'chairs

[68] The base is exceptional for the proximity of its findspot to its original location: Papastamati-von Moock (2007) 282.

[69] *IG* ii² 3555. The base is currently displayed *in situ* at the eastern *parodos* of the Theatre of Dionysus in the Acropolis Archaeological Park in Athens.

[70] The 121st Olympiad began in 292 BC.

[71] See Papastamati-von Moock (2007) 285–6.

[72] Papastamati-von Moock (2007).

[73] Papastamati-von Moock (2007) 289–98, esp. 294–5. See esp. the discussion of Zanker (1995): in the statue of Menander 'The seated motif has now taken on an entirely new set of connotations' (79). No longer reserved for women and dignified, elderly men (as it had been in the classical period: see esp. 53–4), the position was now suggestive of contemplation: 'The poet is presented to us as a private individual who cultivates a relaxed and luxurious way of life' (79); cf. ch. 3 ('The Rigors of Thinking') *passim*. On the statue's appearance and its significance for the original display context see esp. Palagia (2005).

Figure 7 Reconstructed statue of Menander, *in situ* at the eastern *parodos* of the Theatre of Dionysus in Athens (original base *c.* 292 BC)

of state' reserved for those who had been awarded the honour of *prohedria*.[74] The honour which the statue symbolically conferred upon Menander was hence effectively a double one: the honour of the statue itself, but also of imagined *prohedria* in perpetuity. The very position of Menander's statue beside the Lycurgan group of Aeschylus, Sophocles and Euripides also declared the continuity of the Athenian dramatic tradition. Menander now stood (or rather sat) to the viewer's right of the tragedians, in the space closest to the Doric gateway that since Lycurgus' era had crowned the building's entrance. He was visually configured as the most recent representative of an illustrious theatrical heritage that stretched across the *parodos* and back over centuries.[75]

74 Palagia (2005) 291; Papastamati-von Moock (2007) 292–3.

75 Cf. Papastamati-von Moock (2007) 319: 'Hierdurch wurde der Dichter [i.e. Menander] als vierter und letzter der bedeutendsten Vertreter des klassischen Dramas charakterisiert: Rechts neben den drei Tragikern erhielt er seinen – tatsätlichen und

No account, whether literary or epigraphical, informs us of the motivations for the statue's installation at the Theatre of Dionysus. If, as Olga Palagia has suggested, the impetus for the statue came from a pro-Macedonian faction in Athens,[76] then it would be tempting to imagine that this move marked another attempt on the part of Macedon and its supporters to appropriate the Athenian theatrical heritage as part of Macedonian history and tradition. The Macedonian rulers of Athens had likely already been using the occasion of the Great Dionysia to proclaim honours for their own allies, and by the third century BC we find signs that the biography of Euripides had been reconfigured, thanks to the story of Euripides' patronage by King Archelaus, to cast the tragedian as an effectively 'native' Macedonian poet.[77] On the other hand, Papastamati-von Moock contends that the statue must have been erected by a decree of the Assembly, and argues that this decree represented an attempt to give Menander the honour that he had not been paid in his lifetime (perhaps precisely because of his supposed association with Macedonian rulers). In this case, the statue will have marked an attempt on the part of the demos to reclaim the poet for a strictly Athenian narrative of the city's theatrical tradition.[78]

The original politics of the statue may be elusive, but to the theatregoers who thronged to Athens the sight of the statue will have served as an awe-inspiring reminder of Athens' status as the mother and nurse of the theatre (as far as we know, neither Philemon nor Diphilus – both of them foreigners – received the honour in Athens of a portrait statue). When read

symbolischen – Platz im verein mit den bedeutendsten Vertretern des antiken Theaters und legitimierte so seinen Platz am Haupteingang des Theaters.'

[76] Palagia (2005) 293. Menander was remembered in antiquity as an associate and friend of Demetrius of Phaleron: see esp. D.L. 5.79 = Men. T 9 (on Menander's near escape from punishment solely on account of this relationship). Owens (2011) argues the *Dyscolus* (which premiered in 316 = Men. T 50) marked an expression of support for Demetrius of Phaleron's instalment as *epimeletēs* of the city in 317.

[77] See Hanink (2008).

[78] Papastamati-von Moock (2007) 293–4. On Menander's relationship with Macedonian rulers (a controversial point) see Major (1997), an account of Menander as sympathetic to Macedonian rule and Lape (2004), whose guiding thesis is that Menandrian comedy 'had a propensity to preserve and reproduce democratic culture against encroachment from Hellenistic kings and kingdoms' (12).

retrospectively, the physical position of Menander's statue at the end of this line of playwrights, immediately after Euripides, also serves as a kind of material and visual parallel for the 'genealogical' claims of later literary sources that saw the comedies of Menander as the direct descendants of Euripidean tragedy. In Satyrus' *Life of Euripides* the primary speaker of the biographical dialogue lists a number of dramatic conceits and devices: reversals of fortune, violations of young women, recognitions by means of tokens and so on. He continues: 'these, I reckon, are the essence of the newer comedy, which Euripides developed to perfection'.[79] Quintilian would also draw a comparison between the two playwrights as part of his assessment of Athenian dramatists in the *Institutio Oratoria*.[80] He claims that 'Menander admired Euripides to the utmost and, as he himself often indicates, imitated him, though in a different genre'.[81] The configuration of the statues at the eastern *parodos* of the Theatre of Dionysus thus marked an early visual 'dramatisation' of the lineage that was perceived as connecting Menander to Euripides. The concord of the Lycurgan Era tragic statue group symbolically dispelled any perceived conflict between the three fifth-century tragedians, conflict of the sort imagined in Aristophanes' fifth-century *Frogs*. And though Menander alone was depicted in a seated position, the very addition of his portrait went further still in proclaiming the city's unified theatrical tradition. Now at the Theatre of

79 Satyrus F 6 fr. 39 col. VII Schorn: ταῦτα | γάρ ἐστι δήπου | τὰ συνέχον|τα τὴν νεω|τέραν κωμωι|δίαν, ἃ πρὸς | ἄκρον ἤγα[γ]εν | Εὐριπίδης. For commentary see Schorn (2004) 256–68, with 256 n. 473 for bibliography which discusses Euripides' influence upon Menander. Satyrus' biography likely dates to the late third or very early second century BC. Scholarship on the relationship between Menander's comedy and classical tragedy is extensive; for general treatments see Cusset (2003), Hunter (1985) 114–36 and Katsouris (1975).

80 Quint. *Inst.* 10.1.65–72.

81 Quint. *Inst.* 10.1.69: *hunc* [sc. Euripides] *et admiratus maxime est, ut saepe testatur, et secutus, quamquam in opere diverso, Menander*. Cf. Dio 18.6–7 (*On Training for Giving Speeches*) for another implicit comparison of Euripides and Menander: Dio recommends that the aspiring orator read Menander for comedy and Euripides for tragedy and proclaims: 'let no one who fancies himself wiser fault me for preferring Menander to Old Comedy, or Euripides to Old Tragedy' (καὶ μηδεὶς τῶν σοφωτέρων αἰτιάσηταί με ὡς προκρίναντα τῆς ἀρχαίας κωμῳδίας τὴν Μενάνδρου ἢ τῶν ἀρχαίων τραγῳδῶν Εὐριπίδην). On Dio's view of Euripides as a more 'contemporary' playwright see Hunter (2009) 46.

Dionysus the whole illustrious history of Athenian drama was presented in panorama, embodied in a line not just of the three great tragedians but of the city's four greatest playwrights.[82] This visual canon in bronze offered a progressive narrative of the evolution of Athenian drama from the primordial tragic past to the popular comedy of the present day.

From Athens to Alexandria

Philippides, a younger contemporary of Menander, was still an active playwright of comedy when Menander's statue was erected near the entrance of the theatre.[83] He is named as one of the six most notable New Comic poets in an anonymous ancient treatise *On Comedy*,[84] and like the fourth-century Axionicus he was the author of a comedy entitled *Phileuripides*. He was also extraordinarily active in the political life of Athens. In the year 295/4, Demetrius Poliorcetes ousted Athens' short-lived tyrant Lachares and returned to rule in the city. The same Stratocles who was responsible for the decree conferring posthumous honours upon Lycurgus now became a notorious flatterer of Demetrius. Stratocles is said by Plutarch to have (among other things) changed the month of Mounychion to Demetrion, and the name of the Dionysia to the Demetria.[85] Plutarch further claims that Philippides composed scathing comic verses in response to Stratocles' acts of sycophancy.[86]

We also have evidence of Philippides' activism on behalf of Athens with Lysimachus, another of Alexander's 'Successors'.

[82] Cf. Ma (2013) 120. The statue of Astydamas from *c*. 340 BC had been built into the stone construction of the fourth-century theatre, specifically into the western *analemma* (a retaining wall supporting the seating): see page 187 above. Despite the fame that he earned during his lifetime, Astydamas was not assimilated into the arch-narrative of the eastern *parodos*.

[83] *Suda* φ 345 = Philippides T 1.

[84] Philippides F 2–4 ; cf. page 179 above; Philippides T 5 = *Prolegomena on Comedy* II.53 Koster.

[85] Plut. *Dem*. 12.2. For the 'Demetria' cf. Duris *FGrH* 76 T14 ap. Ath. 12.535e–6a. The claim that the Dionysia was transformed into a Demetria likely reflects a misunderstanding in the ancient sources (another festival altogether, the 'Demetria', may have been instituted); for a recent discussion see Versnel (2011) 452–3, with 444–56 for a lively account of how Demetrius 'played (the) god' in Athens.

[86] Plut. *Dem*. 12.4; Philippides F 25.

An unusually long honorific decree survives (from 283/2) which commends Philippides for his intercessions with King Lysimachus of Macedon on behalf of Athens after the Battle of Ipsus in 301.[87] The decree also praises him for his service as *agonothetēs* in the archonship of Isaeus, at the Great Dionysia of 284/3.[88] He is commended in particular for having contributed to the festival freely of his own funds. The decree awards Philippides a gold crown, to be proclaimed 'at the tragic contest of the Dionysia'; it also calls for an honorific statue of him to be erected in the theatre and grants perpetual *prohedria* to him and to his descendants. No mention is made of Philippides' work as a comic poet (though the portrait statue's location at the Theatre of Dionysus surely gestures to it). In the combined testimonia for his life we therefore see, as Wilfred Major has noted, 'a unity of dramatic comedy and political activity unparalleled even among the poets of Old Comedy'.[89]

Only five years after the remarkable decree for Philippides, the first inscribed documents granting privileges to specific associations of *technitai* appear. In this period the Great Dionysia in Athens was still going in full force, as we know both from the record of Philippides' service as *agonothetēs* and from an inscription which attests to a meeting of an Assembly in the Theatre after the festival's celebration in 282/1.[90] This is an honorific decree for Euthius son of Antiphon from the deme of Teithras, who had been archon in 283/2. The decree praises Euthius for, among other things, having commendably overseen the *pompē* of the Great Dionysia during his archonship.[91] Not long afterwards, in around 280, Athens began erecting a monumental, inscribed structure containing the so-called 'Victors' Lists' (or *Catalogi Victorum, IG* ii^2 2325A–H) in the

[87] *IG* ii^2 657.

[88] *IG* ii^2 657.38–40. For other cases of comic insults against Demetrius Poliorcetes see Kurke (2002) 33–40 on the *Chreiai* of Machon (a contemporary of Callimachus). Kurke argues that the courtesans depicted by Machon as quoting lines of Athenian tragedy to humiliate Demetrius Poliorcetes use their command of the Athenian literary past to display 'resistance, contempt, and superiority' in the face of the city's Macedonian rulers.

[89] Major (1997) 48.

[90] *SEG* xxi 89 = *Agora* 16.181.

[91] *SEG* xxi 89 lines 12–13: τῆς πομπῆς τῶ|ι Διονύσωι ἐπεμελήθη φιλοτίμως.

Sanctuary of Dionysus. These recorded the names of victors at the Athenian dramatic festivals and their total number of victories. Benjamin Millis and Douglas Olson suggest, on the basis of the information which the lists record and apparent changes in hands, that these records were first inscribed in 279/8.[92] Their addition to the theatrical landscape would only have served to advance further the project of transforming this structure into a kind of living museum of Athens' theatrical past, a *lieu de mémoire* which nevertheless continued to play host to new performances by contemporary playwrights on each festival occasion. The same year also happens to be the year for which Daniela Summa postulates the introduction of a contest of 'old dramas' (παλαιὰ δράματα) at the Great Dionysia.[93] Summa places both the inscription of the Victors' Lists and the introduction of the new *agon* in the historical context of the Greek defeat of Brennus' Gauls in the winter of that year. A number of Greek states held festivals celebrating the victory over the 'barbarians': Ptolemy II Philadelphus held his first Ptolemaea during the same year and the Delphians instituted the Soteria festival to honour the sanctuary's liberation.[94] The Athenians also marked the victory with festival celebrations, perhaps in part by elaborating their own Dionysia with the new contest of old drama.[95] The addition of contests of old drama will have dramatically increased (from two to perhaps six) the number of old plays performed at the festival and may have served to reorient the emphasis of the occasion towards revivals, and away from dramatic debuts.[96]

[92] For an overview of the inscription see Millis and Olson (2012) 133–5. Millis (forthcoming) 438 argues for the likelihood that the *Didascaliae* and the Victors' Lists 'were roughly contemporary and that the monuments on which they were inscribed were situated so as to speak to one another'.

[93] Summa (2008). The inscription that attests to the contest of *palaia dramata* for both comedy (fr. 1) and tragedy (fr. 2) (*SEG* XXVI 208), gives a record for the competition of 255/4.

[94] Summa (2008) 494.

[95] For these and other ways in which Athens marked the victory see Summa (2008) 494–6.

[96] See however Wilson and Hartwig (2009) 22–3 for the ample evidence that honours continued to be proclaimed before the contest of new tragedies until the mid-first century BC.

Ptolemy II Philadelphus' institution of the Ptolemaea in Alexandria during the same period reminds us that activity in Alexandria was now beginning to foreshadow the significant shift that lay on the horizon for the localization of Athens' theatrical heritage. During his reign Philadelphus put on a splendid *pompē* of his own, one which surely far outshone the brilliance of the procession that Euthius had overseen in Athens.[97] Philadelphus' *pompē* featured a large theatrical presence: the *technitai* of Dionysus (presumably the Egyptian chapter of the association) walked in the parade,[98] which also included a float with a fifteen-foot statue of the god Dionysus pouring a libation. That statue was covered with a canopy from which there hung numerous theatrical masks.[99]

Remarkably, Athens' tragic texts now resurface in a notice preserved by Galen about Philadelphus' successor, Ptolemy III Euergetes, who reigned from 246–222 BC. According to Galen, Euergetes issued an order that any books found on ships that weighed anchor in the Harbour of Alexandria were to be seized and copied. Only the copies would then be returned to the original owners. As proof of Euergetes' great zeal for collecting antique books, Galen tells the story of how he deceived the Athenians into bringing to Alexandria 'the books (βιβλία) of Sophocles and Euripides and Aeschylus' under the pretence that the originals would be returned – as a sign of good faith, the Athenians were even given fifteen talants of silver as a deposit. But Euergetes, predictably, sent back to Athens only the copies of the texts, with the message that the Athenians should keep the silver. The Athenians' hands were tied and they were forced to allow the Egyptian king to keep the precious texts.[100] Nearly a century earlier, the city had attempted to

[97] On the procession see esp. Hazzard (2000) 57–9 and Rice (1983). Foertmeyer (1988) argues that the procession took place at the second celebration of the Ptolemaea in Alexandria, in 275/4.

[98] Callixinus *FGrH* 627 F 2.40–2 ap. Ath 198c. This portion of the procession included floats featuring what Rice (1983) calls 'Tableaux from the "Life" of Dionysus' (59). On the Egyptian association of *technitai* (one of the first, along with those of Athens and of the Isthmus and Nemea) see esp. Le Guen (2001) II.7–9 and 34–6 and Dunand (1986).

[99] Callixinus *FGrH* 627 F 2.55–6 ap. Ath 198d–e.

[100] Gal. *In Hippocratis epidemiarum* iii 17a.607.5–17 Wenkebach.

proclaim its ownership of the patrimony of Aeschylus, Sophocles and Euripides in part by depositing official versions of their dramatic scripts in the archive. If we are to trust any part of Galen's account, it was now precisely the existence of those texts which allowed the Alexandrians, once and for all, to wrest that cultural inheritance from Athens. The Lycurgan law had sent a symbolic message to the rest of Greece about Athens' indisputable ownership of the tragic scripts, and through those very same material texts an equally symbolic transfer of Greece's centre of culture was imagined to have occurred.

Hindsight allows us to see that the Alexandrian editions of the works of the tragedians would become the authoritative versions of the texts in posterity. Nevertheless, the story of how, within a matter of less than a century, the authoritative centre for the preservation of the Athenian theatrical heritage was transplanted from Athens to Alexandria still remains to be told. Here I have only skimmed the surface of the half century between the death of Lycurgus and the creation of the Alexandrian Library, and a detailed account of both the theatre and the theatrical heritage, in all of its aspects (performative, scholarly, cultural, economic, etc.) is needed. This is especially the case given how critical this period was both for the survival of certain tragedies and for the continued formation of retrospective notions about the Athenian theatrical achievement. Ancient sources, too, linked the cultural landscapes of Athens and Alexandria in this period, by means of the story that Menander refused repeated invitations to Ptolemy I Soter's court in Alexandria.[101] Though of dubious credibility, this story further allegorises Macedonian attempts to appropriate for their own cultural programmes aspects of the Athenian theatrical tradition. In an essay on Lycurgus' policies and their foreshadowing of Ptolemaic cultural initiatives, Claude Mossé argued that a crucial bridge between Lycurgus and the first Ptolemies existed in the figure of Demetrius of

[101] Pliny *NH* 7.111 = Men. T 15; Alciphr. 4.18.5–6 = Men. T 20. The *Suda* entry for Menander (μ 589 = Men. T 1) credits Menander with comedies as well as 'letters to King Ptolemy'.

Phaleron. Demetrius himself is said (by not entirely trustworthy sources) to have been largely responsible for the first organisation of the Library.[102] But regardless of the extent to which Demetrius was truly responsible for the Library and Museum in Alexandria, the magnitude of Lycurgus' cultural programme and its impetus for preservation do raise a number of questions about the stretch of the programme's influence. If nothing else, later efforts that were made in Alexandria shared Lycurgus' commitment to preserving that part of the past which, by the last quarter of the fourth century, the Athenians had already come to define as their own 'classical' heritage.

We began with Plutarch and here we might return to him one last time. Plutarch lived centuries after the events that he has described for us, but he has proven an insightful voice regarding the transformations that the Athenian theatre industry underwent in the fourth century BC. His instinct for the theatre as a site and symbol of power in the Greek world is sharp, and the themes that his anecdotes raise – the idea that tragedy had the power to save Athens, the theatrical competition between Athens and Macedon as a microcosm of the larger struggle, etc. – have guided us towards key problems and offered a framework for this study. There is, however, a curious minor work of his that tends to be overlooked, even though it offers antiquity's most extended explicit account of the relationship between classical tragedy and the Athenian empire. This is his *de gloria Atheniensium*, a text which, like his *de fortuna Romanum* and his two works *de fortuna Alexandri*, is written in a highly 'declamatory' style.[103]

Perhaps precisely because it is so rhetorical, *de gloria Atheniensium* has been largely ignored for the insight that it provides into post-classical notions of classical Athens. The long title of the work, *Whether the Athenians were more illustrious*

[102] Mossé (1989) 32–4. For Demetrius of Phaleron's involvement in the Library see SOD T 58–66, on the problems of these sources see Tracy (2000) 343–4, who does allow that 'Demetrius was active in some way in the efforts of the first Ptolemy to create a collection' (344).

[103] For a critical edition and commentary see Thiolier (1985).

in war or wisdom (Πότερον Ἀθηναῖοι κατὰ πόλεμον ἢ κατὰ σοφίαν ἐνδοξότεροι), well captures the central opposition that Plutarch sets out to construct, namely an opposition between Athens' military deeds and cultural achievements. Early on in the treatise Plutarch establishes that 'wisdom' here will stand largely for tragic composition, as 'Athens certainly possessed no illustrious craftsman of either epic or melic poetry'.[104] Departing from that observation, he outlines the terms of his enquiry as follows:

> What profit, then, did these fine tragedies bring to Athens to compare with the shrewdness of Themistocles which provided the city with a wall, with the diligence of Pericles which adorned the Acropolis, with the liberty which Miltiades bestowed upon her, with the supremacy to which Cimon advanced her? If in this manner the wisdom of Euripides, the eloquence of Sophocles, and the poetic magnificence of Aeschylus rid the city of any of its difficulties or gained for her any brilliant success, it is but right to compare their tragedies with trophies of victory, to let the theatre (θέατρον) rival the War Office (στρατήγιον), and to compare the records of dramatic performances (τὰς διδασκαλίας) with the memorials of valour (ταῖς ἀριστείαις). (Plut. *Mor.* 348c–d)

From the beginning Plutarch is clear: the Athenians were great in both art and war, but they ought to have spent less on the theatre and more on military undertakings:

> For, if we reckon up the cost of each tragedy, the Athenian people will be seen to have spent more on productions of Bacchae, Phoenissae, Oedipuses, and Antigones, and the woes of Medea and Electra, than they spent in fighting for their supremacy and for their freedom from the barbarians. (Plut. *Mor.* 349a)

Plutarch's opposition between the Athenians' expenditure on the military and on the theatre has precedent in the third quarter of the fourth century.[105] In his third *Olynthiac*, Demosthenes had urged the Athenians to send expeditions in aid of Olynthus and against Philip. He argued that funds could be levied for these expeditions if only the Athenians would stop allowing the stratiotic fund (τὰ στρατιωτικά) to be used as

[104] Plut. *Mor.* 348b.
[105] Plutarch also complains about the excesses of expenditure at the Great Dionysia of his own day: *Mor.* 527d (*de Cupiditate Divitiarum*).

theōrika, that is as public money spent on (among other things) building projects and theatre subsidies.[106] In his first *Olynthiac* Demosthenes had also reproached the Athenians for wasting monies that should have been earmarked for the military: 'You have money, men of Athens, you have more military funds (στρατιωτικά) than all other men, but you spend it on whatever you please.'[107] Demosthenes delivered his *Olynthiac* speeches in 349, at roughly the same time as construction began again on the stone Theatre of Dionysus. He may even have had the expense of that particular project in mind as he complained about the Athenians' misuse of state funds.[108]

Plutarch, who cites Athenian tragedy throughout the *Lives* and *Moralia*, did clearly recognise the benefits brought by Athens' cultivation of the theatre. Yet in *de gloria Atheniensium* he criticises the city for funding the theatre so extravagantly, and even implies that the Athenians' misplaced priorities had led (as Demosthenes warned would happen) to their ruin. Athens was successful in repelling the Persian invasions of the fifth century, and thus the 'barbarians' to whom Plutarch refers in *Mor.* 349a must be the Macedonians. The implication is therefore that Athenian spending on the theatre in precisely the period that we have examined here massively contributed to the city's downfall. But on this count Plutarch's usually keen analysis somewhat misses the mark. Athens' investment in its drama industry during the third quarter of the fourth century left a cultural legacy at least as great as that of the military empire. The city's care for and investment in its theatre proved attention to a cultural patrimony that would long outlast the Delian League and the Athenian naval fleet. And attempt though Plutarch might to resist fascination with any triumph of Attic tragedy, his own accounts of tragic production, the Great Dionysia and the saving power of Euripidean poetry all speak to drama's prominence in the Athens of

[106] See most recently Csapo and Wilson (forthcoming) 1.1 for an account of *theōrika* in this period.

[107] Dem. 1.19.

[108] Csapo and Wilson (forthcoming) 1.2 suggest that funds for the construction came from the theoric fund.

his own imagination.[109] After all, we began with a passage from his *Life of Lysander* in which he claims that the city escaped complete obliteration thanks only to a few lines from Euripides' *Electra*.[110] Plutarch was himself one of the greatest brokers in the myth of classical tragedy, a myth and idea that Athenians of the fourth century constructed and disseminated even as Macedonian troops loomed at their borders. It is largely to those Athenians that we, like Plutarch, owe our soaring idea of classical tragedy: the gift that ensured, if not the very survival of the city, then at least our enduring belief in an Athenian miracle.

[109] References to Great Dionysia occur at e.g. Plut. *Cim.* 8.7–8, *Phoc.* 30 and *Dem.* 12. For case studies in Plutarch's use of tragedy and tragic quotations in the *Lives* see Papadi (2008) and Mossman (1988).

[110] Plut. *Lys.* 15.3.

BIBLIOGRAPHY

Albini, U. (1985) 'Euripide e le pretese della retorica', *PP* 40: 354–60.

Alemdar, S. (2000) 'Le monument de Lysicrate et son trépied', *Ktema* 25: 199–206.

Allan, W. (2001) 'Euripides in Megale Hellas: some aspects of the early reception of tragedy', *G&R* 48: 67–83.

Allen, D. S. (2000) 'Changing the authoritative voice: Lycurgus' *Against Leocrates*', *ClAnt* 19: 5–33.

(2013) *Why Plato Wrote*. Oxford.

Ampolo, C. (1979) 'Un politico "euergete" del IV secolo a.c.: Xenokles figlio di Xeinis del demo di Sphettos', *PP* 34: 167–78.

Aneziri, S. (2003) *Die Vereine der dionysischen Techniten im Kontext der hellenistischen Gesellschaft*. Stuttgart.

Arnott, W. G. (1996) *Alexis: The Fragments*. Cambridge.

Arrighetti, G. (1964) *Satiro: Vita di Euripide*. Pisa.

(1987) *Poeti, eruditi e biografi: momenti della riflessione dei greci sulla letteratura*. Pisa.

Asmis, E. (1992) 'Plato on poetic creativity', in *The Cambridge Companion to Plato*, ed. R. Kraut. Cambridge: 338–64.

Austin, M. M. (1994) 'Society and economy', in *The Cambridge Ancient History*. Vol. VI: *The Fourth Century B.C.*, ed. D. M. Lewis *et al.* Cambridge: 527–64.

Avery, H. C. (1968) 'My tongue swore, but my mind is unsworn', *TAPA* 99: 19–35.

Azoulay, V. (2009) 'Lycurgue d'Athènes et le passé de la cité : entre neutralisation et instrumentalisation', *CEA* 46: 149–80.

Azoulay, V. and Ismard, P. (eds.) (2011) *Clisthène et Lycurgue d'Athènes. Autour du politique dans la cité classique*. Paris.

Bakola, E. (2010) *Cratinus and the Art of Comedy*. Oxford.

Battezzato, L. (2003) 'I viaggi dei testi', in *Tradizione testuale e ricezione letteraria antica della tragedia greca. Atti del convegno Scuola Normale Superiore, Pisa, 14–15 giugno 2002*, ed. L. Battezzato. Amsterdam: 7–31.

Belfiore, E. (1992) 'Aristotle and Iphigenia', in *Essays on Aristotle's Poetics*, ed. A. O. Rorty. Princeton: 359–78.

Bellah, R. N. (1967) 'Civil religion in America', *Daedalus* 96: 1–21.

Biles, Z. P. (2006–2007) 'Aeschylus' afterlife: reperformance by decree in 5th c. Athens?', *ICS* 31–2: 206–42.

(2011) *Aristophanes and the Poetics of Competition.* Cambridge.
Bing, P. (2011) 'Anecdote, hypothesis, and image in the Hellenistic reception of Euripides', *A&A* 56: 1–17.
Blum, R. (1991) *Kallimachos: The Alexandrian Library and the Origins of Bibliography*, trans. H. H. Wellisch. Madison, Wis.
Bollansée, J. (1999) *Hermippos of Smyrna and His Biographical Writings.* Leuven.
Bosher, K. (2008–2009) 'To dance in the orchestra: a circular argument', *ICS* 33/34: 1–24.
Bosher, K., ed. (2012) *Theater Outside Athens: Drama in Greek Sicily and South Italy*. Cambridge.
Bosworth, A. B. (1996) 'Alexander, Euripides, and Dionysos: the motivation for apotheosis', in *Transitions to Empire: Essays in Greco-Roman History, 360–146 B.C.*, ed. R. W. Wallace and E. M. Harris. Norman, Okla.: 140–66.
Brennan, G. and Pettit, P. (2001) 'The hidden economy of esteem', *Economics and Philosophy* 16: 77–98.
(2004) *The Economy of Esteem: An Essay on Civil and Political Society*. Oxford.
Brivitello, S. (1998) 'Saffo sulla scena', *AFLB* 41: 179–205.
Brown, A. L. (1984) 'Three and scene-painting Sophocles', *PCPS* 110: 1–17.
Brown, T. S. (1967) 'Alexander's book order (Plut. *Alex.* 8)', *Historia* 16: 359–68.
Brun, P. (2000) *L'orateur Démade: Essai d'histoire et d'historiographie.* Bordeaux.
(2005) 'Lycurge d'Athènes: un législateur ?', in *Le législateur et la loi dans l'Antiquité*, ed. P. Sineux. Caen: 187–200.
Burke, E. M. (1977) '*Contra Leocratem* and *De Corona*: political collaboration?', *Phoenix* 31: 330–40.
(2010) 'Finances and the operation of the democracy in the "Lycurgan Era"', *AJP* 131: 393–423.
Burtt, J. O. (1962) *Minor Attic Orators.* Vol. II. Cambridge, Mass.
Büsing-Kolbe, A. (1978) 'Frühe griechische Türen', *JDAI* 93: 66–174.
Cagnazzi, S. (1993) 'Notizie sulla partecipazione di Euripide alla vita pubblica ateniense', *Athenaeum* 81: 165–75.
Calame, C. (2011) 'Myth and performance on the Athenian stage: Praxithea, Erechtheus, their daughters, and the etiology of autochthony', *CP* 106: 1–19.
Canevaro, M. (2013) *The Documents in the Attic Orators: Laws and Decrees in the Public Speeches of the Demosthenic Corpus*. Oxford.
Cantor, P. A. (1991) 'Aristotle and the history of tragedy', in *Theoretical Issues in Literary History*, ed. D. Perkins. Cambridge, Mass.: 60–84.
Capps, E. (1895) 'The chorus in the later Greek drama with reference to the stage question', *AJA* 10: 287–325.

(1900) 'Chronological studies in the Greek tragic and comic poets', *AJP* 21: 38–61.
(1943) 'Greek inscriptions: a new fragment of the list of victors at the City Dionysia', *Hesperia* 12: 1–11.
Capuccino, C. (2005) *Filosofi e rapsodi. Testo, traduzione e commento dello Ione platonico*. Bologna.
Carey, C. (2007a) *Lysiae orationes cum fragmentis*. Oxford.
(2007b) 'Epideictic oratory', in *A Companion to Greek Rhetoric*, ed. I. Worthington. Oxford: 235–62.
Carey, C., *et al.* (2008) 'Fragments of Hyperides' *Against Diondas* from the Archimedes Palimpsest', *ZPE* 165: 1–19.
Carrara, P. (2009) *Il testo di Euripide in antichità*. Florence.
Carter, D. M. (2007) *The Politics of Greek Tragedy*. Bristol.
ed. (2011) *Why Athens? A Reappraisal of Tragic Politics*.
Casolari, F. (2003) *Die Mythentravestie in der griechischen Komödie*. Munster.
Cawkwell, G. L. (1960) 'Aeschines and the Peace of Philocrates', *REG* 73: 416–38.
(1963) 'Eubulus', *JHS* 83: 47–67.
Ceccarelli, P. (2004) '"Autour de Dionysos" : remarques sur la dénomination des artistes dionysiaques', in *Le statut de l'acteur dans l'Antiquité grecque et romaine*, ed. C. Hugoniot, F. Hurlet and S. Milanezi. Tours: 109–42.
(2010) 'Contexts of tragedy: on the place of tragedy in the civic and cultural life of the Greek Poleis', in *Beyond the Fifth Century: Interactions with Greek Tragedy from the Fourth Century BCE to the Middle Ages*, ed. I. Gildenhard and M. Revermann. Berlin: 99–150.
Chaniotis, A. (2007) 'Theatre rituals', in *The Greek Theatre and Festivals: Documentary Studies*, ed. P. J. Wilson. Oxford: 48–66.
(2009) 'Traveling memories in the Hellenistic world', in *Wandering Poets in Ancient Greek Culture: Travel, Locality, Panhellenism*, ed. R. Hunter and I. Rutherford. Cambridge: 249–69.
Chroust, A.H. (1973) *Aristotle: New Light on His Life and on Some of His Lost Works*. Vol. II. London.
Chwe, M.S-Y. (2001) *Rational Ritual: Culture, Coordination, and Common Knowledge*. Princeton.
Cipolla, P. (2003) *Poeti minori del dramma satiresco: testo critico, traduzione e commento. Supplementi di Lexis, XXIII*. Amsterdam.
Clayman, D.L. (1987) 'Sigmatism in Greek poetry', *TAPA* 117: 69–84.
Clinton, K. (2008) *Eleusis: The Inscriptions on Stone. Documents of the Sanctuary of the Two Goddesses and Public Documents of the Deme* (3 vols.). Athens.
Colin, G. (1946) *Hypéride: Discours*. Paris.
Collard, C. (1970) 'On the tragedian Chaeremon', *JHS* 90: 22–34.
Collard, C. and Cropp, M. J. (2008) *Euripides: Fragments: Oedipus–Chrysippus; Other Fragments*. Cambridge.

Collard, C., Cropp, M. J. and Lee, K. H. eds. (1995) *Euripides: Selected Fragmentary Plays*. Vol. 1. Warminster.

Connelly, J. B. (1996) 'Parthenon and *parthenoi*: a mythological interpretation of the Parthenon Frieze', *AJA* 100: 53–80.

Conomis, N. C. (1970) *Lycurgus: Oratio in Leocratem*. Leipzig.

Constantinides, E. (1969) 'Timocles' *Ikarioi Satyroi*: a reconsideration', *TAPA* 100: 49–61.

Cope, E. M. and Sandys, J. E. (1877) *The Rhetoric of Aristotle* (3 vols.). Cambridge.

Cropp, M. J. (1995) 'Erechtheus', in Collard, Cropp and Lee: 148–94.

Csapo, E. (2000) 'From Aristophanes to Menander? Genre transformation in Greek comedy', in *Matrices of Genre: Authors, Canons, and Society*, ed. M. Depew and D. Obbink. Cambridge, Mass.: 115–34.

(2007) 'The men who built the theatres: theatropolai, theatronai, arkhitektones', in *The Greek Theatre and Festivals: Documentary Studies*, ed. P. J. Wilson. Oxford: 87–115.

(2010) *Actors and Icons of the Ancient Theater*. Oxford.

Csapo, E., Goette, H. R., Green, R. and Wilson, P. eds. (forthcoming) *Death of Drama or Birth of an Industry? The Greek Theatre in the Fourth Century BC*. Berlin.

Csapo, E. and Slater, W. J. (1995) *The Context of Ancient Drama*. Ann Arbor.

Csapo, E. and Wilson, P. J. (2010) 'Le passage de la chorégie à l'agonothésie à Athènes à la fin du IVe siècle', in *L'argent dans les concours du monde grec*, ed. B. Le Guen. Saint-Denis: 83–105.

(forthcoming) 'The finance and organisation of the Athenian theatre in the time of Eubulus and Lycurgus', in Csapo, Goette, Green and Wilson (forthcoming). Berlin: 393–424.

Culasso Gastaldi, E. (2003) 'Eroi della città: Eufrone di Sicione e Licurgo di Atene', in *Modelli eroici dall'antichità alla cultura europea*, ed. A. Barzanò *et al*. Rome: 65–98.

Cusset, C. (2003) *Ménandre ou La comédie tragique*. Paris.

Davidson, J. (1990) 'Isocrates against imperialism: an analysis of the *De Pace*', *Historia* 39: 20–36.

Davies, J. K. (1971) *Athenian Propertied Families: 600–300 BC*. Oxford.

(1996) 'Documents and "documents" in fourth-century historiography', in *Le IVe siècle av. J.-C.: Approches historiographiques*, ed. P. Carlier. Nancy: 29–39.

Dearden, C. (1999) 'Plays for export', *Phoenix* 53: 222–48.

de Marcellus, H. (1996) '*IG* XIV 1184 and the ephebic service of Menander', *ZPE* 110: 69–76.

Denniston, J. D. (1929) 'καθάπερ καί, ὥσπερ καί, οἷον καί', *CR* 43: 60.

Depew, D. (2007) 'From hymn to tragedy: Aristotle's genealogy of poetic kinds', in *The Origins of Theater in Ancient Greece and Beyond: From Ritual to Drama*, ed. E. Csapo and M. Miller. Cambridge: 126–49.

Depuydt, L. (1997) 'The time of death of Alexander the Great: 11 June 323 BC, *ca.* 4:00–5:00 pm', *Die Welt des Orients* 28: 117–35.
Develin, R. (1989) *Athenian Officials 684–321 BC*. Cambridge.
Diggle, J. (2004) *Theophrastus: Characters*. Cambridge.
Dillon, S. (2006) *Ancient Greek Portrait Sculpture*. Cambridge.
Dobrov, G. W. (2002) 'Μάγειρος ποιητής: language and character in Antiphanes', in *The Language of Greek Comedy*, ed. A. Willi. Oxford: 169–90.
Dobson, J. F. (1919) *The Greek Orators*. London.
Donini, P. (1997) 'L'universalità della tragedia in Aristolele (e in Platone)', in *Filosofia, storia, immaginario mitologico*, ed. M. Guglielmo and G. F. Gianotti. Alessanaria: 137–47.
Dorjahn, A. P. (1927) 'Poetry in Athenian courts', *CP* 22: 85–93.
(1929) 'Some remarks on Aeschines' career as an actor', *CJ* 25: 223–39.
Dörpfeld, W. and Reisch, E. (1896) *Das griechische Theater*. Athens.
Dougherty, C. (2009) 'Just visiting: the mobile world of classical Athens', in *The Oxford Handbook of Hellenic Studies*, ed. G. Boys-Stones, B. Graziosi and P. Vasunia. Oxford: 391–400.
Dover, K. J. (1974) *Greek Popular Morality in the Time of Plato and Aristotle*. London.
(1978) *Greek Homosexuality*. London.
(1993a) *Aristophanes: Frogs*. Oxford and New York.
(1993b) 'The contest in Aristophanes' *Frogs*: the points at issue', in *Tragedy, Comedy, and the Polis*, ed. A. H. Sommerstein *et al.* Bari: 445–60.
DuBois, P. (2004) 'Toppling the hero: polyphony in the tragic city', *New Literary History* 35: 63–81.
Dué, C. (2001) 'Achilles' golden amphora in *Against Timarchus* and the afterlife of oral tradition', *CP* 96: 33–47.
(2003) 'Poetry and the dēmos: state regulation of a civic possession', in *Dēmos: Classical Athenian Democracy*, ed. C. W. Blackwell. The Stoa [www.stoa.org]. Accessed at http://www.stoa.org/projects/demos/article_poetry_and_demos
Dunand, F. (1986) 'Les associations dionysiaques au service du pouvoir lagide (IIIe s. av. J.-C.)', *Collection de l'Ecole Française de Rome* 89: 85–103.
Duncan, A. (2006) *Performance and Identity in the Classical World*. Cambridge.
Dyck, A. (1985) 'The function and persuasive power of Demosthenes' portrait of Aeschines in the speech *On the Crown*', *G&R* 32: 40–6.
Easterling, P. E. (1993) 'The end of an era? Tragedy in the early fourth century', in *Tragedy, Comedy, and the Polis*, ed. A. H. Sommerstein *et al.* Bari: 559–69.

(1994) 'Euripides outside Athens: a speculative note', *ICS* 19: 73–80.
(1997a) 'A show for Dionysus', in *The Cambridge Companion to Greek Tragedy*, ed. P. E. Easterling. Cambridge: 36–53.
(1997b) 'From repertoire to canon', in *The Cambridge Companion to Greek Tragedy*, ed. P. E. Easterling. Cambridge: 211–27.
(1999) 'Actors and voices: reading between the lines in Aeschines and Demosthenes', in *Performance Culture and Athenian Democracy*, ed. S. Godhill and R. Osborne. Cambridge: 154–66.
(2002) 'Actor as icon', *Greek and Roman Actors: Aspects of an Ancient Profession*, ed. P. E. Easterling and E. Hall. Cambridge: 427–41.
(2006) 'Sophocles: the first thousand years', in *Greek Drama III: Essays in Honour of Kevin Lee*, ed. J. Davidson, F. Muecke and P. J. Wilson. London: 1–16.

Else, G. (1986) *Plato and Aristotle on Poetry*. Chapel Hill: University of North Carolina.
(1968) *Aristotle's Poetics*. Harvard.

Engels, J. (1992) 'Zur Stellung Lykurgs und zur Aussagekraft seines Militär- und Bauprogramms for die Demokratie vor 322 v. Chr.', *AncSoc* 23: 5–29.

Engen, D. T. (2010) *Honor and Profit: Athenian Trade Policy and the Economy and Society of Greece, 415 307 BCE*. Ann Arbor.

Erbse, H. and Kannicht, R. (1991) *Musa Tragica: Die griechische Tragödie von Thespis bis Ezechiel*. Göttingen.

Falappone, M. (2006) 'Citazioni della tragedia attica nelle "archaiologiai"', in *Memoria di testi teatrali antichi*, ed. O. Vox. Lecce: 67–104.

Falkner, T. (2002) 'Scholia versus actors: text and performance in the Greek tragic scholia', in *Greek and Roman Actors: Aspects of an Ancient Profession*, ed. P. E. Easterling and E. Hall. Cambridge: 342–61.

Fantham, E. (2002) 'Actor and/et orator', in *Greek and Roman Actors: Aspects of an Ancient Profession*, ed. P. E. Easterling and E. Hall. Cambridge: 362–76.

Fantuzzi, M. and Hunter, R. L. (2004) *Tradition and Innovation in Hellenistic Poetry*. Cambridge.

Faraguna, M. (1992) *Atene nell'età di Alessandro: problemi politici, economici, finanzari* (2 vols.). Rome.
(2003) 'I documenti nelle "Vite dei X oratori" dei Moralia plutarchei', in *L'uso dei documenti nella storiografia antica*, ed. A. M. Biraschi *et al.* Naples: 481–503.
(2005) 'Scrittura e amministrazione nelle città greche: gli archivi pubblici', *QUCC* 80: 61–86.

Ferrari, G. R. F. (1989) 'Plato and poetry', in *The Cambridge History of Literary Criticism. Vol. 1: Classical Criticism*, ed. G. A. Kennedy. Cambridge: 92–148.

Ferrario, S. B. (2006) 'Replaying *Antigone*: changing patterns of public and private commemoration at Athens *c.* 440–350', *Helios* 33 (supplement): 79–118.

Fisher, N. (2001) *Aeschines: Against Timarchos*. Oxford and New York.

Foertmeyer, V. (1988) 'The dating of the *pompe* of Ptolemy II Philadelphus', *Historia* 37: 90–104.

Fongoni, A. (2005) 'Antifane e Filosseno', *QUCC* 81: 91–8.

Ford, A. (1988) 'The classical definition of ΡΑΨΩΙΔΙΑ', *CP* 4: 300–7.

(1999) 'Reading Homer from the rostrum: poems and laws in Aeschines' *Against Timarchus*', in *Performance Culture and Athenian Democracy*, ed. S. Godhill and R. Osborne. Cambridge: 231–56.

(2003) 'From letters to literature: reading the "song culture" of Ancient Greece', in *Written Texts and the Rise of Literate Culture in Ancient Greece*, ed. H. Yunis. Cambridge: 15–37.

(2009) 'Herodotus and the poets', in *The Landmark Herodotus*, ed. R. B. Strassler. New York: 816–18.

Frangeskou, V. (1999) 'Tradition and originality in some Attic funeral orations', *CW* 92: 315–36.

Friend, J. L. (2009) 'The Athenian Ephebeia in the Lycurgan Period: 334/3–322/1 B.C.' Unpublished University of Texas dissertation, accessed at http://hdl.handle.net/2152/6635

Gagarin, M. (2002) *Antiphon the Athenian: Oratory, Law, and Justice in the Age of the Sophists*. Austin.

(2012) 'Law, politics, and the question of relevance in the case on the crown', *ClAnt* 31: 293–314.

Gagné, R. (2009) 'Mystery inquisitors: performance, authority, and sacrilege at Eleusis', *ClAnt* 28: 211–47.

Garland, R. (2001) *Celebrity in Antiquity: From Media Tarts to Tabloid Queens*. London.

(2004) *Surviving Greek Tragedy*. London.

Garnsey, P. (1988) *Famine and Food Supply in the Greco-Roman World: Responses to Risk and Crisis*. Cambridge.

Garzya, A. (1981) 'Sulle interpolazione degli attori', in *Studi salernitani in memoria di Raffaele Cantarella*, ed. I. Gallo. Salerno: 53–75.

Gehrke, H.-J. (2001) 'Myth, history and collective identity: uses of the past in Ancient Greece and beyond', in *The Historian's Craft in the Age of Herodotus*, ed. N. Luraghi. Oxford: 286–313.

(2010) 'Representations of the past in Greek culture', in *Intentionale Geschichte. Spinning Time*, ed. L. Foxhall, H.-J. Gehrke and N. Luraghi. Stuttgart: 15–34.

Ghiron-Bistagne, P. (1976) *Recherches sur les acteurs dans la Grèce antique*. Paris.

Giuliani, L. (2001) 'Sleeping furies: allegory, narration and the impact of texts in Apulian vase-painting', *Scripta Classica Israelica* 20: 17–38.

Glucker, J. (1969) 'Aeschylus and the third actor', *C&M* 30: 56–77.
Goette, H. R. (1999) 'Die Basis des Astydamas im sogenannten Lykurgischen Dionysos-Theater zu Athen', *AK* 42: 21–5.
(2007a) 'An archaeological appendix', in *The Greek Theatre and Festivals: Documentary Studies*, ed. P. J. Wilson. Oxford: 116–21.
(2007b) 'Choregic monuments and the Athenian democracy', in *The Greek Theatre and Festivals: Documentary Studies*, ed. P. J. Wilson. Oxford: 122–49.
(forthcoming) 'Archaeology of the Rural Dionysia', in Csapo, Goette, Green and Wilson (forthcoming). Berlin: 77–105.
Golden, M. (2004) *Sport in the Ancient World from A to Z*. London.
Goldhill, S. (1987) 'The Great Dionysia and civic ideology', *JHS* 107: 58–76.
(1997) 'The audience of Athenian tragedy', in *The Cambridge Companion to Greek Tragedy*, ed. P. E. Easterling. Cambridge: 54–68.
Gomme, A. W. and Sandbach, F. H. (1973) *Menander: A Commentary*. Oxford.
Gow, A. S. F. (1965) *Machon: The Fragments*. Cambridge.
Graziosi, B. (2002) *Inventing Homer: The Early Reception of Epic*. Cambridge.
Green, J. R. (1990) 'Carcinus and the temple: a lesson in the staging of tragedy', *GRBS* 31: 281–5.
(1994) *Theatre in Ancient Greek Society*. London.
Grethlein, J. (2010) *The Greeks and Their Past: Poetry, Oratory and History in the Fifth Century BC*. Cambridge.
Gribble, D. (1997) 'Rhetoric and history in [Andocides] 4, *Against Alcibiades*', *CQ* 47: 367–91.
(1999) *Alcibiades and Athens: A Study in Literary Presentation*. Oxford.
Griffith, M. (1978) 'Aeschylus, Sicily, and Prometheus', in *Dionysiaca: Nine Studies in Greek Poetry by Former Pupils Presented to Sir Denys Page on His Seventieth Birthday*, ed. R. Dawe *et al.* Cambridge: 105–39.
(1999) *Sophocles: Antigone*. Cambridge.
(2002) 'Slaves of Dionysos: satyrs, audience, and the ends of the *Oresteia*', *ClAnt* 21: 195–258.
Guarducci, M. (1929) 'Poeti vaganti e conferenzieri dell' età ellenistica', *MAL* 6: 629–65.
Gutzwiller, K. J. (2000) 'The tragic mask of comedy: metatheatricality in Menander', *ClAnt* 19: 102–37.
Gwatkin, W. E. (1953) 'The legal arguments in Aischines' *Against Ctesiphon* and Demosthenes' *On the Crown*', *Hesperia* 26: 129–41.
Habicht, C. (1988) 'Die beiden Xenokles von Sphettos', *Hesperia* 57: 323–7.
Hadji, A. and Kontes, Z. (2003) 'The Athenian Coinage Decree: inscriptions, coins and Athenian politics', in *Actas del XIII Congreso*

Internacional de Numismática, ed. C. Alfaro, C. Marcos and P. Otero. Madrid: 263–7.
Hall, E. (1996) 'Is there a polis in Aristotle's Poetics?', in *Tragedy and the Tragic: Greek Theatre and Beyond*, ed. M. S. Silk. Oxford: 295–309.
(2007) 'Greek tragedy 430–380 BC', in *Debating the Athenian Cultural Revolution*, ed. R. Osborne. Cambridge: 264–87.
Halliwell, S. (1984) 'Plato and Aristotle on the denial of tragedy', *PCPS* 30: 49–71.
(1998) *Aristotle's Poetics*. Chicago.
(2011) *Between Ecstasy and Truth: Interpretations of Greek Poetics from Homer to Longinus*. Oxford.
Hammond, N. G. L. (1992) 'The archaeological and literary evidence for the burning of the Persepolis palace', *CQ* 42: 358–64.
Handley, E. (2002) 'Actors, action and words in New Comedy', in *Greek and Roman Actors: Aspects of an Ancient Profession*, ed. P. E. Easterling and E. Hall. Cambridge: 161–88.
Hanink, J. (2008) 'Literary politics and the Euripidean *Vita*', *CCJ* 54: 135–55.
(2010a) 'The classical tragedians, from Athenian idols to wandering poets', in *Beyond the Fifth Century: Interactions with Greek Tragedy from the Fourth Century BCE to the Middle Ages*, ed. I. Gildenhard and M. Revermann. Berlin: 39–67.
(2010b) 'The *Life* of the author in the letters of "Euripides"', *GRBS* 50: 537–64.
(2011) 'Aristotle and the tragic theater in the fourth century: a response to Jennifer Wise', *Arethusa* 44: 311–28.
Hansen M. H. (1987) *The Athenian Democracy in the Age of Demosthenes*. Oxford.
Hansen, P. A. (1983–1989) *Carmina epigraphica graeca* (2 vols.). Berlin.
Harder, A. (1985) *Euripides' Kresphontes and Archelaos*. Leiden.
Harding, P. (1985) *From the End of the Peloponnesian War to the Battle of Ipsus (Translated Documents of Greece and Rome 2)*. Cambridge.
(2008) *The Story of Athens: The Fragments of the Local Chronicles of Attica*. Oxford and New York.
Harris, D. (1992) 'Bronze statues on the Acropolis: the evidence of a Lycurgan inventory', *AJA* 96: 637–52.
Harris, E. M. (1985) 'The date of the trial of Timarchus', *Hermes* 113: 376–80.
(1994) 'Law and oratory', in *Persuasion: Greak Rhetoric in Action*, ed. I. Worthington. London: 130–50.
(1995) *Aeschines and Athenian Politics*. Oxford.
(1996) 'Demosthenes and the theoric fund', in *Transitions to Empire: Essaysin Greco-Roman History, 360–146 BC, in Honor of E. Badian*, ed. R. W. Wallace and E. M. Harris. Norma, Okla.: 57–76.

Harvey, D. and Wilkins, J. eds. (2000) *The Rivals of Aristophanes: Studies in Athenian Comedy*. Swansea.

Hazzard, R. A. (2000) *Imagination of a Monarchy: Studies in Ptolemaic Propaganda*. Toronto.

Heath, M. (1991) 'The universality of poetry in Aristotle's *Poetics*', *CQ* 41: 389–402.

(2009) 'Should there have been a *polis* in the *Poetics*?', *CQ* 59: 468–85.

Heckel, W. (2006) *Who's Who in the Age of Alexander the Great: Prosopography of Alexander's Empire*. Oxford.

Heisserer, A. J. and Moysey, R. A. (1986) 'An Athenian decree honoring foreigners', *Hesperia* 55: 177–82.

Henry, A. S. (1983) *Honours and Privileges in Athenian Decrees*. Zurich and New York.

(1996) 'The hortatory intention in Athenian state decrees', *ZPE* 112: 105–19.

Hintzen-Bohlen, B. (1995) *Die Kulturpolitik des Eubolos und des Lykurg. die Denkmäler- und Bauprojekte in Athen zwischen 355 und 322 v. Chr.* Berlin.

(1997) 'Retrospektive Tendenzen im Athen der Lykurg-Ära', in *Retrospektive. Konzepte von Vergangenheit in der griechisch-römischen Antike*, ed. M. Flashar, H.-J. Gehrke and E. Heinrich. Munich: 87–112.

Hobden, F. (2007) 'Imagining past and present: a rhetorical strategy in Aeschines 3, *Against Ctesiphon*', *CQ* 57: 490–501.

Humphreys, S. C. (1985) 'Lycurgus of Butadae: an Athenian aristocrat', in *The Craft of the Ancient Historian: Essays in Honor of Chester G. Starr*, ed. J. W. Eadie and J. Ober. Lanham, Md. and London: 199–252.

(2004) *The Strangeness of the Gods: Historical Perspectives on the Interpretation of Athenian Religion*. Oxford.

Hunter, R. L. (1983) *Eubulus: The Fragments*. Cambridge.

(1985) *The New Comedy of Greece & Rome*. Cambridge.

(2009) *Critical Moments in Classical Literature: Studies in the Ancient View of Literature and its Uses*. Cambridge.

(2011) 'Plato's *Ion* and the origins of scholarship', in *Ancient Scholarship and Grammar: Archetypes, Concepts and Contexts*, ed. S. Matthaios, F. Montanari and A. Rengakos. Berlin: 27–40.

(2012) *Plato and the Traditions of Ancient Literature: The Silent Stream*. Cambridge.

Hunter, R. L. and Russell, D. (2011) *Plutarch: How to Study Poetry*. Cambridge.

Hunter, R. and Rutherford, I. eds. (2009) *Wandering Poets in Ancient Greek Culture: Travel, Locality, Panhellenism*. Cambridge.

Hurst, A. (1990) 'Ménandre et la tragédie', in *Relire Ménandre*, ed. E. Handley and A. Hurst. Geneva: 93–122.

Huxley, G. (1974) 'Aristotle's interest in biography', *GRBS* 15: 203–13.

Isler, H. P. (2002) 'Das Dionysos-Theater in Athen', in *Die griechische Klassik. Idee oder Wirklichkeit*, ed. W. D. Heilmeyer. Berlin: 533–41.

Jaeger, W. (1923) *Aristoteles: Grundlegung einer Geschichte seiner Entwicklung*. Berlin.

Janko, R. (1984) *Aristotle on Comedy: Towards a Reconstruction of Poetics II*. London.

(1987) *Aristotle: Poetics*. Indianapolis.

(1991) 'Philodemus' *On Poems* and Aristotle's *On Poets*', *Cronache Ercolanesi* 21: 5–64.

Jebb, R. C. (1876) *The Attic Orators from Antiphon to Isaeus*. Vol. II. London.

Jensen, C. (1963) *Hyperides orationes sex: cum ceterarum fragmentis*. Leipzig.

Jocelyn, H. D. (1967) *The Tragedies of Ennius: The Fragments*. London.

Jones, N. F. (1999) *The Associations of Classical Athens: The Response to Democracy*. Oxford.

Jouan, F. and van Looy, H. (2002) *Tragédies: Euripide. Tome 8 Partie 2: Fragments (De Bellérophon à Protésilas)*. Paris.

Kaimio, M. (1999) 'The citizenship of the theatre-makers in Athens', *Würzburger Jahrbücher für die Altertumswissenschaft* 23: 43–61.

Karamanou, I. (2007) 'The *lysis* in Theodectes' *Lynceus*: remarks on Arist. *Poet*. 11, 1452A 27–29 and 18, 1455B 29–32', *QUCC* 87: 119–25.

(2011) 'Aristotle's *Poetics* as a source for lost tragedies', in *Actas del XII Congreso Español de Estudios Clásicos*. Madrid: 389–97.

Katsouris, A. G. (1975) *Tragic Patterns in Menander*. Athens.

Kaufmann, W., ed. and trans. (2000) *Basic Writings of Nietzsche*. New York.

Keim, B. D. (2011) 'The political economies of honour in democratic Athens'. Unpublished University of Cambridge Ph.D. thesis.

Kindstrand, J. F. (1982) *The Stylistic Evaluation of Aeschines in Antiquity*. Uppsala and Stockholm.

Kitto, H. D. F. (1966) 'Aristotle and fourth century tragedy', in *For Service to Classical Studies: Essays in Honour of Francis Letters*, ed. M. Kelly. Melbourne: 113–29.

Knell, H. (2000) *Athen im 4 Jahrhundert v. Chr. – Eine Stadt verändert ihr Gesicht (Archäologisch-kulturgeschichtliche Betrachtungen)*. Darmstadt.

Knöbl, R. (2008) 'Biographical representations of Euripides. Some examples of their development from Classical Antiquity to Byzantium'. Unpublished University of Durham Ph.D. thesis, accessed at http://etheses.dur.ac.uk/2190/1/2190_199.PDF

Konstantakos, I. M. (2000) 'Notes on the chronology and career of Antiphanes', *Eikasmos* 11: 173–96.

(2004) 'Antiphanes' *Agroikos*-plays', *RCCM* 46: 9–40.

(2011) 'Conditions of playwriting and the comic dramatist's craft in the fourth century', *Logeion* 1: 145–82.

Korres, M. (1983) [1989] 'Διονυσιακό Θέατρο (χορηγικό μνημείο *IG* II2 3073)', *Arkhaiologikon Deltion* 38 B1: 10.

Kowalzig, B. (2006) 'An empire of heroes', in *Greek Drama III: Essays in Honour of Kevin Lee*, ed. J. Davidson, F. Muecke and P. J. Wilson. London: 79–98.

(2008) 'Nothing to do with Demeter? Something to do with Sicily! Theatre and society in the early fifth-century West', in *Performance, Iconography, Reception: Studies in Honour of Oliver Taplin*, ed. M. Revermann and P. J. Wilson. Oxford: 128–57.

Krumeich, R. (2002) 'Die "lyukurgische Tragikerweihung"', in *Die griechische Klassik. Idee oder Wirklichkeit*, ed. W. D. Heilmeyer. Berlin: 542–6.

Krumeich, R., Pechstein, N. and Seidensticker, B. eds. (1999) *Das griechische Satyrspiel*. Darmstadt.

Kurke, L. (1997) 'The cultural impact of (on) democracy: decentering tragedy', in *Democracy 2500: Questions and Challenges*, ed. I. Morris and K. Raaflaub. Dubuque, IA: 155–69.

(2002) 'Gender, politics and subversion in the *Chreiai* of Machon', *PCPS* 48: 20–65.

Lane Fox, R. (1994) 'Aeschines and Athenian democracy', in *Ritual, Finance, Politics: Athenian Democratic Accounts Presented to David Lewis*, ed. R. Osborne and S. Hornblower. Oxford: 135–55.

La Spina, L. (1980–1981) 'Poesia e retorica contro Leocrate', *AFLN* 23: 17–41.

Laks, A. (2010) 'Plato's "truest tragedy": *Laws* Book 7, 817a–d', in *Plato's Laws: A Critical Guide*, ed. C. Bobonich. Cambridge: 217–31.

Lamagna, M. (2004) 'Da Filosseno a Euripide in una mossa: Antifane, fr. 205 K.–A.', in *Mathesis e mneme: Studi in memoria di Marcello Gigante*, ed. G. Indelli, G. Leone and F. L. Auricchio. Naples: 33–44.

Lambert, S. D. (2003a) 'IG II2 410: an erasure reconsidered', in *Lettered Attica: A Day of Attic Epigraphy*, ed. D. Jordan and J. Traill. Athens: 55–67.

(2003b) 'The first Athenian *agonothetai*', *ΗΟΡΟΣ* 14–16: 99–105.

(2004) 'Athenian state laws and decrees 352/1–322/1. I. Decrees honouring Athenians', *ZPE* 150: 85–120.

(2006) 'Athenian state laws and decrees. 352/1–322/1: III Decrees honouring foreigners. A. Citizenship, proxeny and evergesy', *ZPE* 158: 115–58.

(2007) 'Athenian state laws and decrees. 352/1–322/1: III Decrees honouring foreigners. B. Other awards', *ZPE* 159: 101–54.

(2008) 'Polis and theatre in Lykourgan Athens: the honorific decrees', in *Μικρός Ιερομνήμων: Μελέτες εις Μνήμνη Michael H. Jameson.*, ed. A. P Matthaiou and I. Polinskaya. Athens: 53–85.

(2010) 'Connecting with the past in Lykourgan Athens: an epigraphical perspective', in *Intentionale Geschichte. Spinning Time*, ed. L. Foxhall, H.-J. Gehrke and N. Luraghi. Stuttgart: 225–38.

(2011) 'Some political shifts in Lykourgan Athens', in *Clisthène et Lycurgue d'Athènes. Autour du politique dans la cité classique*, ed. V. Azoulay and P. Ismard. Paris: 175–90.

(2012) *Inscribed Athenian Laws and Decrees 352/1–322/1 BC: Epigraphical Essays*. Leiden.

Lanni, A. (2006) *Law and Justice in the Courts of Classical Athens*. Cambridge.

Lape, S. (2004) *Reproducing Athens: Menander's Comedy, Democratic Culture, and the Hellenistic City*. Princeton.

Lawton, C. L. (1995) *Attic Document Reliefs: Art and Politics in Ancient Athens*. Oxford.

Lech, M. L. (2009) 'The shape of the Athenian theatron in the fifth century: overlooked evidence', *GRBS* 49: 223–6.

Lefkowitz, M. R. (1981) *The Lives of the Greek Poets*. London.

(2012) *The Lives of the Greek Poets*. 2nd edn. Baltimore.

Le Guen, B. (1995) 'Théâtre et cités à l'époque hellénistique: "Mort de la cité" – "mort du théâtre"?', *REG* 108: 59–80.

(2001) *Les associations de technites dionysiaques à l'époque hellénistique* (2 vols.). Paris.

(2007) '"Décadence" d'un genre? Les auteurs de tragedies et leurs oeuvres à la période hellénistique', in *À chacun sa tragédie? Retour sur la tragédie grecque*, ed. B. Le Guen. Rennes: 85–140.

(2010) 'Les fêtes du théâtre grec à l'époque hellénistique', *REG* 123: 495–520.

(forthcoming) 'Theatre and politics at Alexander's travelling court', in Csapo, Goette, Green and Wilson (forthcoming). Berlin: 249–74.

Liddel, P. (2003) 'The places of publication of Athenian state decrees from the fifth century BC to the 3rd century AD', *ZPE* 143: 79–93.

(2007) *Civic Obligation and Individual Liberty in Ancient Athens*. Oxford.

Lightfoot, J. L. (2002) 'Nothing to do with the *technītai* of Dionysus?', *Greek and Roman Actors: Aspects of an Ancient Profession*, ed. P. E. Easterling and E. Hall. Cambridge: 209–24.

Loraux, N. (1986) *The Invention of Athens: The Funeral Oration in the Classical City*. Trans. A. Sheridan. Cambridge.

Lord, C. (1974) 'Aristotle's history of poetry', *TAPA* 104: 195–229.

Lorenzoni, A. (1994) 'Chaerem. Fr. 10 Sn.-K.', *Eikasmós* 6: 45–56.

Lucas, D. W. (1968) *Aristotle: Poetics*. Oxford.

Luraghi, N. (2010) 'The demos as narrator: public honors and the construction of future and past', in *Intentionale Geschichte. Spinning Time*, ed. L. Foxhall, H.-J. Gehrke and N. Luraghi. Stuttgart: 247–63.

Luraghi, N. and Foxhall, L. (2010) 'Introduction', in *Intentionale Geschichte. Spinning Time*, ed. L. Foxhall, H.-J. Gehrke and N. Luraghi. Stuttgart: 9–14.

Ma, J. (2013) *Statues and Cities: Honorific Portraits and Civic Identity in the Hellenistic World.* Oxford.
Maass, M. (1972) *Die Prohedrie des Dionysostheater in Athen.* Munich.
MacDowell, D. M. (1990) *Against Meidias: Demosthenes.* Oxford.
(2000) *Demosthenes: On the False Embassy (Oration 19).* Oxford.
(2010) *Demosthenes the Orator.* Oxford.
MacFarlane, K. A. (2009) 'Choerilus of Samos' lament and the revitalization of epic', *AJP* 130: 219–34.
Major, W. (1997) 'Menander in a Macedonian world', *GRBS* 38: 41–73.
Mangidis, T. (2003) *Antiphanes' Mythentravestien.* Frankfurt-on-Main and Oxford.
Markle, M. M. (1976) 'Support of Athenian intellectuals for Philip: a study of Isocrates' *Philippus* and Speusippus' *Letter to Philip*', *JHS* 96: 80–99.
Marshall, C. W. (2000) '*Alcestis* and the problem of prosatyric drama', *CJ* 95: 229–38.
Martin, G. (2009) *Divine Talk: Religious Argumentation in Demosthenes.* Oxford.
Mastronarde, D. J. (1990) 'Actors on high: the *skene* roof, the crane, and the gods in Attic drama', *ClAnt* 9: 247–94.
(2010) *The Art of Euripides.* Cambridge.
Meritt, B. D. (1938) 'Greek inscriptions', *Hesperia* 7: 77–160.
(1952) 'Greek inscriptions', *Hesperia* 21: 340–80.
Mette, H. J. (1977) *Urkunden dramatischer Aufführungen in Griechenland.* Berlin.
Michelini, A. N. (1998) 'Isocrates' civic invective: *Acharnians* and *On the Peace*', *TAPA* 128: 115–33.
Mikalson, J. D. (1998) *Religion in Hellenistic Athens.* Berkeley and Los Angeles.
Miles, S. (2009) 'Strattis, comedy, and tragedy'. Unpublished University of Nottingham Ph.D. thesis, accessed at http://etheses.nottingham.ac.uk/887/
Millender, E. G. (2001) 'Spartan literacy revisited', *ClAnt* 20: 121–64.
Millis, B. W. (forthcoming) 'Inscribed public records of the dramatic contests at Athens: IG II2 2318–2323a and 2325', in Csapo, Goette, Green and Wilson (forthcoming). Berlin: 425–45.
Millis, B. W. and Olson, S. D. (2012) *Inscriptional Records for the Dramatic Festivals in Athens.* Leiden.
Mitchel, F. W. (1970) *Lykourgan Athens: 338–322 (Lectures in Memory of Louise Taft Semple, 2nd series).* Cincinnati.
Moloney, E. P. (2003) 'Theatre for a new age: Macedonia and Ancient Greek drama'. Unpublished University of Cambridge Ph.D. thesis.
Moretti, J.-C. (1999–2000) 'The theater of the Sanctuary of Dionysus Eleuthereus in late fifth-century Athens', *ICS* 24–5: 377–98.

Morrow, G. R. (1993) *Plato's Cretan City: A Historical Interpretation of the Laws*. Princeton.

Mosley, D. J. (1973) *Envoys and Diplomacy in Ancient Greece*. Wiesbaden.

Mossé, C. (1989) 'Lycurge l'Athénien. Homme du passé ou précurseur de l'avenir?', *Quad.Stor.* 30: 25–36.

Mossman, J. (1988) 'Tragedy and epic in Plutarch's *Alexander*', *JHS* 108: 83–93.

Most, G. W. (2003) 'Euripide ὁ γνωμολογικώτατος', in *Aspetti di letteratura gnomica nel mondo antico*, ed. M. Funghi. Florence: 141–58.

Murray, P. (1996) *Plato: On Poetry*. Cambridge.

(2013) 'Paides malakon mouson: tragedy in Plato's *Laws*', in *Performance and Culture in Plato's Laws*, ed. A.-E. Peponi. Cambridge: 294–312.

Nagy, G. (1979) *The Best of the Achaeans: Concepts of the Hero in Greek Poetry*. Baltimore.

(1989) 'Early Greek views of poets and poetry', in *The Cambridge History of Literary Criticism.* Vol. I: *Classical Criticism*, ed. G. A. Kennedy. Cambridge: 1–77.

(1990) *Pindar's Homer: The Lyric Possession of an Epic Past*. Baltimore and New York.

(1996) *Homeric Questions*. Austin.

(2002) *Plato's Rhapsody and Homer's Music: The Poetics of the Panathenaic Festival in Classical Athens*. Cambridge, Mass.

Neil, R. A. (1901) *The Knights of Aristophanes*. Cambridge and New York.

Nervegna, S. (2007) 'Staging scenes or plays? Theatrical revivals of "old" Greek drama in antiquity', *ZPE* 162: 14–42.

(2013) *Menander in Antiquity: The Contexts of Reception*. Cambridge.

(forthcoming) 'Performing classics: the tragic canon in the fourth century and beyond', in Csapo, Goette, Green and Wilson (forthcoming). Berlin: 157–87.

Nesselrath, H.-G. (1985) *Lukians Parasitendialog*. Berlin.

(1990) *Die attische Mittlere Komödie*. Berlin.

(1995) 'Myth, parody, and comic plots: the birth of gods and Middle Comedy', in *Beyond Aristophanes: Transition and Diversity in Greek Comedy*, ed. G. W. Dobrov. Atlanta: 1–28.

(1997) 'The polis of Athens in Middle Comedy', in *The City as Comedy: Society and Representation in Athenian Drama*, ed. G. W. Dobrov. Chapel Hill: 271–88.

Nora, P. (1996) 'From lieux de mémoire to realms of memory', in *Realms of Memory: Rethinking the French Past.* Vol. I: *Conflicts and Divisions*, ed. P. Nora and L. D. Kritzman. New York and Chichester: xv–xxiv.

Ober, J. (2001) 'The debate over civic education in classical Athens', in *Education in Greek and Roman Antiquity*, ed. Y. L. Too. Leiden. 175–209.

(2006) 'From epistemic diversity to common knowledge: rational rituals and cooperation in Democratic Athens', *Episteme* 3: 214–33.

(2008) *Democracy and Knowledge: Innovation and Learning in Classical Athens*. Princeton.
Ober, J. and Strauss, B. (1990) 'Drama, political rhetoric, and the discourse of Athenian democracy', in *Nothing to Do with Dionysos? Athenian Drama in its Social Context*, ed. J. J. Winkler and F. I. Zeitlin. Princeton: 237–70.
O'Connor, J. B. (1908) *Chapters in the History of Actors and Acting in Ancient Greece*. Chicago.
Oliver, G. J. (2007) *War, Food, and Politics in Early Hellenistic Athens*. Oxford.
(2011) 'Before "Lykourgan Athens": the origins of change', in *Clisthène et Lycurgue d'Athènes. Autour du politique dans la cité classique*, ed. V. Azoulay and P. Ismard. Paris: 119–31.
Olson, S. D. (1997) 'Was Carcinus I a tragic playwright? A response', *CP* 92: 258–60.
(2006–2010) *The Learned Banqueters: Athenaeus* (6 vols.). Harvard.
Osborne, R. (1999) 'Inscribing performance', in *Performance Culture and Athenian Democracy*, ed. S. Godhill and R. Osborne. Cambridge: 341–58.
O'Sullivan, L. (2009a) *The Regime of Demetrius of Phalerum in Athens, 317–307 BCE*. Leiden.
(2009b) 'History from comic hypotheses: Stratocles, Lachares, and *P. Oxy.* 1235', *GRBS* 49: 53–79.
Owens, W. M. (2011) 'The political topicality of Menander's *Dyskolos*', *AJP* 132: 349–78.
Paga, J. (2010) 'Deme theaters and the Attic trittys system', *Hesperia* 79: 351–84.
Page, D. (1934) *Actors' Interpolations in Greek Tragedy*. Oxford.
Page, D. L. (1981) *Further Greek Epigrams*. Cambridge.
Palagia, O. (2005) 'A new interpretation of Menander's image by Kephisodotos II and Timarchos', *ASAA* 5: 287–97.
Papadi, D. (2008) '*Moralia* in the *Lives*: tragedy and theatrical imagery in Plutarch's Pompey', in *The Unity of Plutarch's Work*, ed. A. G. Nikolaidis. Berlin: 111–23.
Papastamati-von Moock, C. (2007) 'Menander und die Tragikergruppe. Neue Forschungen zu den Ehrenmonumenten im Dionysostheater von Athen', *MDAI(A)* 122: 273–327.
(forthcoming) 'The Theatre of Dionysus in Athens: new data and observations on its "Lycurgan" phase', in Csapo, Goette, Green and Wilson (forthcoming). Berlin: 15–76.
Papillon, T. (1998) 'Isocrates and the Greek poetic tradition', *Scholia* 7: 41–61.
Parker, R. C. T. (1996) *Athenian Religion: A History*. Oxford and New York.
(2005) *Polytheism and Society at Athens*. Oxford.

Perlman, S. (1964) 'Quotations from poetry in Attic orators of the fourth century BC', *AJP* 85: 155–72.

Petrides, A. K. (2010) 'New performance', in *New Perspectives on Postclassical Tragedy*, ed. A. K. Petrides and S. Papaioannou. Newcastle upon Tyne: 79–124.

Petrie, A. (1922) *Lycurgus: The Speech Against Leocrates*. Cambridge.

Pfeiffer, R. (1968) *History of Classical Scholarship: From the Beginnings to the End of the Hellenistic Age*. Oxford.

Pickard-Cambridge, A. (1927) *Dithyramb, Tragedy and Comedy*. Oxford.

(1946) *The Theatre of Dionysus in Athens*. Oxford.

(1953) *The Dramatic Festivals of Athens*. Oxford.

(1962) *Dithyramb, Tragedy and Comedy* (2nd edn, revised by T. B. L. Webster). Oxford.

(1968) *The Dramatic Festivals of Athens* (2nd edn, revised by J. Gould and D. M. Lewis). Oxford.

(1988) *The Dramatic Festivals of Athens 2. Second edition (1968) revised with a new supplement by J. Gould and D.M. Lewis*. Oxford.

Pitcher, L. V. (2005) 'Narrative technique in *The Lives of the Ten Orators*', *CQ* 55: 217–34.

Pitcher, S. M. (1939) 'The *Antheus* of Agathon', *AJP* 60: 145–69.

Podlecki, A. J. (1969) 'The peripatetics as literary critics', *Phoenix* 23: 114–37.

Pöhlmann, E. (1977) 'Der Überlieferungswert der χοροῦ-Vermerke in Papyri und Handschriften', *WJA* 3: 69–81.

Polacco, L. (1990) *Il teatro di Dioniso Eleutero ad Atene*. Rome.

Pontani, F. (2009) 'Demosthenes, parody, and the *Frogs*', *Mnemosyne* 62: 401–16.

Porter, J. I. (2006) 'Feeling classical: classicism and ancient literary criticism', in *Classical Pasts*, ed. J. I. Porter. Princeton: 301–52.

Prauscello, L. (2006) *Singing Alexandria: Music between Practice and Textual Transmission*. Leiden.

Pritchett, W. K. (1996) *Greek Archives, Cults and Topography*. Amsterdam.

Pucci, P. (1987) *Odysseus Polutropos: Intertextual Readings in the Iliad and the Odyssey*. Ithaca.

Reisch, E. (1903) 'Didaskaliai', *RE* cols. 394–401.

Reiske, I. I. (1771) *Oratorum Graecorum [etc.]* Vol. IV. Leipzig.

Renehan, R. (1970) 'The "Platonism" of the Attic orator Lycurgus', *GRBS* 11: 219–31.

Revermann, M. (1999–2000) 'Euripides, tragedy and Macedon: some conditions of reception', *ICS* 24–5: 451–67.

(2006). *Comic Business: Theatricality, Dramatic Technique, and Performance Contexts of Aristophanic Comedy*. Oxford.

Rhodes, P. J. (1993) *A Commentary on the Aristotelian Athenaion Politeia*. Oxford.

(2003) 'Nothing to do with democracy: Athenian drama and the *polis*', *JHS* 123: 104–19.

(2004) 'Keeping to the point', in *The Law and the Courts in Ancient Greece*, ed. E. M. Harris and L. Rubinstein. London: 137–58.

(2005) *A History of the Classical Greek World: 478–323 BC*. Oxford.

(2010) '"Lycurgan" Athens', in *Philathenaios: Studies in Honour of M. J. Osborne*, ed. A. Tamis, C. J. Mackie and S. G. Byrne. Athens: 81–90.

Rhodes, P. J. and Osborne, R. (2003) *Greek Historical Inscriptions: 404–323 BC*. Oxford.

Rice, E. E. (1983) *The Grand Procession of Ptolemy Philadelphus*. Oxford.

Richter, G. M. A. (1965) *The Portraits of the Greeks*. Vol. 1. London.

Ridgway, B. S. (1984) *Roman Copies of Greek Sculpture: The Problem of the Originals*. Ann Arbor.

Rose, V. (1886) *Aristoteles: Fragmenta*. Leipzig.

Roselli, D. K. (2005) 'Vegetable-hawking mom and fortunate son: Euripides, tragic style, and reception', *Phoenix* 59: 1–49.

(2009) '*Theorika* in fifth-century Athens', *GRBS* 49: 5–30.

(2011) *Theater of the People: Spectators and Society in Ancient Athens*. Austin.

Rosen, R. M. (2005) 'Aristophanes, Old Comedy and Greek tragedy', in *A Companion to Tragedy*, ed. R. Bushnell. Malden, Mass.: 251–68.

(2006) 'Aristophanes, fandom and the classicizing of Greek tragedy', in *Playing Around Aristophanes: Essays in Celebration of the Completion of the Edition of the Comedies of Aristophanes by Alan Sommerstein*, ed. L. Kozak and J. Rich. Oxford: 26–47.

Rosivach, V. (1994) *The System of Public Sacrifice in Fourth-Century Athens*. Atlanta.

Rowe, G. (1966). 'The portrait of Aeschines in the oration *On the Crown*', *TAPA* 97: 397–406.

Rusten, J. (ed.) (2011) *The Birth of Comedy: Texts, Documents, and Art from Athenian Comic Competitions, 486–280*. Baltimore, Md. and London.

Rutherford, I. (2008) 'Theoria and theatre at Samothrace: the Dardanos by Damas of Iasos', in *The Greek Theatre and Festivals: Documentary Studies*, ed. P. Wilson. Oxford 279–93.

(2009) 'Aristodama and the Aetolians: an itinerant poetess and her agenda', in *Wandering Poets in Ancient Greek Culture: Travel, Locality, Panhellenism*, ed. R. Hunter and I. Rutherford. Cambridge: 544–68.

Salamone, S. (1976) 'L'impegno etico e la morale di Licurgo', *A&R* 21: 41–52.

Salkever, S. (1986) 'Tragedy and the education of the *dêmos*: Aristotle's response to Plato', in *Greek Tragedy and Political Theory*, ed. J. P. Euben. Berkeley: 274–303.

Samons, L. J. (2000) *Empire of the Owl: Athenian Imperial Finance*. Stuttgart.

Sanders, L. Y. (1987) *Dionysius I of Syracuse and Greek Tyranny*. London.

Šarnina, A. B. (1987) 'Les associations de *technitai* de Dionysos dans les *poleis* hellénistiques', *VDI* 181: 102–17.
Scharffenberger, E. (2012) 'Axionicus, *The Euripides Fan*', in *No Laughing Matter: Studies in Athenian Comedy*, ed. C. W. Marshall and G. Kovacs. London: 159–75.
Schlesinger, A. C. (1937) 'Identification of parodies in Aristophanes', *AJP* 58: 294–305.
Schmitt, O. (1992) *Der lamische Krieg*. Bonn.
Scholl, A. (2002) 'Denkmäler der Choregen, Dichter un Schauspieler des athenischen Theaters', in *Die griechische Klassik. Idee oder Wirklichkeit*, ed. W. D. Heilmeyer. Berlin: 546–64.
Schorn, S. (2004) *Satyros aus Kallatis*. Basle.
Schwenk, C. J. (1985) *Athens in the Age of Alexander: The Dated Laws and Decrees of 'The Lykourgan Era'*. Chicago.
Scodel, R. (2001) 'The poet's career, the rise of tragedy, and Athenian cultural hegemony', in *Gab es das griechische Wunder? Griechenland zwischen dem Ende des 6. und der Mitte des 5. Jahrhunderts v. Chr.*, ed. P. Papenfuss and V. M. Stocka. Mainz: 215–26.
(2007) 'Lycurgus and the state text of tragedy', in *Politics of Orality (Orality and Literacy in Ancient Greece 6)*, ed. C. Cooper. Leiden: 129–54.
Scott, K. (1928) 'The deification of Demetrius Poliorcetes: Part I', *AJP* 2: 137–66.
Scullion, S. (2002) '"Nothing to do with Dionysus": tragedy misconceived as ritual', *CQ* 52: 102–37.
Seidensticker, B. (2002) 'Wie die Tragiker zu Klassikern wurden', in *Die griechische Klassik. Idee oder Wirklichkeit*, ed. W. D. Heilmeyer. Berlin: 526–9.
Sfyroeras, P. (2008) 'πόθος Εὐριπίδου: reading *Andromeda* in Aristophanes' *Frogs*', *TAPA* 129: 299–317.
Shaw, C. A. (2010) 'Middle Comedy and the "satyric style"', *AJA* 131: 1–22.
Shear, T. L. (1995) 'Bouleuterion, metroon, and the archives at Athens', in *Studies in the Ancient Greek Polis*, ed. M. H. Hansen and K. A. Raaflaub. Stuttgart: 157–90.
Sickinger, J. P. (1999) *Public Records and Archives in Athens*. Chapel Hill and London.
Sidwell, K. (1996) 'The Politics of Aeschylus' *Eumenides*', *Classics Ireland* 3: 182–203.
(2000) 'From Old to Middle to New? Aristotle's *Poetics* and the history of Athenian comedy', in Harvey and Wilkins (2000), 247–58.
Sifakis, G. M. (2002) 'Looking for the actor's art in Aristotle', *Greek and Roman Actors: Aspects of an Ancient Profession*, ed. P. E. Easterling and E. Hall. Cambridge: 148–64.

Silk, M. S. (1993) 'Aristophanic paratragedy', in *Tragedy, Comedy, and the Polis*, ed. A. H. Sommerstein *et al.* Bari: 477–504.
Sinclair, R. K. (1988) *Democracy and Participation in Athens*. Cambridge.
Slater, N. W. (1985) 'Play and playwright references in Middle and New Comedy', *LCM* 10: 103–5.
(2005) 'Nothing to do with satyrs? Alcestis and the concept of prosatyric drama', in *Satyr Drama: Tragedy at Play*, ed. G. W. M. Harrison. Swansea: 83–101.
Snell, B. (1971) *Szenen aus griechischen Drama*. Berlin.
Sommerstein, A. H. (1981) *The Knights*. Warminster.
(1993) 'Kleophon and the restaging of the Frogs', in *Tragedy, Comedy, and the Polis*, ed. A. H. Sommerstein *et al.* Bari: 461–76.
(1996) *Aristophanes: Frogs*. Warminster.
Sonnino, M. (2010) *Euripidis Erechthei quae extant*. Florence.
Spina, L. (1980–1981) 'Poesia e retorica contro Leocrate', *AFLN* 23: 17–41.
Stalley, R. F. (1983) *Introduction to Plato's Laws*. Oxford.
Steinbock, B. (2011) 'A lesson in patriotism: Lycurgus' *Against Leocrates*, the ideology of the ephebeia, and Athenian social memory', *ClAnt* 30: 279–317.
(2013) *Social Memory in Athenian Public Discourse: Uses and Meanings of the Past*. Ann Arbor.
Stephanis, I. (1988). *Διονυσιακοὶ Τεχνῖται*. Heraklion.
Stevens, P. T. (1956) 'Euripides and the Athenians', *JHS* 76: 87–94.
Storey, I. (2012) 'Comedy and the crises', in *Crisis On Stage: Tragedy and Comedy in Late Fifth-Century Athens*, ed. A. Markantonatos and B. Zimmermann. Berlin: 303–19.
Stork, P., Max van Ophuijsen, J. and Dorandi, T. (2000) 'Demetrius of Phalerum: the sources, text and translation', in *Demetrius of Phalerum: Text, Translation and Discussion*, ed. W. W. Fortenbaugh and E. Schütrumpf. New Brunswick, NJ: 1–310.
Sullivan, J. F. (1933–1934) 'Aristotle's estimate of Euripides in his *Rhetoric*', *CB* 10: 70–1.
Summa, D. (2003) 'Dalla coregia all' agonotesia attraverso i documenti epigrafici', in *Teatro greco postclassico e teatro Latino: teorie e prassi drammatica*, ed. A. Martina. Rome: 511–32.
(2008) 'Un concours de drames «anciens» à Athènes', *REG* 121: 479–96.
Sutton, D. F. (1987) 'The theatrical families of Athens', *AJP* 108: 9–26.
Takeuchi, K. (2006) 'Reconsidering the relation between the Attic Demes and the Dionysiac Law', *JCS* 54: 42–51.
Tanner, J. (2006). *The Invention of Art History in Ancient Greece: Religion, Society and Artistic Rationalisation*. Cambridge.
Taplin, O. (1976) 'ΧΟΡΟΥ and the structure of post-classical tragedy', *LCM* 1: 47–50.
(1993) *Comic Angels*. Oxford.

(1999) 'Spreading the word through performance', in *Performance Culture and Athenian Democracy*, ed. S. Godhill and R. Osborne. Cambridge: 33–57.

(2007) *Pots & Plays: Interactions between Tragedy and Greek Vase-Painting of the Fourth Century BC.* Los Angeles.

(2009a) 'Hector's helmet glinting in a fourth-century tragedy', in *Sophocles and the Greek Tragic Tradition*, ed. S. Goldhill and E. Hall. Cambridge: 251–63.

(2009b) 'Tragedy', in *The Oxford Handbook of Hellenic Studies*, ed. G. Boys-Stones, B. Graziosi and P. Vasunia. Oxford: 469–80.

(2010) 'Antifane, Antigone, e la malleabilità del mito tragico', in *Antigone e le Antigoni: storia, forme, fortuna di un mito*, ed. A. M. Belardinelli and G. Greco. Florence: 27–36.

Telò, M. (2007) *Eupolidis Demi.* Florence.

Thiolier, J. C. (1985) *De gloria Atheniensium.* Paris.

Thomas, R. (1989) *Oral Tradition and Written Record in Athens.* Cambridge.

Tod, M. N. and Austin, R. P. (1944) 'Athens and the satraps' revolt', *JHS* 64: 98–100.

Todd, O. J. (1938) 'ΤΡΙΤΑΓΩΝΙΣΤΗΣ. A reconsideration', *CQ* 32: 30–8.

Todd, S. C. (2009) 'Hypereides *Against Diondas*, Demosthenes *On the Crown*, and the rhetoric of political failure', *BICS* 52: 161–74.

Townsend, R. F. (1986) 'The fourth-century *skene* of the Theater of Dionysos at Athens', *Hesperia* 55: 421–38.

Tracy, S. (2000) 'Demetrius of Phalerum: who was he and who was he not?', in *Demetrius of Phalerum: Text, Translation and Discussion*, ed. W. W. Fortenbaugh and E. Schütrumpf. New Brunswick, N. J.: 331–45.

Tsagalis, C. C. (2007) '*CEG* 594 and Euripides' *Erechtheus*', *ZPE* 162: 9–13.

Velardi, R. (1989) *Enthousiasmòs.* Rome.

Veligianni-Terzi, C. (1997) *Wertbegriffe in den attischen Ehrendekreten der Klassischen Zeit.* Stuttgart.

Vernant, J.-P. (1972) 'Le moment historique de la tragédie en Grèce', in *Mythe et tragédie en Grèce ancienne*, ed. J.-P. Vernant and P. Vidal-Naquet. Paris: 13–17.

Versnel, H. (2011) *Coping with the Gods.* Leiden.

Vielberg, M. (1991) 'Die religiösen Vorstellungen des Redners Lykurg', *RhM* 134: 49–68.

Vuolo, S. R. (1985) 'Parodia mitologica e filosofica in Antifane', *Euresis* 1: 44–8.

(1989) 'Critica e parodia letteraria in *Antigone*', *Euresis* 5: 31–4.

Walbank, F. W. (1967) *A Historical Commentary on Polybius.* Vol. II: *Commentary on Books 7–18.* Oxford.

Walbank, M. B. (1978) *Athenian Proxenies of the Fifth Century B.C.* Toronto and Sarasota, Fla.

(1990) 'Notes on Attic decrees', *ABSA* 85: 435–47.

Webster, T. B. L. (1954) 'Fourth-century tragedy and the *Poetics*', *Hermes* 82: 294–308.
(1970) *Studies in Later Greek Comedy*, 2nd edn. Manchester.
Wehrli, F. (1944–1959) *Die Schule des Aristoteles: Texte und Kommentar* (10 vols.). Basle.
Wessels, A. (2002) 'Die Didaskalien der Jahre 341 bis 339 v. Chr.', in *Die griechische Klassik. Idee oder Wirklichkeit*, ed. W. D. Heilmeyer. Berlin: 531–2.
West, M. L. (2007) 'A new musical papyrus: Carcinus, *Medea*', *ZPE* 161: 1–10.
West, W. C. (1995) 'The decrees of Demosthenes' *Against Leptines*', *ZPE* 107: 237–47.
White, S. A. (1992) 'Aristotle's favorite tragedies', in *Essays on Aristotle's Poetics*, ed. A. O. Rorty. Princeton: 221–40.
Whitehead, D. (1977) *The Ideology of the Athenian Metic*. Cambridge.
(1983) 'Competitive outlay and community profit: *philotimia* in classical Athens', *C&M* 24: 55–74.
(1986) *The Demes of Attica*. Princeton.
(1993) 'Cardinal virtues: the language of public approbation in democratic Athens', *C&M* 44: 37–75.
Wiles, D. (2000) *Tragedy in Athens: Performance Space and Theatrical Meaning*. Cambridge.
Wilhelm, A. (1906) *Urkunden dramatischer Aufführungen in Athen*. Vienna.
Wilkins, J. (2000) *The Boastful Chef: Discourses of Food in Greek Comedy*. Oxford.
Williams, J. M. (1983) 'Athens without democracy: the oligarchy of Phocion and the Tyranny of Demetrius of Phalerum, 322–307 BC'. Unpublished Yale University Ph.D. thesis.
Wilson, P. J. (1991) 'Demosthenes 21, *Against Meidias*: democratic abuse', *PCPS* 37: 164–95.
(1996) 'Tragic rhetoric: The use of tragedy and the tragic in the fourth century', *Tragedy and the Tragic: Greek Theatre and Beyond*, ed. M. S. Silk. Oxford: 310–31.
(2000) *The Athenian Institution of the Khoregia*. Cambridge.
(2008) 'Costing the Dionysia', in *Performance, Iconography, Reception: Studies in Honour of Oliver Taplin*, ed. M. Revermann and P. J. Wilson. Oxford: 88–122.
(2009) 'Tragic honours and democracy: neglected evidence for the politics of the Athenian Dionysia', *CQ* 59: 8–29.
(2010) 'How did the Athenian demes fund their theatre?', in *L'argent dans les concours du monde grec*, ed. B. Le Guen. Saint-Denis: 37–82.
Wilson, P. J. and Csapo, E. (2009) 'The end of the *khorēgia* in Athens: a forgotten document', in *La Musa dimenticata: Aspetti dell'esperienza musicale greca in età ellenistica. Atti e Seminari delle edizioni della Scuola Normale Pisa*, ed. M. C. Martinelli. Pisa: 47–74.

Wilson, P. J. and Hartwig, A. (2009) '*IG* 13 102 and the tradition of proclaiming honours at the tragic *agon* of the Athenian City Dionysia', *ZPE* 169: 17–27.

Wirth, G. (1997) 'Lykurg und Athen im Schatten Philipps II', in *Volk und Verfassung im vorhellenistischen Griechenland*, ed. W. Eder and K. J. Hölkeskamp. Stuttgart: 191–225.

Wise, J. (2008) 'Tragedy as "an augury of a happy life"', *Arethusa* 41: 381–410.

(2013) 'Aristotle, actors, and tragic endings: a counter-response to Johanna Hanink', *Arethusa* 46: 117–39.

Worthington, I. (2002) *Persuasion: Greek Rhetoric in Action*. London.

Wright, J. H. (1891) 'Review: Gwatkin's Ctesiphontea of Aeschines', *CR* 5: 149–53.

Xanthakis-Karamanos, G. (1979a) 'The influence of rhetoric on fourth-century tragedy', *CQ* 29: 66–76.

(1979b) 'Deviations from classical treatments in fourth-century tragedy', *BICS* 26: 99–102.

(1980) *Studies in Fourth-Century Tragedy*. Athens.

(1982–1983) 'Chaeremon's *Achilles Thersitoctonus*. Reconstruction of a post-classical tragedy', *Platon* 34–5: 55–67.

(1994) 'The comic fragment in PSI 1175: commentary and literary motifs', in *Proceedings of the 20th International Congress of Papyrologists: Copenhagen, 23–29 August, 1992*, ed. A. Bülow-Jacobson. Copenhagen: 332–5.

Young, A. M. (1933) 'The "Frogs" of Aristophanes as a type of play', *CJ* 29: 23–32.

Yunis, H. (2000) 'Politics as literature: Demosthenes and the burden of the Athenian past', *Arion* 8: 97–118.

(2001) *Demosthenes: On the Crown*. Cambridge.

Zagdoun, M.-A. (2006) 'Aristote et Euripide', *REG* 119: 765–75.

Zanker, P. (1995) *The Mask of Socrates: The Image of the Intellectual in Antiquity*. Trans. A. Shapiro. Berkeley and Los Angeles.

Ziegler, K. (1936) 'Timachidas', *RE* 6A: 1052–60.

Ziolkowski, J. E. (1981) *Thucydides and the Tradition of Funeral Speeches at Athens*. New York.

Zwierlein, O. (1966) *Die Rezitationsdramen Senecas*. Meisenheim-on-Glan.

INDEX

Entries found in footnotes are indicated by italicised page numbers.

Index

Index

Index

Index

Index

Made in the USA
Middletown, DE
14 September 2017